Jess in Action

Jess in Action

Rule-Based Systems in Java

ERNEST FRIEDMAN-HILL

MANNING

Greenwich
(74° w. long.)

Manning Publications Co.   Copyeditor: Tiffany Taylor
209 Bruce Park Avenue   Typesetter: Syd Brown
Greenwich, CT 06830   Cover designer: Leslie Haimes

ISBN 1-930110-89-8

Printed in the United States of America

1 2 3 4 5 6 7 8 9 10 – VHG – 06 05 04 03

To my family

brief contents

contents

ix

PART 3 CREATING YOUR FIRST RULE-BASED APPLICATION: THE TAX FORMS ADVISOR ... 147

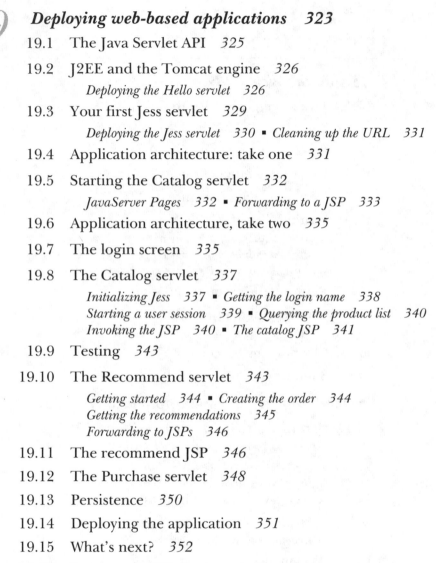

preface

In 1994, I was working in the Scientific Computing department at Sandia National Laboratories in Livermore, California. We had an impressive (for the time) array of heterogeneous computing equipment: workstations from Silicon Graphics and Sun Microsystems, Intel PCs running Linux, Macintoshes galore. I was writing software agents that managed dynamically distributed computations across this network. Agents were running on each machine, and they used a sort of "post and bid" method to decide which machines would run which piece of a computation, based on machine capabilities and load balancing. The agents were fairly intelligent in their decision-making capabilities, and the plans they developed were sometimes surprising. Their "brains" were *rule engines*—software systems that used rules to derive conclusions from premises.

That project led to others, and soon I developed an interest in *mobile agents*— software entities that can travel from node to node in a computer network, maintaining their state as they go. Thus was born the idea for a rule engine whose state could be packaged up, sent across a wire, and reconstituted. The newly released Java language seemed to be a perfect vehicle for this rule engine—and such was the origin of Jess™, the rule engine for the Java Platform.[1]

Jess is a general-purpose rule engine, developed at Sandia National Laboratories. Written in the Java programming language, Jess offers easy integration with

---

[1] Jess is a registered trademark of the Sandia Corporation.

other Java-based software. Jess is free for academic and government use, and it can be licensed for commercial use. You can download a fully functional Home Edition of Jess free of charge if you own a copy of this book (see chapter 3 for download instructions). You can use the Jess Home Edition for noncommercial purposes.

Jess has evolved quite a bit since its original introduction in 1997, largely in response to feedback from a global user community. I've enjoyed working on Jess the whole time, and look forward to its continuing evolution in the future.

acknowledgments

Writing a book is a huge project. This is my second book, and somehow I thought it would be easier this time around. It wasn't. The original four-month estimate to write the manuscript has stretched out into much more than a year. I'm very happy with the results, though. Writing a book about a subject so near and dear as Jess is to me is a dodgy business: I think I've steered clear of the minefields of self-indulgence and created something that will be useful to everyone interested in rule-based software.

Writing a book is *such* a huge project, in any event, that no one does it alone—least of all me. I've had help from many kind, generous, and talented people during the whole time this book was being developed.

One standout has been Bob Orchard of Canada's National Research Council. Bob is the author of the FuzzyJ toolkit and the FuzzyJess extension that adds fuzzy logic to Jess. He's been an active member of the Jess community for years. He generously contributed the essay in chapter 16 showing how to apply the principles of fuzzy logic to the HVAC Controller example. He also served as both a technical reviewer and a technical proofreader for this book and provided an exhaustive list of my (embarrassingly many) typos in the first draft of the manuscript. Thanks, Bob, for everything!

Next I must mention the denizens of the Jess mailing list, a friendly community of smart and generous people who have come together over the years that Jess has existed. The following people have helped find bugs, helped develop new features, or contributed their own projects to the Jess community: Abel Martinez, Al Davis, Alan Moore, Alex Jacobson, Alex Karasulu, Andreas Rasmusson, Andrew Marshall, Ashraf Afifi, Benjamin Good, Blaine Bell, Bob Orchard, Bob Trelease, Bruce Douglas, Chad Loder, Charles May, Cheruku Srini, Dan Larner, Dave Barnett, Dave Carlson, Dave Kirby, David Bruce, David Li, David Young, Drew van Duren, Duane Steward, Ed Katz, Emmanuel Pierre, Eric Eslinger, Fang Liu, George Rudolph, Glen Tarbox, Glenn Williams, Henrik Eriksson, Ian de Beer, J.P. van Werkhoven, Jacek Gwizdka, Jack Fitch, Jack Kerkhof, James Gallogly, James Owen, Jason Smith, Javier Torres, John Callahan, John Collins, Joszef Toth, Juraj Frivolt, Karl Mueller, Ken Bertapelle, Kenny Macleod, Lakshmi Vempati, Lars Rasmusson, Laurence Leff, Mariusz Nowostawski, Matt Bishop, Matthew Johnson, Michael Coen, Michael Friedrich, Michael Futtersack, Michal Fadljevic, Michelle Dunn, Mikael Rundqvist, Mike Finnegan, Mike Isenberg, Mike Lucero, Miroslav Madecki, Nancy Flaherty, Ning Zhong, Norman Ghyra, Oliver Hoffman, Osvaldo Pinali Doederlein, Pau Ortega, Peter Hanson, Peter Klotz, Ralph Grove, Richard Long, Rob Jefson, Robert Gaimari, Russ Milliken, S. S. Ozsariyildiz, Sander Faas, Scott Kaplan, Scott Trackman, Sebastian Varges, Seung Lee, Sidney Bailin, Simon Blackwell, Simon Hamilton, Steve Bucuvalas, Thomas Barnekow, Thomas Gentsch, Travis Nelson, William E. Wheeler, Win Carus, and Yang Xiao. I'm sure I've forgotten someone important; please forgive the oversight.

The staff at Manning Publications, both past and present, are talented people and real professionals. I thank Marjan Bace for his guidance and eye for the big picture; Lianna Wlasiuk for her useful and practical advice in the first stages of writing; Ann Navarro for her expertise in editing; Tiffany Taylor for the tremendous skill and effort she applied to meticulously copy-editing and formatting my ill-formed manuscript; Syd Brown, who produced the beautiful example of the typographer's art you see before you; Maggie Mitchell, for proofreading; Mary Piergies, for overseeing the production of this book; Ted Kennedy for gathering a team of excellent reviewers and organizing the results; Dan Barthel, who got me started on this book in the first place; and, undoubtedly, many others who worked behind the scenes.

Quite a few technical reviewers and friends read the manuscript and provided detailed and useful comments. This book is vastly improved by their input; any remaining problems are, of course, my fault. I thank Andrew Grothe, Bob Trelease, David Young, Jeff Wang, John Crabtree, John Mitchell, Mark Watson, Michael J. Smith, Roedy Green, Said Tabet, Ted Neward, and Daniel Selman (and of course Bob Orchard) for reading and commenting on the manuscript.

I deeply appreciate the support I've received from my management at Sandia, both for encouraging Jess's development over the years and for permission to write this book in my copious free time. Thanks to Paul Nielan, Ken Washington, Jim Costa, Len Napolitano, and Mim John. I'm also deeply indebted to my innovative "business partner" Craig Smith, who handles Jess licensing with aplomb.

Finally, I want to thank my family for their encouragement and support. Every year with a preschooler is an adventure, and this last one has been no exception. My wife Stacia deserves special thanks for picking up the slack when I was busy writing. And to my daughter Danielle: by the time this sentence is printed, I bet you will be able to read it. I love you both; this book is for you.

about this book

This book was originally conceived in August 2001. As I write these words now in May 2003, I feel like I've stayed quite close to the original concept for the book. Then, as now, despite the still-growing prominence of rule-based systems in nearly every field of software development, the few available books on the topic were heavily theoretical and lacking in real-world examples. With this book, I set out to change that pattern. The book you're holding is structured around a series of large, fully developed, and eminently practical examples of rule-based programming in Java.

This book can be used in several ways. First, it is a general introduction to rule-based systems. If you've never encountered rule-based systems before, you'll want to read part 1 closely. This first section of the book introduces the concepts behind rule-based systems, discusses their applications, and shows some first examples of rule-based programs written with Jess. Part 1 also discusses what's involved in adopting a rule-based solution at your company. Although the programming examples in later chapters use Jess as a vehicle, the concepts presented will transfer to other rule engines easily.

Second, this book is a programmer's manual for the Jess rule language. Part 2 is part Jess language reference and part tutorial. It first introduces you to the language, and how the language is integrated with Java. Later chapters in this part discuss rules and working memory elements—the data that rules operate on. There's also a chapter describing some of the theory behind Jess and what makes it run fast.

Finally, this is a cookbook for real rule-based systems. Parts 3 through 6 describe substantial, realistic software systems in enough detail to teach you how to develop similar systems on your own. Each part presents a rule-based system of increasing complexity, and also introduces new programming techniques:

- Part 3 presents an information kiosk, the *Tax Forms Advisor*, that helps customers choose which income tax forms to bring home. You'll learn how to collect expert knowledge and condense it into rules. The kiosk as presented has a simple text-based interface.

- Part 4 is concerned with the development of the *PC Repair Assistant*, a help-desk application with a Swing-based graphical interface. This example builds on and extends some of the software infrastructure developed for the Tax Forms Advisor.

- In Part 5, I'll guide you through the development of the *HVAC Controller*, an intelligent climate-control system for a hypothetical office building. This part shows how rule-based systems can be interfaced to hardware. A special section written by Bob Orchard, developer of the FuzzyJ toolkit and the FuzzyJess extension for Jess, shows how the HVAC Controller can be enhanced by the use of fuzzy logic.

- Part 6 is about web-based e-commerce solutions. This part presents a *Recommendations Agent* that analyzes a customer's past and present purchases to recommend additional items of interest. The Recommendations Agent is embedded in a set of servlets and JavaServer Pages in the Tomcat servlet engine.

- Part 7 is a little different. The two chapters in this last part cover various topics relevant to using rule-based systems in enterprise applications, including using XML as a rule language, and working with application servers, Enterprise Java Beans, and the J2EE environment.

The main text does not try to be an exhaustive guide to all of Jess; instead it concentrates on those features relevant to the example applications. The first two appendices provide some additional detail. Appendix A includes a description of each of the functions built into the Jess language, and appendix B presents the highlights of Jess's Java APIs.

The development methodology used in this book emphasizes testing. Appendix C presents a simple automated testing framework that can be used to test Jess applications. The code for this framework is available from this book's web site.

Who should read this book?

Because this book can be used in several different ways, it has several distinct possible audiences. Part 1 is an introduction to rule-based systems for any student of information technology, practitioners and management alike. The later parts of the book are aimed squarely at programmers. I've assumed an intermediate knowledge of the Java programming language throughout. Occasionally I explain a Java concept, but most of the time, I just imagine that you understand.

The audience I thought of most as I wrote are intermediate Java programmers with little or no exposure to rule-based systems, who are interested in getting that exposure.

This book is also suitable as a text for a university course on practical rule-based systems development. The course prerequisites should include a course on Java programming. The course content would include parts 1, 2, and 3 of the book, followed by either part 5 or part 6. Additional material could be used as time permits, of course.

Source code downloads

The code for all the major examples and applications in this book is available from the book's web site, www.manning.com/friedman-hill. You can also download a special version of Jess from this web site.

Typographical conventions

This book includes listings of code in both the Jess and Java languages. It also contains transcripts of interactive sessions at the Jess prompt. All of these are set in `monospace type`. Keywords, function names, variable names, and symbols in any language are also set in `monospace` when they occur in the main text. It is generally clear from context whether I'm talking about Jess code or Java code, because the two don't look much alike.

In the interactive session transcripts, the Jess prompt and things that you enter are all shown in normal `monospace` type, while responses printed by Jess are shown in *italic*.

In step-by-step examples, text that you are to type appears in **bold**.

author online

Purchase of *Jess in Action* includes free access to a private web forum run by Manning Publications where you can make comments about the book, ask technical questions, and receive help from the author and from other users. To access the forum and subscribe to it, point your web browser to www.manning.com/friedman-hill. This page provides information on how to get on the forum once you are registered, what kind of help is available, and the rules of conduct on the forum.

Manning's commitment to our readers is to provide a venue where a meaningful dialog between individual readers and between readers and the author can take place. It is not a commitment to any specific amount of participation on the part of the author, whose contribution to the AO remains voluntary (and unpaid). We suggest you try asking the author some challenging questions lest his interest stray!

The Author Online forum and the archives of previous discussions will be accessible from the publisher's web site as long as the book is in print.

about the title

By combining introductions, overviews, and how-to examples, the *In Action* books are designed to help learning *and* remembering. According to research in cognitive science, the things people remember are things they discover during self-motivated exploration.

Although no one at Manning is a cognitive scientist, we are convinced that for learning to become permanent it must pass through stages of exploration, play, and, interestingly, retelling of what is being learned. People understand and remember new things, which is to say they master them, only after actively exploring them. Humans learn *in action*. An essential part of an *In Action* guide is that it is example-driven. It encourages the reader to try things out, to play with new code, and explore new ideas.

There is another, more mundane, reason for the title of this book: our readers are busy. They use books to do a job or to solve a problem. They need books that allow them to jump in and jump out easily and learn just what they want just when they want it. They need books that aid them *in action*. The books in this series are designed for such readers.

about the cover illustration

The figure on the cover of *Jess in Action* is a "Muger del Xeque," a sheik's wife. The illustration is taken from a Spanish compendium of regional dress customs first published in Madrid in 1799. A sheik was the head of an Arab clan or tribe and the richness of his wife's robes and jewelry would be considered a testament to his authority and wealth.

The book's title page states:

Coleccion general de los Trages que usan actualmente todas las Nacionas del Mundo desubierto, dibujados y grabados con la mayor exactitud por R.M.V.A.R. Obra muy util y en special para los que tienen la del viajero universal

which we translate, as literally as possible, thus:

General collection of costumes currently used in the nations of the known world, designed and printed with great exactitude by R.M.V.A.R. This work is very useful especially for those who hold themselves to be universal travelers

Although nothing is known of the designers, engravers, and workers who colored this illustration by hand, the "exactitude" of their execution is evident in this drawing. The "Muger del Xeque" is just one of many figures in this colorful collection. Their diversity speaks vividly of the uniqueness and individuality of the world's towns and regions just 200 years ago. This was a time when the dress codes of two regions separated by a few dozen miles identified people uniquely as belonging to one or the other. The collection brings to life a sense of isolation and distance of that period—and of every other historic period except our own hyperkinetic present.

Dress codes have changed since then and the diversity by region, so rich at the time, has faded away. It is now often hard to tell the inhabitant of one continent from another. Perhaps, trying to view it optimistically, we have traded a cultural and visual diversity for a more varied personal life. Or a more varied and interesting intellectual and technical life.

In spite of the current downturn, we at Manning celebrate the inventiveness, the initiative, and, yes, the fun of the computer business with book covers based on the rich diversity of regional life of two centuries ago, brought back to life by the pictures from this collection.

Part 1

Introducing
rule-based systems

What are rule-based systems? What are they good for? Where did they come from? Are they right for you? What should you do if you want to build one? These are the questions we'll begin to address in part 1. You'll learn what rule-based systems are, about their history, and about their many uses. We'll also look at how to decide when a rule-based solution is appropriate for your application. Finally, you'll learn about how rule-based systems are implemented, and some strategies for developing them.

Rules to the rescue

1

In this chapter you'll...

- Be introduced to the Jess programming language
- Analyze a rule-based program
- See familiar examples of rule-based systems

3

Rule-based software is in regular use in practically every business, school, and home. In this chapter, we'll look at some examples of how rules are used to solve common problems. Because most programmers learn best by doing, you'll start by writing a rule-based program of your own.

1.1 Math class melee

"The answer, please?"

The stern voice startles you. You were dozing in Mrs. Rosencrantz's high school math class again. You realize at once that she's been talking to you.

"Well?"

You look at the blackboard. It's one of those word puzzles, the logic kind. Mrs. Rosencrantz is waiting for you to solve it. You quickly scan what she's scrawled on the board with her crone's hand:

- A foursome of golfers is standing at a tee, in a line from left to right. Each golfer wears different colored pants; one is wearing red pants. The golfer to Fred's immediate right is wearing blue pants.

- Joe is second in line.

- Bob is wearing plaid pants.

- Tom isn't in position one or four, and he isn't wearing the hideous orange pants.

- In what order will the four golfers tee off, and what color are each golfer's pants?"

You get the gist of it right away, but how on earth are you supposed to figure it out? There's no formula to use, no analytic procedure for deriving a solution. Algebra was one thing, but this? Why weren't you paying attention in class?

Rules to the rescue! A rule-based program can satisfy Mrs. Rosencrantz by efficiently finding the one combination of names, positions, and colors that fits all the constraints. You can directly translate the problem statement into rules, and the rules will find the solution.

Let's write that program to see how a rule-based system would solve this problem. You'll write the program in the Jess language. Don't be concerned that you don't know the Jess language yet—right now, I'd just like you to understand the approach. You're going to:

1 Choose a way to represent the possible combinations of men's names, positions, and pants colors.

2 Write one rule that describes the problem.

The Jess rule engine will find the solution automatically. Let's get started.

The first step is to define data structures to represent the smallest useful pieces of a possible solution to the problem: a link between a name and either a position or a color:

```
(deftemplate pants-color (slot of) (slot is))
(deftemplate position (slot of) (slot is))
```

A `deftemplate` is a bit like a class declaration in Java. While class objects have member variables, `deftemplates` have *slots*. Each slot is a placeholder for a specific piece of information. For example, the `pants-color` template has a slot named `of` for a person's name and a slot named `is` to hold a color. Whereas a Java class is a definition of a type of object, a template is a definition for a type of *fact* (a fact is basically what it sounds like: a piece of possibly useful information.) A `pants-color` fact represents the idea that one specific golfer (named in the `of` slot) has a certain color pants (named in the `is` slot.)

You'll use these templates to create facts representing each of the possible combinations. There are 32 of them altogether—for example:

```
(pants-color (of Bob) (is red))
(position (of Joe) (is 3))
```

You can write a rule to create all 32 of these facts and put them into *working memory*, a kind of scratch space Jess uses to store the facts it knows:

```
(defrule generate-possibilities
    =>
    (foreach ?name (create$ Fred Joe Bob Tom)
        (foreach ?color (create$ red blue plaid orange)
            (assert (pants-color (of ?name)
                                    (is ?color))))

        (foreach ?position (create$ 1 2 3 4)
            (assert (position (of ?name)
                                (is ?position))))))
```

This code loops (using `foreach`) over the four names given in the problem and creates (using `assert`) a `pants-color` fact for each of the possible name/color pairs and a `position` fact for each name/position pair, for a total of 32 facts. The function `create$` returns a list of its arguments.

Now that you've written a rule to create all the possible combinations, you'll write a second rule to search through them to find the subset of facts that represent the solution. This is the fun part. You'll translate each sentence in the problem statement directly into code. First, note that you use a symbol starting with a question mark, like `?c`, to write a variable in Jess. You'll use the variable `?c` to represent "some color"; ?p to represent "some position"; ?n to mean "some name"; and ?c1...?c4 and ?p1...?p4 to represent Fred, Joe, Bob, and Tom's pants color and position, respectively.

Here's the first useful sentence, *The golfer to Fred's immediate right is wearing blue pants*:

```
(defrule find-solution
    ;; There is a golfer named Fred, whose position is ?p1
    ;; and pants color is ?c1
    (position (of Fred) (is ?p1))
    (pants-color (of Fred) (is ?c1))

    ;; The golfer to Fred's immediate right
    ;; is wearing blue pants.
    (position (of ?n&~Fred)
              (is ?p&:(eq ?p (+ ?p1 1))))
    (pants-color (of ?n&~Fred)
                 (is blue&~?c1))
```

In this code snippet, the variable ?n represents the unknown name of the person to Fred's right, ?p1 is Fred's unknown position, ?c1 is the unknown color of Fred's pants, and ?p is the unknown golfer's position. In these patterns, & means *and* and ~ means *not*, so (name ?n&~Fred) means that this person's name, call it ?n, is not Fred. Here's the next line (*Joe is second in line*):

```
    ;; Joe is in position #2
    (position (of Joe) (is ?p2&2&~?p1))
    (pants-color (of Joe) (is ?c2&~?c1))
```

Note that you must be careful to read between the lines of the problem as you write this rule. You know every golfer is in a different position, so you can say with confidence that ?p2&2&~?p1—Joe's position, call it ?p2, the value of which is 2, is not the same as Bob's position ?p1. It's possible that ?p2 and ?p are the same, though: Joe might be to Fred's immediate right, so you don't mention ?p here.

Now the next line of the problem, *Bob is wearing plaid pants*:

```
    ;; Bob is wearing the plaid pants
    (position (of Bob)
              (is ?p3&~?p1&~?p&~?p2))
    (pants-color (of Bob&~?n)
                 (is plaid&?c3&~?c1&~?c2))
```

By now you know a lot about Bob's position ?p3 and pants color ?c3. You know ?p3 is not the same as ?p1 or ?p2, and you also know it's not the same as ?p. Why? Because the golfer in position ?p wears blue pants, and Bob's pants are plaid, and the golfers in ?p1 and ?p2 are named Fred and Joe, not Bob.

Finally, you know a lot about Tom (*Tom isn't in positions one or four, and he isn't wearing the hideous orange pants*):

```
;; Tom isn't in position 1 or 4
;; and isn't wearing orange
(position (of Tom&~?n)
          (is ?p4&~1&~4&~?p1&~?p2&~?p3))
(pants-color (of Tom)
             (is ?c4&~orange&~blue&~?c1&~?c2&~?c3))
```

There are only four positions, but you know Tom's position is not 1, not 4, and not ?p1, ?p2, or ?p3—more constraints than there are possibilities. This is actually a good sign; it suggests that you have more than enough information to solve the puzzle. You can place a similar number of constraints on Tom's fashion choices.

All that is left is to print out the set of variables ?p1...?p4 and ?c1...?c4 that solves the problem:

```
=>
(printout t Fred " " ?p1 " " ?c1 crlf)
(printout t Joe "  " ?p2 " " ?c2 crlf)
(printout t Bob "  " ?p3 " " ?c3 crlf)
(printout t Tom "  " ?p4 " " ?c4 crlf crlf))
```

The symbol => separates the *if* part of the rule from the *then* part—it specifies what the rule should do if all the requirements are satisfied. Here it prints a table of results. If you enter the code for the problem into Jess and then run it, you get the answer directly. The source for this problem is in the file `rosencrantz.clp`, and you can run it like this:

```
C:\Jess61> java -classpath jess.jar jess.Main rosencrantz.clp
Fred 1 orange
Joe  2 blue
Bob  4 plaid
Tom  3 red
```

You see that exactly one set of variables satisfies the problem. Joe turns out to be the mysterious man in the blue pants, and Fred (the tasteless golfer in the orange ones) will tee off first.

What would happen if some of the information was missing? For example, suppose you didn't know that Joe was second at the tee—how would this affect the results? Let's give it a try. If you change Joe's section of the program like so:

```
;; We don't know anything about Joe, really
(position (of Joe) (is ?p2&~?p1))
(pants-color (of Joe) (is ?c2&~?c1))
```

and then run it, you get the following result:

```
Fred 3 orange
Joe  4 blue
Bob  1 plaid
Tom  2 red

Fred 2 orange
Joe  4 blue
Bob  1 plaid
Tom  3 red

Fred 2 orange
Joe  1 blue
Bob  4 plaid
Tom  3 red

Fred 1 orange
Joe  2 blue
Bob  4 plaid
Tom  3 red

Fred 1 orange
Joe  3 blue
Bob  4 plaid
Tom  2 red

Fred 1 orange
Joe  4 blue
Bob  3 plaid
Tom  2 red
```

Now there are six different solutions, and Jess finds and reports them all. This is another strength of rule-based programming: Rule-based systems can degrade gracefully in the presence of incomplete information. You didn't have to build this quality into the program—it's just *there*.

1.1.1 Beyond logic puzzles

When you wake up from the recurring math-class nightmare, you may be relieved to think that solving logic puzzles is a far cry from your normal duties as a programmer. But that's really not so. Ill-defined problems like this logic puzzle abound in business environments. A human-resources application may need to flag personnel with a suspicious pattern of insurance claims. A requirement for a financial application might be to recommend buying securities that look promising. Manufacturing software could raise an alarm and shut down an assembly line if quality-assurance results indicate there may be a production problem.

What do *suspicious, promising,* and *may be a problem* mean, exactly? They probably can't be expressed as equations—it's possible they can't be given a precise definition at all. If they each can be described as a set of constraints and guidelines, however, then a rule-based program can implement them easily. In the rest of this chapter, we'll look at some common applications of rule-based programming.

1.2 *Some real-world examples*

You are probably affected by rule-based software every day, whether you realize it or not. Many commonplace activities in a modern office are controlled by rules. Let's look at a few examples.

1.2.1 *Mail filtering*

"I can't keep up with all the email I get!" is a common complaint in this Net-connected world. Huge numbers of email messages are sent, delivered, and read every day. *Rules to the rescue!* There are many technological solutions to the problem of sorting email, and almost without exception, these solutions are simple rule-based systems.

The venerable program `sendmail` (http://www.sendmail.org/) delivers most of the email on the Internet. It sports a famously cryptic rule-based configuration language. The following example is lifted verbatim from the `sendmail` web site. It shows a `sendmail` rule that translates BITNET addresses like decvax!user and research!user into user@decvax.dec.com and user@research.att.com, respectively:

```
# translate UUCP addresses to SMTP ones
LOCAL_RULE_3
UUCPSMTP(`decvax', `decvax.dec.com')
UUCPSMTP(`research', `research.att.com')
```

Microsoft Outlook, Eudora, Netscape Messenger, OS X Mail, and other popular mail clients include the ability to automatically sort messages into mailboxes according to the sender's address, the recipient's address, the subject, and other characteristics. In all cases, the user programs the filter in a rule-based language. For these graphical mail clients, the rule language is generally a pattern of checkboxes and pop-up menus in a mail-filtering dialog box.

Programs like `procmail` (http://www.procmail.org/) and `filter` (http://www.math.fu-berlin.de/~guckes/elm/elm.index.html) do this same kind of filtering in batch mode on Unix systems. I'd personally perish under the weight of the hundreds of messages I receive each day without `procmail` to sort through and organize my mail. Instead of dialog boxes, these programs offer a simple textual language. For example, here are two of the rules in my `procmail` configuration:

```
# Put all messages mentioning Jess in their subject line
# into the IN.jess-users folder.
:0:
* ^Subject:.*jess
Mail/IN.jess-users

# Send all messages from "Out-of-Office Autoreply" to
# /dev/null - the UNIX "Trash can."
:0:
* ^From:.*Autoreply
/dev/null
```

Other programs exist that can automatically filter mail at a mail server to remove spam or to strip viruses from attachments. Again, these programs offer a wide range of features and interfaces, generally programmed via rules.

Email handling is one common example of how rules can make life easier for individuals. Now let's look at some applications of rules in the enterprise.

1.2.2 *Product configuration*

When a complex, customizable product like a computer is sold to a customer, the seller must make sure the order corresponds to a functional system. If a given peripheral requires a specific cable, then the order must include that cable. Likewise, if the chassis can hold only two full-height disk drives, then the order better not include four of them. For many kinds of custom-manufactured goods, hundreds or thousands of these kinds of restrictions exist, making order validation a difficult and painstaking process.

The XCON system and its predecessors,[1] developed at Digital Equipment Corporation (DEC), are well-known examples of using rule-based systems in this application area. The original XCON included 210 rules for validating orders for DEC hardware. By 1989, XCON included 17,500 rules and knew about 31,000 hardware components. The estimated savings to DEC at the time was $40 million annually due to increased accuracy, reduced testing costs, and higher customer satisfaction, compared to configuration by human workers. Such systems have become common not only in manufacturing but in the mail-order and Internet sales industry, where rule-based systems help to recommend related products,

---

[1] D. O'Connor and V. Barker, "Expert Systems for Configuration at Digital: XCON and Beyond," *Communications of the ACM* 32, no. 3 (1989).

optimize packaging, and perform other routine order-configuration tasks. Part VI of this book describes a series of web-enabled systems for order configuration built around the Jess rule engine using Java servlets and JavaServer pages.

1.2.3 *Implementing business rules*

Corporations invariably define policies and strategies that specify how the business should respond to events ranging from individual sales to hostile takeover attempts. A *business rule* is a policy or strategy written in executable form, such that a computer can follow it. Here are two simple examples of business rules governing common situations:

```
IF
    employee's length of service > 1 year
AND employee category is regular employee
AND employee contributes to 401k plan
THEN
    employee is vested in 401k plan
END

IF
    customer order is more than ten units
AND customer type is wholesaler
THEN
    deduct 10 percent from order
END
```

If a company's business rules are *implicit*—not written as rules per se, but embedded in procedural logic—and scattered throughout corporate computer applications, then a change in a single policy might require significant programmer effort to implement. Furthermore, if business rules are to be embedded directly into application software, it becomes difficult to use commercial, off-the-shelf (COTS) products, increasing the company's development costs. The corporation will be forced to make a choice between containing development costs and making policy adjustments in response to changing circumstances.

The solution to this dilemma is to remove the business rules from the individual applications, make them *explicit*, and embed them in a centralized *rule engine* for execution. Any business policy can then theoretically be changed at a single point. The rule engine is often embedded in a network-based server so that it can be accessible across an enterprise.

This enterprise-level use of a rule engine is probably the fastest growing and most visible market for rule-based systems programming today. Some application servers, like BEA's WebLogic, include integrated rule engines. Other vendors like ILOG sell rule engines meant to be used with third-party servers. There are literally dozens of rule engines to choose from, targeted toward this product niche. Part VII of this book discusses the use of rule engines in general and the Jess rule engine in particular in enterprise applications based on the Java 2 Enterprise Edition (J2EE) architecture.

1.3 Summary

Rule-based programs are everywhere. Their applications include everything from mail filtering to order configuration, and from monitoring chemical plants to diagnosing medical problems. Rule-based programs excel at solving problems that are difficult to solve using traditional algorithmic methods, and they work even when the input data is incomplete.

In the next chapter, we'll refine our definition of a rule-based system. You'll learn about the history of rule-based systems and about their architecture. We'll also look at the development cycle for rule-based programs. By the end of the next chapter you'll be ready to begin learning how to write your own rule-based software.

What are rule-based systems?

In this chapter you'll...

- Be introduced to declarative programming
- Learn the architecture of a typical rule-based system
- See a method for developing rule-based systems
- Read about industry standards for rules and rule engine APIs

There's an old saying that "when all you've got is a hammer, everything looks like a nail." In computer programming, too, it's important to choose the right tool for the right job. Some problems can be solved easily using traditional programming techniques, whereas writing a rule-based system is the easiest way to solve others. Other problems are in the middle, and either technique will work equally well. This chapter will help you understand which problems are well suited to being solved with a rule-based system, and what this type of software is all about.

2.1 The cooking/driving robot

Imagine your first day on the job at Acme Advanced Robotics Corporation. Acme has built some great humanoid robot prototypes, but the company is having trouble teaching its robots to survive in the real world. You've been brought in to write some high-level robot control software so that Acme can begin selling robot butlers to the masses. You decide to start with something simple: breakfast.

How do you teach a robot to prepare a bowl of breakfast cereal? Assume for the moment that the robot knows how to recognize, pick up, and interact with objects, and that the robot will operate in a closed, controlled, optimal environment. It is be a straightforward program: Tell the robot to get a bowl, a spoon, and a napkin, and set them on the table. Then, the robot should open a box of cereal, fill the bowl, and add milk. If you were writing a computer program for a sophisticated cereal-serving robot, it might look something like this:

```
START
putOnTable(Bowl)
putOnTable(Spoon)
putOnTable(Napkin)
open(Cereal)
pour(Cereal)
open(Milk)
pour(Milk)
eat(Cereal, Spoon)
END
```

The cereal program, with its predictable linear control flow, is typical of many small computer programs. Calculating the value of an equation, computing a customer's bill at a shopping mall, even rendering a single frame of a complex video game, are all variations on the same sort of linear, deterministic process, in which each step follows inevitably from the last. Such programs are often called *procedural* programs—they solve a problem in a straightforward, predictable way. Traditional software development techniques can be used to write programs such as the cereal program to good effect. You wouldn't write a rule-based program to solve the cereal problem. In general, problems that have a well-known algorithmic solution should be solved using a traditional procedural approach.

Emboldened by your success, you now think about teaching the same robot how to drive a car in the real world. You have to tell the robot to search for its keys and driver's license—but only if it isn't already carrying them. You tell the robot how to start the car, put the car in reverse, and back out of the garage—but only if the garage door is already open! The instructions probably need to cover the different behaviors of cold motors and warm motors, how to use both manual and automatic transmissions, and different types of emergency brakes. And the instructions will become far more complex once the car begins to move.

This time, the instructions are filled with many context-sensitive decisions—in fact, there are more decisions than actions. The control flow includes many loops and branches. It would be next to impossible to write a single list of instructions covering every situation that might possibly arise, considering that circumstances interact to constantly change the correct outcomes of each decision. For example, seeing a child's ball roll into the road is not a serious situation when the car isn't moving, but it requires prompt and decisive action when the car is driving toward the bouncing ball.

If it's impossible to write a procedural program to control your robot, how *can* you do it? You can use *declarative programming* instead.

2.1.1 *Declarative programming: a different approach*

Much of the programming we do is procedural. Rule-based programming, however, is *declarative*.

In procedural programming, the programmer tells the computer what to do, how to do it, and in what order. Procedural programming is well suited for problems in which the inputs are well specified and for which a known set of steps can be carried out to solve the problem. Mathematical computations, for example, are best written procedurally.

Note that I'm using *procedural* in a slightly different way than is conventional. Although *object-oriented programming* is traditionally contrasted with the older procedural programming, for the purposes of this discussion, the two are equivalent. In both procedural and object-oriented programming, the programmer writes all the logic that controls the computer, although it is partitioned differently in an object-oriented program.

A purely declarative program, in contrast, describes what the computer should do, but omits much of the instructions on how to do it. Declarative programs must be executed by some kind of runtime system that understands how to fill in the blanks and use the declarative information to solve problems. Because declarative programs include only the important details of a solution, they can be easier to understand than procedural programs. Furthermore, because the control flow is chosen by the runtime system, a declarative program can be more flexible in the face of fragmentary or poorly conditioned inputs (when you removed some of the information from Mrs. Rosencrantz's problem in chapter 1, the same program, unchanged, was still able to find the possible solutions). Declarative programming is often the natural way to tackle problems involving control, diagnosis, prediction, classification, pattern recognition, or situational awareness—in short, many problems without clear algorithmic solutions. Programming a cooking, driving robot declaratively will be a breeze!

Although the driving program would be hard to write in a procedural style, it is an ideal candidate to be written as a declarative program. A rule-based program doesn't consist of one long sequence of instructions; instead, it is made up of discrete rules, each of which applies to some subset of the problem. A few rules plucked from the robot's driving program might look like these:

```
IF
    the engine has stalled
THEN
    start car
END

IF
    you hear sirens
AND you are driving
THEN
    pull over to curb
END

IF
    you see brake lights
AND you are getting closer to them
THEN
    depress the brake pedal
END
```

In a rule-based program, you write only the individual rules. Another program, the *rule engine*, determines which rules apply at any given time and executes them as appropriate. As a result, a rule-based version of a complex program can be shorter and easier to understand than a procedural version. Writing the program is simpler, because you can concentrate on the rules for one situation at a time. Modifying the program is also simpler—if you've ever had to work on a program containing a dozen levels of nested `if` statements, you'll understand why. In the rest of this chapter, we'll formalize some of the ideas behind rule-based systems and see how they are constructed.

2.2 *Rules and rule engines*

A *rule* is a kind of instruction or command that applies in certain situations. "No chewing gum in school," "no running with scissors," and other rules of that ilk, are some of the first explicit rules we learn. "Where there is smoke, there's fire" and Murphy's Law ("Whatever can go wrong, will go wrong") are others that we learn throughout our lives.[1] Using this very general definition, you might conclude that all the knowledge you have about the world can be encoded as rules. Experience shows that this is often (but not always) the case. In general, any information you can think about in logical terms can be expressed as rules.

Rules are a lot like the *if-then* statements of traditional programming languages. You might write a gum-chewing rule like this, in an English-like pseudocode:

```
IF
    I am in school
AND I am chewing gum
THEN
    spit out the gum
END
```

The *if* part of a rule written in this form is often called its *left-hand side* (often abbreviated *LHS*), *predicate*, or *premises*; and the *then* part is the *right hand side* (*RHS*), *actions*, or *conclusions*.

The *domain* of a rule is the set of all information the rule could possibly work with. In this hypothetical case, the domain of the chewing rule is a set of facts about the location and oral fixations of one particular person.

A *rule-based system* is a system that uses *rules* to derive *conclusions* from *premises*: Given the gum-chewing rule and the premise that you are in school, you (as an advanced kind of rule-based system yourself) might conclude that it's time to spit out your gum. In this book, the systems we're talking about are a specific category

---

[1] One reviewer pointed out that this popular proverb is properly called *Finagle's Law*, and that the original formulation of Murpny's Law was, "If there are two or more ways to do something, and one of those ways can result in a catastrophe, then someone will do it." I chose not to go against popular usage here, but the pedant in me appreciated this fact enough to add a footnote. For more information, see The Jargon File—for instance, http://info.astrian.net/jargon/terms/f/Finagle_s_Law.html.

of computer programs. These programs are sometimes called *rule engines*. <u>A rule engine doesn't contain any rules until they are programmed in. A rule engine knows how to follow rules, without containing any specific knowledge itself.</u>

A rule engine is generally part of a *rule development and deployment environment*. The features offered by these environments vary widely, depending on the intended applications for the rule engine and on the type of programmer intended to develop the systems. This book will show you how to develop and deploy rule-based systems in general. To do so, it will use the Jess rule engine in all its examples.

2.2.1 Expert systems

Expert systems, rule-based computer programs that capture the knowledge of human experts in their own fields of expertise, were a success story for artificial intelligence research in the 1970s and 1980s. Early, successful expert systems were built around rules (sometimes called *heuristics*) for medical diagnosis, engineering, chemistry, and computer sales. One of the early expert system successes was *MYCIN*,[2] a program for diagnosing bacterial infections of the blood. Expert systems had a number of perceived advantages over human experts. For instance, unlike people, they could perform at peak efficiency, 24 hours a day, forever. There are numerous dramatic examples in the computer science literature of these early systems matching or exceeding the performance of their human counterparts in specific, limited situations. Predictions were made that someday, sophisticated expert systems would be able to reproduce general human intelligence and problem-solving abilities.

Over time, of course, the drama receded, and it became clear that researchers had vastly underestimated the complexity of the common-sense knowledge that underpins general human reasoning. Nevertheless, excellent applications for expert systems remain to this day. Modern expert systems advise salespeople, scientists, medical technicians, engineers, and financiers, among others.

Today, general rule-based systems, both those intended to replace human expertise and those intended to automate or codify business practices or other activities, are a part of virtually every enterprise. These systems are routinely used to order supplies, monitor industrial processes, prescreen résumés, route telephone calls, and process web forms. Many commercial application servers

---

[2] R. Davis, B. G. Buchanan, and E. H. Shortliffe, "Production Systems as a Representation for a Knowledge-Based Consultation Program," *Artifical Intelligence* 8 (1977): 15–45.

incorporate a rule engine, and most others explicitly or implicitly offer integration with one. Expert systems really have become ubiquitous—we just don't call them by that name anymore.

2.3 Architecture of a rule-based system

The rules in the first expert systems were intertwined with the rest of the software, so that developing a new expert system meant starting from the ground up. The folks who wrote MYCIN, recognizing this fact, created a development tool named EMYCIN.[3] EMYCIN (Empty MYCIN) was developed by removing all the medical knowledge from MYCIN, leaving behind only a generic framework for rule-based systems. EMYCIN was the first *expert system shell*. An expert system shell is just the inference engine and other functional parts of an expert system with all the domain-specific knowledge removed. Most modern rule engines can be seen as more or less specialized expert system shells, with features to support operation in specific environments or programming in specific domains. This book is about this kind of rule engine.

A typical rule engine contains:

- An inference engine
- A rule base
- A working memory

The inference engine, in turn, consists of:

- A pattern matcher
- An agenda
- An execution engine

These components are shown schematically in figure 2.1.

---

[3] W. Van Melle, "A Domain-Independent Production Rule System for Consultation Programs," *International Joint Conference on Artificial Intelligence* (1979): 923–925.

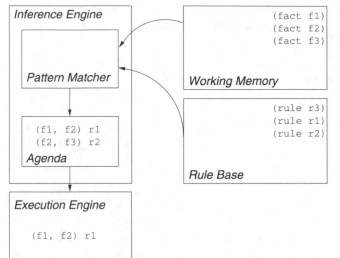

```
(fact f1)
(fact f2)
(fact f3)
```
Working Memory

```
(rule r3)
(rule r1)
(rule r2)
```
Rule Base

Figure 2.1
The architecture of a typical rule-based system. The pattern-matcher applies the rules in the rule-base to the facts in working memory to construct the agenda. The execution engine fires the rules from the agenda, which changes the contents of working memory and restarts the cycle.

2.3.1 *The inference engine*

If you wanted to write your own rule engine, where would you start? You might begin with the most important component. The primary business of a rule engine is to apply rules to data. That makes the *inference engine* the central part of a rule engine.

The inference engine controls the whole process of applying the rules to the working memory to obtain the outputs of the system. Usually an inference engine works in discrete cycles that go something like this:

1. All the rules are compared to working memory (using the *pattern matcher*) to decide which ones should be *activated* during this cycle. This unordered list of activated rules, together with any other rules activated in previous cycles, is called the *conflict set*.

2. The conflict set is ordered to form the *agenda*—the list of rules whose right-hand sides will be executed, or *fired*. The process of ordering the agenda is called *conflict resolution*. The conflict resolution strategy for a given rule engine will depend on many factors, only some of which will be under the programmer's control.

3. To complete the cycle, the first rule on the agenda is fired (possibly changing the working memory) and the entire process is repeated. This

repetition implies a large amount of redundant work, but many rule engines use sophisticated techniques to avoid most or all of the redundancy. In particular, results from the pattern matcher and from the agenda's conflict resolver can be preserved across cycles, so that only the essential, new work needs to be done.

Many beginning rule programmers have difficulty with the idea that the rule engine will decide the order in which the rules will be fired, but this is actually one of the great strengths of rule-based programming. The rule engine can more or less create a custom program for each situation that arises, smoothly handling combinations of inputs the programmer might not have imagined.

2.3.2 *The rule base*

Your rule engine will obviously need somewhere to store rules. The *rule base* contains all the rules the system knows. They may simply be stored as strings of text, but most often a *rule compiler* processes them into some form that the inference engine can work with more efficiently. For an email filter, the rule compiler might produce tables of patterns to search for and folders to file messages in. Jess's rule compiler builds a complex, indexed data structure called a *Rete network*. A Rete network is a data structure that makes rule processing fast. Chapter 8 describes how Jess's rule compiler works.

In addition, the rule compiler may add to or rearrange the premises or conclusions of a rule, either to make it more efficient or to clarify its meaning for automatic execution. Depending on the particular rule engine, these changes may be invisible to the programmer.

Some rule engines allow (or require) you to store the rule base in an external relational database, and others have an integrated rule base. Storing rules in a relational database allows you to select rules to be included in a system based on criteria like date, time, and user access rights.

2.3.3 *The working memory*

You also need to store the data your rule engine will operate on. In a typical rule engine, the *working memory*, sometimes called the *fact base*, contains all the pieces of information the rule-based system is working with. The working memory can hold both the premises and the conclusions of the rules. Typically, the rule engine maintains one or more indexes, similar to those used in relational databases, to make searching the working memory a very fast operation.

It's up to the designer of the rule engine to decide what kinds of things can be stored in working memory. Some working memories can hold only objects of a specific type, and others can include, for example, Java objects.

2.3.4 *The pattern matcher*

Your inference engine has to decide what rules to fire, and when. The purpose of the *pattern matcher* is to decide which rules apply, given the current contents of the working memory. In general, this is a hard problem. If the working memory contains thousands of facts, and each rule has two or three premises, the pattern matcher might need to search through millions of combinations of facts to find those combinations that satisfy rules. Fortunately, a lot of research has been done in this area, and very efficient ways of approaching the problem have been found. Still, for most rule-based programs, pattern matching is the most expensive part of the process. Beginning rule programmers often overlook this fact, expecting the procedural right-hand sides of their rules to represent all the computational effort in their program. The solution to Mrs. Rosencrantz's problem involved lots of pattern matching and no procedural code at all (except to print a report at the end). Often the pattern-matching technique used by a particular rule engine will affect the kinds of rules you write for that engine, either by limiting the possibilities or by encouraging you to write rules that would be particularly efficient.

2.3.5 *The agenda*

Once your inference engine figures out which rules should be fired, it still must decide which rule to fire first. The list of rules that could potentially fire is stored on the *agenda*. The agenda is responsible for using the conflict strategy to decide which of the rules, out of all those that apply, have the highest priority and should be fired first. Again, this is potentially a hard problem, and each rule engine has its own approach. Commonly, the conflict strategy might take into account the specificity or complexity of each rule and the relative age of the premises in the working memory. Rules may also have specific priorities attached to them, so that certain rules are more important and always fire first.

As an example, the driving robot's control program might have two rules like these:

```
IF
    the light is green
THEN
    go
END
```

```
IF
     a person is in front of you
THEN
     stop
END
```

If the robot is stopped for a red light, and the light turns green when someone is still in the crosswalk, then both rules will apply. It is important that the second rule fire before the first, or the future of driving robots will be in serious peril. This second rule should therefore be given a very high priority.

2.3.6 *The execution engine*

Finally, once your rule engine decides what rule to fire, it has to execute that rule's action part. The *execution engine* is the component of a rule engine that fires the rules. In a classical production system such as MYCIN, rules could do nothing but add, remove, and modify facts in the working memory. In modern rule engines, firing a rule can have a wide range of effects. Some modern rule engines (like Jess) offer a complete programming language you can use to define what happens when a given rule fires. The execution engine then represents the environment in which this programming language executes. For some systems, the execution engine is a language interpreter; for others, it is a dispatcher that invokes compiled code.

2.4 *Developing rule-based systems*

This book is a hands-on guide to building useful rule-based systems. Each individual project in this book covers some aspect of this task, presenting realistic examples of every step along the way. In this section, we look at an overview of the development process we will follow in later chapters.

2.4.1 *Knowledge engineering*

The first step in the development of any rule-based system is to begin collecting the knowledge from which the rules will be derived. People who do this for a living are called *knowledge engineers*. Knowledge engineering can be tricky, particularly if the knowledge has to come from human experts. Experts aren't always cooperative, and even if they are, they don't always know how to explain the procedures they follow. On the other hand, many experts respond well to interviews, and you can ask questions to fill in gaps in the expert's explanations.

If you are developing a rule-based system that is strictly based on a procedures manual or other document, or if a human expert is not available, then the knowledge may be collected directly from written sources. Collecting knowledge from books and other reference material has its own advantages and disadvantages. Although books are generally more organized than human experts, they can be lacking in the kind of practical rules of thumb (or *heuristics*) that a practitioner can supply. On the other hand, you rarely have scheduling and other logistical problems when attempting to read a book, but these can be annoying obstacles when working with a human expert.

Another important aspect of knowledge engineering is organizing and structuring knowledge. A typical rule-based system contains hundreds or thousands of rules. Organizing the collected knowledge so that translation to rules will be straightforward is a challenging task for the knowledge engineer.

We'll discuss the knowledge engineering process in greater detail in chapter 9.

2.4.2 *Structuring data*

When all the knowledge has been collected, the task of programming the system begins. The best first step is to examine the knowledge and design data structures that will make it easy to implement the rules clearly and directly. This process resembles *object-oriented analysis*. First, the major concepts are identified. For an employee benefits consultant, these might include *employee*, *health plan*, *claim*, *time*, and *money*. The important thing at this stage is to identify all the concepts referred to in the collected knowledge—the irrelevant ones can be removed later.

Then, you list all the variable characteristics of each concept: Employees have a *name*, a *health plan*, *years of service*, and a *salary*, among other things. Again, at this stage you try to identify all the characteristics mentioned in the collected knowledge. The `pants-color` and `position` templates in chapter 1 were simple examples of data structures for working memory elements. Designing data structures for rule-based systems is discussed in chapter 10.

2.4.3 *Testing*

You may wonder why I'm mentioning testing now, when you haven't written any code yet. Actually, this is the perfect time to begin testing a rule-based system: at the beginning. If rigorous tests are applied to the system at every stage of its development, it will naturally be more robust, more modular, and better understood than a system that wasn't tested until the end. Therefore, before writing a group of rules, you should develop an automated test to exercise them. You can write tests in Java, in your rule language, or in a convenient scripting language. You should run all the tests you have written quite often, ideally each time a change is made to the system. When the final system is delivered, the tests can be part of the deliverable—they will be a great help to anyone who needs to modify the system in the future.

How do you develop tests? Some tests will be very small and check intermediate results, whereas others will be fully worked problems. In the former case, you might develop the test by yourself. The larger tests, though, should be based when possible on actual case studies of how problems were solved in the past.

It is important that the tests be automated, so no human checking of results is required; otherwise the tests will require too much effort to run and will not be used. It helps to have an automated test framework—you can often quickly develop one yourself using Perl, shell scripts, or similar scripting facilities. This testing technique, known as *test-driven development*, is one facet of *eXtreme Programming*,[4] a methodology that is rapidly gaining acceptance in many computer programming fields. An automated test framework that I use for testing Jess programs is described in appendix C.

2.4.4 *Interface building*

For most rule-based systems to do any useful work, they need to be connected in some way to their environment. Sometimes this means database access; other times it means directly reading values from sensors and sending commands to embedded hardware. Before you begin to code your rules, you try to develop a picture of what your system will need to realize these connections. Depending on your development environment, your rules may already have a built-in ability to connect to all the data sources and sinks they'll need to reach, directly from the rule language. In other situations, you may need to write interface code in another language. If you do, I hope you'll use test-first programming to develop it. We'll look at interface building many times throughout this book.

2.4.5 *Writing the rules*

Once the data structures are defined, the interfaces are specified, and the tests are in place, it's time to begin writing the rules. As in all programming, this process involves a significant amount of art; there are always multiple ways to accomplish a task. The good news is that because each rule can be independent of the others, rule-based programs can be developed iteratively: code a little, test a little, and then code some more. The bad news is that it's relatively easy to write unstructured rule-based programs, which can become hard to understand.

---

[4] K. Beck, *Extreme Programming Explained: Embrace Change* (Reading, Mass.: Addison-Wesley), 2000.

You can give structure to your rule-based programs by thinking in terms of *phases* or *modules*, groups of rules that are the only ones relevant at specific phases of the execution of your system. Most rule development languages offer explicit support for this kind of modularity, and it's a good idea to use it whenever possible. The driving robot's rules might be divided into separate modules devoted to starting the car, parking the car, city driving, highway driving, passing other cars, and so on. By breaking rules into small groups, you can make a rule-based program easier to write and to understand. We'll first study writing rules for a real application (an information kiosk) in chapter 11.

2.4.6 Iterative development

Once you've developed some rules, you'll often find that you don't have all the information you need to write more. When this happens, you'll need to go back to the source and do some more knowledge engineering. The development of a rule-based system lends itself well to this sort of iterative procedure. You can show the early incarnations of the system to the human experts, if they exist, and ask them for corroboration of the results. You might have to change your tests, if the experts disagree with what they are testing.

It's also worthwhile to have another knowledge engineer look over your work at this point. Code reviews are amazingly effective at finding problems with software before a release, and they work for rule-based software as well. Whether you hold formal code reviews or just ask a friend for advice, a second pair of eyes can really help to increase the quality of your work.

2.5 Rule engine standards

Various commercial off-the-shelf products (other than application servers) can be designed to work together with rule engines. Historically, there has been a certain amount of vendor lock-in, because each rule engine has its own programmer's interface. The Java Rule Engine API (http://www.jcp.org/jsr/detail/94.jsp), defined by the `javax.rules` package, is a standard enterprise API for accessing rule engines, currently being developed by a consortium of rule engine vendors under the Java Community Process. The `javax.rules` package will allow the host program to interact generically with multiple rule engines, the same way the Java Database Connectivity (JDBC) API makes it possible to write vendor-neutral database programs. The API will include mechanisms for creating and managing sets of rules; for adding, removing, and modifying objects in working memory; and for initializing, resetting, and running the engine. Soon (perhaps even by the time you read this), most popular rule engines, including Jess, will be accessible using the `javax.rules` API. In fact, the official reference implementation of the `javax.rules` API is currently slated to be a driver for Jess.

The `javax.rules` API will not specify a standard rule language, however. Other groups are working on developing standardized rule languages,[5] although less consensus exists in this area. For the same reason there is no one standard general programming language, it is likely that vendor-specific rule languages will be with us for a long time. Each rule language has its own strengths and weaknesses, and the expressiveness, elegance, and power of a rule language can be a major factor in choosing an engine.

2.6 *Summary*

A rule-based system is a computer program that uses rules to reach conclusions from a set of premises. Its historical roots include production systems and expert systems, but nowadays their broad range of applications includes everything from real-time control of embedded systems to enterprise resource planning for multinational corporations.

Rule based systems are not procedural, but declarative programs. They require a different approach to programming in which a runtime system is used to make scheduling and control-flow decisions. Modern rule-based systems often include hybrid procedural/declarative languages, broadening their applicability.

A wide range of commercial rule development and deployment environments is available, but all have an essential architecture in common. Efforts are underway to standardize rule engine APIs and rule programming languages.

These first two chapters provided an introduction to the fundamental concepts of rule-based programs. This is really a practitioner's book, however, so we want to begin writing new rule-based programs as soon as possible. You will learn the Jess programming language in the next part of this book. You'll start by learning about the Jess software itself in chapter 3 and proceed from there.

---

[5] See, for example, http://www.dfki.uni-kl.dc/ruleml/.

## Part 2

Jess: A rule-based programming environment

If you're going to develop rule-based systems, first you'll need to pick a rule engine. For the rest of this book, you'll be working with the *Jess* rule engine that you first met in chapter 1. In chapter 3, you'll learn about Jess's origins, how to get a copy, and how to write the Jess version of the famous "Hello, World" program. In the next few chapters, you'll learn a lot about writing programs in Jess's rule language. Chapter 4 is a general introduction to the Jess language. Chapter 5 teaches you how to work with Java objects from Jess programs. The next two chapters talk about Jess's working memory and how to write rules, respectively. Finally, chapter 8 explains some of the nuts and bolts that make Jess work. All together, part 2 of this book is a comprehensive tutorial on both the Jess language and the Jess rule engine; it will get you ready to start developing rule-based applications in part 3.

Introducing Jess 3

In this chapter you'll...

- Learn how to obtain and install your copy of Jess
- Learn how to run Jess programs
- See how Jess applications are structured

This is a hands-on book. It walks you through the development of several large software systems that use rule-based technology. You'll see how each system is architected, and you'll see the detailed implementation of each one. All the example systems use the Jess rule engine. In this chapter, we'll take a closer look at Jess itself. Jess is an interpreter for the *Jess rule language*. The syntax of the Jess rule language is similar to that of Lisp, so it might look strange to you at first; but Jess's language is simple, easy to learn, and well-suited to both defining rules and procedural programming. Although Jess is in some sense fairly small, it's a very rich environment. Even after you've spent the next few chapters learning about Jess and its rule language, there will be plenty more to learn on the fly as you develop the major applications.

Although previous experience with Lisp might help you begin to understand the Jess rule language, it is not necessary; this book explains all you need to know. On the other hand, I assume you have some familiarity with Java, and I assume you have a Java environment installed and know how to use it to compile and run Java applications.

3.1 *The Jess rule engine*

Jess (`http://herzberg.ca.sandia.gov/jess`) is a rule engine and scripting language developed at Sandia National Laboratories in Livermore, California in the late 1990s. It is written in Java, so it is an ideal tool for adding rules technology to Java-based software systems.

The CLIPS expert system shell (`http://www.ghgcorp.com/clips/CLIPS.html`), an open-source rule engine written in C, was the original inspiration for Jess. Jess and CLIPS were written by entirely different groups of people, however, and their implementations have always been very different. Jess is dynamic and Java-centric, so it automatically gives you access to all of Java's powerful APIs for networking, graphics, database access, and so on; CLIPS has none of these facilities built in. Still, there is a strong similarity between the rule languages supported by these two systems. Many of the core concepts of Jess were originally derived from CLIPS, which was itself influenced by early rule engines like OPS5 and ART.

NOTE FOR CLIPS USERS Jess's syntax is quite similar to CLIPS', but Jess and CLIPS are different and unrelated systems. Some Jess constructs (defclass, definstance, defmodule) have very different semantics in CLIPS, whereas others (defrule) are virtually identical. Jess has many features (defquery, the ability to directly call functions in the host language) that CLIPS doesn't, and Jess does not implement everything that CLIPS does (COOL, the CLIPS Object Oriented Language, is one notable example). If you have previous experience using CLIPS, don't assume you can skip over this part of the book.

3.1.1 Obtaining Jess

You can download a specially licensed version of Jess from the Manning Publications web site, at http://www.manning.com/friedman-hill. The license lets you use Jess for educational purposes, so you can try out and experiment with the examples in this book. In this chapter I'll assume you're using that version of Jess.

Jess is also available from the Jess web site, http://herzberg.ca.sandia.gov/jess. There you can immediately download a trial version, or you can obtain a Jess license and then download a full version with source code. Jess licenses are available free of charge for academic use. You can also purchase a commercial license. See the web site for details.

3.1.2 Installing Jess

To run Jess, you need to have the Java 2 Platform installed. If you don't already have it, you can download a free implementation directly from Sun Microsystems at http://java.sun.com. Versions are available for Windows, Linux, and Solaris. Apple has its own version, which is included in Macintosh OS X. If Java is properly installed, you should be able to execute the command `java -version` in a command window and see version information about your installed Java software. If the version number is 1.2.0 or greater, you're ready to go.

The Jess distribution is a Zip file, and you can open it with many popular archiving tools. (WinZip [http://www.winzip.com] is one useful program for working with Zip files on Microsoft operating systems.) The Zip file contains a single item: a directory named JessXX, where *XX* is a number (currently *61*, for Jess 6.1). Use your archiving tool to unpack that directory to a convenient location—`C:\JessXX`, for example. The unpacked directory will contain:

- A Java archive file `jess.jar`, which contains the Jess software.
- The directory `examples/`, which contains some simple examples of Jess programs.
- A copy of the Jess manual in the directory `docs/`. Open `docs/index.html` in your web browser to view the manual.

To complete your installation, add `jess.jar` to your CLASSPATH environment variable. CLASSPATH tells the Java program where to find installed Java software.

> **NOTE**   The details of setting environment variables vary between platforms. For older versions of Windows, it involves editing the `C:\AUTOEXEC.BAT` file. For newer Microsoft operating systems, you can set environment variables in the System control panel. For Unix-like systems, editing your `.cshrc` or `.profile` will do the trick. Refer to your operating system's documentation for details.

`CLASSPATH` consists of a series of filenames joined by the character your operating system uses to separate filenames in other kinds of lists. On Windows, this is the semicolon (;) character, and on Unix-like systems it is the colon (:). Make sure that `CLASSPATH`, at a minimum, includes the full path to the `jess.jar` file and a period (.), which represents the current directory. So, on Windows, if there is no pre-existing `CLASSPATH` setting, you set this variable to `.;C:\Jess61\jess.jar`. If you find that your system already has a `CLASSPATH` variable defined, you can simply add these two entries to the existing list.

3.1.3 *Running Jess*

Jess is primarily intended as a library that can be embedded in other Java software. However, when you're developing Jess code, it's nice to have an interactive environment to work with, so Jess comes complete with a simple command prompt. To run Jess as a standalone command-line application, execute the class `jess.Main` from the JAR file like this:

```
C:\> java jess.Main
Jess, the Java Expert System Shell
Copyright (C) 2003 E.J. Friedman Hill and the Sandia Corporation
Jess Version 6.1 4/9/2003
Jess>
```

Jess displays a welcome banner and then the `Jess>` prompt. When Jess displays this prompt, it is waiting for you to enter a Jess program. You can probably guess what's coming next: You're going to write the Jess version of "Hello, World".

3.1.4 *"Hello, World"*

You can enter a Jess program directly at the command prompt, and Jess will execute it immediately:

```
Jess> (printout t "Hello, World!" crlf)
Hello, World!
Jess>
```

You can also pass the name of a file that contains Jess code as an argument when you start `jess.Main`. Jess executes the code in the file and then exits:

```
C:\Jess61> java jess.Main hello.clp
Hello, World!
C:\Jess61>
```

We will begin our study of the Jess language in the next chapter, but if you're curious: `printout` is a function that prints formatted output; `t` tells `printout` to print to standard output; and the argument `crlf` starts a new line, like printing a \n in Java. This parenthesized list of symbols is the Jess way of calling a function. Jess immediately evaluates the call to `printout`, producing the side effect of printing "Hello, World!" to the console.

In addition to `jess.Main`, the class `jess.Console` presents the same command-line interface in a graphical console window (see figure 3.1). If you would like a more elaborate graphical interface, you can try JessWin, a free graphical development environment for Jess written by William Wheeler. JessWin (which is also written in Java) is menu-driven and contains an integrated graphical editor (see figure 3.2). You can download JessWin from the Jess web site (http://herzberg.ca.sandia.gov/jess/user.html).

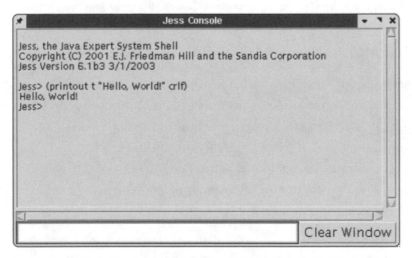

Figure 3.1 The `jess.Console` interface for Jess. This as an alternative to the command-line `jess.Main` interface. You can enter Jess code in the small text field at the bottom left, and Jess output appears in the scrolling text area at the top.

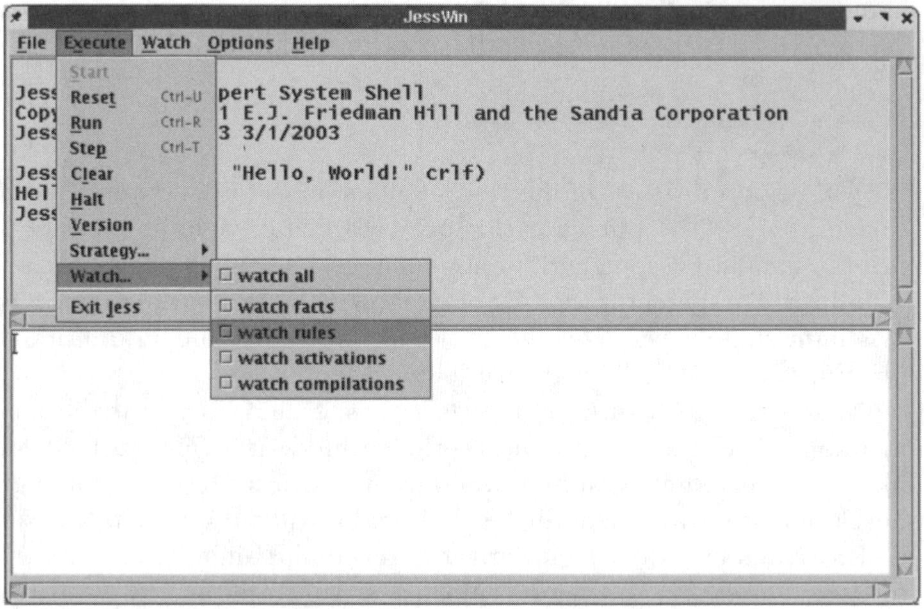

Figure 3.2 The JessWin developer's environment for Jess. JessWin is a third-party add-on that provides a graphical interface to many functions that are useful to Jess programmers.

3.2 *Jess applications*

Jess has been used to develop a broad range of commercial software, including:

- Expert systems that evaluate insurance claims and mortgage applications
- Agents that predict stock prices and buy and sell securities
- Network intrusion detectors and security auditors
- Design assistants that help mechanical engineers
- Smart network switches for telecommunications
- Servers to execute business rules
- Intelligent e-commerce sites
- Games

You'll develop some fairly large applications in this book: the Tax Forms Advisor (an intelligent information kiosk), the PC Repair Assistant (a graphical help desk application), an HVAC Controller (a soft real-time control system), and the Recommendations Agent (a smart e-commerce web site).

You can program with Jess in two different but overlapping ways. First, you can use Jess as a rule engine. A rule-based program can have hundreds or even thousands of rules, and Jess will continually apply them to your data. Often the rules represent the heuristic knowledge of a human expert in some domain, and the knowledge base represents the state of an evolving situation (perhaps an interview or an emergency). In this case, the rules are said to constitute an *expert system*. Expert systems are widely used in many domains. The newest applications of expert systems include being used as the reasoning part of intelligent agents, in enterprise resource planning (ERP) systems, and in order validation for electronic commerce.

The Jess language is also a general-purpose programming language, and it can directly access all Java classes and libraries. For this reason, Jess is also frequently used as a dynamic scripting or rapid application development environment. Whereas Java code generally must be compiled before it can be run, <u>Jess interprets code and executes it immediately upon being typed</u>. This allows you to experiment with Java APIs interactively and build up large programs incrementally. It is also easy to extend the Jess language with new commands written in Java or in Jess itself, so the Jess language can be customized for specific applications.

Jess is therefore useful in a wide range of situations. In this book, you will see Jess used primarily for its rule engine capabilities—but there will be plenty of scripting along the way. How can you choose an architecture for a specific application? As with many things in Jess, lots of choices are available.

3.2.1 *Command line, GUI, or embedded?*

Given its flexibility, Jess can be used in command-line applications, GUI applications, servlets, and applets. Furthermore, Jess can provide the Java `main()` function for your program, or you can write it yourself. You can develop Jess applications (with or without GUIs) without compiling a single line of Java code. You can also write Jess applications that are controlled entirely by Java code you write, with a minimum of Jess language code. Jess has been deployed in everything from enterprise applications using J2EE on mainframes to personal productivity applications on handheld devices. If you can think of it, you can probably implement it with Jess.

The most important step in developing a Jess application is to choose an architecture from among the almost limitless range of possibilities. You must make this choice early in the development of your application. One way to organize the possibilities is to list them in increasing order of the amount of Java programming involved:

1   Pure Jess language, with no Java code.

2   Pure Jess language, but the program accesses Java APIs.

3   Mostly Jess language code, but with some custom Java code in the form of new Jess commands written in Java.

4   Half Jess language code, with a substantial amount of Java code providing custom commands and APIs. Jess provides the `main()` function (the entry point for the program).

5   Half Jess language code, with a substantial amount of Java code providing custom commands and APIs. You write the `main()` function.

6   Mostly Java code, which loads Jess language code at runtime.

7   All Java code, which manipulates Jess entirely through its Java API.

The sample applications presented in the later parts of this book start at the beginning of this continuum (the Tax Forms Advisor developed in part 3 consists entirely of Jess code) and work their way toward the end (the business-rules systems are mostly written in Java). Experiencing the development of each type of application will help you decide what route to take in future development, based both on the requirements of the application and on the abilities of the programming team that will write it.

3.2.2 *Jess performance*

Some people will tell you that Java is slow. They're wrong. Modern Java virtual machines are extremely powerful and sophisticated. In many applications, Java is as fast as comparable C or C++ code. For Jess, being written in Java is not a liability.

Jess is *fast*. The algorithm used for pattern matching, which we'll study in chapter 8, is very efficient, and Jess can plow through large piles of rules and facts in little time. Using Sun's HotSpot JVM on an 800 MHz Pentium III, Jess can fire more than 80,000 rules per second; it can perform almost 600,000 pattern-matching operations per second; it can add more than 100,000 facts to working memory per second; and a simple counting loop can do 400,000 iterations per second. Independent benchmarks have shown that Jess is significantly faster than many rule engines written in the "faster" C language. For example, on many problems, Jess outperforms CLIPS by a factor of 20 or more on the same hardware.[1]

---

[1]   See http://aaaprod.gsfc.nasa.gov/teas/Jess/JessUMBC/sld025.htm and http:// www.mail-archive.com/ jess-users@sandia.gov/msg03278.html for some benchmarks.

Jess's rule engine uses an improved form of a well-known method called the *Rete algorithm* (*Rete* is Latin for *net*) to match rules against the working memory. We'll look at the Rete algorithm in detail in chapter 8. The Rete algorithm explicitly trades space for speed, so Jess can use a lot of memory. Jess does contain commands that let you sacrifice some performance to decrease memory usage. Nevertheless, Jess' memory usage is not ridiculous, and fairly large programs will fit easily into Java's default heap size of 64 megabytes.

Because Jess is a memory-intensive application, its performance is sensitive to the behavior of the Java garbage collector. Recent JVMs from Sun feature an advanced Java runtime called HotSpot, which includes a flexible, configurable garbage collection (GC) subsystem. The garbage collector is the part of the JVM that is responsible for finding and deleting unused objects. Excellent articles on GC performance tuning are available at Sun's web site.[2] Although every Jess rule base is different, in general, Jess benefits if you adjust two parameters: the *heap size* and the *object nursery size*. For example, on my machine, Jess' performance on the Miranker `manners` benchmark (http://www-2.cs.cmu.edu/afs/cs/project/ai-repository/ai/areas/expert/bench/bench/0.html) with 90 guests is improved by 25% by adjusting the initial heap size and nursery size to 32MB and 16MB, respectively, from their defaults of 64MB and 640KB. In this case, you make the default heap size *smaller*, which makes the garbage collector run faster because there is less memory to search. You can tune the HotSpot virtual machine in this way using the following command:

```
java -XX:NewSize=16m -Xms32m -Xmx32m jess.Main <scriptfile>
```

The object nursery is a subset of the Java heap set aside for recently allocated objects. The total heap size in this example is 32MB, not 48MB.

3.3 *Summary*

Jess is a powerful environment for processing rules and scripting the Java platform. You can use it in a wide range of applications, built purely using the Jess rule language, purely in Java, or with some mixture of the two.

You can run Jess as an interactive command-line application during development using the `jess.Main` class. Jess programs can also be stored as plain text files and executed by `jess.Main`.

---

[2] See in particular http://developer.java.sun.com/developer/TechTips/2000/tt1222.html#tip2.

Jess works with any Java 2 virtual machine. Jess is very fast, but its performance is sensitive to the detailed operation of the Java garbage collector. You can often tune the performance of a Jess application by tuning the behavior of the garbage collector.

The next five chapters will teach you the Jess language in detail. First you'll learn to use Jess as a pure programming language, and then you'll see how to write rules. Along the way, especially in chapter 8, we'll peer under the hood and see how Jess works. Let's get started!

Getting started with
the Jess language

In this chapter you'll...

- Learn the basic syntax of Jess
- Work with basic Jess control structures
- Find out how to define functions in Jess

This chapter is an introduction to the Jess rule language. It will not teach you how to write rules—that will have to wait for chapter 7—but it will explain how to write code in the Jess rule language, and you'll need this ability to write the right-hand sides of rules. The Jess rule language is also a general-purpose programming language, and you can use it even without writing any rules.

The next few chapters contain *syntax diagrams* to concisely describe the syntax of some of the more complicated expressions. In these diagrams:

- Text in *<angle-brackets>* is a description of some kind of data that you must supply.
- Things ending with + can appear one or more times.
- Things ending with * can appear zero or more times.
- Things in [square brackets] are optional. Square brackets are also used to group expressions together, so that one of the repeating operators can be applied to a group.

4.1 The basics

Just as books are made up of words, code is made up of *tokens*. A token is a sequence of characters that a computer language recognizes as a fundamental unit. Jess understands only a few different kinds of tokens: symbols, numbers, strings, and comments. Once you know about these, you can begin to do some programming.

4.1.1 Whitespace

Input to Jess is free-form. Newlines and whitespace are not significant except inside quoted strings. You can use newlines and indentation to highlight the structure of the code you write, just as in Java; for example, the following code

```
(if (< ?x 3) then (printout t "?x is less than three" crlf))
```

would usually be written

```
if (< ?x 3) then
    (printout t "?x is less than three" crlf))
```

4.1.2 Symbols

The *symbol* is a core concept of the Jess language. Symbols are tokens that are very much like identifiers in Java. A Jess symbol can contain letters, numbers, and the following punctuation marks: $, *, ., =, +, /, <, >, _, ?, and #. A symbol may not begin with a number. Some of the punctuation marks ($, ?, and =) cannot be used as the first character of a symbol, but can appear in other positions. The other punctuation marks listed can appear as the first character or any character of a symbol. Jess symbols are case sensitive: foo, FOO, and Foo are all different symbols. The best symbols consist of letters, numbers, underscores, and hyphens; hyphens are traditional word separators. The following are all valid symbols:

```
foo    first-value    contestant#1    _abc
```

Jess gives special meaning to a few symbols; they are like Java keywords. The symbol nil is like null in Java, and TRUE and FALSE are Jess's Boolean values. Note that case is significant: TRUE and FALSE must be uppercase, and nil must be lowercase. Other symbols have special meanings only in certain contexts; for example, the symbol crlf is translated into a newline when printed.

4.1.3 *The jess.Value class*

Internally, all Jess values—symbols, numbers, strings, and others—are represented by instances of the jess.Value Java class. You will work extensively with this class when you interface Jess and Java code. jess.Value objects are *immutable*—once one is created, the value it represents cannot be changed. Every jess.Value object knows the type of the datum it holds, and you can fetch this type using the type() member function. The possible values are enumerated by a set of constants in the jess.RU class (RU stands for *Rete Utilities*). Symbols are of type RU.ATOM.

4.1.4 *Numbers*

Jess's parser uses the Java parsing functions java.lang.Integer.parseInt and java.lang.Double.parseDouble to parse integer and floating-point numbers, respectively. (See the Java API documentation for those methods for a precise syntax description.) The following are all valid numbers:

```
3    4.    5.643    6.0E4    1D
```

The Jess language has three numeric types: RU.INTEGER (corresponding to Java int), RU.FLOAT (corresponding to Java double), and RU.LONG (like the Java type long). The type of a numeric value is inferred when it is parsed. The type RU.LONG isn't used much; in fact, you can't type a long literal in Jess. We'll talk about a function that turns a string into an RU.LONG value after we've discussed functions and strings.

4.1.5 *Strings*

Character strings in Jess are denoted using double quotes ("). Typical strings look like this:

```
"foo"
"Hello, World"
```

You can use backslashes (\) to escape embedded quote symbols, just like in Java:

```
"\"Nonsense,\" he said firmly."
```

Jess strings do not recognize any other Java-style escape sequences. In particular, you cannot embed a newline in a string using \n. On the other hand, real newlines are allowed inside double-quoted strings; they become part of the string. This Jess string is equivalent to the Java string "Hello, \nThere".

```
"Hello,
There"
```

Strings are represented as jess.Value objects of type RU.STRING.

4.1.6 *Comments*

You can add descriptive comments to your Jess code. Programmer's comments in Jess begin with a semicolon (;) and extend to the end of the line of text. Here is an example of a comment:

```
; This is a number
1.2345
```

Comments can appear anywhere in a Jess program; they are simply ignored.

Note that Jess comments can nest—a semicolon can appear in a comment without trouble. Many Jess programmers use multiple semicolons on a line for visual emphasis:

```
;;;;;;;;;;;;;;;;;;;;;;;;;;;;;;;;;;
;; Rules added 2/3/2003
;;;;;;;;;;;;;;;;;;;;;;;;;;;;;;;;;;
```

Although you'll see this usage often in Jess code, it has no special meaning.

Whitespace, symbols, numbers, strings, and comments are the fundamental elements of Jess syntax. Now you're ready to learn how to put these elements together into code.

4.2 *Adding some structure*

Tokens by themselves aren't terribly interesting, any more than isolated words have much to say. Tokens become meaningful when they are put together into code. In the following sections, you'll see how to put together "sentences" in the Jess language.

4.2.1 *Lists*

The basic unit of structure in Jess code is the *list*. A list is a group of tokens that includes an enclosing set of parentheses and zero or more tokens or other lists. The following are all valid lists:

```
(+ 3 2)
(a b c)
("Hello, World")
()
(1 2 3)
(deftemplate foo (slot bar))
```

Lists are a little like arrays in Java and other languages. In Jess, they're the central way of structuring both code and data. The first element of a list is called the list's *head*, and in many contexts it is special. For example, Jess function calls are lists where the head is the name of a function, and rules are written as lists where the head is the special symbol `defrule`.

Lists remind many new Jess programmers of scopes in Java—the parentheses group the items in a Jess list just as pairs of brackets delimit Java methods and classes. As a result, some people tend to write Jess code by lining up opening and closing parentheses vertically as they might do in Java. In the worst cases, that might look like this:

```
(bind ?x (+
            (* 20 3
            )
            (- 37 23
            )
         )
)
```

In addition to being aesthetically awkward, it can be confusing. It's better style to simply put the closing parentheses on the last line of the list they close, like this:

```
(bind ?x (+
    (* 20 3)
    (- 37 23)))
```

This is generally more readable, not less. Whether you use a text editor that helps you balance parentheses may influence your choice of code format. The open-source Emacs editor is available on the Windows, Linux, and Macintosh platforms, and makes editing Jess code easy. A special Jess mode for Emacs is available (http://jess-mode.sourceforge.net).

Jess interprets lists in many different ways depending on where in your program they appear. A list might be a rule, a fact, a pattern on a rule's left-hand side, a function definition, or a function call, among other things. You'll see ways to use lists as this chapter continues, but let's pick just one to get started. The simplest Jess program consists of a single function call—and you're probably anxious to write a program, so let's learn about function calls. Later in this chapter we'll return to the study of lists in general.

4.2.2 *Calling functions*

If you type an arbitrary list at the Jess> prompt, Jess will assume you're trying to call a function:

```
Jess> (+ 2 2)
4
```

Here the function + is being called. Jess prints the result (4) on the next line. The result is like the return value of a Java function. The process of executing a function call to determine the result is called evaluating the function call. Every Jess function has a result—there are no void functions, as there are in Java, that don't have a return value.

Jess function calls use a prefix notation: the head of the list is the name of the function being called, and the other items in the list are the arguments of the function. The arguments of a function call can be numbers, symbols, strings, or other function calls—that is, function calls can be nested:

```
Jess> (+ (+ 2 3) (* 3 3))
14
```

The two arguments to + are (+ 2 3) and (* 3 3). Jess evaluates the arguments in left-to-right order before the outer sum is computed.

Jess comes with a large number of built-in functions that compute mathematical quantities, control program flow, manipulate strings, give you access to Java APIs, and perform other useful tasks. Appendix A describes all the functions that are built in to Jess. In section 4.4, you'll also learn how to define new functions by writing Jess language code. In chapter 15, you'll even learn how to extend the Jess language by adding functions written in Java. All code in Jess (control structures, assignments, declarations) takes the form of a function call. You have already seen most of the Jess language's built-in syntax; virtually everything else is accomplished by functions that use these basic elements. Let's look at some simple functions that are used in most Jess programs. In section 4.3, you'll learn about more complex functions that implement control structures.

One of the most commonly used functions is printout. The printout function is used to send text to Jess's standard output or to a file. The first argument tells printout where to send its output. The subsequent arguments are printed one after another, with no spaces between. A complete explanation of the first argument will have to wait, but for now, all you need to know is that if you use the symbol t, printout sends its output to the console. The special symbol crlf is printed as a newline. Here's an example of printing several arguments:

```
Jess> (printout t "The answer is " 42 "!" crlf)
The answer is 42!
```

Another useful function is batch, which evaluates a file of Jess code. To run the Jess source file examples/hello.clp (which comes with the standard Jess distribution), you can enter the following command:

```
Jess> (batch examples/hello.clp)
Hello, World!
```

Another simple function is long. You can't enter a literal long value in Jess as you can in Java. Instead, you must use the Jess long function to create one from a string. In Java, you can write

```
long aLongValue = 123456789L;
```

The equivalent in Jess is

```
(bind ?aLongValue (long "123456789"))
```

As you can see, even assigning a value to a variable is done using a function call. The bind function assigns a value to a Jess variable. Let's learn more about variables in Jess.

4.2.3 *Variables*

A Jess *variable* is a named container that can hold a single value, much like a variable in Java. Jess variables, however, are *untyped*. This means a Jess variable can hold a value of any data type, and it can hold values of any number of different types during its lifetime. A variable can refer to a single symbol, number, string, list, or other value.

Most variables in Jess are written as symbols that begin with a question mark (?). The question mark is part of the variable's name. Although it is legal to do so, it is considered bad style to use any other punctuation marks except dashes (-) or underscores (_) in a variable name. In particular, don't use asterisks (*), because asterisks are used to name global variables (which we'll discuss soon).

You don't need to declare variables in the Jess language; they come into being when they are first given a value. To assign a value to a variable, use the bind function:

```
Jess> (bind ?x "The value")
"The value"
```

To see the value of a variable at the Jess> prompt, you can simply type the variable's name:

```
Jess> (bind ?a (+ 2 2))
4
Jess> ?a
4
```

You can use a variable anywhere a value is expected. For example, variables can be passed as arguments in function calls:

```
Jess> (+ ?a 2)
6
```

Global variables

Any variables you create at the Jess> prompt or at the top level of any Jess language program are cleared whenever the reset command is issued. Because reset is an important function—it is used to reinitialize the working memory of Jess's rule engine—this makes these top-level variables somewhat transient. They are fine for scratch variables while you are working interactively at the Jess> prompt, but they are not persistent global variables in the normal sense of the word. To create global variables that are not destroyed by reset, you can use the defglobal construct:

```
(defglobal [?*<global variable name>* = <value>]+)
```

This syntax diagram says that you can declare one or more defglobals in a single defglobal construct. Each declaration consists of a *global variable name*, an equals sign, and a value. Global variable names must begin and end with *. Valid global variable names look like this:

```
?*a*      ?*all-values*      ?*counter*
```

Aside from the special naming convention, defglobals are similar to ordinary variables and can be used in the same ways.

When a global variable is created, it is initialized to the given value. When the reset command is subsequently issued, the variable *may* be reset to this same value, depending on the current setting of Jess's reset-globals property. You can use the set-reset-globals function to set this property. An example will help:

```
Jess> (defglobal ?*x* = 3)
TRUE
Jess> ?*x*
3
Jess> (bind ?*x* 4)
4
Jess> ?*x*
4
Jess> (reset) ;; Jess will reset ?*x* to its initial value of 3
TRUE
Jess> ?*x*
3
Jess> (bind ?*x* 4)
4
Jess> (set-reset-globals nil)
FALSE
Jess> (reset) ;; This time, ?*x* will not be changed.
TRUE
Jess> ?*x*
4
```

You can read about set-reset-globals and the accompanying get-reset-globals function in appendix A.

Multifields

Multifields are another special kind of variable. A *multifield* is a variable whose first characters are $? (for example, $?x). Multifields have special meaning in only two contexts: in the argument lists of deffunctions (see section 4.4) and on the left-hand-sides of rules (see chapter 7). They are otherwise equivalent to regular variables. In fact, the variable ?x and a multifield $?x refer to the same storage location—they're two names for the same thing.

Now that you understand Jess variables, you're ready to learn more about the structure of Jess code in general. We return now to our study of lists.

4.2.4 *More about lists*

As you've seen, if you type a list directly at the Jess prompt, Jess assumes it's a function call; if you nest a list inside a function call, Jess assumes that nested list is a function call, too. So how can you create a list that's *not* a function call? You use special functions like create$ to make a list, and then you bind the list to a variable:

```
Jess> (bind ?grocery-list (create$ eggs bread milk))
(eggs bread milk)
```

The variable ?grocery-list now holds a list of three items.

This kind of list, which just contains data, is called a *plain list*. Plain lists are useful data structures in Jess. They're a lot like Java arrays. You can access the elements of a Java array using square brackets with a numeric subscript: For example, arr[0] is the first element of an array named arr. To access an element of a plain list in Jess, you call the nth$ function, which returns a single list element:

```
Jess> (printout t (nth$ 2 ?grocery-list) crlf)
bread
```

You may have noticed that many of the Jess functions that deal explicitly with lists have names ending in $—this is just a convention, but a useful one. Two other list-related functions are first$ and rest$:

```
Jess> (first$ ?grocery-list)
(eggs)
Jess> (rest$ ?grocery-list)
(bread milk)
```

The function first$ returns a list containing just the first element of its single argument, and rest$ returns a list holding the second and subsequent elements.

You might be tempted to use lists to build trees or other nested data structures. Plain lists can't be nested, however. Jess will flatten out any nested plain list you attempt to create:

```
Jess> (bind ?more-groceries (create$ ?grocery-list salt soap))
(eggs bread milk salt soap)
```

Usually, when you have a grocery list, you walk through a grocery store, find each item on the list, and put it into your shopping cart. This involves *iterating* over the list—performing an action for each item of the list. To do this, you need to learn about control structures in Jess.

4.3 *Control flow*

Up until this point, the code you've written executes sequentially, one statement at a time. It's hard to write interesting programs this way. Luckily, the Jess language has a number of functions that affect the flow of control and let you group statements, make decisions, and execute loops.

In describing these control-flow functions, I'll use the term *expression*. An expression is any Jess value: a symbol, number, string, variable, or function call. To *evaluate* an expression means to use the value of the constant expression, take the value that the variable represents, or evaluate the function and use its result.

We'll discuss the following control-flow functions in this section:

- apply—Calls a function on a given set of arguments
- build—Parses and executes a function call from a string
- eval—Parses and executes a function call from a string
- foreach—Executes a block of code once for each item in a list
- if/then/else—Chooses among alternative courses of action
- progn—Executes a group of function calls
- while—Executes a block of code while an expression is true

You'll use some of these control-flow functions (like foreach, while, and if/then/ else) all the time, and some of them only rarely. We'll look at the most common ones first.

4.3.1 *foreach*

The foreach function provides the perfect way to shop for each item on your grocery list. It evaluates a block of expressions once for each element in a plain list. Each time through the block, a variable you supply is set equal to the corresponding entry from the list you also supply. The syntax diagram looks like this:

```
(foreach <variable> <list> <expression>+)
```

Here's an example of using foreach to print each item on your grocery list on a separate line:

```
Jess> (bind ?grocery-list (create$ eggs milk bread))
(eggs milk bread)
Jess> (foreach ?e ?grocery-list
    (printout t ?e crlf))
eggs
milk
bread
```

The foreach function is useful when you already have a list of values for the loop variable. Often, though, you need a more general kind of looping construct, such as while.

4.3.2 *while*

The `while` function lets you repeatedly evaluate a group of one or more expressions as long as some condition remains true:

```
(while <Boolean expression> do <expression>+)
```

The first argument in the `while` function must be a *Boolean expression*—an expression that evaluates to TRUE or FALSE. The `while` function evaluates the Boolean expression, and if the expression is not FALSE, all other expressions in the body of the `while` (except the optional symbol do) are evaluated. The Boolean expression is then reevaluated, and the cycle repeats until the expression becomes FALSE. The value of the last expression evaluated is the return value—invariably, it is FALSE. Here is an example of using `while` to add the numbers from 1 to 10:

```
Jess> (bind ?i 1)
1
Jess> (bind ?sum 0)
0
Jess> (while (<= ?i 10) do
    (bind ?sum (+ ?sum ?i))
    (bind ?i (+ ?i 1)))
FALSE
Jess> ?sum
55
```

Note that if the Boolean expression is FALSE the first time it is evaluated, the body of the `while` is never executed.

The `while` loop implicitly makes a decision about what code to execute each time it evaluates the Boolean expression. The `if/then/else` function lets you make this kind of choice explicitly.

4.3.3 *if/then/else*

You can use the `if` function to choose what code to execute next. The syntax of Jess's `if` function is similar to the `if` statement in Java:

```
(if <Boolean expression> then <expression>+ [else <expression>+])
```

The first argument to `if` is a Boolean expression. If the value of the expression is not FALSE, the `if` function evaluates the group of expressions that follows the symbol then, in order. If the expression is FALSE, then the statements after else are evaluated (if the optional else clause is present.)

This example uses the function member$, which accepts a value and a plain list as arguments and returns TRUE if the value appears in any position of the list:

```
Jess> (bind ?grocery-list (create$ eggs milk bread))
(eggs milk bread)
Jess> (if (member$ eggs ?grocery-list) then
        (printout t "I need to buy eggs" crlf)
     else
        (printout t "No eggs, thanks" crlf))
I need to buy eggs
```

Either the if block or the else block can be terminated early using the return function. The return value of the whole if function call is the value of the last expression evaluated.

You can chain if functions together, much as you can in Java. All you need to do is to use a second if function call as the body of an else block. In this example, three if function calls are nested together:

```
Jess> (bind ?x 1)
1
Jess> (if (= ?x 3) then
        (printout t "?x is three." crlf)
     else
        (if (= ?x 2) then
          (printout t "?x is two." crlf)
        else
          (if (= ?x 1) then
            (printout t "?x is one." crlf))))
?x is one.
```

The if function, like the while function, takes a single Boolean expression as its first argument. What if you need to write several expressions to compute a Boolean value? The progn function is there to help.

4.3.4 progn

The progn function evaluates a list of expressions and returns the value of the last one:

```
(progn <expression>+)
```

The progn function is useful when you need to group multiple expressions together into one expression, usually due to syntax restrictions of other functions, as in the following example:

```
Jess> (bind ?n 2)
2
Jess> (while (progn (bind ?n (* ?n ?n)) (< ?n 1000)) do
     (printout t ?n crlf))
4
16
256
FALSE
```

Of course, this particular example could also be written more succinctly as follows:

```
Jess> (bind ?n 2)
2
Jess> (while (< (bind ?n (* ?n ?n)) 1000) do
    (printout t ?n crlf))
```

However, in many important cases progn is the only real alternative. Many of these cases come up during pattern matching on the left-hand sides of rules, which you will see in chapter 7.

The next few functions are used less frequently than the ones we've covered so far in this section—but when you need them, you need them *badly.* These functions have no equivalents in Java; they are powerful features available only in the Jess environment. They are used to convert directly between data and code, something that can't be done in a compiled language like Java.

4.3.5 *apply*

In Java, you write a different line of code to add two numbers than you would to multiply them, print them, or save them in a file. In Jess, you can write one line of code that, depending on the values of some arguments, can do any of these things, and more.

The first argument of apply is the name of a function. Invoking apply calls that function with all the other expressions as arguments:

```
(apply <function-name> <expression>+)
```

The function name can be held in a variable or can itself be the return value of a function. In this example, the user is prompted for the name of a function, which is then called with a list of numbers as arguments; the result is then printed. The user enters + when prompted:

```
Jess> (apply (read) 1 2 3)
+
6
```

Because the user typed +, apply added the numbers and displayed the result. If the input had been − instead, the result would have been −4. The apply function therefore turns a bit of data—the name of a function—into code for Jess to execute. The eval and build functions take this idea one step further.

4.3.6 *eval and build*

Because Jess is an interpreted language, it doesn't much care where the code it's executing comes from. The code can come from a file, from the keyboard, or even from a variable. The eval and build functions convert arbitrary Jess data into Jess code, making it simple to write a Jess program that writes other Jess programs. This means a rule-based program can create and incorporate new rules as it runs—it can *learn*. This is a powerful feature!

The eval function accepts a single argument: a string containing a complete Jess expression, including parentheses if the expression is a function call. When you call eval, the string is parsed, the expression is evaluated, and the result is returned. In this example, a string is bound to a variable, and then the eval function is used to evaluate the string and produce a result, just as if the contents of the string had been typed at the command line:

```
Jess> (bind ?x "(+ 1 2 3)")
"(+ 1 2 3)"
Jess> (eval ?x)
6
```

The build function is a synonym for eval. For historical reasons, build is generally used to assemble rules, and eval is used for function calls—but they're identical.

Altogether, Jess has almost 200 built-in functions, including these control structures. If that's not enough (and of course, it never is) you can define your own functions, too, as described in the next section.

4.4 *Defining functions with deffunction*

Suppose that some time in the near future, you find yourself in Dallas, working on the AI module for a new martial arts video game (you're using Jess, of course). You're writing many different rules that have to reason geometrically; in particular, many rules care about the distance between two combatants. If the variables ?X1, ?Y1, and ?Z1 hold the coordinates of one ninja, and ?X2, ?Y2 and ?Z2 the coordinates of another, the Jess code to compute distance in three dimensions looks like this:

```
(bind ?x (- ?X1 ?X2))
(bind ?y (- ?Y1 ?Y2))
(bind ?z (- ?Z1 ?Z2))
(bind ?distance (sqrt (+ (* ?x ?x) (* ?y ?y) (* ?z ?z))))
```

The formula takes the difference of each of the X, Y, and Z coordinate pairs, adds them, and takes the square root. It is long and messy, and you surely don't want to type it more than once. Many different rules need to do the same computation, so you can define a function named distance and call it from each rule as needed.

You can write your own functions in the Jess language using the deffunction construct. Once you define a deffunction, you can use it like any other Jess function. deffunction looks like this:

```
(deffunction <name> (<parameter>*) [<comment>] <expression>*)
```

The name of the deffunction must be a symbol. Each parameter must be a variable name, complete with the question mark. A function can have as many parameters as you need to use.

The optional comment is a double-quoted string that can describe the purpose of the function. This special comment is included when a deffunction is displayed. It's a good idea to provide a comment that succinctly describes the purpose of the function. The comment, like any Jess string, can span multiple lines.

The body of a deffunction is composed of any number of expressions. The return value of the deffunction is the value of the last expression evaluated, unless you use the return function to provide an explicit return value. Here's what the distance calculation looks like as a deffunction:

```
Jess> (deffunction distance (?X1 ?Y1 ?Z1 ?X2 ?Y2 ?Z2)
        "Compute the distance between two points in 3D space"
        (bind ?x (- ?X1 ?X2))
        (bind ?y (- ?Y1 ?Y2))
        (bind ?z (- ?Z1 ?Z2))
        (bind ?distance (sqrt (+ (* ?x ?x) (* ?y ?y) (* ?z ?z))))
        (return ?distance))
    TRUE
```

You can now call distance just as if it were built in to Jess:

```
Jess> (distance 10 0 0 2 0 0)
8
```

Besides being shorter and easier to type, the function call is much easier to understand—the reader immediately knows what's being computed, instead of needing to puzzle out those subtractions, multiplications, additions, and square root functions.

The distance function computes a single value. More complex deffunctions can use the control-flow functions like foreach, if, and while that you learned about in section 4.3. Your video-game rules will need to make decisions based on which of several rival ninjas is closest to the player. The following example is a deffunction that returns the smaller of its two numeric arguments:

```
Jess> (deffunction min (?a ?b)
        (if (< ?a ?b) then
          (return ?a)
        else
          (return ?b)))
    TRUE
```

Note that this could also be written as

```
Jess> (deffunction min (?a ?b)
    (if (< ?a ?b) then
      ?a
    else
      ?b))
  TRUE
```

because the expressions in the body of a `deffunction` do not have to be function calls, and a `deffunction` returns the value of the last expression evaluated.

One limitation of `min` is that it takes only two arguments, but your video game will contain scenes with dozens of rival ninjas. A version of `min` that takes an unlimited number of arguments would be very useful, and you can write such a function in Jess. In the definition of a `deffunction`, the last parameter can be a multifield (a variable starting with $, as in $?x.) If it is, then the `deffunction` will accept a variable number of arguments; any arguments in excess of the number of named parameters are compiled into a list, and that list is assigned to the multi-field. Here's a version of `min` that uses this feature:

```
Jess> (deffunction min ($?args)
    "Compute the smallest of a list of positive numbers"
    (bind ?minval (nth$ 1 ?args))
    (foreach ?n ?args
  (if (< ?n ?minval) then
    (bind ?minval ?n)))
    (return ?minval))
  TRUE
Jess> (min 10 100 77 6 43)
  6
```

4.4.1 *Late binding*

Jess uses *late binding* for function names, meaning the link between the name of a function and the code it represents can be changed right up until the instant the function is called. In Java, of course, code won't compile if it calls a function that hasn't been defined yet. In Jess, you can write code that calls a function, even if you haven't written that second function yet. Jess won't try to find the undefined function until the code that calls it is executed. If the undefined function hasn't been defined at that time, an error will result.

Late binding is a useful property because it also means you can redefine a function at any time, and any code that called the old function will automatically call the new one. To redefine a function, you simply define a new function by the same name, and the old one is replaced. You can even redefine any of the built-in functions this way (although doing so is not recommended). If you want to change the behavior of a built-in function, you can do so using defadvice, described in the next section.

4.5 *Fine-tuning a function's behavior*

If you're a Java programmer, it probably bothers you that functions like nth$ number list items starting at one rather than zero. In some languages, you'd be stuck. But Jess makes it easy to fine-tune the behavior of any function, so if you'd like nth$ to use zero-based indices, you can have it your way by using *advice*. Advice is code that you add to a function to change its behavior.

The function defadvice lets you easily wrap advice around any Jess function, such that it executes before (and thus can alter the argument list seen by the real function, or short-circuit it completely by returning a value of its own) or after the real function (and thus can see the return value of the real function and possibly alter it). This is a great way for Jess add-on authors to extend Jess without needing to change any internal code. It was named after a similar feature in Emacs Lisp.

To make nth$ accept a zero-based index, all you need to do is intercept any call to nth$ and add one to the first argument before nth$ sees it. That way, when you call nth$, you can pass zero-based indices, but nth$ will see one-based indices.

Imagine that the variable ?argv holds a copy of a function call to nth$ using a zero-based index; that is, it's a list like this:

```
(nth$ 0 ?grocery-list)
```

You need to write some Jess code to change this list to use a one-based index:

```
(nth$ 1 ?grocery-list)
```

The code to make this change looks like this:

```
;; Strip off the function name
(bind ?tail (rest$ ?argv))
;; Convert zero-based to one-based index
(bind ?index (+ 1 (nth$ 1 ?tail)))
;; Put the argument list back together.
(bind ?argv (create$ nth$ ?index (rest$ ?tail)))
```

You saw the rest$ function in section 4.2.4: It strips the first element from a list and returns the remainder. You needed to use nth$ to write this code, and you used a one-based index, because that's what nth$ wants by default.

Now you can use this block of code to modify the behavior of nth$. In the body of a defadvice call, the variable ?argv is special: It points to the actual function call being executed. By modifying the contents of ?argv, you can modify the arguments the built-in nth$ function sees.

First, let's watch the default behavior of nth$ in action:

```
Jess> (bind ?grocery-list (create$ peas beans butter milk))
(peas beans butter milk)
Jess> (nth$ 1 ?grocery-list)
peas
```

Now, you add some advice to nth$, and then call it again:

```
Jess> (defadvice before nth$
          ;; Strip off the function name
          (bind ?tail (rest$ ?argv))
          ;; Convert zero-based to one-based index
          (bind ?index (+ 1 (nth$ 1 ?tail)))
          ;; Put the argument list back together.
          (bind ?argv (create$ nth$ ?index (rest$ ?tail))))
TRUE
Jess> (nth$ 1 ?grocery-list)
beans
```

The result is different this time—the index is interpreted as one-based, and the answer is beans instead of peas. The nth$ function will continue to behave this way until Jess is restarted, the clear function (discussed in chapter 6) is called, or the advice is removed with undefadvice:

```
Jess> (undefadvice nth$)
TRUE
Jess> (nth$ 1 ?grocery-list)
peas
```

You may be surprised that you were able to call nth$ in the previous advice code. It looks as though you're redefining nth$ in terms of itself—a recipe for an infinite loop. To prevent this kind of problem, Jess doesn't apply advice to any function calls invoked in an advice block. That's why your call to nth$ inside the advice block uses a one-based index.

In the nth$ example, the advice code executes before the built-in nth$ function is invoked. If the first argument to defadvice were after instead of before, the advice would execute after nth$. In this case, the special variable ?retval is also defined; it holds the result returned by the adviced function. The advice code can modify this variable if it wants to return a different value.

4.5.1 *Take my advice, please*

You can only apply advice to actual functions (built-in or user-defined), not to function-like *constructs* like deffunction, defglobal, deftemplate, defrule, or defquery. Here's a short deffunction to confirm whether something is a function:

```
Jess> (deffunction is-a-function (?name)
    (neq FALSE (member$ ?name (list-function$))))
TRUE
Jess> (is-a-function printout)
TRUE
Jess> (is-a-function deftemplate)
FALSE
```

Let's figure out how this function works—it'll be good practice in reading Jess code, and it includes calls to a couple of built-in functions you haven't seen before. To read complex nested Jess language expressions, it's usually best to start from the inside and work your way out. The innermost function call in this deffunction is to list-function$, which returns (not surprisingly) a list of all the functions currently defined in Jess, including all deffunctions and user-defined functions written in Java. The member$ function returns FALSE if the first argument is not found in the second argument (which must be a list), and returns the index at which the first argument was found otherwise. Finally, is-a-function uses neq (Not EQual) to convert member$'s somewhat odd return value into a simple TRUE or FALSE. The whole deffunction then returns TRUE if the argument appears in the list of defined functions or FALSE otherwise. The two examples confirm that it works.

4.6 *Summary*

The Jess language has a simple and regular syntax. It's rather different from Java's syntax, but it's easy to learn. It is a full-featured programming language in which you can write real programs. Given that it is an interpreted language, it is surprisingly fast.

The Jess language has only a few built-in data types, including INTEGER, FLOAT, SYMBOL, STRING, and LONG. There are several simple control structures, some of which let you transform data into executable code. All of the control structures are actually functions. Jess comes with almost 200 built-in functions, and you can define your own functions using the deffunction construct. You can modify the behavior of the built-in functions using defadvice.

On top of all that, you can also call any Java function you want from Jess. How to do so is the topic of the next chapter.

Scripting Java with Jess

In this chapter you'll...

- Create Java objects
- Call Java methods
- Access Java member data
- ... all from the Jess language

Arguably, the most powerful features of Jess are those that allow it to be easily integrated with Java. From Java code, you can access all parts of the Jess library, so that it's very easy to embed Jess in any Java application, servlet, applet, or other system. Likewise, from the Jess language, the full power of Java is directly available. This capability is shown schematically in figure 5.1.

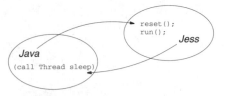

Figure 5.1　You can use Jess from Java, and call Java methods from Jess.

We'll discuss embedding Jess in larger Java systems in great depth later in this book. This chapter describes how you can create Java objects, call their methods, and otherwise interact with Java without writing any Java code.

Jess is therefore a kind of *scripting language* for Java. Aside from using Jess to build rule-based systems, you can also use Jess for experimenting with Java APIs, as a prototyping tool, or even to build entire applications. Want to find out what a particular API method does with a specific argument? It's usually faster to start the Jess command prompt and type in a single line of Jess code than it would be to write, compile, and run a short Java program to do the same experiment. Want to try different arrangements of a graphical interface? You can create the windows, buttons, and other graphical components with a few lines of Jess code, and then interactively assemble and rearrange them to your liking. This is a great way to experiment with the sometimes surprising behavior of Java's layout managers—the classes that arrange components inside an on-screen container.

5.1　*Creating Java objects*

In chapter 4, you learned about plain lists. Although lists are useful, they are not as powerful as the `Map` and `Set` containers in Java's Collections API. A plain list is a good choice for holding a grocery list, but you really need something like a `HashMap` to hold a grocery price lookup table. The `HashMap` would let you easily look up the price of any item in the table.

Jess's <u>new</u> function lets you create instances of Java classes. For instance, you can create a Java `HashMap` and store it in a variable with the following function call:

```
Jess> (bind ?prices (new java.util.HashMap))
<External-Address:java.util.HashMap>
```

Jess uses the type `RU.EXTERNAL_ADDRESS` for the `jess.Value` objects that hold arbitrary Java objects. When you display an `RU.EXTERNAL_ADDRESS` type, you see a string that contains the name of the class. You might expect instead that Jess would call the Java `toString` method on the contained object—if Jess did this, however, the results could be confusing. A `java.lang.Integer` object and a Jess value of type `RU.INTEGER` act very differently, but if Jess used `toString` to display EXTERNAL_ADDRESS objects, they'd both print as a number.

The fully qualified name `java.util.HashMap` requires a lot of typing, and typing package names like `java.util` can be error-prone. In Java, you can avoid using package prefixes with the `import` keyword. Jess has an `import` function you can use to do the same thing:

```
Jess> (import java.util.*)
TRUE
Jess> (bind ?prices (new HashMap))
<External-Address:java.util.HashMap>
```

This example uses the wildcard character "*" to mean "import all the classes in this package," but you can also import one class at a time by using the fully qualified name. Just as in Java, the entire `java.lang` package is implicitly imported, so you can create `Integer` and `String` objects without importing that package explicitly.

So far, you've used `HashMap`'s default constructor. Of course, you can create objects using a class's other constructors as well. `HashMap` has a constructor that takes a Java `int` and a Java `float` as arguments. If you invoke this constructor and pass normal Jess numbers, Jess will make it work:

```
Jess> (bind ?prices (new HashMap 20 0.5))
<External-Address:java.util.HashMap>
```

Jess, like any Java code, can only invoke the public constructors of public classes in other packages. If you want Jess to be able to construct instances of the classes you define, be sure to make both the class and its constructors public.

When you call a Java method, Jess converts the arguments from Jess data types to Java types, as indicated in table 5.1. Generally, when converting in this direction, Jess has some idea of a *target type*. The target type is the Java type that is needed in a given situation. In the `HashMap` example, the target types are `int` and `float`, because those are the types of the formal parameters of the only `HashMap` constructor that takes two arguments. When passing an argument to a Java constructor or method, Jess has the `java.lang.Class` object that represents the formal parameter's type and a `jess.Value` object that contains the value you passed, and wants to turn the `Value`'s contents into something assignable to the type named by the `Class`. Hence the symbol `TRUE` could be passed to a function expecting a `boolean` argument, or to one expecting a `String` argument, and the call would succeed in both cases.

Table 5.1   **Standard conversions from Jess types to Java types**

Jess type	Possible Java types
`RU.EXTERNAL_ADDRESS`	The wrapped object
The symbol `nil`	A null reference
The symbol `TRUE` or `FALSE`	`String`, `java.lang.Boolean`, or `boolean`
`RU.ATOM` (a symbol), `RU.STRING`	`String`, `char`, or `java.lang.Character`
`RU.FLOAT`	`float`, `double`, and their wrappers
`RU.INTEGER`	`long`, `short`, `int`, `byte`, `char`, and their wrappers
`RU.LONG`	`long`, `short`, `int`, `byte`, `char`, and their wrappers
`RU.LIST`	A Java array

You've created a `HashMap`, but you haven't done anything with it. Let's turn it into a lookup table by filling it with grocery price data.

5.2   *Calling Java methods*

If you have a reference to a Java object in a Jess variable, you can invoke any of that object's methods using the `call` function. Let's work with the `HashMap` you created in the previous section. `HashMap.put` associates a *key* with a *value*, and `HashMap.get` lets you look up a value by key. In this example, the keys are the names of grocery items, and the values are the prices:

```
Jess> (call ?prices put bread 0.99)
Jess> (call ?prices put peas 1.99)
Jess> (call ?prices put beans 1.79)
Jess> (call ?prices get peas)
1.99
```

The first argument to `call` is a Java object, and the second argument is the name of a method to invoke. The remaining arguments to `call` are the arguments to be passed to the Java method. The arguments are converted to Java types according to table 5.1.

In this example, you ignore the return value of `HashMap.get` and allow Jess to simply display it. Often, though, you'll want to do something with the return type: binding it to a variable or calling another method on it in turn are two common alternatives. Jess converts the return values of Java methods to Jess types according to table 5.2. These conversions are generally the reverse of those in table 5.1.

Table 5.2   Standard conversions from Java types to Jess types

Java type	Jess type
A null reference	The symbol `nil`
A void return value	The symbol `nil`
`String`	`RU.STRING`
`boolean` or `java.lang.Boolean`	The symbol `TRUE` or `FALSE`
`byte`, `short`, `int`, or their wrappers	`RU.INTEGER`
`long` or `java.lang.Long`	`RU.LONG`
`double`, `float`, or their wrappers	`RU.FLOAT`
`char` or `java.lang.Character`	`RU.ATOM` (a symbol)
An array	A list
Anything else	`RU.EXTERNAL_ADDRESS`

You can call virtually any Java method this way. There are a few special cases: Static methods, methods returning or accepting arrays, and overloaded methods all require special care. We'll discuss these cases in the next few sections. First, let's look at a shortcut that will improve the readability of the last example.

5.2.1 *Nesting function calls, and a shortcut*

The symbol `call` in the following example is a little distracting:

```
(call ?prices put bread 0.99)
```

It is actually no more verbose than the equivalent Java code:

```
map.put("bread", new Double(0.99));
```

(In fact, the Jess code is a little shorter.) But still, `call` seems like extra baggage. The good news is that Jess lets you omit it:

```
(?prices put bread 0.99)
```

When the first element of a function call is a Java object, Jess assumes you meant to include the symbol `call` and invokes a function on the object. This works even if the first element of the function call is another function call:

```
((bind ?prices (new HashMap)) put bread 0.99)
```

This single line of code creates a `HashMap`, binds it to a variable, and adds a name/value pair. Be careful with nesting function calls this way, however; combining logically separate operations into one line of code can make your programs hard to understand. Used wisely, though, such compact code can be readable and efficient.

For most method calls, the `call` is optional. However, you can't leave it out when you're calling a static method.

5.2.2 *Calling static methods*

Static or *class* methods in Java are those methods that can be called without reference to a specific object. In both Java and Jess code, you can use just the name of a Java class to invoke any of its static methods. One well-known example is the `java.lang.Thread.sleep` method:

```
Jess> (call Thread sleep 1000)
(pause for one second)
Jess>
```

You don't need to use the fully qualified name `java.lang.Thread`, because the classes in Java's `java.lang` package are implicitly imported in Jess.

When you call a static method, you must include the `call` function name, as shown in the example; therefore, the most common use of `call` is to invoke static methods. Jess includes other functions, analogous to `call`, to help you invoke other categories of methods, as you'll see in the next section.

5.2.3 *Calling set and get methods*

Special Java objects called *JavaBeans* play an important role in Jess, as you'll see in chapter 6. Therefore, Jess includes many tools for working with them. One of these tools is a pair of methods to simplify accessing their data. Methods that look like the following are fairly common in most object-oriented languages:

```
public String getName() {
    return name;
}
public void setName(String n) {
    name = n;
}
```

They are often called *accessors* and *mutators*, or *getters* and *setters*. They are very common in Java and form an important part of the JavaBeans specification.[1] We'll talk more about JavaBeans in chapter 6, but for now, we'll only be concerned with setters and getters. Many of the Java library classes (especially in the graphical libraries) use this method naming convention.

---

[1] The JavaBeans project page is at http://java.sun.com/products/javabeans/; it offers the JavaBeans specification for download.

Jess includes the functions `set` and `get`, which can be used as an alternative to `call` for setters and getters. The following pairs of function calls are equivalent:

```
Jess> (bind ?b (new javax.swing.JButton))
<External-Address:javax.swing.JButton>

Jess> (?b setText "Press Me") ;; or...
Jess> (set ?b text "Press Me")

Jess> (?b getText ) ;; or...
"Press Me"
Jess> (get ?b text)
"Press Me"
```

The name of a setter or getter method includes a property name, which is `text` in these examples. The property name is passed as the second argument to the `set` or `get` functions. To derive the property name to use, remove the prefix from the Java method name and make the initial capital letter of the rest of the name lowercase. The one exception is for names like `getURL`, where the property name is `URL` in all uppercase. This convention is the same as that used by the JavaBeans specification.

So far we've dealt only with single Java objects and values. Jess also lets you work with Java arrays.

5.2.4 *Working with arrays*

The grocery price table can also serve as a simple grocery list. You can ask a Java `Map` for its collection of keys, and you can ask that collection to convert itself to an array. If you could convert that array to a plain list in Jess, you'd be able to recreate the simple grocery list you worked with in earlier chapters of this book.

As noted in tables 5.1 and 5.2, Jess automatically converts Java arrays to plain lists (Values of type `RU.LIST`). You can use the method `toArray` in `java.util.Collection` to extract all the keys from your `HashMap` into a Jess list:

```
Jess> (bind ?grocery-list ((?prices keySet) toArray))
(bread peas beans)
```

If you want to put your list of groceries into a pop-up menu component, you can pass this list of items as a constructor argument to the `javax.swing.JComboBox` class. `JComboBox` wants an array as a constructor argument, but Jess converts your plain list back into an array automatically:

```
Jess> (import javax.swing.JComboBox)
Jess> (bind ?jcb (new JComboBox ?grocery-list))
<External-Address:javax.swing.JComboBox>
```

This system works well for small arrays (less than a few dozen items), but converting between arrays and lists is inefficient for large arrays, because the Jess data structures to represent the plain list must be created or destroyed on each conversion. A better way of working with large Java arrays is planned for a future version of Jess. Meanwhile, if you need to work with large arrays in your Jess programs, you can write the code to do the work in Java and then call it from Jess.

Jess also has no special interface for working with multidimensional arrays, so again, Java code may be necessary. You can either write ordinary Java functions and call them using the techniques from this chapter, or you can use functions written in Java to extend the Jess language itself. You'll learn how to do this in chapter 15.

The JComboBox class has several constructors, but in the previous example Jess knew which one you wanted to call based on the list you passed as an argument. Let's see how Jess decides which method to invoke based on the function calls you write.

5.2.5 *How Jess chooses among overloaded methods*

Jess is much less picky about data types than Java is. In Java, you can't store a float into a HashMap, but you can store a Jess float—because Jess obligingly converts the number you provide into a java.lang.Double automatically, and that can be stored just fine. Most of the time, these automatic conversions are helpful; but occasionally they cause problems. One problem area is when you need to call one of a set of overloaded Java methods.

A Java method name is said to be *overloaded* if multiple methods with the same name but different argument lists are available on the same object. The many overloads of java.io.PrintWriter.println are an extreme example. All these methods appear in the PrintWriter class:

```
void println()
void println(boolean x)
void println(char x)
void println(char[] x)
void println(double x)
void println(float x)
void println(int x)
void println(long x)
void println(Object x)
void println(String x)
```

When you call an overloaded method in Java code, the Java compiler chooses an overload based on the exact compile-time types of the parameters. Java chooses the most specific applicable method.[2] Sometimes, if there's no clear choice, you get a Java compiler error, but the important point is that there's always a right answer.

Jess is much more relaxed about choosing between overloads, because it has to be: It doesn't have the same kind of strict type information that Java has. One simple example: Looking at the list of overloaded `println` methods, you can see that there are versions for both `double` and `float`. Jess has only one floating-point type, so it can't be sure which one you'd rather call.

When you call an overloaded method such as `println`, Jess looks at each of the overloads in turn, trying to match the parameter types of the method to the types of the arguments you passed. The first overload Jess finds that can be invoked with the given argument list will be called. Jess does *not* search for a best match—it uses the first matching method it finds. Because Jess knows so many different ways to convert between Jess and Java values, the whole idea of a best match is too vague to be useful.

Often, it doesn't matter which of a set of overloaded methods is called; a set of overloaded methods usually all do the same thing, and the overloading is just for the sake of convenience. This is the case with `java.io.PrintWriter.println`. Sometimes, however, you may want to call a specific overloading of a method, and circumstances may conspire to make this impossible. For example, if you pass the string `"TRUE"` to a Java method that is overloaded to take either a `boolean` or a `String`, it is generally impossible to predict which overload Jess will choose. In these cases, you can usually resort to using an explicit wrapper class. For example, suppose that in this case you want to invoke the `boolean` overload but Jess calls the `String` one instead; creating and passing a `java.lang.Boolean` object should fix the problem, because Jess will automatically convert `java.lang.Boolean` to `boolean`, but not to `String`.

Sometimes calling Java methods isn't enough—you may need to work directly with an object's member variables or the static member variables of a class. Jess lets you do that, too.

5.3 *Accessing Java member data*

Some Java classes have public variables you may need to work with. Sometimes these are objects like the familiar `System.out`. More commonly, they are static constants like `MAX_PRIORITY` in `java.lang.Thread` or `NORTH` in `java.awt.BorderLayout`. Of

---

[2] See the Java Language Specification, section 15.11.2.2.

course, some classes have public member variables, like the x and y members of java.awt.Point, which you'll want to both read and modify.

Instance variables are members of a class that belong to individual objects; each object has its own copy of an instance variable. Jess can access public instance variables of Java objects using the get-member and set-member functions. In this example, a Point object is allocated, and its x and y members are set and then read:

```
Jess> (bind ?pt (new java.awt.Point))
<External-Address:java.awt.Point>
Jess> (set-member ?pt x 37)
37
Jess> (set-member ?pt y 42)
42
Jess> (get-member ?pt x)
37
```

The set-member and get-member functions also work on *class variables*. There is only a single copy of each class variable, and all objects of a class share it. Class variables are also called *static variables* in Java. You can access class variables by using the name of the class instead of an object as the first argument to set-member or get-member:

```
Jess> (get-member System out)
<External-Address:java.io.PrintStream>
Jess> (get-member java.awt.BorderLayout NORTH)
"North"
```

Jess converts values for all kinds of member variables between Java and Jess types according to tables 5.1 and 5.2—that is, using the same rules as are used for method arguments and return values.

When you're working with Java objects, methods usually return a value to their caller, and everything works fine. Sometimes, though, methods don't return—they throw exceptions instead. In the next section, you'll see how Jess handles exceptions.

5.4 *Working with exceptions*

Java methods can signal an error by *throwing an exception*. An exception is just a Java object, and it's intended to be treated as a message from the failed code to the caller. When a Java constructor or method throws an exception, Jess receives or *catches* the message and makes it available to you. Jess signals errors in your Jess code and failures in its own functions using exceptions, too, so this section is relevant even when you aren't explicitly working with Java objects.

When Jess catches an exception in a Jess function or a Java method, its default action is to print a detailed message, including either one or two stack traces, to the console. If there is only one stack trace, it shows where in Jess's own Java code the problem occurred. If the exception occurred in a Java method you called from Jess, a second stack trace pinpoints the error in the Java method. Together, these stack traces tell you exactly what happened in your Jess program.

Although these messages are useful to you, the programmer, they're generally not what you want to happen in a deployed system, when a user would see them. Therefore, whenever you call a method that might throw an exception, you should supply a *handler* to execute in response to the exception in place of Jess's default handler. You can do this using the `try` function. As a first example, let's call the function `parseInt` in the `java.lang.Integer` class, which throws `NumberFormatException` if its argument can't be parsed as the string representation of an integer:

```
Jess> (deffunction parseInt (?string)
    (try
        (bind ?i (call Integer parseInt ?string))
        (printout t "The answer is " ?i crlf)
     catch
        (printout t "Invalid argument" crlf)))
TRUE
Jess> (parseInt "10")
The answer is 10
Jess> (parseInt "1O")
Invalid argument
```

Lowercase "ell",
uppercase "oh"

The `try` function evaluates the expressions in the first block, one at a time. If one of those expressions throws an exception, that block is abandoned, and `try` begins evaluating expressions that follow the symbol `catch`, if it appears. You can also have a `finally` block following the `catch` block, just like in Java. The `finally` expressions are evaluated regardless of whether the `try` statements throw any exceptions. A good use for a `finally` block is to close a file, as in this Jess rendering of some typical Java file I/O code:

```
Jess> (import java.io.*)
TRUE
Jess> (bind ?file nil)
Jess> (try
        (bind ?file
            (new BufferedReader
                (new java.io.FileReader "data.txt")))
        (while (neq nil (bind ?line (?file readLine)))
            (printout t ?line crlf))
     catch
```

```
        (printout t "Error processing file" crlf)
    finally
        (if (neq nil ?file) then
            (?file close)))
Error processing file
```

You must have either a `catch` or a `finally` block, or both, in every `try` function call.

You can access the actual exception object that was thrown using the special variable `?ERROR`, which is always defined for you in a `catch` block and is initialized by Jess to point to the caught exception. Whereas in Java you can define multiple `catch` blocks in a single `try`, differentiated by exception type, you can have only one `catch` block in a `try` in Jess. If you want to distinguish between exception types, you can use the `?ERROR` variable and the `instanceof` function, which can tell you whether a given object belongs to a given Java class. For example, you may want to call the static method `lookup` in the `java.rmi.Naming` class. This method is used to contact remote objects via the RMI protocol. The `lookup` method can throw `NotBoundException`, `RemoteException`, and `AccessException` (all from the `java.rmi` package), as well as `java.net.MalformedURLException`. You can issue specific error messages for each of these cases; the code might look like listing 5.1.

Listing 5.1   Using `instanceof` in `catch` blocks

```
Jess> (import java.rmi.*)
TRUE                                          Lets you use
Jess> (import java.net.MalformedURLException)  short class
TRUE                                          names           Service
Jess> (try                                                    misspelled;
    (bind ?server                                             throws
        (call Naming lookup "rmi://snarf.blat.com/Survice"))  NotBound-
        (printout t "Connection established." crlf)           Exception
    catch
        (if (instanceof ?ERROR NotBoundException) then     Check exception
            (printout t "No such service at host" crlf)    type; print
        else (if (instanceof ?ERROR MalformedURLException) then  custom
                (printout t "Address has a syntax error" crlf)   message
            else (if (instanceof ?ERROR AccessException) then
                    (printout t "You don't have permission" crlf)
                else (if (instanceof ?ERROR RemoteException) then
                        (printout t "Network error" crlf)
                    else
                    (printout t "Unknown Error" crlf))))))  Default error
No such service at host.                                    message
```

Jess's `throw` function lets you throw Java exceptions from Jess code. It works just like the `throw` keyword in Java: The single argument must be an instance of a Java class that extends `java.lang.Throwable`. Here's an example:

```
Jess> (throw (new Exception "Testing"))
Jess reported an error in routine throw
    while executing (throw (new Exception "Testing")).
Message: Exception thrown from Jess language code.
Program text: (throw (new Exception "Testing")) at line 1.
Nested exception is:
java.lang.Exception: Testing
    at jess.TryCatchThrow.call(Funcall.java:827)
    at jess.FunctionHolder.call(FunctionHolder.java:37)
```

5.5 *Summary*

Jess can create Java objects, call their methods, and access their data. Jess can also work with Java primitives by converting between Java and Java types. With a few exceptions (particularly working with large or multidimensional arrays), most Java code can be directly translated to Jess. Even these exceptions can easily be overcome by extending Jess with functions written in Java; you'll learn how to do this in part 5 of this book.

In chapters 6 and 7, you'll see how Jess's ability to work with Java objects comes into play in rule-based programming as we study Jess's working memory and learn how to write Jess rules. And as you'll see later in this book, these capabilities make integrating Jess into a Java application extraordinarily easy.

Representing facts in Jess

Now that we've looked at the basic syntax of the Jess language, it's time to begin our study of Jess's rule-based programming features. In this chapter, we'll look at how to create and manage the data that rules can act on—the *working memory* we first discussed in chapter 1. The working memory, sometimes called the *fact base*, contains all the pieces of information Jess is working with. The working memory can hold both the premises and the conclusions of your rules.

Jess stores the contents of working memory using a set of customized indices that make looking up a particular piece of information very fast—much as a relational database does. Even though Jess uses a data-centric index internally, your view of working memory will look like a simple list. Each item in working memory appears on this list in the order in which it was added. We'll begin our study of working memory by looking at the individual items it contains—the working memory elements, or *facts*.

6.1 *Jess's working memory*

Jess maintains a collection of information nuggets called *facts*. This collection of facts is known as the *working memory*. All the pieces of information your rules work with are represented as facts in the working memory. For example, if your program is a smart environmental control system for an office building, the facts in the working memory may be temperature and humidity readings from around the building, and sensor readings and switch settings from the building's air-conditioning systems (see figure 6.1). The contents of Jess's working memory are held in your computer's RAM.

Facts come in different types. However, like most other constructs in Jess, facts are stored as lists. Each of the following is a valid fact:

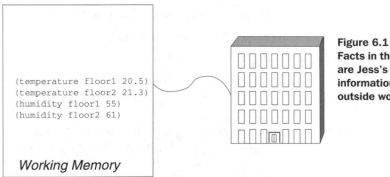

```
(temperature floor1 20.5)
(temperature floor2 21.3)
(humidity floor1 55)
(humidity floor2 61)
```

Working Memory

Figure 6.1
Facts in the working memory are Jess's representation of information about the outside world.

```
(initial-fact)
(little red Corvette)
(groceries milk eggs bread)
```

As it happens, these are all examples of *ordered facts*, which will be discussed in section 6.4.

It is important to recognize that we're using the word *fact* in a specific, technical sense, and the meaning differs slightly from the colloquial English usage. In rule-based systems terminology, <u>*fact* is another word for *working memory element*. A fact is therefore the smallest unit of information that can be separately added to or removed from the working memory of a rule-based system.</u> Jess facts aren't generally *atomic*; rather, they have some structure to them, as you'll see in the following sections.

6.1.1 *Manipulating the working memory*

Intuitively, a collection is a group of items you can add to or remove from. Depending on your tastes as a collector, you can acquire new baseball cards, or discard a chipped ceramic unicorn. Working memory is a collection of facts, and if you were to write a rule-based program about trading cards, each card in your collection might be represented by a single fact.

Jess offers a set of functions to let a program perform the basic collection operations (add, remove, modify, duplicate) on the working memory. You can also use these functions interactively while you're programming, along with others that let you examine, initialize, and clear the working memory. This section describes the following functions and constructs; as a Jess programmer, you'll use all of these frequently:

- assert—Adds facts to working memory
- clear—Clears all of Jess
- deffacts—Defines the initial contents of working memory
- facts—Displays the contents of working memory
- reset—Initializes the working memory
- retract—Removes facts from working memory
- watch—Tells Jess to print diagnostics when interesting things happen

Jess includes several functions that let you peer into working memory and see what's happening. We'll cover these first so you'll be able to follow the action in later sections.

The watch function

Many Jess programs are developed interactively by typing at the Jess> prompt and watching the results. It would therefore be useful to be able to see when Jess's working memory has changed. You can use the watch function to tell Jess to print messages when various interesting things happen. Depending on the arguments you pass to watch, you can get Jess to report on several different kinds of events, including changes to the working memory. If you type the expression **(watch facts)**, then you'll see a message whenever any facts are added or removed from then on. The reset function initializes the working memory and creates the fact (MAIN::initial-fact), and you can see the fact being added to working memory if (watch facts) is in effect:

```
Jess> (watch facts)
TRUE
Jess> (reset)
==> f-0 (MAIN::initial-fact)
TRUE
Jess> (unwatch facts)
TRUE
```

The ==> symbol given by Jess in a response means the fact is being added to working memory, whereas a <== symbol is printed to show a fact being removed.

In the rest of this chapter, we'll show Jess's output as if the watch function has not been issued, but you can use it whenever you want to keep an eye on what's happening with working memory. As you may have inferred from the example, the unwatch function reverses the effect of watch.

The facts function

Although watch can tell you when new facts appear and old ones are removed, it can't give you the big picture. You can get that using facts. You can see a list of all the facts in the working memory using the facts function. If you continue the previous example by typing **(facts)** at the prompt, you'll see that the fact (MAIN::initial-fact) is the only one in working memory:

```
Jess> (facts)
f-0 (MAIN::initial-fact)
For a total of 1 facts.
```

The (initial-fact) turns out to be useful, but it's not especially interesting. Let's add some more facts to working memory so you have something worth looking at.

Creating facts with assert

Rules can only act on information that is represented by facts in Jess's working memory. In any nontrivial program, then, you need to create new facts of your own. New facts are added to the working memory using the `assert` function:

```
Jess> (reset)
TRUE
Jess> (assert (groceries milk eggs bread))
<Fact-1>
Jess> (facts)
f-0 (MAIN::initial-fact)
f-1 (MAIN::groceries milk eggs bread)
For a total of 2 facts.
```

The grocery list has been added to the working memory and assigned an index 1, called the *fact-id*. Every fact in the working memory has a fact-id, assigned in order starting with 0, so that a fact with a larger fact-id was always added to working memory at a later time than a fact with a smaller fact-id. Here the fact-id 0 was assigned to (MAIN::initial-fact). The fact-id serves as a convenient way to refer to a fact when you want to modify it or remove it from working memory. Jess also uses fact-ids when it decides the order in which rules will be fired.

The qualifier MAIN:: that was prepended to the first field in the list (called the fact's *head*; see chapter 4) is the name of the current *module*. A module is a named subset of the rules, facts, and other constructs you've entered into Jess. Modules are often used to divide rules and facts into functional groups, and we'll study them in detail in chapter 7. For now, it's enough to know that MAIN is the default module name and all the facts you define belong to it.

The `assert` function takes any number of facts as arguments and returns the fact-id of the last fact asserted, or FALSE if the last fact couldn't be asserted. Typically, this means the argument was a duplicate of a fact that was already in working memory. (Jess's working memory contains only unique facts.)

Real collections both grow and shrink: You can sell baseball cards as well as buy them. Facts, likewise, come and go. When you're through with your grocery shopping, you'll want to erase the list from working memory.

Removing facts with retract

If a fact represents a true statement about the world, then when the world changes, that fact needs to be removed from the working memory. You can remove individual facts from the working memory using the `retract` function. Arguments for `retract` can be actual facts—that is, a `jess.Value` object of type RU.FACT, which holds a reference to a `jess.Fact` Java object—or they can be numeric fact-ids. Let's retract the two facts you currently have in working memory, one at a time:

```
Jess> (facts)
f-0 (MAIN::initial-fact)
f-1 (MAIN::groceries milk eggs bread)
For a total of 2 facts.
Jess> (retract 1)
TRUE
Jess> (facts)
f-0 (MAIN::initial-fact)
For a total of 1 facts.
Jess> (bind ?f (fact-id 0))      ◁──┐  Fetch Fact object
<Fact-0>                              │  with fact-id 0
Jess> (retract ?f)
TRUE
Jess> (facts)
For a total of 0 facts.
```

This example retracts the grocery-list fact using its fact-id and the initial-fact fact by using the Fact object directly (you first have to look up the Fact object using the fact-id function). Both approaches work, but if you already have a reference to a Fact object, then using that reference is faster. Using fact-ids is more convenient when you're working interactively at the Jess> prompt.

You retracted two facts, one at a time. It would have been possible to get the same effect using a single call to the clear function, as you'll see in the next section.

Clearing and initializing working memory

As you work interactively in Jess, the working memory tends to become full of bits and pieces of information that are no longer relevant. When this happens, you might want to clean things up to make it easier to see what you're doing. Similarly, a running program might want to periodically start from a known state—for instance, when a particular customer signs on to your e-commerce site, the program should have on hand only the information relevant to that customer.

You can remove all the facts from working memory using the clear function. However, clear goes beyond just erasing working memory; it also erases all variables, rules, and deffunctions from Jess. Because clear essentially deletes the entire active program, it's not used very often—generally only if you're in an interactive session and want to start from a clean slate.

To restore the initial state of an application without erasing it completely, you can use reset. The reset function puts working memory into a known state. By default, working memory is empty except for the special fact (MAIN::initial-fact), as you've seen in the earlier examples. This initial fact is special because Jess uses it internally. Many rules implicitly expect it to be there and won't work correctly without it. Before you use the working memory, it's important to use the reset function at least once, while your program is starting up or at the beginning of an interactive session. You (or your program) can issue reset again whenever you want to reinitialize the working memory.

You can specify the initial contents of working memory, in addition to (MAIN::initial-fact), using the deffacts construct.

The deffacts construct

Typing separate assert functions for each of many facts is rather tedious. It's also common to initialize the Jess engine using the reset function, which clears the working memory, and then immediately want to put the working memory into a known state containing a number of initial facts. For example, in an e-commerce program, the initial facts might include the product catalog.

To make this process easier, Jess includes the deffacts construct. A deffacts construct is a simply a named list of facts. You can define any number of deffacts constructs. The facts in all existing deffacts are asserted into the working memory whenever the reset function is issued. Listing 6.1 demonstrates the operation of deffacts.

Listing 6.1 A deffacts construct in action

```
Jess> (clear)
TRUE
Jess> (deffacts catalog "Product catalog"
    (product 354 sticky-notes "$1.99")
    (product 355 paper-clips "$0.99")
    (product 356 blue-pens "$2.99")
    (product 357 index-cards "$0.99")
    (product 358 stapler "$5.99"))
TRUE
Jess (facts)
For a total of 0 facts.
Jess> (reset)
TRUE
Jess> (facts)
f-0 (MAIN::initial-fact)
f-1 (MAIN::product 354 sticky-notes "$1.99")
f-2 (MAIN::product 355 paper-clips "$0.99")
f-3 (MAIN::product 356 blue-pens "$2.99")
f-4 (MAIN::product 357 index-cards "$0.99")
f-5 (MAIN::product 358 stapler "$5.99")

For a total of 6 facts.
```

Whenever `reset` is called, the facts in the `deffacts` are asserted. This is a convenient way to set up the product catalog in working memory for the first time and to restore it after working memory has been cleared.

Using the functions we've discussed in this section, you add and remove facts from Jess's working memory and see the effects of your changes. Now let's examine the individual facts themselves in more detail.

6.2 *Just the facts, ma'am*

Jess's working memory is stored in a complex data structure with multiple indexes, so that searching the working memory is a very fast operation. The working memory is therefore something like a relational database, and the individual facts are like rows in a database table (see figure 6.2). This implies that facts, like table rows, must have a specific structure so that they can be indexed. Jess offers three different kinds of facts; each kind has its own structure and is indexed and used in a different way.

Unordered facts are the workhorses of the working memory. An unordered fact is quite literally like a row in a relational database table, with individual named data fields corresponding to the table's columns. When you assert an unordered fact, you can specify the slots in any order—hence the name *unordered*. Unordered facts are the most common kind of fact and a good choice for most situations. An unordered fact looks like this:

```
(person (name "John Q. Public") (age 34) (height 5 10) (weight 170))
```

An *ordered fact* lacks the structure of named fields—it is just a short, flat list—but ordered facts are convenient for simple bits of information that don't need structure. All the facts we've used as examples so far have been ordered facts. If you used an ordered fact to represent the same "person" data, it would look like this:

```
(person "John Q. Public" 34 5 10 170)
```

Finally, *shadow facts* are unordered facts that are linked to Java objects in the real world—they provide a way to reason about events as they occur outside of Jess. In the following sections, we'll cover each of these categories of fact in detail.

Figure 6.2
Working memory is something like a relational database.

6.3 *Unordered facts*

A table in a relational database has a name and a set of named columns. Each row of data in a table provides a value for each of the columns. *Unordered facts* are working memory elements that behave like rows in a database table (although the columns are traditionally called *slots*). Here are some examples of unordered facts:

```
(person (name "Bob Smith") (age 34) (gender Male))
(automobile (make Ford) (model Explorer) (year 1999))
(box (location kitchen) (contents spatula))
```

The person fact has slots name, age, and gender; the automobile fact has slots make, model, and year. The head of an unordered fact (person, automobile, box) is like the table name, and the slot names are like the column names.

Before you can work with unordered facts, you have to specify their structure using the deftemplate construct. Once you have created some unordered facts and put them in working memory, functions such as modify and duplicate let you change or copy them.

6.3.1 *The deftemplate construct*

Typically, a relational database contains many tables, one for each type of information the database holds. In a real relational database, to create a new table, you have to specify the names of the columns that will be found in the table. Thereafter, every row in the table has those same columns—no more and no less.

Similarly, in Jess, you define many different kinds of unordered facts. Before you can assert an unordered fact with a given head, you have to use the deftemplate construct to define the slots that kind of fact. This example defines an unordered fact type with three slots:

```
Jess> (deftemplate person "People in actuarial database"
    (slot name)
    (slot age)
    (slot gender))
TRUE
Jess> (assert (person (age 34) (name "Bob Smith")
                (gender Male)))
<Fact-1>
Jess> (facts)
f-0 (MAIN::initial-fact)
f-1 (MAIN::person (name "Bob Smith") (age 34)
    (gender Male))
For a total of 2 facts.
```

The *name* of the deftemplate (person) is used as the head of the facts. You can define as many slots as you want in your deftemplate. You can also include a short description, as shown in the example.

When you assert an unordered fact, you can specify the slots in any order, and you don't have to include every slot. When Jess displays an unordered fact (for instance, when you type the (facts) function), the slots are always displayed in a standard order—the order in which you defined them in the deftemplate.

If you omit any slots when you assert an unordered fact, they're filled in using *default values*.

6.3.2 *Default slot values*

Most relational databases support the idea of a "don't care" value in a particular column. If you add a row to a table and don't specify a value for one or more columns, then this default value—usually called NULL—is used. Jess lets you do the same thing with unordered facts. When you assert unordered facts, you can omit values for any number of slots, and Jess will fill in the default value nil:

```
Jess> (assert (person (age 30) (gender Female)))
<Fact-2>
Jess> (facts)
f-0 (MAIN::initial-fact)
f-1 (MAIN::person (name "Bob Smith") (age 34)
    (gender Male))
f-2 (MAIN::person (name nil) (age 30)
    (gender Female))
For a total of 3 facts.
```

Sometimes nil is an acceptable default value, but often it's not. You can specify your own default value by using a *slot qualifier*:

```
Jess> (clear)
TRUE
Jess> (deftemplate person "People in actuarial database"
    (slot name (default "OCCUPANT"))
    (slot age)
    (slot gender))
TRUE
```

NOTE If you're following along, you may have entered a previous definition for the person template. You can't redefine a deftemplate until you use the clear function to completely erase Jess's internal state, as this example does.

Notice that when you assert a `person` fact and don't specify a value for the `name` slot, the default value OCCUPANT is used:

```
Jess> (assert (person (age 30) (gender Female)))
<Fact-0>
Jess> (facts)
f-0 (MAIN::person (name "OCCUPANT") (age 30)
    (gender Female))
For a total of 1 facts.
```

What if the appropriate default value isn't constant, but changes over time? As an example, a slot might be initialized to hold a timestamp indicating when the fact was asserted. The default-dynamic qualifier lets you accomplish this. Jess evaluates the given value each time a new fact is created using this template. Usually you'll use a function call with `default-dynamic`. For example, to create the timestamp, you could use `(default-dynamic (time))`.

The slots we've looked at so far have all contained single values. Slots that hold multiple values are useful, too. You'll learn how to create them next.

6.3.3 *Multislots*

The normal slots we've looked at so far can each hold only a single value. Sometimes, though, it's handy to keep a list of things in a slot. For example, if you wanted to keep track of a person's hobbies in a `hobbies` slot, you'd need to be able to handle people who have more than one way to spend their free time. You can create slots that can hold multiple values by using the multislot keyword:

```
Jess> (clear)
TRUE
Jess> (deftemplate person "People in actuarial database"
    (slot name (default OCCUPANT))
    (slot age)
    (slot gender)
    (multislot hobbies))
TRUE
Jess> (assert (person (name "Jane Doe") (age 22)
    (hobbies snowboarding "restoring antiques")
    (gender Female)))
<Fact-0>
```

Now Jane has two hobbies, both listed in the single `hobbies` multislot.

If you don't specify a default value for a multislot, Jess uses an empty list. Usually this is what you want, but you can specify a different default if you need to.

The values contained in the slots of an unordered fact are not fixed; you can change them whenever you want using the `modify` function.

6.3.4 *Changing slot values with modify*

Very often, a rule acts on a fact by updating it. For example, a rule about the passage of time might occasionally need to update the age slot of all the persons in the working memory. You can change the values in the slots of an unordered fact using the modify function. Continuing the previous example:

```
Jess> (modify 0 (age 23))
<Fact-0>
Jess> (facts)
f-0 (MAIN::person (name "Jane Doe") (age 23)
    (gender Female)
    (hobbies snowboarding "restoring antiques"))
For a total of 1 facts.
```

The first argument to modify is either a Fact object or a numeric fact-id, and all the other arguments are *slot name, value* pairs that specify a new value for the named slot. You can modify any number of slots in a fact with a single modify function. You can use modify on multislots, too.

Note that the fact-id of a fact does not change when you use the modify function. It's the same fact—it just has new slot values. If you've used CLIPS, you might notice that this is an important difference between CLIPS and Jess; in CLIPS, the fact-id changes when you use modify. This simple property is extremely useful. A slot of one fact can hold the fact-id of another fact as slot data, and in this way, you can build structures of related facts. Because the fact-id of a fact is constant, the relationships won't be broken if the facts are modified.

6.3.5 *Copying facts with duplicate*

If you know that John Doe is the same age as Jane and likes the same things, but is male instead of female, you can create a fact representing him using the duplicate function. The duplicate function is similar to modify, except that instead of modifying an existing fact, it makes a copy, and then modifies the copy. Continuing the previous example, let's make a copy of the Jane Doe fact (fact-id 0):

```
Jess> (duplicate 0 (name "John Doe") (gender Male))
<Fact-1>
Jess> (facts)
f-0 (MAIN::person (name "Jane Doe") (age 23)
    (gender Female) (hobbies snowboarding "restoring antiques"))
f-1 (MAIN::person (name "John Doe") (age 23)
    (gender Male) (hobbies snowboarding "restoring antiques"))
For a total of 2 facts.
```

Just like modify, duplicate does nothing if the new fact would be an exact copy of an existing fact. The duplicate function returns the fact-id of the newly created fact, or FALSE if no fact was created. The modify and duplicate functions only work with unordered facts, because they require a slot name as an argument, which ordered facts don't have. Let's look at some things that ordered facts *can* do.

6.4 *Ordered facts*

Although unordered slots are a great way to organize data when you need many slots per fact, if you only need one slot, they can seem redundant. For example, here's a deftemplate to hold a fact representing a single number:

```
Jess> (deftemplate number (slot value))
TRUE
Jess> (assert (number (value 123)))
<Fact-0>
```

The name value doesn't add any information—it just clutters things up. For simple cases like this, it would be nice to be able to omit the notion of a slot name altogether—and Jess allows this:

```
Jess> (clear)
TRUE
Jess> (assert (number 123))
<Fact-0>
```

You can assert facts that look like simple, flat lists, without explicitly defining a deftemplate for them, as long as no deftemplate using that same head has already been defined. All the facts you used in the first section of this chapter were ordered facts. We'll use the following functions to take a closer look at ordered facts and their templates:

- ppdeftemplate—Displays a pretty-printed deftemplate
- show-deftemplates—Lists all the deftemplates currently defined

When you assert the first ordered fact with a given head, Jess automatically generates an *implied* deftemplate for it. The ppdeftemplate function lets you see the definition of any deftemplate. Let's use it to examine the implied deftemplate for number:

```
Jess> (ppdeftemplate number)
"(deftemplate MAIN::number extends MAIN::__fact \"(Implied)\"
    (multislot __data))"
```

ppdeftemplate (the *pp* stands for *pretty print*) returns its result as a string, so the definition is enclosed in double quotes and the quotes around the documentation string are escaped with backslashes. The implied deftemplate number contains a single slot named __data. Jess treats facts created from these deftemplates specially. The name of the __data slot is normally hidden when the facts are displayed. This is really just syntactic shorthand, though; ordered facts are unordered facts with a single multislot. Jess understands that the name __data doesn't add any information and so should normally be hidden.

In practice, the most common kind of ordered facts is the head-only kind like (initial-fact). They are often used for transient information that will soon be retracted and for one-of-a-kind statements like (shutdown-now) and (found-solution). If your fact will hold more than one piece of slot data, unordered facts offer a lot more flexibility and lend structure to the information they hold, so they are generally preferable in most situations. In addition, unordered facts lead to fewer coding errors. The explicit slot labels serve as a sanity check during programming and help prevent mistakes. Finally, unordered facts give better pattern-matching performance, as you'll learn in chapter 7.

The show-deftemplates function lists any implied deftemplates along with any explicitly created ones. You can also use show-deftemplates to see Jess's built-in deftemplates:

```
Jess> (show-deftemplates)
(deftemplate MAIN::__clear extends MAIN::__fact "(Implied)")
(deftemplate MAIN::__fact "Parent template")
(deftemplate MAIN::__not_or_test_CE
    extends MAIN::__fact "(Implied)")
(deftemplate MAIN::initial-fact extends MAIN::__fact "(Implied)")
(deftemplate MAIN::number extends MAIN::__fact "(Implied)"
    (multislot __data))
FALSE
```

In this example you can see the three special templates Jess uses internally: __clear, __fact, and __not_or_test_CE, as well as the initial-fact template and your number template.

The third and final category of facts is perhaps the most interesting, because these facts connect Jess's working memory to the real world outside.

6.5 *Shadow facts*

A *shadow fact* is an unordered fact whose slots correspond to the properties of a Java-Bean. JavaBeans are a kind of normal Java object; therefore, shadow facts serve as a connection between the working memory and the Java application inside which Jess is running. They're called *shadow facts* because they are like images, or shadows, of JavaBeans outside of Jess. The function defclass lets you create a special `deftemplate` to be used with shadow facts, and `definstance` lets you create an individual shadow fact. Let's briefly look at what JavaBeans are, and then see how they can be connected to Jess's working memory. We'll discuss these Jess functions:

- `defclass`—Creates a `deftemplate` from a JavaBean class
- `definstance`—Adds a JavaBean to Jess's working memory

6.5.1 Jess and JavaBeans

You can view Jess's working memory as sort of an electronic organizer for your rule-based system. A piece of data must be part of the working memory for it to be used in the premises of a Jess rule. Ordered and unordered facts are useful in many situations, but in many real-world applications, it's useful to have rules respond to things that happen outside of the rule engine. Jess lets you put regular Java objects in working memory—instances of your own classes that can serve as hooks into a larger software system—as long as those objects fulfill the minimal requirements necessary to be JavaBeans.

As previously mentioned, unordered facts look a bit like Java objects. Specifically, they look a lot like JavaBeans. The JavaBean component architecture specification (http://java.sun.com/products/javabeans/) defines a JavaBean simply as a self-contained, reusable component that can be used from a graphical builder tool. JavaBeans, like other kinds of software components (for instance, Visual Basic controls), often serve as interfaces to more complex systems such as databases or special hardware.

6.5.2 JavaBeans have "slots"

The similarity between JavaBeans and unordered facts is that both have a list of slots (for JavaBeans, they're called *properties*) containing values that might change over time. There's plenty more to JavaBeans than just properties; however, those features go beyond the scope of this book.[1]

A JavaBean property is most often a pair of methods named in a standard way. If the property is a `String` named `label`, the Java methods look like this:

```
String getLabel();
void setLabel(String);
```

The `get` method is used to read the value of the property, and the `set` method to change it. The `java.beans` API includes a class named `Introspector` that can

---

[1] Plenty of great books on JavaBeans are available if you're interested. For example: Lawrence Rodrigues, *The Awesome Power of Java Beans* (Greenwich, CT: Manning Publications, 1998).

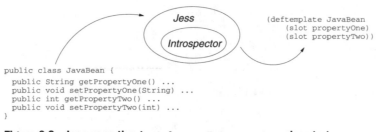

```
public class JavaBean {
  public String getPropertyOne() ...
  public void setPropertyOne(String) ...
  public int getPropertyTwo() ...
  public void setPropertyTwo(int) ...
}
```

Figure 6.3 Jess uses the `java.beans.Introspector` class to turn JavaBeans into `deftemplates`.

examine JavaBeans and find properties defined according to this get/set naming system. There are a few wrinkles having to do with capitalization and other details, but this simple convention works most of the time.

Jess can use `Introspector` to automatically generate a `deftemplate` that represents any specific JavaBean class (see figure 6.3). A fact created from this `deftemplate` can then serve as a sort of adapter to store the JavaBean in working memory, the shadow facts. A shadow fact has one slot for each JavaBean property. If a JavaBean has array properties, those properties become multislots, and all other properties become normal slots. The slots are automatically populated with the values of the JavaBean's properties. In the next section, you'll watch Jess use `Introspector` to create a custom template for a JavaBean.

6.5.3 *An example JavaBean*

Now let's work through an example of how a JavaBean can be connected to Jess's working memory. Listing 6.2 shows a simple JavaBean class. This JavaBean has one property called `brightness`. Note that when you set the `brightness` property, the Bean calls the method `adjustTriac` that brightens or dims an attached lighting fixture (the code for `adjustTriac` presumably uses the Java Native Interface to access code written in another language, like C). The value you read using the `getBrightness` method is thus always tied to the brightness of the light. If you had a `DimmerSwitch` object in Jess's working memory, then your rules would be able to reason in real time about the lighting in a building.

Listing 6.2 A simple JavaBean with one property: `brightness`

```
public class DimmerSwitch {
    private int brightness = 0;
    public int getBrightness() { return brightness; }
    public void setBrightness(int b) {
        brightness = b;
        adjustTriac(b);
    }
}
```

```
    private void adjustTriac(int brightness) {
        // Code not shown
    }
  }
```

You need a special `deftemplate` to plug a `DimmerSwitch` into Jess—let's learn how to create one.

6.5.4 *Creating a deftemplate for DimmerSwitch*

The Jess functions that let you put JavaBeans into working memory are `defclass` and `definstance`. The `defclass` function tells Jess to generate a special template to represent a specific JavaBean class, whereas `definstance` puts a shadow fact connected to one particular JavaBean instance into working memory.

Before you can insert an instance of `DimmerSwitch` into Jess's working memory, you need a `deftemplate` to represent the class. You use `defclass` to tell Jess to generate it:

```
Jess> (defclass dimmer DimmerSwitch)
DimmerSwitch
Jess> (ppdeftemplate dimmer)
"(deftemplate MAIN::dimmer extends MAIN::__fact
    \"$JAVA-OBJECT$ DimmerSwitch\"
    (slot brightness
        (default <External-Address:jess.SerializablePD>))
    (slot class (default <External-Address:jess.SerializablePD>))
    (slot OBJECT (type 2048)))"
```

To run this code, you first need to compile the `DimmerSwitch` class and make the `.class` file available on your CLASSPATH. The resulting template is a bit strange looking (especially the default values). It does have a slot called `brightness`, as you'd expect, which arises from the `brightness` property of the JavaBean. All shadow facts have the other slots in common. The slot `class` comes from the method `getClass` that every Java object inherits from `java.lang.Object`, and the slot OBJECT is added by Jess. This special OBJECT slot always contains a reference to the JavaBean to which a given shadow fact. The first argument to `defclass`—dimmer, here—is used as the `deftemplate` name. (Some people like to use the name of the Java class itself; my personal preference is to use a shorter name with a lowercase initial.)

6.5.5 *Putting a DimmerSwitch into working memory*

Now you can put a `DimmerSwitch` into working memory. Here you'll create one from Jess code, but it could come from anywhere (later in this book, you'll learn many strategies for passing objects back and forth between Jess and Java code). After you create a `DimmerSwitch`, you use the `definstance` function to add it to the working memory:

```
Jess> (bind ?ds (new DimmerSwitch))
<External-Address:DimmerSwitch>
Jess> (definstance dimmer ?ds static)
<Fact-0>
Jess> (facts)
f-0 (MAIN::dimmer
    (brightness 0)
    (class <External-Address:java.lang.Class>)
    (OBJECT <External-Address:DimmerSwitch>))
For a total of 1 facts.
```

The first argument to `definstance` is the name of a template created by `defclass`, and the second argument is a corresponding JavaBean. We'll discuss the meaning of `static` in the next section.

As soon as you call the `definstance` function, a shadow fact representing the Bean appears in the working memory. Rules can react to this `dimmer` fact just as they can to any other fact in working memory. If you imagine thousands of `dimmer` facts, representing the brightness of every light fixture in a large office building, you can see how letting Jess reason about `DimmerSwitch` objects could be useful.

6.5.6 *Static vs. dynamic shadow facts*

The working memory representation of a JavaBean can be either *static* (changing infrequently, like a snapshot of the properties at one point in time) or *dynamic* (changing automatically whenever the JavaBean's properties change). The `definstance` you have defined already is `static`. What happens if you change the `brightness` property of your Bean, turning on the light? You can invoke the `setBrightness` method using the `call` function you learned about in chapter 5:

```
Jess> (call ?ds setBrightness 10)
Jess> (facts)
f-0 (MAIN::dimmer
    (brightness 0)
    (class <External-Address:java.lang.Class>)
    (OBJECT <External-Address:DimmerSwitch>))
For a total of 1 facts.
```

Nothing changed. The working memory still thinks the Bean's `brightness` is set at 0, even though you changed it to 10. This is expected behavior for a `static` `definstance`. Obviously, though, you'd like the shadow fact to track changes in the Bean's properties. What happens if you call `reset`?

```
Jess> (reset)
TRUE
Jess> (facts)
f-0 (MAIN::initial-fact)
f-1 (MAIN::simple
    (brightness 10)
    (class <External-Address:java.lang.Class>)
    (OBJECT <External-Address:DimmerSwitch>))
For a total of 2 facts.
```

The reset function updates the shadow fact to match the JavaBean. This behavior is what you get when you specify static in the definstance function as you did earlier. Static shadow facts are refreshed only when a reset is issued. In between reset calls, their properties do not change in response to property changes in their JavaBean.

If you want to have a shadow fact continuously track property changes in a Java-Bean, Jess needs to be notified whenever a property changes in that JavaBean. The JavaBean can notify Jess by sending it a special kind of Java event, a java.beans.PropertyChangeEvent. Many commercially available JavaBeans already support this kind of notification, and you can easily add it to Beans you write yourself. If DimmerSwitch offered support for PropertyChangeListeners, then it could notify Jess when its brightness changed, and the shadow facts could stay in sync with the Beans. Let's add that support now.

6.5.7 *Adding PropertyChangeListener support to DimmerSwitch*

Let's modify the DimmerSwitch class to send PropertyChangeEvents. The modified class DimmerSwitchDynamic is shown in listing 6.3. The interesting method in DimmerSwitchDynamic is setBrightness. This method saves the original value of the brightness member variable, then gives it its new value, and then sends a property change notification using the PropertyChangeSupport utility class. The addPropertyChangeListener and removePropertyChangeListener methods are boilerplate code that is always used with PropertyChangeSupport. These methods allow interested external code like Jess to register to be notified when a property changes.

Listing 6.3   A JavaBean that sends property change notifications

```
import java.beans.*;
public class DimmerSwitchDynamic {
    private int brightness = 0;
    public int getBrightness() {
        return brightness;
    }
```

```
public void setBrightness(int b) {
    int old = brightness;
    brightness = b;
    adjustTriac(b);
    pcs.firePropertyChange("brightness",
                     new Integer(old), (new Integer(b)));
}
```

Calls fireProperty-Change to indicate brightness property is changing

```
private void adjustTriac(int brightness) {
    // Code not shown
}

private PropertyChangeSupport pcs =
    new PropertyChangeSupport(this);
public void
addPropertyChangeListener(PropertyChangeListener p) {
    pcs.addPropertyChangeListener(p);
}
public void
removePropertyChangeListener(PropertyChangeListener p) {
    pcs.removePropertyChangeListener(p);
}
```

Boilerplate code you can reuse in JavaBeans

```
}
```

Now if you use `definstance` without the `static` qualifier to register a `Dimmer-SwitchDynamic` instance with Jess, the shadow fact tracks the `brightness` property whenever it changes, as listing 6.4 demonstrates. This time, calling `setBrightness` to change the JavaBean changes the shadow fact, too; Jess receives a `Property-ChangeEvent` and modifies the shadow fact accordingly.

Listing 6.4   A demonstration of dynamic `definstances`

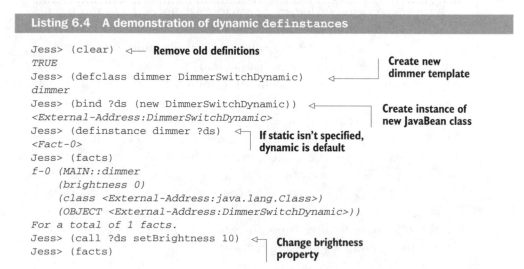

```
Jess> (clear)   ◁── Remove old definitions
TRUE
Jess> (defclass dimmer DimmerSwitchDynamic)   ◁──┐  Create new
dimmer                                             dimmer template
Jess> (bind ?ds (new DimmerSwitchDynamic))   ◁──┐  Create instance of
<External-Address:DimmerSwitchDynamic>            new JavaBean class
Jess> (definstance dimmer ?ds)   ◁── If static isn't specified,
<Fact-0>                              dynamic is default
Jess> (facts)
f-0 (MAIN::dimmer
    (brightness 0)
    (class <External-Address:java.lang.Class>)
    (OBJECT <External-Address:DimmerSwitchDynamic>))
For a total of 1 facts.
Jess> (call ?ds setBrightness 10)   ◁── Change brightness
Jess> (facts)                             property
```

```
f-0  (MAIN::dimmer                    Brightness slot updated
        (brightness 10)  ◁─────┐      to match Bean
        (class <External-Address:java.lang.Class>)
        (OBJECT <External-Address:DimmerSwitchDynamic>))

For a total of 1 facts.
```

6.5.8 *Shadow facts and working memory functions*

Many of the functions and constructs you've seen so far work on shadow facts just as they work on other kinds of facts, but there are some differences. Most of these differences are obvious. For example, you can't use the `assert` function to assert a shadow fact; you use `definstance` instead. You can, however, use `retract` to remove a shadow fact. You also can't put a shadow fact in a `deffacts` construct. Note, though, that each individual `definstance` behaves like its own `deffacts`—when you call `reset`, the shadow fact for every instance is reinitialized.

The `modify` function operates on shadow facts just as it works on regular facts. Furthermore, if you modify the contents of a slot of a shadow fact, Jess automatically updates the corresponding JavaBean property. This happens for both static and dynamic `definstance`s.

Finally, the `duplicate` function cannot be used with shadow facts. Jess throws an exception if you try to duplicate one.

6.6 *Summary*

Jess's working memory can contain *ordered facts*, *unordered facts*, and *shadow facts*; each type of fact is useful in certain situations. Unordered facts are general-purpose facts, whereas ordered facts are useful for small bits of information. Shadow facts are used to connect a JavaBean in your Java application to Jess's working memory, so that rules can react to things that happen outside of your Jess program. You can write rules that operate on any or all of these working memory elements; in the next chapter, you'll see how.

All facts are created from a `deftemplate`, which defines the slots a fact can have. Sometimes you define this `deftemplate` yourself, and sometimes Jess creates it for you. The `deftemplate`s in a rule-based system are like the schema of a database; they define a way of looking at the data relevant to the system.

Now that you know the Jess language and understand something about Jess's working memory, you're ready to learn how to write rules. In the next chapter, you'll learn about writing rules and about *pattern matching*—how to make rules react to the contents of working memory.

Writing rules in Jess

7

In this chapter you'll...

- Learn to write rules
- Learn the difference between forward and backward chaining
- Learn how to partition your rules with modules
- Learn to probe working memory with queries

Now that you've learned how to populate the working memory, you can develop a *knowledge base* to go with it. This is the whole reason you're here: The knowledge base is the collection of *rules* that make up a rule-based system. Rules can take actions based on the contents of working memory.

There are two main classes of rules in Jess: *forward-chaining* and *backward-chaining* rules. Forward-chaining rules are somewhat like if ... then statements in a procedural language, and they're the most common and important kind of rule in Jess. Backward-chaining rules, on the other hand, don't have a clear analogy in procedural programming. They are also similar to if ... then statements, but a backward-chaining rule actively tries to satisfy the conditions of its if part.

You can access working memory directly with *queries*. You can design queries to search working memory, to find specific facts, and to explore their relationships. Queries have a lot in common with rules—if you can write one, you know how to write the other. You'll learn how to write and invoke queries in section 7.7.

7.1 Forward-chaining rules

A *forward-chaining rule* is something like an if ... then statement in a procedural language, but it is not used in a procedural way. Whereas if ... then statements are executed at a specific time and in a specific order, according to how the programmer writes them, a Jess rule's then part can be executed whenever the if part is satisfied. This makes rules less obviously deterministic than a typical procedural program, because Jess decides the order in which to fire the rules. (See section 8.3's discussion of the *Rete algorithm* for an explanation of why this architecture can be many orders of magnitude faster than an equivalent set of traditional if ... then statements.)

This section discusses the following functions and constructs:

- defrule—Defines a new rule
- ppdefrule—Pretty-prints a rule
- run—Begins firing activated rules from the agenda
- undefrule—Deletes a rule
- watch rules—Prints a diagnostic when a rule fires
- watch activations—Prints a diagnostic when a rule is activated

All Jess rules are defined using the defrule construct. The simplest possible rule looks like this:

```
Jess> (defrule null-rule
  "A rule that does nothing"
  =>
)
TRUE
```

The symbol `null-rule` is the name of the rule. A hyphen (-) is often used to separate words in a symbol. Rules are uniquely identified by their name. If a rule named `my-rule` exists, and you define another rule named `my-rule`, the first version is deleted. There is also an undefrule function that can delete a rule by name.

The name is followed by an optional documentation string that describes the purpose of the rule. The symbol => (an equals sign followed by a greater-than sign) separates the rule's *left-hand side* (*LHS,* or `if` part) from its *right-hand side* (*RHS,* or `then` part). The symbol => can thus be read as *then*. The previous rule has no conditions on its LHS and no actions on its RHS. It will therefore always execute, and it will accomplish nothing.

The following example uses two new arguments to the `watch` function, `activations` and `rules` (you used `(watch facts)` in chapter 6):

```
Jess> (watch facts)
TRUE
Jess> (watch activations)
TRUE
Jess> (watch rules)
TRUE
Jess> (reset)
==> f-0 (MAIN::initial-fact)
==> Activation: MAIN::null-rule : f-0
Jess> (run)
FIRE 1 MAIN::null-rule f-0
1
```

The function call (watch activations) tells Jess to print a message whenever an *activation record* is placed on, or removed from, the agenda. An activation record associates a set of facts with a rule. It means the given set of facts matches the LHS of the given rule, and so the rule should be executed. In this case, because `null-rule` doesn't specify a LHS, Jess has automatically made it conditional on the presence of the initial fact. You'll recall from chapter 6 that the `reset` function places a fact (initial-fact) in working memory. This is one important role for (initial-fact): to serve as a trigger for rules with an empty LHS. You can see the change using the `ppdefrule` function, which pretty-prints a rule by re-creating its text from Jess's internal representation:

```
Jess> (ppdefrule null-rule)

"(defrule MAIN::null-rule
\"A rule that does nothing\"
  (MAIN::initial-fact)
  =>) "
```

The return value of `ppdefrule` is a string, so when it is displayed to the console, the embedded quotation marks are escaped with a backslash character. It is important to note that all the work of pattern matching—comparing the LHSs of rules to a given fact—is done while that fact is being asserted. Because (`initial-fact`) is asserted by the `reset` function, `null-rule` is activated whenever the reset function is called, and that's what happens here.

The function call (`watch rules`) tells Jess to print a message whenever a rule is *fired*. A rule is said to be fired when the actions on its RHS are executed. The `run` function tells Jess to start firing rules; no rules will fire except during a call to `run`. Jess's rule engine then fires the rules on the agenda, one at a time, until the agenda is empty. `run` returns the number of rules fired—so 1 is printed in the previous example.

Now let's look at a more complex rule:

```
Jess> (defrule change-baby-if-wet
    "If baby is wet, change its diaper."
    ?wet <- (baby-is-wet)
    =>
    (change-baby)
    (retract ?wet))
TRUE
```

This rule again has two parts, separated by =>. The LHS consists of the *pattern* (baby-is-wet). The RHS consists of two function calls, to `change-baby` and `retract`. Note that the definition of `change-baby` isn't shown here. Although you might at first find it hard to tell due to the Lisp-like syntax, the LHS of a rule consists of patterns that are used to match facts in the working memory, while the RHS contains function calls.

Let me say that again: The left-hand side of a rule (the `if` part) consists of patterns that match facts; they are *not* function calls. The right-hand side of a rule (the `then` clause) is made up of function calls. The following rule does *not* work:

```
Jess> (defrule wrong-rule
(eq 1 1)
=>
(printout t "Just as I thought, 1 == 1!" crlf))
```

Many novice Jess users write rules like this, intending (eq 1 1) to be interpreted as a function call. This rule will *not* fire just because the function call (eq 1 1) would evaluate to TRUE. Instead, Jess tries to find a fact in the working memory that looks like (eq 1 1). Unless you have previously asserted such a fact, this rule will not be activated and will not fire. If you want to fire a rule based on the evaluation of a function, you can use the *test conditional element*, described in section 7.3.4.

The example rule, then, will be activated when the fact `(baby-is-wet)` appears in the working memory. When the rule fires, the function `(change-baby)` is called, and the `(baby-is-wet)` fact is retracted. This rule forms part of a complete program in listing 7.1.

Listing 7.1 A simple but complete Jess program

```
Jess> (clear)
TRUE
Jess> (watch all)
TRUE
Jess> (reset)
==> f-0 (MAIN::initial-fact)
TRUE
Jess> (deffunction change-baby ()
    (printout t "Baby is now dry" crlf))
TRUE
Jess> (defrule change-baby-if-wet
    "If baby is wet, change its diaper."
    ?wet <- (baby-is-wet)
    =>
    (change-baby)
    (retract ?wet))
change-baby-if-wet: +1+1+1+t
TRUE
Jess> (assert (baby-is-wet))
==> f-1 (MAIN::baby-is-wet)
==> Activation: MAIN::change-baby-if-wet : f-1
<Fact-1>
Jess> (run)
FIRE 1 MAIN::change-baby-if-wet f-1
Baby is now dry
<== f-1 (MAIN::baby-is-wet)
1
```

The <u>watch all</u> command in listing 7.1 <u>tells Jess to print diagnostics for everything</u> <u>important that happens while this program runs.</u> Many of the diagnostics in the listing are interesting. You first see how issuing the `reset` command again asserts the fact `(initial-fact)`. Although this rule won't need the initial fact, in most programs the initial fact will be needed by many rules, so you should always issue a `reset` command at some point before running a program.

When the rule is entered at the Jess prompt, you see the line +1+1+1+t. This result tells you something about Jess interprets the rule internally (see chapter 8 for more information). When the fact `(baby-is-wet)` is asserted, you see the diagnostic `Activation: MAIN::change-baby-if-wet : f-1`. This means Jess has noticed that all the LHS conditions of the rule `change-baby-if-wet` are met by the given list of facts—here the single fact `f-1`—and an activation record has been created. Note how the activation record associates the specific fact with the rule; this action will be important later.

Again, the rule doesn't fire until you issue the `run` command. As soon as you enter `(run)`, the activated rule fires. Because you entered the `watch all` command, Jess prints the diagnostic `FIRE 1 MAIN::change-baby-if-wet f-1` to notify you of this action. The `f-1` is a list of the facts that matched this rule's LHS.

You then see the output of the rule's RHS actions. First the function `change-baby` is called. Second, the fact `f-1` is retracted. The variable `?wet` is called a *pattern binding*; the `<-` operator stores a reference to the fact (baby-is-wet) in this variable, and the `retract` function can then access this variable on the rule's RHS. Note, then, that rules cannot only react to the contents of working memory—they can change it. Thus one rule can put information into working memory, which in turn can cause another rule to fire.

The final number 1 is the number of rules that fired (the return value of the `run` command). The `run` function returns when there are no more activated rules to fire.

What would happen if you entered `(run)` again? Nothing. Jess activates a rule only once for a given working memory state. Once the rule has fired, it will not fire again for the same list of facts. You won't change the baby again until a new `baby-is-wet` fact is asserted.

7.1.1 *Patterns and shadow facts*

Jess's working memory can hold JavaBeans as well as facts. Actually, you'll recall that this isn't quite correct: The working memory contains only facts; but some of those facts, called *shadow facts,* are stand-ins for JavaBeans. A shadow fact has a slot for every property of a JavaBean, and for dynamic shadow facts—defined using the `definstance dynamic` function—those slots track the contents of the Java-Bean's properties in real time.

Therefore, everything about patterns in this chapter applies equally to patterns that match facts and to patterns that match JavaBeans. There's no way to tell by looking at a pattern whether it's intended to match `deftemplate` facts or shadow facts.

7.2 *Constraining slot data*

The `baby-is-wet` fact in the previous section didn't have any slot data. Most facts do, however, and most patterns need to specify some particular set of slot values for the facts they match. These specifications are called *constraints*, because they constrain the values a slot can have in a fact that matches the pattern. A number of different kinds of constraints can be used to match slot data:

- *Literal constraints*—Specify exact slot values
- *Variable constraints*—Bind a matched value to a variable
- *Connective constraints*—Let you combine conditions to match A *and* B, or A *or* B
- *Predicate constraints*—Let you call a function to test for a match
- *Return value constraints*—Test for an exact match between a slot's contents and the result of a function call

7.2.1 Literal constraints

Literal slot values can be included in patterns as constraints. A pattern including a literal value matches *only* facts that include that value. In the following example, although both facts have the head letters, only the one with slot data that exactly matches the pattern activates the rule:

```
Jess> (clear)
TRUE
Jess> (defrule literal-values
    (letters b c)
    =>)
TRUE
Jess> (watch activations)
TRUE
Jess> (assert (letters b d))    <— This doesn't activate the rule...
<Fact-0>
Jess> (assert (letters b c))    <— ... but this does
==> Activation: MAIN::literal-values: f-1
<Fact-1>
```

Remember that an ordered fact is implemented as an unordered fact with a single multislot named __data (a multislot, you'll recall, can hold any number of items). You could therefore write the previous rule as

```
Jess> (assert (letters b c))
<Fact-0>
Jess> (defrule literal-values
    (letters (__data b c))
    =>)
TRUE
```

and it would behave the same way (I asserted a letters fact first to emphasize that Jess only defines the implicit deftemplate for letters when it sees an ordered letters fact; the rule won't be parsed correctly until this deftemplate exists). It's important to keep this relationship in mind as you read this chapter; remember that everything that applies to ordered facts applies equally well to the multislots of unordered facts. The same goes for the regular slots of unordered facts, with the restriction that they can hold only one value at a time.

Finally, note that literal constraints have to match *exactly*; no conversions are done. Thus the floating-point literal 1.0 doesn't match the integer 1, and the symbol xyz doesn't match the string "xyz". This is a common source of problems when using shadow facts (see section 6.5).

7.2.2 *Variables as constraints*

If all the patterns of a rule had to be given literally, Jess would not be very powerful. However, patterns can also include variables and various kinds of *predicates* (comparisons and boolean functions), and can be modified by *conditional elements*. We'll consider variables and predicates here and conditional elements in the following sections.

You can specify a variable instead of a literal value for any part of the slot data in a pattern. A variable matches any value in that position within the facts that match that pattern. For example, the rule

```
Jess> (defrule simple-variables
    (a ?x ?y)
    =>
    (printout t "Saw 'a " ?x " " ?y "'" crlf))
```

is activated each time an ordered fact with head a having two fields is asserted: (a b c), (a 1 2), (a a a), and so forth. The variables thus matched on the LHS of a rule are available on the RHS of the same rule; you can think of them as the arguments to the rule's RHS when it fires. For example, if the previous rule matched the fact (a b c), then when the rule fired, ?x would have the value b and ?y would have the value c. You can mix literal values and variables in the same pattern, of course.

The same variable can appear in more than one pattern in the same rule, or in several places within one pattern, or both. Every time the variable is used, it must match the same value. In listing 7.2, although two facts could match each pattern individually, only one pair can activate the rule: the fact (a 2) and (b 2).

Listing 7.2   Example of repeating a variable constraint

```
Jess> (defrule repeated-variables
    (a ?x)
    (b ?x)
    =>
    (printout t "?x is " ?x crlf))
```

```
TRUE
Jess> (watch activations)
TRUE
Jess> (deffacts repeated-variable-facts
    (a 1)
    (a 2)
    (b 2)
    (b 3))
TRUE
Jess> (reset)
==> Activation: MAIN::repeated-variables : f-2, f-3
TRUE
Jess> (run)
?x is 2
1
```

Note that in Jess 6.1, you can't use a variable to match the head of a fact or the name of a slot; these things must always be specified as literal values. This capability is planned for a future release, however.

Multifields

Regular variables match exactly one value. *Multifields* can match any number of values—zero, one, or more. You write a multifield by preceding a variable name with the characters $?—for example, $?mf is a multifield. You can only use multifields in multislots. They can be used alone, in which case the multifield matches any number of values in that multislot, or in combination with regular variables or literal values. If you use multifields together with single values, the multifields expand to match everything not matched by the other values. For example, the pattern in this rule matches a shopping-cart fact with any number of values in the contents multislot:

```
(defrule any-shopping-cart
    (shopping-cart (contents $?items))
    =>
    (printout t "The cart contains " ?items crlf))
```

The pattern in this rule matches any shopping-cart fact with a contents slot that contains milk preceded by any number (zero or more) of items and followed by any number of additional items:

```
(defrule cart-containing-milk
    (shopping-cart (contents $?before milk $?after))
    =>
    (printout t "The cart contains milk." crlf))
```

As shown here, multifields are accessible on the RHS of the rules that use them in patterns (just as normal variables are). A multifield always contains the matched values as a list, even if it matches zero or one value. You can (and generally should, as a matter of style) leave the $ sign off a multifield when you refer to it on the RHS of a rule, because there it is acting as a normal variable.

Blank variables

You can match a field without binding it to a variable by omitting the variable name and using a question mark (?) as a placeholder. This is generally only useful as a way to specify that a multislot contains a certain arrangement of values without caring what those values are. For example, a pattern like (poker-hand ten ? ? ? ace) matches any poker-hand starting with a ten, ending with an ace, and containing a total of five cards. You can have blank multifields, too—just use bare $? characters.

Matching global variables

If you match to a defglobal with a pattern like (score ?*x*), the match only considers the value of the defglobal when the fact is first asserted. Subsequent changes to the defglobal's value will *not* invalidate the match—if the rule was activated based on the value of the defglobal, it stays activated even if the defglobal's value changes. The match does not reflect the current value of the defglobal, but only the value at the time the matching fact was asserted.

7.2.3 Connective constraints

Quite often, matching with a literal value or a variable isn't enough. You might want a pattern to match if a client is located in either Boston or Hartford, for example, or you might want a pattern to match as long as the client is not from Bangor. You can write these patterns, and many others, using the *connective constraints* & (*and*), | (*or*), and ~ (*not*).

Any single constraint preceded by a tilde (~) matches the opposite of what the constraint would originally have matched. For example, the following pattern matches any client facts with a city slot that doesn't contain Bangor:

```
(client (city ~Bangor))
```

This pattern matches clients that have purchased exactly two items, which must not be the same:

```
(client (items-purchased ?x ~?x))
```

The other connective constraints let you form groups of single constraints. Ampersands (&) represent logical *and*, and pipes (|) represent logical *or.* For example, this pattern matches any client that hails from Boston or Hartford:

```
(client (city Boston|Hartford))
```

And this one again matches any client not from Bangor, and in addition remembers the contents of city in the variable ?c:

```
(client (city ?c&~Bangor))
```

When you use several connective constraints together in a single expression, you should pay attention to *operator precedence*, or the way Jess groups the constraints together as it evaluates the expression. The ~ connective constraint has the highest precedence, followed by & and |, in that order. ~ always applies to the single constraint immediately following it, so the following (redundant) pattern matches all clients that are not from Bangor and *are* from Portland:

```
(client (city ~Bangor&Portland))
```

This pattern does *not* mean "all clients that are from neither Bangor nor Portland," which would be written

```
(client (city ~Bangor&~Portland))
```

There are no grouping symbols that you can use with constraints—you can't use parentheses to change their precedence. If you can't express what you want using connective constraints, you can do it instead using *predicate constraints*, as described in the next section.

7.2.4 *Constraining matches with predicate functions*

Literal constraints, variables, and connectives suffice for many situations, but there are some things they can't express. Perhaps you want to match any shopping-cart that contains an odd number of items, or a client that lives in a city whose name contains more than 10 letters. Jess lets you specify these constraints, and virtually any other constraint you can imagine, using *predicate functions*. For our purposes, a predicate function is just a Boolean function—a function that returns TRUE or FALSE. You can use any predicate function as a constraint by preceding it with a colon (:). If you want to use the value of a slot as an argument to the function (and you almost always do), you should bind that value to a variable first, and then connect that binding to the function using the & connective:

```
Jess> (defrule small-order
    (shopping-cart (customer-id ?id)
```

```
                          (contents $?c&:(< (length$ $?c) 5)))
        (checking-out-now ?id)
        =>
        (printout t "Wouldn't you like to buy more?" crlf))
    TRUE
```

The `length$` function returns the length of a list. This rule delivers a special message to any customers who go to the checkout with fewer than five items in their cart.

You can use the and, or, and not predicate functions to express complex logical conditions. Although they are more verbose than the simple connective constraints, they are more powerful because you can group them into arbitrary structures. For example, this rule fires if a customer is checking out with more than 50 items, but his cart contains neither milk nor butter:

```
Jess> (defrule large-order-and-no-dairy
    (shopping-cart (customer-id ?id)
                   (contents $?c&
                     :(and (> (length$ $?c) 50)
                           (not (or (member$ milk $?c)
                                    (member$ butter $?c))))))
    (checking-out-now ?id)
    =>
    (printout t "Don't you need dairy products?" crlf))
    TRUE
```

Note that internally, Jess implements the | connective by transforming the whole pattern for that slot into predicate functions, and then using or to represent the |.

When evaluating a predicate constraint, Jess interprets any return value except FALSE as if it were TRUE. The `member$` function returns FALSE if the given value is not a member of the list argument; otherwise it returns the position of the value in the list. Even though `member$` never returns TRUE, it works perfectly well as a predicate function, because the non-FALSE values are interpreted as TRUE.

7.2.5 *Return value constraints*

Often you'll want to constrain the contents of slot to match the return value of a function. For example, if you wanted to find a pair of grocery items such that the price of one was exactly twice the price of another, you might use a predicate constraint like this:

```
(item (price ?x))
(item (price ?y&:(eq ?y (* ?x 2))))
```

(The eq function returns TRUE if the arguments are all equal, or FALSE otherwise.) Although this approach works, it's not especially pretty. It would be more convenient to write this using a *return value constraint*. A return value constraint includes an arbitrary function, and the slot data must match whatever the function returns. When you're writing a return value constraint, the function is preceded by an equals sign (=). You can rewrite the previous example using a return value constraint like so:

```
(item (price ?x))
(item (price =(* ?x 2)))
```

The return value constraint version is simpler because you don't need the variable ?y or the call to eq.

In fact, pretty-printing a rule containing a return value constraint always shows that Jess has transformed it into an equivalent predicate constraint using eq, so the two forms are equivalent. Which one to use is a matter of taste.

7.2.6 *Pattern bindings*

To use retract, modify, or duplicate on a fact matched by the LHS of a rule, you need to pass a handle to the fact to the RHS of the rule. To do this, you use a pattern-binding variable:

```
Jess> (defrule pattern-binding
    ?fact <- (a "retract me")
    =>
    (retract ?fact))
```

A reference to the jess.Fact object that activates this rule is bound to the variable ?fact when the rule is fired.

You can retrieve the name of a fact, its integer ID, and other useful data by calling the Java member functions of the jess.Fact class directly, like this:

```
Jess> (defrule call-fact-methods
    ?fact <- (initial-fact)
    =>
    (printout t "Name is " (call ?fact getName) crlf)
    (printout t "Id is " (call ?fact getFactId) crlf))
TRUE
Jess> (reset)
TRUE
Jess> (run)
Name is MAIN::initial-fact
Id is 0
1
```

Note that because pattern bindings have to refer to specific facts, you must be careful when using them with some of the grouping conditional elements described in the following sections. You can't use them with not or test conditional elements, for example; and when using them with or and and conditional elements, you must be careful that the binding will apply to only one fact. Jess lets you write ambiguous bindings, but they may lead to errors at runtime, depending on how the patterns are matched. The next section presents some additional details on this issue.

7.3 *Qualifying patterns with conditional elements*

We've just been looking at increasingly sophisticated ways to match the data within individual facts. Now we'll look at ways to express more complex relationships *between* facts, and to qualify the matches for entire facts. *Conditional elements* (CEs) are *pattern modifiers*. They can group patterns into logical structures, and they can say something about the meaning of a match. There's even one conditional element, test, that doesn't involve matching a fact at all.

Before we begin, let me caution you that many of these conditional elements have the same names as predicate functions we looked at in the last section. There's an and conditional element, and there's an and predicate function. Although they may look similar, they're entirely unrelated. The and predicate function operates on Boolean expressions, but the and conditional element operates on patterns. You can always tell which you're dealing with by the context—predicate functions can appear only as constraints on slot data. The following are all of Jess's conditional elements:

- and—Matches multiple facts
- or—Matches alternative facts
- not—Matches if no facts match
- exists—Matches if at least one fact matches
- test—Matches if a function call doesn't evaluate to FALSE
- logical—Matching facts offer logical support to new facts

7.3.1 *The and conditional element*

The LHS of every rule consists of a list of zero or more patterns. Each of those patterns must match for the whole LHS to match. You might recognize this as the *intersection* operation from formal logic. You can express the intersection of a group of patterns in Jess using the and conditional element. The entire LHS of every rule is enclosed in an implicit and.

Any number of patterns can be enclosed in a list with and as the head. The resulting pattern is matched if and only if all of the enclosed patterns are matched. The following rule matches only if (flaps-up) and (engine-on) both match:

```
Jess> (defrule ready-to-fly
    (and (flaps-up)
         (engine-on))
    =>)
```

Of course, this rule would behave precisely the same way if the and CE was omitted, so by itself, and isn't very interesting. Combined with or and not conditional elements, though, you can use the and CE to construct complex logical conditions.

7.3.2 *The or conditional element*

Any number of patterns can be enclosed in a list with or as the head. The or CE matches if one or more of the patterns inside it matches. If more than one of the patterns inside the or matches, the entire or is matched more than once:

```
Jess> (clear)
TRUE
Jess> (deftemplate used-car (slot price) (slot mileage))
TRUE
Jess> (deftemplate new-car (slot price) (slot warrantyPeriod))
TRUE
Jess> (defrule might-buy-car
    ?candidate <- (or (used-car (mileage ?m&:(< ?m 50000)))
                      (new-car (price ?p&:(< ?p 20000))))
    =>
    (assert (candidate ?candidate)))
Jess> (assert (new-car (price 18000)))
<Fact-0>
Jess> (assert (used-car (mileage 30000)))
<Fact-1>
Jess> (run)
2
```

The rule fires twice: once for the new car and once for the used car. In this rule, only one of the two branches of the or conditional element will match at a time, but the rule can be activated separately as many times as there are facts to match. Each of the vehicles listed matches only one or the other of the branches. For some activations, the first branch of the or will match, and for others, it will be the second branch. Note that the variable ?candidate is bound to whatever fact matches the or in each particular activation. If might-buy-car's RHS tried to modify the mileage slot of the used-car template, runtime errors would occur whenever ?candidate was bound to a new-car fact, because the new-car template doesn't have such a slot.

If the RHS of a rule uses a variable defined by matching on the LHS of that rule, and the variable is defined by one or more branches of an or pattern but not all branches, then a runtime error may occur. For example, if the RHS of `might-buy-car` used the variable `?m` (which is defined only when the rule matches a `used-car` fact), then when it fired in response to a `new-car` fact, you'd see an error message and Jess would stop firing rules.

The `and` group can be used inside an `or` group and vice versa. In the latter case, Jess rearranges the patterns so that there is a single `or` at the top level. For example, the rule

```
Jess> (defrule prepare-sandwich
      (and (or (mustard)
               (mayo))
         (bread))
     =>)
```

is automatically rearranged as follows:

```
Jess> (defrule prepare-sandwich
      (or (and (mustard) (bread))
          (and (mayo) (bread)))
     =>)
```

Jess rearranges the patterns of any rule that has `or` conditional elements in it so that in the end, there is at most one `or` per rule, and it appears at the top level. Jess may use DeMorgan's rules to accomplish this result. DeMorgan's rules are a set of two formulas that describe legal ways of substituting logical expressions. Written in Jess syntax, they can be stated as follows:

```
(not (or (x) (y)))  is the same as (and (not (x)) (not (y)))
(not (and (x) (y))) is the same as (or (not (x)) (not (y)))
```

Jess does this rearrangement so that it can form *subrules*, which are the topic of the next section.

Subrule generation and the or conditional element

A rule containing an `or` conditional element with *n* branches is precisely equivalent to *n* rules, each of which has one of the branches on its LHS. In fact, this is how Jess implements the `or` conditional element: Jess internally divides the rule, generating one rule for each branch. Each of these generated rules is a *subrule*. For a rule named `rule-name`, the first subrule is also named `rule-name`, the second is `rule-name&1`, the third is `rule-name&2`, and so on. Each of these subrules is added to the Rete network individually. If you execute the `(rules)` command, which lists all the defined rules, you will see each of the subrules listed separately. If you use the `ppdefrule` function to see a pretty-print representation of a subrule, you will see only the representation of that particular subrule. Note that because `&` is a token delimiter in the Jess grammar, you can only refer to a subrule with an ampersand in the name by placing the whole name in quotes—for example, (ppdefrule "rule-name&6").

Jess knows that the subrules created from a given rule are related. If the original rule is removed (either using undefrule or implicitly by defining a new rule with the same name as an existing one), every subrule associated with that rule is also removed.

A note regarding subrules and efficiency: You'll learn in chapter 8 that similar patterns are shared between rules in the Rete network, avoiding duplicated computation. Therefore, splitting a rule into subrules does *not* mean the amount of pattern-matching work is increased; much of the splitting may indeed be undone when the rules are compiled into the network.

On the other hand, keep the implementation in mind when you define your rules. If an or conditional element is the first pattern on a rule, all the subsequent pattern-matching on that rule's LHS won't be shared between the subrules, because sharing occurs only as far as two rules are similar reading from the top down. Placing or conditional elements near the end of a rule leads to more sharing between the subrules, and thus more efficient pattern matching.

Finally, I should mention that although subrules will probably always be part of the implementation of the or conditional element in Jess, it is likely that they will no longer be user-visible at some time in the future.

7.3.3 *The not conditional element*

You may have heard the saying "two wrongs don't make a right" when you were growing up. How can the opposite of the opposite of something not be the same as the original thing? Well, as it turns out, it's quite often not. Such is the case in real-world logic: The concept of *negation* is a tricky thing. It's tricky in Jess, too.

Imagine that you want a rule to fire when no red cars are available. Your first try might look something like this:

```
Jess> (defrule no-red-cars
    (auto (color ~red))
    =>)
```

But this rule fires for each car that is not red. If there are no cars at all, it won't fire. This result isn't the same as firing when there are no red cars.

Luckily, Jess has the not conditional element. Most patterns can be enclosed in a list with not as the head. In this case, the pattern is considered to match if a fact (or set of facts) that matches the pattern is *not* found. For example, this rule will fire if there are no cars at all, or if there are only blue cars, but not if there are any red ones:

```
Jess> (defrule no-red-cars-2
    (not (auto (color red)))
    =>)
```

Because a <u>not</u> pattern matches the *absence* of a fact, it cannot define any variables that are used in subsequent patterns on the LHS. You can introduce variables in a <u>not pattern as long as they are used only within that pattern</u>:

```
Jess> (defrule no-odd-numbers
    (not (number ?n&:(oddp ?n)))
    =>
    (printout t "There are no odd numbers." crlf))
```

Similarly, a not pattern <u>can't have a pattern binding</u>; again, because it doesn't match an actual fact, there would be no fact to bind to the variable.

Now, here comes the tricky part I alluded to earlier. You already know that pattern matching is driven by facts being asserted—the matching computation happens during the assert, definstance, modify, duplicate, or reset function that creates the fact. Because a not CE matches the absence of a fact, when can it be evaluated? The answer is that a <u>not CE is evaluated only in these cases</u>:

- When a fact matching it is asserted (in which case the pattern match fails)
- When a fact matching it is removed (in which case the pattern match succeeds)
- When the pattern immediately before the not on the rule's LHS is evaluated

If a not CE is the first pattern on a rule's LHS, the first pattern in an and group, or the first pattern on a given branch of an or group, the pattern (initial-fact) is inserted before the not to become this important preceding pattern. Therefore, <u>the initial fact created by the reset command is necessary for the proper</u> <u>functioning of many not patterns</u>. For this reason, it is especially important to issue a reset command before attempting to run the rule engine when working with not patterns.

The not CE can be used in arbitrary combination with the and and or CEs. You can define complex logical structures this way. For example, suppose you want a rule to fire once, and only once, if for every car of a given color, there exists a bus of the same color. You could express that as follows:

```
Jess> (defrule forall-example
    (not (and (car (color ?c)) (not (bus (color ?c)))))
    =>)
```

Decoding complex logical expressions is easier if you start from the inside and work your way out. The innermost pattern here is (bus (color ?c)), which matches any bus fact. The not around that matches only when there are no bus facts. The `(car (color ?c))` pattern matches any `car` facts, and the `and` groups these two patterns together. The entire `and` thus matches when there is a `car`, but no `bus` of the same color. Putting the `and` group into the outermost `not` means the whole pattern matches only when the `and` doesn't; thus the whole thing can be translated as "It is not true that for some color `?c`, there is a `car` of that color but no `bus` of that same color."

In the next section we'll look at another interesting way to combine `not` CEs into more complex groups.

The exists conditional element

You can nest multiple `not` CEs to produce some interesting effects. Two nots nested one inside the other are so useful that there's a shorthand notation: the `exists` CE. A pattern can be enclosed in a list with `exists` as the head. An `exists` CE is true if there exist any facts that match the pattern, and false otherwise—which is precisely the meaning of two nested nots. The `exists` CE is useful when you want a rule to fire only once, although there may be many facts that could potentially activate it:

```
Jess> (defrule exists-an-honest-man
    (exists (honest ?))
    =>
    (printout t "There is at least one honest man!" crlf))
```

If there are any honest men in the world, the rule will fire once and only once. The `exists` CE is implemented as two nested `not` CEs; that is, `(exists (A))` is exactly the same as `(not (not (A)))`. Therefore, you can't bind any variables in an `exists` CE for use later in the rule, and you also can't use pattern bindings with `exists`.

7.3.4 The test conditional element

A pattern with `test` as the head is special; the body consists not of a pattern to match against the working memory but of a Boolean function. The result determines whether the pattern matches. A `test` pattern fails if and only if the function evaluates to the symbol FALSE; if it evaluates to TRUE, the pattern succeeds. For example, suppose you wanted to find people whose age is less than 30 years old:

```
Jess> (deftemplate person (slot age))
TRUE
Jess> (defrule find-trustworthy-people-1
    (person (age ?x))
    (test (< ?x 30))
    =>
    (printout t ?x " is under 30!" crlf))
TRUE
```

A `test` pattern, like a `not`, cannot contain any variables that are not bound before that pattern, and it can't have a pattern binding.

Because a `test` CE, like a `not` CE, doesn't match an actual fact, its implementation is similar to the way `not` is implemented. A `test` CE is evaluated every time the preceding pattern on the rule's LHS is evaluated, just like a `not`. Therefore the following rule is equivalent to the previous one:

```
Jess> (defrule find-trustworthy-people-2
    (person (age ?x&:(< ?x 30)))
    =>
    (printout t ?x " is under 30!" crlf))
```

Which form you use here is mostly a matter of taste. I tend to use the `test` CE only for long or complex functions that would be hard to read if they were written as predicate constraints. Of course, the `test` CE can also be used to write tests that are unrelated to any facts:

```
(import java.util.Date)
(defrule fire-next-century
    (test ((new Date) after (new Date "Dec 31 2099")))
    =>
    (printout t "Welcome to the 22nd century!" crlf))
```

For rules like this, in which a `test` CE is the first pattern on the LHS, or the first pattern in an `and` CE, or the first pattern in any branch of an `or` CE, Jess inserts the pattern (initial-fact) to serve as the preceding pattern for the `test`. The fact (initial-fact) is therefore also important for the proper functioning of the `test` conditional element; the caution about `reset` in the preceding section applies equally to `test`. The rule `fire-next-century` won't fire until `reset` is called *after* the twenty-second century begins.

The `test` and `not` conditional elements may be combined, so that

```
(not (test (eq ?x 3)))
```

is equivalent to

```
(test (neq ?x 3))
```

The conditional elements we've looked at so far affect how a rule matches working memory. There is one conditional element we haven't covered yet, and it's unusual in that instead of affecting how a rule matches, it affects what happens when a rule fires.

7.3.5 *The logical conditional element*

When you turn on your kitchen faucet, you expect water to come out (if it doesn't, you've got a plumbing problem). When you turn off the faucet, the flow of water stops as a result. This kind of relationship is called a *logical dependency*—the water flowing is logically dependent on the faucet being open. To express this idea in Jess, you could write the following two rules:

```
Jess> (defrule turn-water-on
      (faucet open)
      =>
      (assert (water flowing)))
TRUE
Jess> (defrule turn-water-off
      (not (faucet open))
      ?water <- (water flowing)
      =>
      (retract ?water))
TRUE
```

Given these two rules, asserting `(faucet open)` will automatically cause `(water flowing)` to be asserted as well, and retracting `(faucet open)` will retract `(water flowing)`—if you call `run` so the rules can fire, of course. The fact `(water flowing)` can therefore be said to be logically dependent on `(faucet open)`.

Writing two rules to express the one idea of logical dependency gets the job done, but there is an easier way. The `logical` conditional element lets you specify these logical dependencies among facts more concisely. All the facts asserted on the RHS of a rule are logically dependent on any facts that matched a pattern inside a `logical` CE on that rule's LHS. If any of the matches later become invalid—for instance, because one of the facts is deleted—the dependent facts are retracted automatically. In the simple example in listing 7.3, the `(water-flowing)` fact is again logically dependent on the `(faucet-open)` fact, so when the latter is retracted, the former is removed, too.

Listing 7.3 An example of using the `logical` CE

```
Jess> (clear)
TRUE
Jess> (defrule water-flows-while-faucet-is-open
    (logical (faucet open))
    =>
    (assert (water flowing)))
TRUE
Jess> (assert (faucet open))
<Fact-0>
Jess> (run)                    <-- Rule water-flows-while-
1                                  faucet-is-open fires
Jess> (facts)
f-0 (MAIN::faucet open)
f-1 (MAIN::water flowing)
```

```
For a total of 2 facts.
Jess> (watch facts)
TRUE
Jess> (retract 0)
<== f-0 (MAIN::faucet open)
<== f-1 (MAIN::water flowing)       Jess retracts fact (water
TRUE                                flowing) automatically
Jess> (facts)
For a total of 0 facts.
```

If fact 1 is logically dependent on fact 2, you can also say that fact 1 "receives logical support from" fact 2. A fact may receive logical support from multiple sources—it may be asserted multiple times with a different set of logical supports each time. Such a fact isn't automatically retracted unless each of its logical supports is removed. If a fact is asserted without explicit logical support, it is said to be *unconditionally supported*. If an unconditionally supported fact also receives explicit logical support, removing that support will not cause the fact to be retracted. You can find out what logical support a fact is receiving with the dependencies function. The dependents function tells you what facts are dependent on another given fact. Both functions take either a single fact object or an integer fact ID as an argument.

If one or more logical CEs appear in a rule, they must be the first patterns in that rule; a logical CE cannot be preceded in a rule by any other kind of CE. You can use the logical CE together with all the other CEs, including not and exists. A fact can thus be logically dependent on the nonexistence of another fact or on the existence of some category of facts in general.

Shadow facts from definstances are no different than other facts with regard to the logical CE. Shadow facts can provide logical support and can receive logical support.

7.4 *Backward-chaining rules*

The rules you've seen so far have been *forward-chaining* rules; as I've said, that means the rules are treated as if … then statements, with the engine simply executing the RHSs of activated rules. Some rule-based systems, notably Prolog and its derivatives, support *backward chaining*. In a backward-chaining system, rules are still if … then statements, but the engine actively tries to make rules fire. If the if clause of one rule is only partially matched and the engine can determine that firing some other rule would cause it to be fully matched, the engine tries to fire that second rule. This behavior is often called *goal seeking*.

As an example, think about the ways Sherlock Holmes might solve a mystery. He has a collection of evidence (a handkerchief, a fingerprint, a dead body) and can proceed in two different ways. First, he can draw conclusions from the available evidence, adding his conclusions to the available information, and continue until he's found a link between the evidence and the crime. This is a forward-chaining method. Alternatively, he can start from the circumstances of the crime, form a hypothesis about how it happened, and then search for clues that support this hypothesis. This latter technique is an example of backward chaining. Holmes generally used both techniques in combination to solve a mystery; as a Jess programmer, you'll do the same.

Jess supports both forward and backward chaining, but Jess's version of backward chaining is not transparent to the programmer. You have to declare which kinds of facts can serve as backward-chaining triggers, and only specific rules you define can be used in backward chaining. In truth, Jess's reasoning engine is strictly a forward-chaining engine, and so backward chaining is effectively simulated in terms of forward-chaining rules. Still, the simulation is quite effective, and Jess's backward-chaining mechanism has many useful applications. You will apply it in several of the systems you develop later in this book.

Backward chaining is often used as a way to pull required data into Jess's working memory from a database on demand. In the example given here, backward chaining is used to avoid computing the factorial of a number more than once (the *factorial* of an integer is the product of every integer between 1 and the number itself, inclusive; for large numbers this value can be expensive to compute). You use the `deftemplate factorial` to store computed factorials. The fact (`factorial 5 125`) signifies that the factorial of 5 is 125. Figure 7.1 shows how this example works: The rule `print-factorial-10` won't fire unless a fact giving the factorial of 10 is present. Because `factorial` has been registered for backward chaining with the `do-backward-chaining` function, Jess automatically asserts the fact (`need-factorial 10 nil`). This fact matches the `need-factorial` pattern in the `do-factorial` rule, which fires and asserts the fact (`factorial 10 3628800`). Finally, this fact activates the `print-factorial-10` rule, which fires and prints its output.

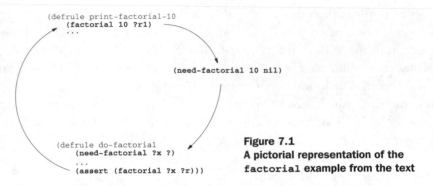

```
(defrule print-factorial-10
    (factorial 10 ?r1)
    ...


                              (need-factorial 10 nil)




(defrule do-factorial
    (need-factorial ?x ?)
    ...
    (assert (factorial ?x ?r)))
```

Figure 7.1
A pictorial representation of the
factorial example from the text

To use backward chaining in Jess, you must first declare that specific `deftemplates` are *backward-chaining reactive* using the `do-backward-chaining` function:

```
Jess> (do-backward-chaining factorial)
TRUE
```

If the template is unordered—if it is explicitly defined with a `deftemplate` or `defclass` construct—then you must define it *before* calling `do-backward-chaining`. You can use `do-backward-chaining` on ordered `deftemplates` before they are created, however.

Once you have declared your reactive `deftemplates`, you can define rules with patterns that match facts of the corresponding types. Note that you must call `do-backward-chaining` *before* defining any rules that use the template.

This rule prints the factorial of 10, assuming a fact recording this information exists:

```
Jess> (defrule print-factorial-10
    (factorial 10 ?r1)
    =>
    (printout t "The factorial of 10 is " ?r1 crlf))
TRUE
```

Patterns that match backward-chaining reactive `deftemplates` are called *goals*. When the rule compiler sees a goal pattern, it rewrites the rule and inserts some special code into the internal representation of the rule's LHS. If, when the rule engine is reset, there are no matches for this pattern, the code asserts a fact into working memory that looks like this:

```
(need-factorial 10 nil)
```

The head of the fact is constructed by taking the head of the reactive pattern and adding the prefix `need-`. These `need-x` facts are called *goal-seeking* or *trigger* facts. This particular trigger fact means that another fact (`factorial 10 ?`) is needed to satisfy some rule. Jess got the number 10 directly from the pattern in `print-factorial-10`; `nil` is a placeholder that means "any value."

Now, let's write a rule that calculates the factorial of a number when it is needed. The rule should directly match the `need-factorial` trigger facts:

```
Jess> (defrule do-factorial
    (need-factorial ?x ?)
    =>
    ;; compute the factorial of ?x in ?r
    (bind ?r 1)
    (bind ?n ?x)
    (while (> ?n 1)
        (bind ?r (* ?r ?n))
        (bind ?n (- ?n 1)))
    (assert (factorial ?x ?r)))
TRUE
```

The rule compiler rewrites rules like this too: It adds a negated match for the `(factorial ?x ?)` pattern to the rule's LHS, so the rule won't fire if both the goal fact and the corresponding goal-seeking fact are both present.

The end result is that you can write rules that match on `factorial` facts, and if they are close to firing except they need a `factorial` fact to do so, any `need-factorial` rules may be activated. If these rules fire, then the needed facts appear, and the `factorial`-matching rules fire. This, then, is backward chaining! Note that any needed `factorial` facts are created only once, so the expensive computation need not be repeated. Often, avoiding redundant computation is one of the main benefits of backward chaining.

Jess chains backward through any number of reactive patterns. In the example in listing 7.4, imagine you have a database that allows you to look up the price of an item given its item number, or the item number given its name. To find the price given the name, you need to do two separate queries. When the `price-check` fact is first asserted, none of the rules can be activated. Jess sees that `price-check` could be activated if there were an appropriate `price` fact, so it generates the trigger `(need-price waffles nil)`. This matches part of the LHS of rule `find-price`, but this rule cannot be activated because there is no `item-number` fact. Jess therefore creates a `(need-item-number waffles nil)` request. This matches the LHS of the rule `find-item-number`, which fires and asserts something like `(item-number waffles 123)`. This fact activates `find-price`, which fires and asserts `(price waffles "$1.99")`, thereby activating rule `price-check`, which then fires. The price is reported. Each of the rules has fired once. The definitions of the functions `fetch-price-from-database` and `fetch-number-from-database` are not shown; they are presumably written in Java using JDBC.

Listing 7.4   Multilevel backward chaining

```
Jess> (clear)
TRUE
Jess> (do-backward-chaining item-number)
TRUE
Jess> (do-backward-chaining price)
TRUE
Jess> (defrule price-check
    (do-price-check ?name)
    (price ?name ?price)
    =>
    (printout t "Price of " ?name " is " ?price crlf))
TRUE
Jess> (defrule find-price
    (need-price ?name ?)
    (item-number ?name ?number)
    =>
    (bind ?price (fetch-price-from-database ?number))
    (assert (price ?name ?price)))
TRUE
Jess> (defrule find-item-number
    (need-item-number ?name ?)
    =>
    (bind ?number (fetch-number-from-database ?name))
    (assert (item-number ?name ?number)))
TRUE
Jess> (reset)
TRUE
Jess> (assert (do-price-check waffles))
<Fact-1>
Jess> (run)
Price of waffles is $1.99
3
```

You can wrap a special conditional element, (explicit), around a pattern to inhibit backward chaining on an otherwise reactive pattern. explicit can be used in any combination with all other conditional elements.

Most rule-based systems consist of dozens if not hundreds of rules. While such a program is running, at any one time a large number of rules may be simultaneously activated. How does Jess decide which rule to fire next? Read on to find out.

7.5   *Managing the agenda*

In section 7.1, you used (watch activations) and (watch rules) to observe the operation of a simple rule. In particular, you learned that a rule is *activated* when its

LHS matches working memory, but it won't immediately fire. The *agenda* is the list of rules that have been activated but haven't fired yet. For some applications, the agenda never contains more than one activated rule, and so managing the agenda isn't a very interesting topic. But in most applications, the agenda contains multiple rules at once. When this is the case, managing the agenda becomes important. In this section, we'll study how Jess chooses which rule to fire next from among all the activated rules on the agenda, and how you can influence this choice.

7.5.1 *Conflict resolution*

A typical rule-based system may contain hundreds or thousands of rules. It's very likely that at any given moment, more than one rule is activated. The set of activated rules that are eligible to be fired is called the *conflict set*, and the process of putting the rules in firing order is called *conflict resolution*. The output of the conflict-resolution process is the ordered list of activations called the *agenda*. You can see this ordered list of activated, but not yet fired, rules with the agenda function.

Conflict resolution in Jess is controlled by pluggable *conflict-resolution strategies*. Jess comes with two strategies: *depth* (the default) and *breadth*. You can set the current strategy with the set-strategy command. Using (set-strategy depth) causes the most recently activated rules to fire first, and (set-strategy breadth) makes rules fire in activation order—the most recently activated rules fire last. In many situations, the difference does not matter, but for some problems the conflict-resolution strategy is important. Although the default strategy is intuitive and correct in most situations, it runs into trouble if every rule that fires activates another rule. The oldest activations then get pushed far down the agenda and never get a chance to fire. The breadth strategy avoids this problem, but the "first-in, first-out" firing order can be confusing.

You can write your own strategies in Java by implementing the jess.Strategy interface and then calling set-strategy with the name of your class as the argument. The Strategy interface has a single nontrivial method compare that compares two activations and returns -1, 1, or 0 to signify that the first activation, the second activation, or either one should fire first.

The conflict-resolution strategy determines how activations are ordered based on when they are added to the agenda. Sometimes, though, you may find that you want to fine-tune the ordering a bit. You can use *salience* to accomplish this.

7.5.2 *Changing rule priority with salience*

Sometimes you may find that a particular rule should be treated as a special case by the conflict-resolution strategy. A rule that reports a security breach might need to fire immediately, regardless of what else is on the agenda. On the other hand, a rule that cleans up unused facts might only need to run during the idle time when no other rules are activated. You can tell the conflict resolver to treat these rules specially using *rule salience.*

Each rule has a property called `salience` that acts as a priority setting for that rule. Activated rules of the highest salience always fire first, followed by rules of lower salience. Within a set of rules with identical salience, the order is determined as described in the previous section. You can use a *salience declaration* to set the salience of a rule:

```
Jess> (defrule defer-exit-until-agenda-empty
    (declare (salience -100))
    (command exit-when-idle)
    =>
    (printout t "exiting..." crlf))
TRUE
```

This rule won't fire until no other rules of higher salience are on the agenda. Declaring a low salience value for a rule makes it fire after all other rules of higher salience. A high value makes a rule fire before all rules of lower salience. The default salience value is 0, so if this is the only rule with an explicit salience value, it will not fire until the agenda is empty.

You can specify salience values using literal integers, global variables, or function calls. How the salience values are evaluated depends on the current value of the *salience evaluation method.* These values are as follows:

- `when-defined`—(Default.) A fixed salience value is computed when the rule is defined.

- `when-activated`—The salience of a rule is reevaluated each time the rule is activated.

- `every-cycle`—The salience value of every rule on the agenda is recomputed after every rule firing. Evaluating `every-cycle` is *very* computationally expensive and isn't used much.

You can query or set the salience evaluation method with the `set-salience-evaluation` and `get-salience-evaluation` functions.

Note that extensive use of salience is generally discouraged, for two reasons. First, use of salience has a negative impact on performance, at least with the built-in conflict-resolution strategies. Second, it is considered bad style in rule-based programming to try to force rules to fire in a particular order. If you find yourself using salience on most of your rules, or if you are using more than two or three different salience values, you probably need to reconsider whether you should be using a rule-based approach to your problem. If you want strict control over execution order, then you're trying to implement a procedural program. Either change your rules to be less sensitive to execution order, or consider implementing your algorithm as one or more `deffunctions` or as Java code. Alternatively, you might consider structuring your program using modules.

7.6 *Partitioning the rule base with defmodule*

A typical rule-based system can easily include hundreds of rules, and a large one can contain many thousands. Developing such a complex system can be a difficult task, and preventing such a multitude of rules from interfering with one another can be hard too.

You might hope to mitigate the problem by partitioning a rule base into manageable chunks. The `defmodule` construct lets you divide rules and facts into distinct groups called *modules*. Modules help you in two ways: First, they help you physically organize large numbers of rules into logical groups. The commands for listing constructs (`rules`, `facts`, and so on) let you specify the name of a module and can then operate on one module at a time. Second, modules provide a control mechanism: The rules in a module fire only when that module has the *focus*, and only one module can be in focus at a time (you'll learn about module focus in section 7.6.3).

We'll discuss the following functions and constructs in this section:

- `clear-focus-stack`—Empties the focus stack
- `defmodule`—Defines a new module
- `focus`—Sets the focus module
- `get-current-module`—Returns the current module
- `get-focus-stack`—Returns the focus stack's contents as a list
- `list-focus-stack`—Displays the focus stack's contents
- `pop-focus`—Pops a module from the focus stack

7.6.1 *Defining constructs in modules*

So far in this book, you haven't explicitly used modules. If you don't specify a module by name when defining a rule or template, it belongs by default to the *current module*. If you never explicitly define any modules, the current module is always the *main module,* which is named MAIN. All the constructs you've seen so far have been defined in MAIN, and therefore are often preceded by MAIN:: when displayed by Jess.

You can define a new module using the defmodule construct:

```
Jess> (defmodule WORK)
TRUE
```

You can then place a deftemplate, defrule, or deffacts into a specific module by qualifying the name of the construct with the module name:

```
Jess> (deftemplate WORK::job (slot salary))
TRUE
Jess> (list-deftemplates WORK)
WORK::job
For a total of 1 deftemplates.
```

Once you have defined a module, it becomes the *current module*:

```
Jess> (get-current-module)
WORK
Jess> (defmodule COMMUTE)
TRUE
Jess> (get-current-module)
COMMUTE
```

If you don't specify a module, all deffacts, templates, and rules you define automatically become part of the current module:

```
Jess> (deftemplate bus (slot route-number))
TRUE
Jess> (defrule take-the-bus
    ?bus <- (bus (route-number 76))
    (have-correct-change)
    =>
    (get-on ?bus))
TRUE
Jess> (ppdefrule take-the-bus)
"(defrule COMMUTE::take-the-bus
    ?bus <- (COMMUTE::bus (route-number 76))
    (COMMUTE::have-correct-change)
    =>
    (get-on ?bus))"
```

Note that the implied deftemplate have-correct-change was created in the COMMUTE module, because that's where the rule was defined. You can set the current module explicitly using the set-current-module function.

7.6.2 *Modules, scope, and name resolution*

A module defines a *namespace* for templates and rules. This means two different modules can each contain a rule with a given name without conflicting—for example, rules named MAIN::initialize and COMMUTE::initialize could be defined simultaneously and coexist in the same program. Similarly, the templates COM-PUTER::bus and COMMUTE::bus could both be defined. Obviously, then, Jess needs a way to decide which template the definition of a rule or query is referring to.

When Jess is compiling a rule, query, or deffacts definition, it looks for templates in three places, in order:

 1. If a pattern explicitly names a module, only that module is searched.

2. If the pattern does not specify a module, then the module in which the rule is defined is searched first.

3. If the template is not found in the rule's module, the module MAIN is searched last. Note that this makes the MAIN module a sort of global namespace for templates.

The example in listing 7.5 illustrates each of these possibilities. In this example, three deftemplates are defined in three different modules: MAIN::mortgage-payment, WORK::job, and HOME::hobby. Jess finds the WORK::job template because the rule is defined in the WORK module. It finds the HOME::hobby template because it is explicitly qualified with the module name. And the MAIN::mortgage-payment template is found because the MAIN module is always searched as a last resort if no module name is specified.

Listing 7.5 Examples of Jess's template lookup rules

```
Jess> (clear)
TRUE
Jess> (assert (MAIN::mortgage-payment 2000))
<Fact-0>
Jess> (defmodule WORK)
TRUE
Jess> (deftemplate job (slot salary))
TRUE
Jess> (defmodule HOME)
TRUE
Jess> (deftemplate hobby (slot name) (slot income))
TRUE
Jess> (defrule WORK::quit-job
    (job (salary ?s))
    (HOME::hobby (income ?i&:(> ?i (/ ?s 2))))
    (mortgage-payment ?m&:(< ?m ?i))
    =>
    (call-boss)
    (quit-job))
TRUE
```

```
Jess> (ppdefrule WORK::quit-job)
"(defrule WORK::quit-job
    (WORK::job (salary ?s))
    (HOME::hobby (income ?i&:(> ?i (/ ?s 2))))
    (MAIN::mortgage-payment ?m&:(< ?m ?i))
    =>
    (call-boss)
    (quit-job))"
```

Commands that accept the name of a construct as an argument (like `ppdefrule`, `ppdeffacts`, and so on) search for the named construct as described earlier. Note that many of the commands that list constructs (such as `facts`, `list-deftemplates`, and `rules`) accept a module name or `*` as an optional argument. If no argument is specified, these commands operate on the current module. If a module name is given, they operate on the named module. If `*` is given, they operate on all modules (see appendix A for full descriptions of all Jess functions and the arguments they accept).

7.6.3 *Module focus and execution control*

You've learned how modules provide a kind of namespace facility, allowing you to partition a rule base into manageable chunks. You can also use modules to control execution. In general, although any Jess rule can be activated at any time, only rules in the *focus module* will fire. Note that the *focus module* is independent from the *current module* discussed earlier.

Initially, the module `MAIN` has the focus, so only rules in the `MAIN` module can fire:

```
Jess> (defmodule DRIVING)
TRUE
Jess> (defrule get-in-car
    =>
    (printout t "Ready to go!" crlf))
TRUE
Jess> (reset)
TRUE
Jess> (run)
0
```

In this example, the rule doesn't fire because the `DRIVING` module doesn't have the focus. You can move the focus to another module using the `focus` function (which returns the name of the previous focus module):

```
Jess> (focus DRIVING)
MAIN
Jess> (run)
Ready to go!
1
```

Note that you can call `focus` from the RHS of a rule to change the focus while the engine is running. The focus can move many times during a single run of a program.

Jess maintains a *focus stack* containing an arbitrary number of modules. The `focus` command pushes the new focus module onto the top of this stack; the focus module is, by definition, the module on top of the stack. When there are no more activated rules in the focus module, it is popped from the stack, and the next module underneath becomes the focus module. The module `MAIN` is always at least on the bottom of the stack; it can also be explicitly pushed onto the focus stack.

You can manipulate the focus stack directly with the functions `pop-focus`, `clear-focus-stack`, `list-focus-stack`, and `get-focus-stack`. `pop-focus` removes the focus module from the focus stack, so that the next module on the stack becomes active. `clear-focus-stack` removes all the modules from the focus stack. The other functions let you examine the contents of the focus stack.

Rule bases are commonly divided into modules along functional lines. For example, you might put all your input-gathering rules into one module, your data-processing rules into another, and your reporting rules into a third. Then, changing the focus from input, to processing, to output represents a natural progression through well-defined phases of your application's execution.

The auto-focus declaration

When a rule that declares the `auto-focus` property is activated, its module automatically gets the focus, as illustrated in listing 7.6. In this example, the rule `crash` fires even though its module `PROBLEMS` didn't have the focus and the agenda of the previous focus module `DRIVING` was not empty. Modules with `auto-focus` rules make great background tasks in conjunction with using `return` from a rule, as described next.

Listing 7.6 An example of using *auto-focus*

```
Jess> (defmodule PROBLEMS)
TRUE
Jess> (defrule crash
    (declare (auto-focus TRUE))
    (DRIVING::me ?location)
    (DRIVING::other-car ?location)
    =>
    (printout t "Crash!" crlf)
    (halt))
TRUE
Jess> (defrule DRIVING::travel
    ?me <- (me ?location)
    =>
```

```
            (printout t ".")
            (retract ?me)
            (assert (me (+ ?location 1)))))
    TRUE
    Jess> (assert (me 1))
    <Fact-1>
    Jess> (assert (other-car 4))
    <Fact-2>
    Jess> (focus DRIVING)
    MAIN
    Jess> (run)
    ...Crash!
    4
```

Returning from a rule's RHS

If the function `return` is called from a rule's RHS, the execution of that rule's RHS is immediately terminated. Furthermore, the current focus module is popped from the focus stack. This suggests that you can call a module like a subroutine. You can call a module from a rule's RHS using `focus`, and the module can return from the call using `return`. Alternatively, a module can act as a kind of background process or periodic task by using `auto-focus` rules to wake itself and `return` to put itself back to sleep.

Both forward- and backward-chaining rules can only react to the contents of working memory. They are passive in the sense that they wait for facts to appear before they can take action, and then nothing happens until they get to the top of the agenda. Sometimes you may want to take a more active stance and deliberately search through working memory to find particular information. Jess lets you do this easily, as you'll see in the next section.

7.7 Searching working memory with defquery

Jess's working memory is a lot like a relational database. Each `deftemplate` is like a *relation*—a table in the database. The individual slots are the columns of the tables. If you're familiar with industrial-strength relational databases, you're probably aware of *database triggers*, which are a lot like forward-chaining rules attached to a database that fire when the data matches some criterion. You can apply rules to relational databases, so it's a reasonable question to ask whether you can make queries against the working memory of a rule-based system. Jess offers the `defquery` construct, which lets you do just that.

A `defquery` is a special kind of rule with no RHS. Jess controls when regular rules fire, but queries are used to search the working memory under direct program control. A rule is activated once for each matching set of facts, whereas a query gives you a `java.util.Iterator` of all the matches. An example should make this clear. Suppose you have defined the query `find-affordable-gifts`:

```
Jess> (deftemplate gift (slot name) (slot price))
TRUE
Jess> (defquery find-affordable-gifts
    "Finds all gifts in a given price range"
    (declare (variables ?lower ?upper))
    (gift (price ?p&:(and (> ?p ?lower) (< ?p ?upper)))))
TRUE
```

The pattern here matches all the gifts whose `price` slot holds a number between `?lower` and `?upper`.

Now you define some facts, including some that match the criterion and some that don't:

```
Jess> (deffacts catalog
    (gift (name red-scarf) (price 20))
    (gift (name leather-gloves) (price 35))
    (gift (name angora-sweater) (price 250))
    (gift (name mohair-sweater) (price 99))
    (gift (name keychain) (price 5))
    (gift (name socks) (price 6))
    (gift (name leather-briefcase) (price 300)))
TRUE
```

You can invoke the query to find the perfect gift using concrete upper and lower price limits:

```
Jess> (reset)
TRUE
Jess> (bind ?it (run-query find-affordable-gifts 20 100))
<External-Address:java.util.AbstractList$Itr>
Jess> (while (?it hasNext)
    (bind ?token (call ?it next))
    (bind ?fact (call ?token fact 1))
    (bind ?name (fact-slot-value ?fact name))
    (printout t ?name crlf))
leather-gloves
mohair-sweater
FALSE
```

Here you're looking for gifts between $20 and $100, and the query finds `mohair-sweater` and `leather-gloves`.

Let's break down this code to see what it's doing. As previously stated, (run-query) returns the query results as a Java `java.util.Iterator` object. The `Iterator` interface has a method `next()` that you call to retrieve each individual result; it also has a `hasNext()` method that returns `true` as long as there are more results to return. That explains the `(while (?it hasNext) ...(call ?it next))` control structure; it steps through each of the results returned by the query.

Each individual result is a `jess.Token` object. A `Token` is just a collection of `jess.Fact` objects; each `Token` holds one match for the query. You call the `fact()` method of `jess.Token` to retrieve the individual `jess.Fact` objects within the `Token`. Each match begins with an extra fact, a *query trigger* fact that initiates the matching process; it is asserted by the `run-query` command (this fact is retracted automatically after the query is run). Hence the argument to the call to `fact()` is 1, not 0. Once you have the right fact, you use the `fact-slot-value` function to extract the contents of the `name` slot. Printing the `name` slot of each fact leads to the output shown earlier.

The `defquery` construct can use virtually all the same features that `defrule` LHSs can, including all the special conditional elements described in this chapter. The function `ppdefrule` can also pretty-print queries. Jess treats a `defquery` as a special kind of `defrule` in many contexts; for instance, the `rules` command lists `defquery`s as well as `defrule`s.

As you can see, the `run-query` function lets you pass parameters to a query; you passed numbers representing the upper and lower limits of a price range to the `find-affordable-gifts` query. Let's examine this process a little more closely.

7.7.1 *The variable declaration*

You might have already realized that two different kinds of variables can appear in a query: those that are internal to the query, like `?p` in `find-affordable-gifts`, and those that are external, or to be specified in the `run-query` command when the query is executed. Jess assumes all variables in a query are internal by default; you must declare any external variables explicitly using this syntax:

```
(declare (variables ?x ?y ...))
```

When you invoke a query using the `run-query` function, you must supply exactly as many variables as are listed in the `variables` declaration. Some queries may not have any external variables; in this case, the `variables` declaration is optional.

7.7.2 *Query trigger facts*

When Jess compiles a `defquery`, it inserts an extra pattern as the first one in the query. This first pattern is of the form

```
(__query-trigger-name ?x ?y ...)
```

where *name* is the name of the query and `?x`, `?y`, and so on are the variables named in the `variables` declaration for the query. `run-query` works by asserting a fact to match this pattern, using the arguments you supply to instantiate the variables. This fact completes any pending matches of the `defquery`'s LHS, and `run-query` collects these matches and returns them.

7.7.3 *The count-query-results function*

To obtain just the number of matches for a query, rather than a full `Iterator` over all the matches, you can use the `count-query-results` function. This function accepts the same arguments as `run-query` but returns an integer specifying the number of matches.

7.7.4 *Backward chaining and queries*

It can be convenient to use queries as triggers for backward chaining. For example, look back at the backward-chaining example in section 7.4. If you were writing a `deffunction` that needed to use factorials, that `deffunction` might want to use a `defquery` to fetch the ones that are already available from working memory, rather than recomputing them. The backward-chaining rules would then compute missing values.

For this technique to be useful, `(run)` must somehow be called while the query is being evaluated, to allow the backward chaining to occur. Facts generated by rules fired during this run may appear as part of the query results.

By default, no rules fire while a query is being executed. If you want to allow backward chaining to occur in response to a query, you can include the `max-background-rules` declaration in that query's definition. For example, this query allows a maximum of five rules to fire while it is being executed:

```
Jess> (defquery find-factorial
    (declare (max-background-rules 5)
         (variables ?arg))
    (factorial ?arg ?))
```

7.8 *Summary*

You can define rules to take action based on the contents of Jess's working memory, and you can write queries to investigate it procedurally. Both rules and queries can use *constraints* (conditions on the slot data of facts) and *conditional elements* (relationships between facts) to express specify detailed requirements on working memory elements.

You can write both forward- and backward-chaining rules. Roughly, you can say that forward-chaining rules discover the conclusions that can be drawn from an existing set of facts, and backward-chaining rules search for the premises from which existing facts can be derived. You can also write queries to probe working memory directly.

In real systems, many rules are activated simultaneously. *Conflict resolution,* or choosing which rule to fire next, is an important part of any rule-based system. Jess lets you influence conflict resolution in a number of ways: by setting the *conflict-resolution strategy,* by using *salience,* or by partitioning your rule base into *modules.*

Under the hood:
how Jess works

In this chapter you'll...

- Learn how Jess compiles rules
- Be introduced to the Rete algorithm
- Use the `view` and `matches` functions
- Learn how to make your rules more efficient

133

You can drive a car without understanding anything about what's under the hood. But if you're driving through a desert, miles from a phone, and your engine starts to sputter and cough, a little knowledge and a full toolbox could go a long way.

So it is with much of the software you use as a developer. As long as everything is working well, you can get by without much knowledge of its internal workings. When something starts to go wrong, however, you may need extra knowledge and a few tools to fix it. This chapter gives you both, as far as Jess is concerned. We'll look at the *Rete algorithm*, the technique that Jess uses to do fast pattern matching. You'll also learn about some tools built into Jess that let you kick the tires and look under the hood.

Some of the information in this chapter is generally true of any system based on the Rete algorithm, and a little is specific to one version of Jess. I'll try to make the distinction as we go along. In general, the version-specific parts of Jess are in nonpublic Java classes, so you'd have to go out of your way to use them. If you do, though, consider yourself warned that they are internal implementation details, and any Java code you write that uses them may well break each time a new version of Jess is released.

8.1 *Review of the problem*

Before looking at Jess's implementation, let's review the problem Jess is meant to solve. Jess is a shell for rule-based systems. In the simplest terms, this means Jess's purpose is to continuously apply a set of if...then statements (*rules*) to a set of data (the *working memory*). Each system built from the shell defines its own rules. Jess rules look like this:

```
(defrule library-rule-1
    (book (name ?x) (status late) (borrower ?y))
    (borrower (name ?y) (address ?z))
    =>
    (send-late-notice ?x ?y ?z))
```

This rule might be translated into pseudo-English as follows:

```
Library rule #1:
IF
    A late book X exists, borrowed by a person Y
AND That borrower's address is known to be Z
THEN
    Send a late notice to Y at Z about the book X.
END
```

The information about books and borrowers would be found in the working memory, which is therefore a kind of database of bits of factual knowledge about the world. Entities like books and borrowers are called *facts*. Facts have attributes called *slots*, like a name, a status, and so on. Each kind of fact can have only a fixed set of slots. The allowed slots for a given type are defined in Jess statements called `deftemplates`. *Actions* like `send-late-notice` can be defined in user-written functions in the Jess language (`deffunctions`) or in Java (see chapter 15). For more information about rule syntax, you can refer to chapter 7.

Therefore, the main problem Jess must solve is that of matching the rules in the rule base to the facts in working memory. Jess has to perform the following steps in an infinite loop:

1 Find all the rules that are satisfied by a set of facts in working memory.

2 Form *activation records* out of these rule/fact associations.

3 Choose one activation record to execute.

8.2 An inefficient solution

The obvious implementation of pattern matching would be to keep a list of the rules and simply check each one's left-hand side (LHS) in turn against the working memory, forming a set of activation records for any that match. After choosing one rule and executing it, you could discard the set of activation records and start again. You might call this the *rules finding facts* approach. It is obviously not very efficient and doesn't scale well. After every rule firing, the system must recheck every fact against every rule. Doubling the number of facts or the number of rules roughly halves the performance of the system.

It is difficult to analyze pattern-matching algorithms like this one in the general case, because the actual performance is dependent on the makeup of working memory and on the exact nature of the rules. For the example rule in the previous section, though, we can say that this naive algorithm will take time proportional to the product B_1B_2 on each cycle, where B_1 is the number of books and B_2 is the number of borrowers. This is easy to see; on each cycle, every book must be checked to see if it is overdue, and the overdue ones must be checked against every borrower to find the right address. On the average, for many rules, the worst-case performance of this simple algorithm will be something like the B_1B_2 expression, extended to deal with any number of patterns and multiplied by the number of rules. We could write the result RF^P, where R is the number of rules, F is the total number of facts, and P is the average number of patterns per rule. If P is 2, then the runtime will scale as the square of the number of facts; doubling the number of facts will multiply the runtime by a factor of 4.

8.3 *The Rete algorithm*

We can improve on the performance of this simple but inefficient pattern-matching algorithm by thinking about the source of its inefficiency. The typical rule-based system has a more or less fixed set of rules, whereas the working memory changes continuously. However, it is an empirical fact that in most rule-based systems, much of the working memory is also fairly fixed over time. Although new facts arrive and old ones are removed as the system runs, the percentage of facts that change per unit time is generally fairly small.

The *rules finding facts* algorithm is therefore needlessly inefficient, because most of the tests made on each cycle will have the same results as on the previous iteration. An algorithm that could somehow remember previous pattern-matching results between cycles, only updating matches for facts that actually changed, could do far less work and get the same results.

Jess uses a very efficient version of this idea, known as the *Rete algorithm.* Charles Forgy's classic paper describing the Rete algorithm[1] became the basis for several generations of fast rule-based system shells: OPS5, its descendant ART, CLIPS, Jess, and others. Each system has enhanced and refined the algorithm to improve performance or flexibility. This chapter describes the algorithm as implemented in Jess.

Briefly, the Rete algorithm eliminates the inefficiency in the simple pattern matcher by remembering past test results across iterations of the rule loop. Only new or deleted working memory elements are tested against the rules at each step. Furthermore, Rete organizes the pattern matcher so that these few facts are only tested against the subset of the rules that may actually match.

8.3.1 *How Rete works*

Rete is Latin for *net* (it's pronounced "ree-tee"). The Rete algorithm is implemented by building a network of interconnected *nodes.* Every node represents one or more tests found on the LHS of a rule. Each node has one or two inputs and any number of outputs. Facts that are being added to or removed from the working memory are processed by this network of nodes. The input nodes are at the *top* of the network, and the output nodes are at the *bottom*. Together, these nodes form the *Rete network*, and this network is how Jess's working memory is implemented.

---

[1]   Charles L. Forgy, "Rete: A Fast Algorithm for the Many Pattern / Many Object Pattern Match Problem," *Artificial Intelligence* 19 (1982): 17–37.

At the top of the network, the input nodes separate the facts into categories according to their *head*—for example, books go through one path, and borrowers go through another. Inside the network, finer discriminations and associations between facts are made, until the facts get to the bottom. At the bottom of the network are nodes representing individual rules. When a set of facts filters all the way down to the bottom of the network, it has passed all the tests on the LHS of a particular rule; this set, together with the rule itself, becomes either a new activation record or a command to cancel a previously existing activation record (recall that an activation record is an association of a list of facts with a rule that they activate).

Between the inputs and the outputs, the network is composed of two broad categories of nodes: *one-input nodes* and *two-input nodes*. One-input nodes perform tests on individual facts, and two-input nodes perform tests across multiple facts. An example would probably be useful at this point. The following rules might be compiled into the network shown in figure 8.1:

```
Jess> (deftemplate x (slot a))
TRUE
Jess> (deftemplate y (slot b))
TRUE
Jess> (deftemplate z (slot c))
TRUE
Jess> (defrule example-1
    (x (a ?v1))
    (y (b ?v1))
    => )
TRUE
Jess> (defrule example-2
    (x (a ?v2))
    (y (b ?v2))
    (z)
    => )
TRUE
```

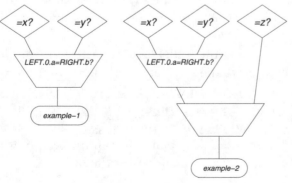

Figure 8.1
An unoptimized Rete network for the two rules example-1 and example-2

In this diagram, each box represents a node. A node's inputs are shown on the top, and its outputs are on the bottom. The diamond-shaped nodes marked =*q*? are one-input or *pattern* nodes. The pattern nodes in this example test if the head of a fact is *q*. Facts that pass this test are sent to the node's output; others are ignored.

The trapezoidal nodes are two-input or *join* nodes. Each join node joins the results of matching the first *n-1* patterns (coming from upper left in the diagram) with the *nth* pattern (attached at upper right in the diagram). Join nodes remember all facts or groups of facts that arrive on either of their two inputs. The network is built so that the left input can receive groups of one or more facts; the right input receives only single facts. Every join node produces groups of two or more facts as at its output. The arrivals from the two inputs are kept in separate memory areas, traditionally called the *alpha* and *beta* memories. We'll refer to them as the *left* and *right* memories instead, because it's easier to keep these names straight! The notation LEFT.*p*.*q*==RIGHT.*r*? indicates a test comparing the contents of slot *q* in the *p*th fact in a group from the left memory to the slot *r* in a fact from the right memory. Join nodes produce one output for each ordered pairing of a left-memory element and a right-memory element that passes the tests in that node.

The oval nodes at the bottom of the network are the *terminal nodes* that represent individual rules. They have a single input and no outputs. When they receive an input, they build an activation record from the input item and the rule they represent and place it on the agenda. Note that any facts that reach the top of a join node could potentially contribute to an activation; they have already passed all the tests that can be applied to single facts.

To run the network, you present every new fact to each node at the top of the network. The example pattern network eliminates all facts except the x, y, and z ones. The join network then sends all {x, y} pairs with x.a == y.b to the terminal node for example-1, and all {x, y, z} triples (given the same restriction) to the terminal node for example-2. The terminal nodes thus know what activation records to create.

What happens if, after processing the initial facts, we assert an additional fact (z (c 17))? The fact is presented to the =z? pattern node and sent down to the join node below. The left memory of that join node already contains all the acceptable x, y pairs, so the correct x, y, z triples can be formed without repeating the pattern matching computation done on the first cycle. One new activation will be created for each precomputed x, y pair. You can now see how the Rete architecture lets you avoid repeating computation over time.

8.3.2 *Handling retract*

So far, you've seen how the Rete algorithm can be used to efficiently handle the pattern matching that happens during `assert` commands; but what about `retract`? Rete can handle removing activation records as easily as it can handle creating them. The trick to doing so is that you don't send facts through the network: You send *tokens*. A token is an association between one or more facts and a *tag*, or command. The tag tells the individual nodes how to interpret the token. Jess uses four different tags, defined as constants in the `jess.RU` class: ADD, REMOVE, CLEAR, and UPDATE. ADD is used for asserting facts, as you've already seen. The behavior described so far only applies for token with a tag value of ADD.

The REMOVE tag is used for retractions. If a REMOVE token arrives at a join node, the node looks in the appropriate memory to find a matching token. If it finds one, the token is deleted. All allowed pairings between that token and all the tokens in the opposite memory are then composed, also with the REMOVE tag. These tokens are sent to the join node's output. Finally, if a terminal node receives a REMOVE token, the corresponding activation record is found and deleted.

The remaining two tags are more subtle. UPDATE is used when a new rule has been added to a preexisting Rete network, and the join nodes belonging to that new rule have to be populated with facts. The UPDATE tag lets the nodes that already existed know they can safely ignore a token, because it's a duplicate of one sent some time in the past; this prevents the preexisting nodes from storing duplicate tokens in their memories. Finally, the CLEAR tag tells the join and terminal nodes to flush their memories; it is used to implement the (reset) command efficiently.

8.4 *Easy optimizations for Rete*

That's it for the basic Rete algorithm. There are many optimizations, however, which can make it even better. Two easy ones work by introducing *node sharing* into the network. The first optimization is to share nodes in the pattern network. In figure 8.1, there are five nodes across the top, although only three are distinct. You can modify the network to share these nodes across the two rules. The result is shown in figure 8.2.

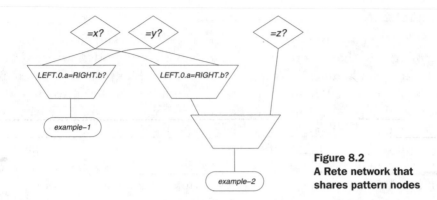

Figure 8.2
A Rete network that
shares pattern nodes

But that's not all the redundancy in the original network. Looking at figure 8.2, you can see that one join node is performing exactly the same function (integrating x, y pairs) in both rules; you can share that also, as shown in figure 8.3. Sharing join nodes is an especially fruitful optimization. Because joining involves comparing facts to one another, the tests in join nodes tend to be executed many more times than those in pattern nodes—so much so that the time spent in the join network generally dominates the running time of the system. By sharing this one join node, then, you've effectively doubled the performance of your program.

The pattern and join networks in figure 8.3 are collectively only half the size they were in the first version. This kind of sharing comes up frequently in real systems and is a significant performance booster.

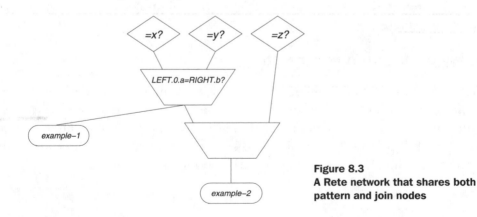

Figure 8.3
A Rete network that shares both
pattern and join nodes

8.5 *Performance of the Rete algorithm*

The Rete algorithm's performance is even harder to analyze precisely than the simple rules finding facts algorithm. In general, the performance on the first cycle is basically the same for the two algorithms; Rete has to do pattern matching for every fact in working memory, because there are no previous results to consult. In the worst case, where every fact changes on every cycle and there is no network sharing between rules, then the performance for later cycles is the same as well. This means Jess won't be very efficient if you populate the working memory, run the pattern matcher for just one cycle, and then reset working memory and repopulate it again from scratch. But in the typical case of a slowly changing working memory, moderate sharing in the network, and effective indexing, Rete will vastly outperform the naive algorithm for all cycles after the first. The runtime will be proportional to something like $R'F'^{P'}$, where R' is a number less than R, the number of rules; F' is the number of facts that change on each iteration; and P' is a number greater than one but less than the average number of patterns per rule.

8.5.1 *Node index hash value*

Jess uses a fairly sophisticated data structure to represent the two memories in each join node. It is basically a hash table with a fixed number of buckets. The interesting feature here is that the hash function uses the part of each token that is most relevant to the specific tests in each join node. This lets Jess presort the tokens before running the join node tests. In many cases, running some or all of the tests can be avoided altogether, because once the tokens are sorted into the hash buckets, questions involving comparisons of slot data can often be answered categorically for a whole bin.

The *node index hash value* is a tunable performance-related parameter that can be set globally or on a per-rule basis. It is simply the number of buckets to use in each individual hash table. A small value saves memory, possibly at the expense of performance; a larger value uses more memory but leads (up to a point) to faster pattern matching. The default, used if you don't declare an explicit value, is chosen for optimal performance.

In general, you might want to declare a large value for a rule that is likely to generate many partial matches. Conventional wisdom has it that prime numbers are the best choices. Experimentation is the only way to determine the best value for a particular rule. If n is the number of item facts, then the following rule will need n^3 tokens in the left memory of its third join node; it's an excellent candidate for a large node index hash value if you expected there to be more than a few item facts:

```
Jess> (defrule many-matches
    (declare (node-index-hash 167))
    (item ?a)
    (item ?b)
    (item ?c)
    (item ?d)
    =>
    (printout t ?a " " ?b " " ?c " " ?d crlf))
TRUE
```

The `set-node-index-hash` function sets the default value for this parameter, used for rules without a specific declaration. If you don't set a value, the default is 101.

8.6   *More complexity and initial-fact*

A number of pattern-matching situations can't be handled by what we've discussed so far. Studying them is enlightening because it explains some otherwise seemingly arbitrary properties of software like Jess that is based on the Rete algorithm.

8.6.1   *Implementing the not conditional element*

The `not` conditional element matches the absence of a fact. Its implementation involves a special kind of join node and a special field in every token. The special field is called the *negation count*. The special NOT join node uses the negation count to keep track of the number of times the node's conditions are met for each token in the left memory. The count is incremented whenever the node's tests pass for a given token and decremented whenever they do not. When the count reaches zero for a given left-memory token, a new token is formed from it and a special *null fact* (which represents the nonexistent right-memory input) and sent to the node's output.

The important thing to notice about this description is that although the facts matching the pattern in the `not` conditional element arrive at the NOT node's *right* input, only the tokens arriving at the *left* input form part of the output tokens. A moment's reflection shows that it has to be this way; the `not` conditional element is matched when there is no matching fact. If there are no tokens in the right memory, that means the `not` conditional element will always succeed, so the NOT node will pass every token received on the left input directly to its output.

Now, what should a NOT node do if it doesn't have a left input? Such a case would arise if a `not` conditional element was the first pattern on the LHS of a rule or the first pattern in a given branch of an `or` conditional element. The NOT node clearly can't function without a left input; it can't create output tokens without left input tokens as seeds. For this reason, Jess inserts the `(initial-fact)` pattern into rules that have this problem. Without this pattern, the `not` conditional element wouldn't work.

8.6.2 *Implementing the test conditional element*

The `test` conditional element doesn't match a fact; it simply evaluates a function. To implement `test`, Jess uses another special join node that ignores its right input. For each token arriving on the left input, the `TEST` join node evaluates its function. If the function doesn't evaluate to `FALSE`, the left input token and a null fact are composed to make a new token, which is then sent to the node's output. The `TEST` node, just like the `NOT` node, clearly can't work properly without a left input. Therefore, `test` conditional elements can also cause Jess to insert `(initial-fact)` patterns into rules.

8.6.3 *Implementing backward chaining*

Jess implements backward chaining on top of the forward-chaining Rete algorithm. The basic problem is detecting when the LHS of a rule has been matched up to, but not including, a pattern that matches a backward-chaining reactive template (see section 7.4). At this point, a signal must be sent describing the fact that would complete the match; as you might guess, having read section 7.4, that signal is a `need-X` fact. Once this fact is asserted, rules that match it can once again be processed in a forward-chaining fashion.

To implement this functionality, the join nodes that receive facts from a backward-chaining reactive template must act specially. Each time a new left input token is received, the number of successful pairings with right input tokens is counted. If the count is zero, a `need-X` fact is generated. The left input token represents the facts that match a rule up to, but not including, the pattern for the reactive template. Once again, you see that the left input token is crucial to the correct operation of this special type of join node, and so Jess inserts `(initial-fact)` patterns as necessary to provide them.

8.7 *Exploring the Rete network in Jess*

The compiled Rete network is a complex and (often) large data structure. Sometimes, understanding it can mean the difference between an efficient program and a dreaded `OutOfMemoryError`. In this section, we'll look at some functions that will help you explore the Rete network: `watch compilations`, `view`, and `match`.

8.7.1 *The (watch compilations) command*

You can see the amount of node sharing in a Rete network by using Jess's `(watch compilations)` function. Executing this function tells the rule compiler to print some diagnostics to the screen when each rule is compiled. For each rule, Jess prints a string of characters something like this, the actual output from compiling rule *example-1* from section 8.3.1:

```
MAIN::example-1: +1+1+1+2+t
```

Each time +1 appears in this string, it means a new one-input node was created. +2 indicates a new two-input node. +t indicates a terminal node.

Now, watch what happens when we compile example-2 from the same section:

```
MAIN::example-2: =1=1+1=1=2+2+t
```

The string =1 is printed whenever a preexisting one-input node was shared; similarly, =2 means a two-input node was shared. You can see from these diagnostics that, as expected, one of the two join nodes in example-2 was shared, along with most of the pattern nodes. If you want to study what happens more precisely, you can use the view command, described in the next section.

8.7.2   *The view function*

The view command (see figure 8.4) is a graphical viewer for the Rete network. By giving you feedback about the data structures Jess builds from your rule definitions, it may help you to design more efficient rule-based systems. Issuing the view command after entering the rules example-1 and example-2 from section 8.3.1 produces a very good facsimile of the diagram in figure 8.3 (with some subtle differences). The various nodes are color-coded according to their roles in the network. Nodes in the pattern network are red, normal join nodes are green, not nodes are yellow, and terminal nodes are blue. The bottom node in the left column of the figure is a *right to left adapter*; one of these is always used to connect the first pattern on a rule's LHS to the network. Passing the mouse over a node displays information about the node and the tests it contains. Double-clicking on a node brings up a dialog box containing additional information; for join nodes, the memory contents are also displayed (the same information displayed by the matches function), and for terminal nodes, a pretty-print representation of the rule is shown. You can move the individual nodes around by dragging them with your mouse. In figure 8.4, the nodes have been dragged into position by hand to resemble the diagrams in the other figures.

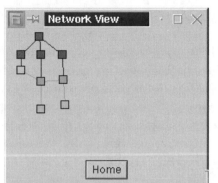

Figure 8.4
Jess's `view` command displays
the Rete network in a window.

To fully appreciate what's happening in the `view` command's display, you need to know something about how Jess implements the Rete algorithm. Jess's network is literally a network of interconnected `Node` objects. Network nodes are represented by subclasses of the abstract type `jess.Node`. Pattern network nodes, which perform tests on single facts, have `Node1` as part of their name. There are also three classes of join nodes—`jess.Node2`, `jess.NodeNot2`, and `NodeTest`—that implement normal joins, the `not` conditional element, and the `test` conditional element, respectively. Terminal nodes are instances of `jess.NodeTerm`.

There are quite a few different `Node1` classes. `jess.Node1TECT` nodes, for example, test the head of a fact, and therefore provide the entrance route into the network. `Node1TEQ` nodes compare the value of a single slot to a constant value, and `Node1TEV1` nodes test whether two slots within a single fact contain the same value. There are separate multislot variations of these types; their names begin with `Node1M`. `Node1MTEQ` nodes, for example, compare a single datum at a particular location in a multislot to a constant value. Finally, there are negated versions, too: `Node1TNEV1` nodes test that two slots in a single fact do *not* contain the same value.

Besides the menagerie of nodes types listed here, other types serve a structural role in the network: `Node1RTL` nodes, for example, adapt an output that would normally lead to the right input of a join node so that it connects to the left input instead, and `Node1NONE` nodes serve as stand-ins for nodes that aren't really there—specifically, for the part of the pattern network that leads to the right input of a `NodeTest`. The information that the `matches` or `view` functions display about individual nodes is generally fairly descriptive of each node's function.

8.7.3 *The matches function*

The matches function lets you see the contents of the left and right memories of the join nodes used by any rule. It can be an invaluable aid in determining why a particular rule isn't behaving the way you expect. It also is a good way to check for computational hot spots that might be slowing down your programs.

The matches function is easy to use. Give it the name of a rule as an argument, and it will show you information about each of the rule's join nodes in left-to-right order. In the following example, the rule matches-demo's single join node has one token in its left memory and one in its right; each memory gets its input from one pattern of the original rule:

```
Jess> (defrule matches-demo
    (a)
    (b)
    =>)
TRUE
Jess> (deffacts matches-demo-facts (a) (b))
TRUE
Jess> (reset)
TRUE
Jess> (matches matches-demo)
>>> [Node2 ntests=0 ;usecount = 1;unique = false]
*** Left Memory:
[Token: size=1;sortcode=1;tag=ADD;negcnt=0;facts=(MAIN::a);]
*** RightMemory:
[Token: size=1;sortcode=2;tag=ADD;negcnt=0;facts=(MAIN::b);]

TRUE
```

8.8 *Summary*

Jess uses the fast, efficient Rete algorithm for pattern matching. The strength of Rete is that it uses a set of *memories* to retain information about the success or failure of pattern matches during previous cycles.

The Rete algorithm involves building a *network* of pattern-matching *nodes*. Jess uses many different kinds of nodes to represent the many different kinds of pattern-matching activities. There are also special nodes to handle some conditional elements like not and test, as well as special behavior in some nodes to handle backward chaining.

This chapter concludes the introduction to Jess. In the next part of this book, and in each subsequent part, you will develop a nontrivial application. Each application is standalone, but each part of the book builds on the knowledge and skills developed during the previous parts.

Part 3

Creating your first rule-based application: the Tax Forms Advisor

Using a classic expert system is something like being interviewed: The program asks you a series of questions and then provides some advice or information. In part 3, you'll develop your first nontrivial program to follow this model. We'll concentrate on the mechanics of rule-based system development. There are special sections on knowledge engineering and on testing.

The system you'll be developing is called the *Tax Forms Advisor*. Given some information about your personal finances, the program will recommend which income tax forms you may need to file. It is suitable for installation in a kiosk in the lobby of a post office.

Collecting the knowledge

A journey of a thousand miles begins with the first step.

—Lao Tzu

The first step in developing any rule-based system is collecting the knowledge the system will embody. In this chapter, your major concern will be to learn how this can be accomplished. As a practical example, you'll gather the knowledge you'll build into your first nontrivial rule-based program.

9.1 *The Tax Forms Advisor*

For the next three chapters, you'll be developing a simple rule-based application that recommends United States income tax forms. The application asks the user a series of questions and, based on the answers, tells the user which paper Internal Revenue Service forms she will likely need. You will populate the application with enough data to make it realistic, although you won't try to make it exhaustive. Your application might be used in an information kiosk at the post office.

You'll follow a realistic development process as you create this application, starting in this chapter by collecting the actual knowledge. In chapters 10 and 11 you'll write the application using an iterative methodology, including lots of testing.

The Tax Forms Advisor has a command-line interface. You'll concentrate on developing the rules themselves, so the entire program will be written in the Jess rule language without using any Java reflection capabilities. In the next part of this book, we'll examine one way to add a graphical interface to applications like this one.

DISCLAIMER The system you're developing is intended only to provide guidelines about what tax forms a taxpayer might need to file. It is not intended to give authoritative legal advice about tax filing.

9.2 *Introduction to knowledge engineering*

Every rule-based system is concerned with some subset of all the world's collected knowledge. This subset is called the *domain* of the system. The process of collecting information about a domain for use in a rule-based system is called *knowledge engineering*, and people who do this for a living are called *knowledge engineers*. On small projects, the programmers themselves might do all the knowledge engineering, whereas very large projects might include a team of dedicated knowledge engineers.

Professional knowledge engineers may have degrees in a range of disciplines: obvious ones like computer science or psychology, and domain-related ones like physics, chemistry, or mathematics. Obviously it helps if the knowledge engineer knows a lot about rule-based systems, although she doesn't have to be a programmer.

A good knowledge engineer has to be a jack of all trades, because knowledge engineering is really just learning—the knowledge engineer must learn a lot about the domain in which the proposed system will operate. A knowledge engineer doesn't need to become an expert, although that sometimes happens. But the knowledge engineer does have to learn something about the topic. In general, this information will include:

- *The requirements*—Looking at the problem the system needs to solve is the first step. However, you might not fully understand the problem until later in the process.
- *The principles*—You need to learn the organizing principles of the field.
- *The resources*—Once you understand the principles, you need to know where to go to learn more.
- *The frontiers*—Every domain has its dark corners and dead ends. You need to find out where the tough bits, ambiguities, and limits of human understanding lie.

The knowledge engineer can use many potential sources of information to research these points. Broadly, though, there are two: *interviews* and *desk research*. In the rest of this section, we'll look at techniques for mining each of these information sources to gather the four categories of information we just listed.

9.2.1 *Where do you start?*

When you're starting on a new knowledge engineering endeavor, it can be difficult to decide what to do first. Knowledge engineering is an *iterative* process. You usually can't make a road map in advance; instead you feel your way along, adjusting your course as you go. As the saying goes, though, a journey of a thousand miles begins with a single step, and taking that first step can be hard.

With most projects, you should first talk to the customers—the people who are paying you to write the system. Find out what their needs are and what resources they can make available. This isn't knowledge engineering per se, but *requirements engineering*—part of planning any software project. But the customer might point you to particular sources of technical information and help you plan your approach to knowledge engineering. After talking to the customers, you should have a rough idea of what the system should do and how long development is expected to take.

Next, it's best to seek out general resources you can use to learn about the fundamentals of the domain and do a bit of self-study. Being at least vaguely familiar with the jargon and fundamental concepts in the domain will let you avoid wasting the time of people you interview later. You should learn enough about the fundamentals to have a rough idea of what kinds of knowledge the system needs to have.

Once you've developed an understanding of the basics, you're ready to begin the iterative process. Based on your initial research, write down a list of questions about the domain which, if answered, would provide knowledge in the areas you previously identified. Seek out a cooperative subject-matter expert, briefly explain the project to him, and ask him the questions (often the customer will provide the expert; otherwise they should pay the expert a consulting fee to work with you). Usually the answers will lead to more questions.

After the initial interview, you can try to organize the information you've gathered into some kind of structure—perhaps a written outline or a flowchart. As you do this, you can begin to look for what might turn out to be individual rules. For the Tax Forms Advisor, an individual rule you might encounter early in the process would be (in the Jess language):

```
(defrule use-ez-form
    ; If filing status is "single", and...
    (filing-status single)
    ; user made less than $50000
    (income ?i&:(< ?i 50000))
    =>
    ; recommend the user file Form 1040EZ
    (recommend 1040EZ))
```

Detailed comments like those shown here will help non-technical people read and understand the rules, if necessary. Buy a stack of white index cards and write each potential rule on one side of an individual card. Use pencil so you can make changes easily. The cards are useful because they let you group the rules according to function, required inputs, or other criteria. When you have a stack of 100 cards or more, the utility becomes obvious. You can use the reverse sides of the cards to record issues regarding each rule. This stack of cards might be the final product of knowledge engineering, or the cards' contents might be turned into a report. The cards themselves are often the most useful format, though.

After organizing the new knowledge on index cards, you may see obvious gaps that require additional information. Develop a new set of interview questions and meet with the expert again. The appropriate number of iterations depends on the complexity of the system.

Knowledge engineering doesn't necessarily end when development begins. After an initial version of a system is available, the expert should try it out as a user and offer advice to correct its performance. If possible, a prototype of the system should be presented to the expert at every interview—except perhaps the first one.

Likewise, development needn't be deferred until knowledge engineering is complete. For many small projects, the knowledge engineer is one of the developers, and in this case you may be able to dispense with the cards and simply encode the knowledge you collect directly into a prototype system. This is what you'll do for the Tax Forms Advisor.

More on writing cards

To write down the rule `use-ez-form` on a card, I had to make up the `deftemplate` names `filing-status` and `income` and also define an imaginary function `recommend`. In general, you will write rules on these cards in *pseudocode*; they're meant to suggest how the real rules might be coded, but they're just guides. When actual development begins on the system, these early guesses will help the developers figure out what `deftemplates` and other infrastructure they need to define.

Finally, note that although I wrote `use-ez-form` in Jess syntax, it would be perfectly OK for a knowledge engineer to use natural language, or pseudocode that looks like some other programming language. If you are a knowledge engineer but not a programmer, writing rules in your native language may be the only option, and that's fine.

9.2.2 *Interviews*

People are the best source of information about the requirements for a system. Many projects have *requirements documents*: written descriptions of how a proposed system should behave. Despite the best intentions, such documents rarely capture the expectations for a system in enough detail to allow the system to be implemented. Often, you can get the missing details only by talking to stakeholders: the customers and potential users of the system.

People can also direct you to books, web sites, and other people who will help you learn about the problem domain. These days it's common to suffer from *information overload* when you try to research a topic—there are so many conflicting resources available that it's hard to know what information to believe. The stakeholders in the system can tell you which resources they trust and which ones they don't.

If you find conflicting information among otherwise trustworthy references during your research, or hear conflicting statements during interviews, don't be afraid to ask for clarification. You'll need a strategy for resolving conflicts that hinge on matters of opinion. Sometimes you can do this by picking a specific person as the ultimate arbiter. Other times, especially on larger projects, it's appropriate to hold meetings to get the stakeholders to make decisions in a group setting.

Interviewing strategies

Cultivating a good relationship with the people you interview is important. This sounds so simple, you might not think it needs to be said—but it does. Computer people have a culture all their own, and it's different enough from mainstream culture that programmers can be perceived as rude. If you're a computer programmer working as a knowledge engineer, you may have to alter your accustomed behavior when you're interviewing nonprogrammers. Here are a few things to watch out for:

- *Speak their language*—It can be difficult for a programmer to remember that stacks, loops, shifts, and pointers are not part of the everyday vocabulary of most nonprogrammers. Don't use programming terms if you can avoid it. You'll also want to avoid geek words like *grok*, *kludge*, and *lossage*, which will only distance you from the interviewee. Instead, work hard to learn the technical jargon of the problem domain, and use it properly.

- *Show respect*—No matter how trivial the domain may seem, the interviewee knows more about it than you, so don't look down on people just because they don't have the same education you do. Your knowledge of programming is not more important than their knowledge of inventory procedures. Your time is not more valuable than theirs. They're doing you a favor by talking to you, so be grateful.

- *Be interested*—Make eye contact when you talk to the interviewee. Ask follow-up questions to show that you're listening. Take notes so you don't ask the same question twice (unless, of course, you didn't understand the answer the first time). Generally look as though you're happy to be talking to the person—or they won't talk to you again.

- *Dress for the occasion*—Gone are the days when all white-collar workers wore white collars (and ties). But if you're interviewing someone older than you, she might remember those days quite clearly. If you're going to interview a client at a bank, don't show up in sandals and a t-shirt. Dressing appropriately will help your interviewee relate to you.

Be reassuring—Often the interviewee is not the customer. A manager may be asking you to capture knowledge from an employee, and that employee may be afraid of being replaced by the proposed new system. Reassure the employee that he's smarter than any computer, and explain that although the system may take over routine tasks, it will free the employee's time to work on more important things. You don't want anyone to perceive you, or the system you're building, as an enemy.

Customers

The *customer*s are the people who are paying you to build the system. Sometimes they know a lot about the problem, and other times they just want the problem solved. If the customer is also a domain expert, then your job is easy, because the customer can direct you to all the information you need. If the customer doesn't know much about the problem domain, then the hardest part of your job may be identifying someone who is.

For the forms advisor application, the customer may be the postal service. No one at the post office will be able to supply much domain knowledge, but they will be able to describe the problem well enough. Luckily, it's obvious in this case who the domain expert should be: a tax accountant. An accountant knows better than anyone else which tax forms people need under various circumstances. The customer should be willing to pay for some of an accountant's time, or perhaps provide access to their own accountants.

Users

The *users* are the people who will interact with the system on a day-to-day basis. Like the customers, the users may or may not know much about the domain in which the system works. A particular category of user, the *expert user*, knows the domain very well. Expert users are people who will use your system to automate tasks they already know how to do. They are often the best kind of interviewee to work with, because they understand the problem and simultaneously know how they want the system to react.

The users for the forms advisor are not expert users—they are just people who wander in to the post office to pick up tax forms. This kind of user isn't particularly useful to interview for knowledge-engineering purposes; however, it can be useful to talk to naïve users about things like user-interface issues.

Experts

A *domain expert* is someone who has technical knowledge in the relevant problem area for your system. A good domain expert is worth her weight in gold, so it is important to seek one out and develop a good working relationship. Most of knowledge engineering consists of extracting information from domain experts.

For the forms advisor application, potential experts include accountants and Internal Revenue Service (IRS) workers. An accountant can tell you what forms are required most often by her clients, whereas an IRS employee may have statistics on form usage by the whole U.S. population. Both can help you understand the tax rules.[1]

9.2.3 Desk research

Not all of your information should come from people. When possible, you should instead collect basic or rote knowledge from written materials, so as not to waste other people's time. Of course, you can't believe everything you read—make sure the experts you talk to would trust the resources you use.

Books and journals

You might use two broad categories of written material: paper publications and electronic ones. With the explosion of the World Wide Web during the last decade, the amount of electronic research material available has mushroomed. Still, scholarly books and periodicals have a significant advantage over most electronic publications: They are usually *peer reviewed*. In the peer-review process, material destined for publication is read and critiqued by impartial experts. This process improves the accuracy and trustworthiness of the information.

In many scientific and engineering fields, college textbooks are an excellent way to get an overview of a domain. Introductory textbooks are often aimed at a general audience, so you can read them without a specialized background. The best textbooks have gone through several editions, honing their language and presentation. Monographs on specific topics can also be useful; these are used as texts for advanced college and graduate-level courses. They are sometimes less well written and aimed at an audience with specific technical background. University and technical libraries are a good source for textbooks and monographs.

Professional and scholarly journals are published several times each year, and they are an excellent way to keep up with advances in a particular field. They can be very expensive, so you'll want to find them in a library as well.

Newsletters, circulars, and other publications aren't usually peer-reviewed, but they can provide useful information. In particular, many government publications

---

[1] Or maybe not. The U.S. General Accounting Office released a much-publicized report in 2001 relating its findings that IRS telephone personnel give out incorrect tax information 47% of the time.

are an invaluable way to learn about laws, regulations, and practices; they combine and distill information from various laws, orders, legal decisions, and policies to produce practical guides.

Web sites and electronic media

You can often find hundreds or even thousands of references by typing a few key words describing your domain into an Internet search engine. There are online encyclopedias of every description, guides to technical fields, troves of engineering data, and countless other valuable resources.

Although the Internet is full of information, it is important to realize that not all of it is correct or unbiased. In particular, many search engines either accept payment for highly placed listings or use a ranking system that is easily fooled into placing a particular page at the top of your search results. Before using a general search engine, learn a little about how it is implemented and operated. Select one that, to the extent possible, ranks results only on their relevance to your search topic. You should also scrutinize individual web pages; check for the source of the information, and try to verify it against another reference.

Sometimes, published electronic reference works on CD-ROM are useful, although they are often simply expensive alternatives to (or worse, a repackaging of) material already available on the Web. Again, you can often find and use these references in libraries.

9.3 Collecting knowledge about tax forms

The domain for the example program is "distributing income tax forms." The project sponsors might describe it like this:

> The system should ask the user a series of questions and then recommend a list of income tax forms the user might need. The list doesn't need to be exhaustive, but it should be generous—that is, if in doubt, recommend the form. The series of questions should be as short as possible and should never include irrelevant or redundant questions.

This simple statement is certainly enough to get you started on the knowledge engineering phase of the project.

9.3.1 An interview

If you've ever filed your own income taxes, you have a reasonable understanding of the concepts behind this application. So, you probably don't need to do any advance desk work—in fact, you can probably gather all the necessary information from one or two interviews and from reading the forms themselves. The first step is to talk to an accountant and ask her to list the 10 most-used income tax forms. She gives you this list, in no particular order:

- *Form 1040*—Income tax
- *Form 1040A*—Income tax
- *Form 1040EZ*—Income tax
- *Form 2441*—Child and dependent care expenses
- *Form 2016EZ*—Employee business expenses
- *Form 3903*—Moving expenses
- *Form 4684*—Casualties and thefts
- *Form 4868*—Application for filing extension
- *Form 8283*—Noncash charitable distributions
- *Form 8829*—Home office expenses

With the list in hand, you can begin asking questions about individual forms. The most relevant question for each form is, "Who needs it?" The accountant's answers are reproduced here:

- *Form 1040* is the standard long form. Everyone needs it.
- *Form 1040A* is the short form. You can use it instead of Form 1040 if your taxable income is less than $50,000. You can't itemize deductions if you use this form, but you *can* get a credit for child-care expenses.
- *Form 1040EZ* is the *really* short form. You can use it instead of Form 1040A if you made less than $50,000, you have no dependents, and you don't itemize deductions. If you're married, you and your spouse must file a joint return or you can't use this form.
- *Form 2441* lets you claim a credit for daycare expenses.
- With *Form 2016EZ*, you can deduct the unreimbursed part of any expenses you incurred for your employer, primarily travel (except commuting). You can use this short form only if you weren't reimbursed for any expenses; otherwise you have to use the long form.
- *Form 3903* gets you a deduction for unreimbursed moving expenses if you moved this year because of your job.
- *Form 4684* lets you recover some of your losses during the year—the part that was not covered by insurance. Many people use this form to deduct costs due to car accidents.

- You fill out *Form 4868* to get an extension for filing your taxes. Note that you still have to *pay* your taxes on time; you can pay an estimated amount with this form.

- You need to file *Form 8283* to get credit for donating more than $500 worth of property to charity.

- You can file *Form 8829* if you have a home office and you want to deduct expenses associated with that office. The rules are fairly restrictive, though—you have to be careful, or you will trigger an audit. You usually shouldn't file this form unless you are self-employed or your home is your primary workplace.

The accountant's expert knowledge is evident in a few of these answers, particularly the descriptions of Forms 2016EZ, 4684, and 8829. Also evident, however, are some of the common problems with interview data. The information is not very precise; for example, it is not true that "everyone needs" Form 1040, because there are two alternative forms.

After hearing these interview replies, a few follow-up questions suggest themselves immediately—for instance, you might want to confirm that the long version of Form 2016EZ is Form 2016 (it is). Otherwise, you should be able to get the rest of the information from the forms themselves; if you have questions about the forms, you can arrange another interview.

9.3.2 Reviewing the forms

You can obtain copies of IRS forms from the IRS web site.[2] Studying the forms turns up a few potentially useful facts that the accountant didn't specify:

- You can't file *Form 1040EZ* if you earned more than $400 in taxable interest. People with more than a certain bank balance (depending on current interest rates) might not be able to use this form.

- You can only file *Form 3903* if you changed work locations and if your new workplace is more than 50 miles further from your old home than your old workplace.

- With *Form 2441*, you can get credit for care for an elderly parent or other dependent, not just care for children.

---

[2] The IRS web site is at http://www.irs.gov. Alternatively, you can get the forms directly at ftp://ftp.fedworld.gov/pub/irs-pdf/.

9.3.3 *Next steps*

You've now amassed enough knowledge about the problem domain to write the application, which you will begin to do in the next chapter. You first need to organize the data by defining `deftemplates` and organize the rules by defining `defmodules`. You also need to write some infrastructure: functions for input and output, for example. In chapter 11, with the infrastructure in place, you will write the rules and deploy the application.

9.4 *Summary*

The application area for a rule-based system is called its *problem domain*. The process of collecting information about a problem domain is called *knowledge engineering*. Knowledge engineering can include gathering data from interviews, books and other publications, the Internet, and other sources.

You've begun work on an application that advises people about the forms they need to use to file their United States federal income taxes. In this chapter, you did the preliminary knowledge engineering, and the end result is several lists of information chunks in prose form.

Designing the application

In this chapter you'll...

- Design `deftemplate`s for the Tax Forms Advisor
- Partition the application with `defmodule`s
- Write code to ask questions of the user

In this chapter, you will begin to develop the Tax Forms Advisor system described in chapter 9. You will decide what the facts should look like and how to divide the rules into modules (when you write them in the next chapter). You'll also design some I/O functions and other infrastructure the rules in the system need. In chapter 11, you'll write the actual rules on the foundation you develop here.

The design process you'll follow in this chapter is idealized: There are no false starts or backtracking. In truth, designing a system like this usually involves experimentation, especially when you're still gaining experience. Don't be discouraged; on the contrary, feel free to experiment with different approaches to implementing this application and to the others in this book.

In previous chapters of this book, you've entered code directly at the Jess> prompt. This approach is great for experimenting, but when you're developing an application, you'll want to save the code in a text file instead. You can then execute your code either by using Jess's (batch) function (which executes the contents of a file full of Jess code) or by specifying the filename on the command line like this:

```
C:\> java -classpath jess.jar jess.Main taxes.clp
```

The .clp extension is traditional but not required. Using a specific extension consistently is helpful, because you may be able to train your programmer's editor to recognize Jess code by the filename.

10.1 *Organizing the data*

As you know, Jess rules work by pattern-matching on facts. Therefore, before you can write any rules, you need to have some idea what the facts will look like. Of course, in one of those classic chicken-and-egg problems, you don't know what the facts should look like until you see the rules. How do you get started?

Generally, the knowledge-engineering effort suggests some possible fact categories. If you record the knowledge as proposed rules or rule-like pseudocode (perhaps using the index-card method described in chapter 9), the possible fact types will be explicitly laid out. Otherwise, you'll have to read through the collected knowledge to get a feel for the kinds of facts that are required. The whole process is subjective, and there is no "right" answer. With practice, you'll get a feeling for what will work and what will not.

Looking through chapter 9's collected knowledge for the Tax Forms Advisor, you can see some possible candidates for deftemplate types:

- form—A specific tax form
- user—The operator of the system

- deduction—A way of reducing your taxable income
- credit—A way of reducing your tax burden
- dependent—A person the user cares for

Thinking about the general organization of the application suggests a few more possibilities:

- question—A question the system might ask the user
- answer—An answer given by the user
- recommendation—A note that the system will recommend a specific form

These eight templates are good candidates for inclusion in the system. Next you need to decide what form they will take—ordered or unordered facts? And for the unordered ones, what slots should they have?

10.2 *Filling in details*

Most facts in this system will represent physical or conceptual *objects*, rather than commands or actions. An object generally has observable properties—color, mass, and so on. To represent an object and its properties as a fact, you can use an unordered fact, declaring an explicit `deftemplate` with multiple slots, one for each property.

The user fact will clearly play a central role. If you look back at the knowledge collected in section 9.3.1, you can see that the user's income and number of dependents are each fairly important and are each referenced in more than one place. These two items are therefore good candidates to be slots in a user *deftemplate*, which might look like this:

```
(deftemplate user
    (slot income)
    (slot dependents))
```

This is a good start, but you need to worry about one detail: default slot values.

10.2.1 *Default slot values*

Jess's mathematical functions generally throw an exception to report the error if you pass in a nonnumeric argument:

```
Jess> (+ 1 2)
3
Jess> (+ one two)
Jess reported an error in routine Value.numericValue
    while executing (+ one two).
```

```
Message: Not a number: "one" (type = ATOM).
Program text: ( + one two ) at line 2.
......
```

An empty slot in an unordered fact contains the value `nil`, which is a symbol, not a number. If you write a rule that matches this empty slot and uses a mathematical function to do it, an exception will be thrown during pattern-matching, like this:

```
Jess> (deftemplate number (slot value))
TRUE
Jess> (defrule print-big-numbers
    (number (value ?v&:(> ?v 10000)))
    =>
    (printout t ?v " is a big number." crlf))
TRUE
Jess> (assert (number))
Jess reported an error in routine Value.numericValue
    while executing (> ?v 10000)
    while executing rule LHS (TEQ)
    while executing rule LHS (TECT)
    while executing (assert (MAIN::number (value nil))).
    Message: Not a number: "nil" (type = ATOM).
    Program text: ( assert ( number ) ) at line 13.
    ...
```

If you plan to use mathematical functions on the left-hand side (LHS) of a rule, it makes sense to add numeric defaults to any slots intended to hold numeric values. The `income` and `dependents` slots of the `user` template will hold numbers, so you should modify the template to look like this:

```
(deftemplate user
    (slot income (default 0))
    (slot dependents (default 0)))
```

Now the `income` and `dependents` slots will be created holding numeric values, and you won't encounter this kind of error.

10.3 *More templates*

A `form` has a code name like *1040A*. It also has a descriptive name, like *Federal income tax short form*. Therefore, the `form` template might look like this:

```
(deftemplate form (slot name) (slot description))
```

Because the system will ask the user a number of questions, you need a generic way to represent a question and its answer. Although you don't know yet what the question-asking mechanism will look like, because you haven't written the code, you can guess that the following two templates might be a good start:

```
(deftemplate question (slot text) (slot type) (slot ident))
(deftemplate answer (slot ident) (slot text))
```

The `question` template ties a symbolic name for a question (in the slot `ident`) to the text of the question. You'll use the working memory as a convenient database in which to look up the question text by identifier, so that if two rules might need to ask the same question, you won't have to duplicate the text. You'll use the `type` slot to hold an indication of the expected category of answer (numeric, yes or no, and so on). The `answer` template ties the answer to a question. A question and its corresponding answer will have the same symbolic value in their `ident` slots. Once an answer for a given question exists, you won't ask it again. (You'll develop the code that uses these templates in section 10.6.)

Finally, a `recommendation` needs a slot to hold a form, and perhaps an explanation:

```
(deftemplate recommendation (slot form) (slot explanation))
```

You've defined templates named `user`, `form`, `question`, `answer`, and `recommendation`. It turns out that this collection is sufficient for your needs. Let's consider why these templates are enough.

10.4 *Templates you don't need*

The other possible templates (`dependent`, `credit`, and `deduction`) probably won't be a part of the application. Looking back at chapter 9, you don't see anything about the collected knowledge that requires you to store information about individual dependents—only the total number of dependents, which you'll store in the `user` template. As a result, you won't need a `dependent` template after all.

The argument for not including `credit` and `deduction` is more involved, and it's related to an important architectural decision. If you stored credits and deductions as facts, you could write a generic set of rules to operate on these facts. The advantage to this architecture is that new forms could be added simply by augmenting the set of credits and deductions—that is, by asserting new facts. You could do this by extending a set of `deffacts` that would be read at application startup. In general, adding new facts would be an easier way to add new tax forms than modifying the rules. If you hard-coded the credit and deduction information into the rules, though, then you could only extend the application by modifying the rules.

On the other hand, the generic rules might be hard to understand, and that would itself make the code more difficult to modify. For the small set of forms this application will work with, I think hard-coding the tax information will lead to a cleaner, simpler application. If you needed to work with 100 forms, or 1,000, the other approach would be worth considering. For this system, though, you won't need `credit` or `deduction` facts; all the tax laws will be encoded directly in the rules.

10.5 *Organizing the rules*

You've defined five templates to serve as data structures for the application. Now let's turn our attention from data to actual code. The first order of business is to sketch out a rough structure for how the rules will be organized.

The Tax Forms Advisor needs to do four things:

1 Initialize the application

2 Conduct an interview with the user to learn about her tax situation

3 Figure out what tax forms to recommend

4 Present the list of forms to the user, removing any duplicate recommendations in the process

These four steps map nicely onto four separate processing phases, each with an independent set of rules. You can put the rules for each phase into a separate `defmodule` (as described in section 7.6) and take advantage of the support Jess offers for partitioning a problem into steps. The four modules are named `startup`, `interview`, `recommend`, and `report`, respectively.

*Defmodule*s partition not only the rules of an application, but also the facts. You need to decide which of the templates ought to go into which of the modules. You can do this by looking at which module's rules need access to the data. Remember that if two or more modules need to share a `deftemplate`, it should go into the module `MAIN`. Examination of the list of templates and of the modules listed here shows that every template will be needed by at least two modules. For instance, the `question` and `answer` templates need to be shared between the `interview` and `recommend` modules, whereas `recommendation` is needed by both `recommend` (which asserts `recommendation` facts) and by `report` (which displays information derived from them). As a result, all of the `deftemplates` you define will be in module `MAIN`. This is not unusual.

10.6 *Building the infrastructure*

Very often, many of the rules in a rule-based system follow a repeating pattern. You know this application needs to ask the user a series of questions and record the answers in the working memory. You can develop code to ask a question and receive an answer as a kind of subroutine, and all the rules that need this capability can call it. Not only does this approach simplify the code for your system, but it also makes it easier to change the interface—if you need to upgrade from a text-based to a graphical kiosk, then you may only need to change this one part of the system.

10.6.1 *Simple text-based I/O*

Recall (from section 3.1.4) Jess's printout function, which you can use to print to standard output. This function can accept any number of arguments and can perform rudimentary formatting (you can control where newlines go by using the special symbol crlf as an argument). There is also a function read that reads a single input token from standard input, returning what it reads. This suggests you can put these two functions together into a deffunction that emits a prompt and reads the response, like this:

```
(deffunction ask-user (?question)
    "Ask a question, and return the answer"
    (printout t ?question " ")
    (return (read)))
```

You should test this function to make sure it works (assuming you've entered the code for ask-user in the file taxes.clp):

```
Jess> (batch taxes.clp)
TRUE
Jess> (ask-user "What is the answer?")
What is the answer? 42
42
```

I entered **42** as the answer, and the function returned *42*; it appears to work fine.

So far, ask-user doesn't do any error checking. You'd like it to only accept answers appropriate to the given question—for example, only *yes* or *no*, or only a number. You need another function—one that can check the form of an answer. Here's one:

```
(deffunction is-of-type (?answer ?type)
    "Check that the answer has the right form"
    (if (eq ?type yes-no) then
      (return (or (eq ?answer yes) (eq ?answer no)))
    else (if (eq ?type number) then
          (return (numberp ?answer)))
        else (return (> (str-length ?answer) 0)))))
```

The second parameter ?type to this function can be yes-no, number, or anything else. If it is yes-no, the function returns FALSE unless ?answer is "yes" or "no". If

?type is number, then the function returns *true* only if ?answer is a number (using the built-in numberp function to test for this condition). If ?type is anything else, is-of-type returns TRUE unless ?answer is the empty string.

Now it is easy to rewrite ask-user to use is-of-type for error checking. While you're at it, you can use the new ?type parameter to enhance the prompt by adding a hint about the possible answers:

```
(deffunction ask-user (?question ?type)
   "Ask a question, and return the answer"
   (bind ?answer "")
   (while (not (is-of-type ?answer ?type)) do
     (printout t ?question " ")
     (if (eq ?type yes-no) then
        (printout t "(yes or no) "))
     (bind ?answer (read)))
   (return ?answer))
```

Again, you should test these new functions:

```
Jess> (is-of-type yes yes-no)
TRUE
Jess> (is-of-type no yes-no)
TRUE
Jess> (is-of-type maybe yes-no)
FALSE
Jess> (is-of-type number abc)
FALSE
Jess> (is-of-type number 123)
TRUE
Jess> (ask-user "What is the answer?" yes-no)
What is the answer? (yes or no) 42
What is the answer? (yes or no) yes
yes
```

This time when I entered **42** as the answer, the function rejected it. When I typed **yes** instead, the function returned yes.

10.6.2 *Fetching the question text*

The question template has a slot to hold the text of a question and another slot to hold a unique identifier. Similarly, the answer template associates that same identifier with an answer. You'd like to call something from the right-hand side (RHS) of a rule in the interview module using just the identifier, and have that something look up the question text, ask the question, and assert an answer fact.

There are two ways to fetch something in working memory: using a defquery or using a defrule. Of the two, rules are cheaper computationally, because invoking a query always involves clearing part of the Rete network and asserting one or

<u>more facts</u>. Therefore, your subroutine could take the form of a single `defrule` in its own `defmodule`. If that `defrule` has the `auto-focus` property (so that it fires as soon as it's activated, regardless of what other rules may be on the agenda) and uses `return` on its RHS to resume the previous module focus as soon as it ran, then the `interview` module can call it as a subroutine just by asserting a fact to activate it. The trigger fact looks like `(ask id)`, where `id` is a question identifier. Such a rule can look like this:

```
(defmodule ask)
(defrule ask::ask-question-by-id
    "Ask a question and assert the answer"
    (declare (auto-focus TRUE))
    ;; If there is a question with ident ?id...
    (MAIN::question (ident ?id) (text ?text) (type ?type))
    ;; ... and there is no answer for it
    (not (MAIN::answer (ident ?id)))
    ;; ... and the trigger fact for this question exists
    ?ask <- (MAIN::ask ?id)
    =>
    ;; Ask the question
    (bind ?answer (ask-user ?text ?type))
    ;; Assert the answer as a fact
    (assert (MAIN::answer (ident ?id) (text ?answer)))
    ;; Remove the trigger
    (retract ?ask)
    ;; And finally, exit this module
    (return))
```

I've explicitly qualified all the fact names with `MAIN::`. Although doing so may not be strictly necessary, it helps to avoid confusion. All of your templates are defined in the module *MAIN*, and therefore they can be shared by all the other modules you define.

You can test this rule after defining a `deffacts` to hold a few sample questions. You should definitely put this test `deffacts` into a file, rather than just entering it interactively—you'll use it again and again to test the rules as you develop them.

NOTE   You should be thinking about putting together a complete test harness now. The details here will vary depending on your platform. On UNIX, you might write a shell script to execute your test code, and on a Windows operating system, you might use a .BAT file (or run the same UNIX scripts using Cygwin).[1] The important thing is to make it convenient to

---

[1] Cygwin is a porting layer that lets UNIX tools run on Windows. The Cygwin home page is at http://www.cygwin.com.

run your test code, and run it often, ideally after each change you make to the developing system. Watch for changes that lead to test failures; if you catch them right away, it is easy to back them out while they are still fresh in your mind. Appendix C describes one technique for automated testing of Jess language code.

Here are some test facts you can use to test `ask-question-by-id`:

```
(deffacts MAIN::test-facts
    (question (ident q1) (type string)
              (text "What is your name?"))
    (question (ident q2) (type number)
              (text "What is your estimated annual income?"))
    (question (ident q3) (type number)
              (text "How many dependents do you have?")))
```

To test the rule, you just need to `reset`, assert an appropriate `ask` fact, and run. You can use `(watch all)` to help see what happens:

```
Jess> (batch taxes.clp)
TRUE
Jess> (reset)
TRUE
Jess> (assert (ask q2))
<Fact-4>
Jess> (watch all)
TRUE
Jess> (run)
FIRE 1 ask::ask-question-by-id f-2,, f-4
What is your estimated annual income? 15000
==> f-5 (MAIN::answer (ident q2) (text 15000))
<== Focus ask
<== f-4 (MAIN::ask q2)
==> Focus MAIN
<== Focus MAIN
1
```

When you enter **(run)**, the rule `ask-question-by-id` grabs the module focus and fires. It asks the question and asserts a new fact holding the answer. Then the focus returns to the original module (`MAIN`, in this case). The subroutine, then, consists of one module, one rule, and two functions, and you can call it just by asserting a fact.

10.7 Summary

In this chapter, you began to turn the knowledge you developed in chapter 9 into a concrete rule-based system. You determined the form the data in working memory will take, you partitioned the system into modules that represent the phases of processing, and you developed some input/output functionality you will use later.

In the next chapter, you will develop the rules that form the actual application. We'll pay special attention to testing techniques, so that you'll trust the components of the application to work well individually and as a complete system.

Writing the application 11

You've done the research, laid the groundwork, and sketched out a design, so now it's time to write the rules that implement the Tax Forms Advisor application. In this chapter, you'll write the rules, test them, and then test the completed application.

As you'll recall from chapter 10, the completed application will consist of five modules: ask, startup, interview, recommend, and report. You developed the ask module in chapter 10. In this chapter, you'll write the rules for the other four modules one module at a time. The code for the complete application is available from this book's web site (http://www.manning.com/friedman-hill).

11.1 Welcoming the user

The startup module for this application is very simple. It doesn't really have any work to do, other than serving as a launching point. You want to print a welcome banner when the user first sees the application, so you can define a rule in startup to display one:

```
(defmodule startup)

(defrule print-banner
    =>
    (printout t "Type your name and press Enter> ")
    (bind ?name (read))
    (printout t crlf "******************************" crlf)
    (printout t "Hello, " ?name "." crlf)
    (printout t "Welcome to the tax forms advisor" crlf)
    (printout t "Please answer the questions and" crlf)
    (printout t "I will tell you what tax forms" crlf)
    (printout t "you may need to file." crlf)
    (printout t "******************************" crlf crlf))
```

11.1.1 Testing the startup module

Whenever you write a rule or cooperating group of rules, you should make sure they work. To test the simple rule print-banner, you can just reset working memory, set the focus, and run (text in bold indicates characters you type in response to a prompt):

```
Jess> (reset)
TRUE
Jess> (focus startup)
MAIN
Jess> (run)
Type your name and press Enter> Fred
**********************************
 Hello, Fred.
 Welcome to the tax forms advisor
```

```
Please answer the questions and
I will tell you what tax forms
you may need to file.
**********************************
1
Jess>
```

11.2 Asking the user questions

The first set of rules you'll write form the `interview` module. As defined, the purpose of this module is to ask questions of the user to collect the inputs for the `recommend` module. The `interview` module should ask the minimum number of questions, and if a question becomes moot, it shouldn't be asked at all. For example, looking back at the knowledge collected in chapter 9, you can see that it's irrelevant how much interest income the user had if his total income is greater than $50,000.

To handle this requirement, you won't ask questions blindly. The rule that asks each question will often need to match the existence or absence of some other fact, so that a question won't be asked unless certain conditions are met.

All the questions you'll ask are represented by facts using the `question` template defined in chapter 10. A `deffacts` containing all the potential questions is shown in listing 11.1.

Listing 11.1 deffacts linking questions to corresponding IDs

```
(deffacts question-data
    "The questions the system can ask."
    (question (ident income) (type number)
      (text "What was your annual income?"))
    (question (ident interest) (type yes-no)
      (text "Did you earn more than $400 in interest?"))
    (question (ident dependents) (type number)
      (text "How many dependents live with you?"))
    (question (ident childcare) (type yes-no)
      (text "Did you have dependent care expenses?"))
    (question (ident moving) (type yes-no)
      (text "Did you move for job-related reasons?"))
    (question (ident employee) (type yes-no)
      (text "Did you have unreimbursed employee expenses?"))
    (question (ident reimbursed) (type yes-no)
      (text "Did you have reimbursed employee expenses, too?"))
    (question (ident casualty) (type yes-no)
      (text "Did you have losses from a theft or an accident?"))
    (question (ident on-time) (type yes-no)
      (text "Will you be able to file on time?"))
```

```
(question (ident charity) (type yes-no)
  (text "Did you give more than $500 in property to charity?"))
(question (ident home-office) (type yes-no)
  (text "Did you work in a home office?")))
```

11.2.1 *Income and dependents*

The user's income determines whether she can use either of the short forms, so the system should ask about income first. If the income is below $50,000, the number of dependents and the amount of interest income determine which of the short forms can be used. Although the number of dependents is needed for other purposes, the interest income is relevant only if the user's income is less than $50,000; therefore, you make asking about interest income conditional on the user's income being below this limit. To ask a question, you assert an `ask` fact that indicates the question to be asked; the `ask` module you developed in section 10.6.2 asks the question and asserts an `answer` fact. The rules to ask these questions are shown in listing 11.2, along with a rule to construct the `user` fact once the necessary information is available. The rules `request-income` and `request-num-dependents` have no patterns on their left-hand sides (LHS); they are activated unconditionally.

Listing 11.2 Some rules from the `interview` module

```
(defmodule interview)

(defrule request-income
    =>
    (assert (ask income)))

(defrule request-num-dependents
    =>
    (assert (ask dependents)))

(defrule request-interest-income
    ;; If the total income is less than 50000
    (answer (ident income) (text ?i&:(< ?i 50000)))
    ;; .. and there are no dependents
    (answer (ident dependents) (text ?d&:(eq ?d 0)))
    =>
    (assert (MAIN::ask interest)))

(defrule assert-user-fact
    (answer (ident income) (text ?i))
    (answer (ident dependents) (text ?d))
    =>
    (assert (user (income ?i) (dependents ?d))))
```

These rules have no patterns and are activated by a call to reset

11.2.2 *Dealing with special circumstances*

The rest of the `interview` rules ask the user about special circumstances in her life during the past year. In general, if some of these special circumstances apply, the user may want to fill out the long form and take the corresponding deductions, even if her income qualifies her to use one of the short forms. These special circumstances include moving and unreimbursed employee expenses. Some of the questions about special circumstances are again asked conditionally, based on other answers; for example, the form for deducting child-care expenses won't be needed if the user has no dependents. The rules that ask about special circumstances are shown in listing 11.3. Many of these rules are fired unconditionally, but a few depend on other answers. The rule `request-childcare-expenses` won't be activated if the user doesn't have dependents, and `request-reimbursed-expenses` will fire only if the user has unreimbursed expenses.

Listing 11.3   Rules that ask about special circumstances

```
(defrule request-childcare-expenses
    ;; If the user has dependents
    (answer (ident dependents) (text ?t&:(> ?t 0)))
    =>
    (assert (ask childcare)))

(defrule request-employee-expenses
    =>
    (assert (ask employee)))

(defrule request-reimbursed-expenses
    ;; If there were unreimbursed employee expenses...
    (answer (ident employee) (text ?t&:(eq ?t yes)))
    =>
    (assert (ask reimbursed)))

(defrule request-moving
    =>
    (assert (ask moving)))

(defrule request-casualty
    =>
    (assert (ask casualty)))

(defrule request-on-time
    =>
    (assert (ask on-time)))

(defrule request-charity
    =>
    (assert (ask charity)))

(defrule request-home-office
    =>
    (assert (ask home-office)))
```

When the `interview` module executes, it asks the user a series of questions and leaves behind a `user` fact and a collection of `answer` facts. These facts serve as input to the next module, `recommend`, which decides which forms the user needs.

11.2.3 *Testing the interview module*

Testing the `interview` module is easy. You can create a series of test cases, each of which should contain the following:

- A hypothetical tax situation
- The expected set of relevant questions
- The expected set of result facts

Once you've developed this set of test data, run the program once (by resetting, setting the focus to `interview`, and invoking `run`) for each test case, supplying the appropriate user answers for that hypothetical case. Then check the results. Make sure the system asks you all the questions on your list for that case, and only those questions. Use the `facts` command (you'll need to use `(facts *)` to see the facts in all modules) to make sure all the expected facts are present and correct. If you can capture your whole terminal session in a file (by using the `script` command on UNIX, for example), then you can save the file and use it as part of an automated test script. The program should produce the same output each time it is run; you can use your automated script to check that changes you make later haven't broken the behavior of this module.

NOTE   Many books have been written on the subject of software testing, and although such books are often useful, they can be discouraging to read. They generally concentrate on teaching you to find *spanning sets* of tests, or lists of tests that cover every possible path through your application. For most real applications, of course, such a spanning set is impossibly large. The testing books often forget to tell you that *some* tests, although perhaps not as good as *all* possible tests, are infinitely better than *no* tests. Don't be discouraged by the sense that you can't completely test a rule-based application. Remember that some testing is a lot better than none at all.

11.3 *Recommending forms*

Writing the rules for the `recommend` module is a bit more challenging, but also more fun. Each of the rules examines the `user` and `answer` facts and recommends one or more forms. These rules directly encode the knowledge gleaned from the interview with a tax expert in chapter 9.

The first set of rules in this module determines which variants of Form 1040 the user might need. In keeping with the design description in chapter 9, your strategy will be to recommend all the forms the user might need; if in doubt, you will recommend the form. This means the system may recommend that the user bring home several versions of the same form, and that's OK.[1]

Recall that the user can file Form 1040EZ if and only if:

- Her income is less than $50,000, and
- She has no dependents, and
- Her interest income is less than $400

You can directly translate these requirements into a rule as follows:

```
(defmodule recommend)

(defrule form-1040EZ
    (user (income ?i&:(< ?i 50000))
          (dependents ?d&:(eq ?d 0)))
    (answer (ident interest) (text no))
    =>
    (assert (recommendation
        (form 1040EZ)
        (explanation "Income below threshold, no dependents"))))
```

Similarly, Form 1040A can be filed if the user's income is below the same threshold, but she has either dependents, or excess interest income, or both. You can write this as two rules:

```
(defrule form-1040A-excess-interest
    (user (income ?i&:(< ?i 50000)))
    (answer (ident interest) (text yes))
    =>
    (assert (recommendation
        (form 1040A)
        (explanation "Excess interest income"))))

(defrule form-1040A
    (user (income ?i&:(< ?i 50000))
          (dependents ?d&:(> ?d 0)))
    =>
    (assert (recommendation
        (form 1040A)
        (explanation "Income below threshold, with dependents"))))
```

---

[1] The U.S. Federal Tax Code is famously complicated. It's common practice for U.S. residents to try filling out several different combinations of tax forms, because each combination can result in a slightly different calculated tax liability. The taxpayer then files the combination of forms that leads to the smallest tax bill.

You recommend the long Form 1040 if the user needs to itemize deductions, or if the user's income is above the threshold. The rule to handle this latter condition is simply

```
(defrule form-1040-income-above-threshold
    (user (income ?i&:(>= ?i 50000)))
    =>
    (assert (recommendation
        (form 1040)
        (explanation "Income above threshold"))))
```

The rest of the rules in this module handle the various special circumstances. The user can take the credit for dependent-care expenses if she files either Form 1040A or Form 1040 (dependent care is special in this regard; all the other special circumstances can only be claimed on Form 1040). The rule to recommend the dependent care expenses form is therefore as follows:

```
(defrule form-2441
    (answer (ident childcare) (text yes))
    =>
    (assert (recommendation
        (form 2441)
        (explanation "Child care expenses"))))
```

You know that if the `childcare` question has been asked and answered, the user must have dependents and therefore isn't filing Form 1040EZ. See the rule `request-childcare-expenses` in listing 11.3.

For most of the other special circumstances, you recommend Form 1040 along with the special form. Here's a representative rule:

```
(defrule form-4684
    (answer (ident casualty) (text yes))
    =>
    (bind ?ex "Losses due to casualty or theft")
    (assert
        (recommendation (form 4684) (explanation ?ex))
        (recommendation (form 1040) (explanation ?ex))))
```

You may notice a problem here: Form 1040 may be recommended multiple times. You need a rule to combine multiple recommendations into one. The following rule does the trick. The separate explanations are concatenated with a newline (represented in Jess as a double-quoted string containing a line break) between them:

```
(defrule combine-recommendations
    ?r1 <- (recommendation (form ?f) (explanation ?e1))
    ?r2 <- (recommendation (form ?f) (explanation ?e2&~?e1))
    =>
    (retract ?r2)
    (modify ?r1 (explanation (str-cat ?e1 "
" ?e2))))
```

Listing 11.4 shows the remainder of the rules that handle special circumstances. These rules are all in the recommend module.

Listing 11.4   Additional rules for special circumstances

```
(defrule form-2016EZ
    (answer (ident employee) (text yes))
    (answer (ident reimbursed) (text no))
    =>
    (bind ?ex "Unreimbursed employee expenses")
    (assert
        (recommendation (form 2016EZ) (explanation ?ex))
        (recommendation (form 1040) (explanation ?ex))))

(defrule form-2016
    (answer (ident employee) (text yes))
    (answer (ident reimbursed) (text yes))
    =>
    (bind ?ex "Reimbursed employee expenses")
    (assert
        (recommendation (form 2016) (explanation ?ex))
        (recommendation (form 1040) (explanation ?ex))))

(defrule form-3903
    (answer (ident moving) (text yes))
    =>
    (bind ?ex "Moving expenses")
    (assert
        (recommendation (form 3903) (explanation ?ex))
        (recommendation (form 1040) (explanation ?ex))))

(defrule form-4868
    (answer (ident on-time) (text no))
    =>
    (assert (recommendation (form 4868)
        (explanation "Filing extension"))))

(defrule form-8283
    (answer (ident charity) (text yes))
    =>
    (bind ?ex "Excess charitable contributions")
    (assert
        (recommendation (form 8283) (explanation ?ex))
        (recommendation (form 1040) (explanation ?ex))))

(defrule form-8829
    (answer (ident home-office) (text yes))
    =>
    (bind ?ex "Home office expenses")
    (assert
        (recommendation (form 8829) (explanation ?ex))
        (recommendation (form 1040) (explanation ?ex))))
```

11.4 *Explaining the results*

When the `recommend` module is finished, the working memory includes a series of `recommendation` facts representing the application's suggestions for the user. All the `report` module needs to do is display the data from these facts in a sensible way. In particular, the forms should be listed in alphabetical order; note that then the main forms (1040, 1040A, 1040EZ) are displayed first.

Each `recommendation` fact includes a bit of text rationalizing the recommendation in the `explanation` slot. You'll display these explanations, too. Because the explanations can span multiple lines, you can't easily display the program's output in tabular form—at least, not if you have to stick to plain text. If you could use HTML, the display would be easy. You'll be developing web-based systems later in the book, so for simplicity's sake you'll display each recommended form and its explanation together, one on top of the other.

Sorting data is an old and well-studied topic, and there are many ways to accomplish a sorting task. A simple, if not particularly efficient, technique is the *selection sort*. To perform a selection sort, you search through a collection for the smallest (or largest) item, and then remove it and make it the first item in a new, sorted collection. Repeat this process to find the second and later items. For small collections, a selection sort is a perfectly reasonable choice, and you'll use it here. This rule-based implementation of a selection sort compares the names of forms in `recommendation` facts. The single rule prints information about a fact and then retracts it if and only if there are no other `recommendation` facts with a form that comes alphabetically earlier. Each time you retract a fact, a different `recommendation` becomes the new alphabetically first one, until all the `recommendation` facts are exhausted. You can use the `str-compare` function, which takes two strings as arguments and returns -1 if the first one is alphabetically first, +1 if the second string should come first, and 0 if the arguments are equal:

```
(defmodule report)

(defrule sort-and-print
    ?r1 <- (recommendation (form ?f1) (explanation ?e))
    (not (recommendation (form ?f2&
                     :(< (str-compare ?f2 ?f1) 0))))
    =>
    (printout t "*** Please take a copy of form " ?f1 crlf)
    (printout t "Explanation: " ?e crlf crlf)
    (retract ?r1))
```

11.4.1 *Testing the report module*

The report module, like the startup module, contains only one rule. You can test it by asserting some recommendation facts yourself:

```
Jess> (assert (recommendation (form f3) (explanation ef3))
    (recommendation (form f1) (explanation ef1))
    (recommendation (form f2) (explanation ef2))
    (recommendation (form f4) (explanation ef4)))
<Fact-3>
Jess> (focus report)
MAIN
Jess> (run)
*** Please take a copy of form f1
Explanation: ef1

*** Please take a copy of form f2
Explanation: ef2

*** Please take a copy of form f3
Explanation: ef3

*** Please take a copy of form f4
Explanation: ef4

4
Jess>
```

Note that the forms are listed in alphabetical order, and each one is displayed with its explanation. The application is now basically done; you just need to handle a few remaining details.

11.5 *Finishing touches*

Now that all the rules are written, you need a way to start your program. Because the module focus must be shifted several times during each run of the application, it is helpful to define a deffunction to perform the proper sequence of operations:

```
(deffunction run-system ()
    (reset)
    (focus startup interview recommend report)
    (run))
```

The single call to focus sets up the focus stack so the four modules become active in the right order. The program can then be executed with a single call to run-system. This application is intended to run continuously in a kiosk at the post office, so you call this function in a loop:

```
(while TRUE
    (run-system))
```

This loop restarts the application each time it terminates.

11.6 *Testing the full application*

Now that the whole application is written, dust off the sample scenarios you developed for testing the `interview` and `recommend` modules and run them again. This time you only need to look at the output of the system. A complete run of the application is shown in listing 11.5.

Listing 11.5   A typical session with the Tax Forms Advisor

```
% java jess.Main taxes.clp

Jess, the Java Expert System Shell
Copyright (C) 2001 E.J. Friedman Hill and the Sandia Corporation
Jess Version 6.1 4/9/2003

Type your name and press Enter> Bertram

**********************************
 Hello, Bertram.
 Welcome to the tax forms advisor
 Please answer the questions and
 I will tell you what tax forms
 you may need to file.
**********************************

What was your annual income? 14000
Did you work in a home office? (yes or no) yes
Did you give more than $500 in property to charity? (yes or no) no
Will you be able to file on time? (yes or no) yes
Did you have losses from a theft or an accident? (yes or no) no
Did you move for job-related reasons? (yes or no) no
Did you have unreimbursed employee expenses? (yes or no) yes
Did you have reimbursed employee expenses, too? (yes or no) no
How many dependents live with you? 7
Did you have dependent care expenses? (yes or no) yes
*** Please take a copy of form 1040
Explanation: Home office expenses
Unreimbursed employee expenses

*** Please take a copy of form 1040A
Explanation: Income below threshold, with dependents

*** Please take a copy of form 2016EZ
Explanation: Unreimbursed employee expenses
```

```
*** Please take a copy of form 2441
Explanation: Child care expenses

*** Please take a copy of form 8829
Explanation: Home office expenses
```

Now would be a good time to take the system to the tax expert to let her play with it. She very well may have some important changes or additions you need to integrate—it is the nature of software development that no set of requirements is ever complete. You should also show this system to the customer to get some feedback.

11.7 Summary

Over the last three chapters, you've gone from concept to research to design and finally to execution of a system for recommending tax forms. Although the program you've developed is somewhat simplistic, the process you followed was representative of rule-based system development. And although the user interface of the application you developed here is unsuitable for real use, the underlying logic is perfectly respectable and includes features like input validation and a simple explanation facility. The routines you developed for asking questions and validating input will serve as a foundation on which you'll build more sophisticated tools later in this book.

In this chapter, you saw how a good design and sturdy infrastructure help simplify programming a system. You learned to write a modular application using processing phases implemented using `defmodules`, and you got some practice writing simple pattern-matching expressions. You even learned how to implement a simple sorting algorithm in a rule-based language. Note, however, that good design decisions don't happen spontaneously; the Jess programmer will become more proficient over time, just as in any discipline. Experience and experimentation will help you develop good design skills.

In the next part of this book, you'll research, design, and build another complete system. This one will be considerably more polished and will include a Java-based graphical user interface. You'll also see how backward chaining lets you easily write programs for problem diagnosis and troubleshooting.

Part 4

Writing a diagnostic application: the PC Repair Assistant

Having developed one realistic application, you're ready to move on to something bigger. The application you'll develop next includes both more knowledge and more features: It's a *PC Repair Assistant* with a graphical interface. It's meant to guide a technician through the process of diagnosing computer hardware problems.

In this part of the book, we'll refine your understanding of engineering knowledge by introducing a new tool—flowcharting. The program you'll write is much more sophisticated than the last one; it is multithreaded and uses Jess's reflection capabilities to build a Swing-based graphical interface directly from a Jess script.

12

Writing the PC Repair Assistant

In this chapter, you'll write a rule-based system with a command-line interface, just like the Tax Forms Advisor. You'll obtain the necessary knowledge by interviewing computer repair technicians, develop the rules, and test the system. This application reuses some techniques you developed for the Tax Forms Advisor. For instance, you'll modify and then reuse the `ask` module to ask the user for input. You'll again use modules to represent processing phases: The main knowledge base is in the `MAIN` module, and we'll introduce a new control module named `trigger`.

Of course, this application showcases some new techniques as well. To model the technician's reasoning when diagnosing computer problems, you'll use *backward chaining*, which we first discussed in section 7.4. Based on an initial description of the behavior of a computer, the system will form a *hypothesis* about what might be wrong with it. Backward chaining rules will then be triggered to either prove or disprove that hypothesis. Along the way, the program will make recommendations for things the user might try to potentially fix the broken computer.

Many of the earliest rule-based systems were backward-chaining diagnostic programs like this one. For example, the *MYCIN* program[1] discussed in section 2.2.1 diagnosed blood infections based on information about bacterial cultures.

In chapter 13, you'll package the application with a graphical user interface suitable for use by office personnel. You'll use Jess's powerful Java scripting capabilities to build a Swing-based graphical interface without writing any Java code. The interface hooks into an enhanced version of the `ask` module, so in adding the interface you won't need to modify the knowledge base you develop here.

12.1 *Using flowcharts in knowledge engineering*

Diagnostic knowledge can be represented fairly well using *flowcharts*. A lot of information can be compactly represented by a few symbols, as shown in table 12.1. A simple flowchart for dealing with automotive problems is shown in figure 12.1.

Table 12.1 Symbols used in flowcharts

Symbol	Meaning	Example
Square box	A simple action	Repairing or replacing a component
Diamond box	A choice or decision	Is the screen dark?

---

[1] R. Davis, B. G. Buchanan, and E. H. Shortliffe, "Production Systems as a Representation for a Knowledge-Based Consultation Program," *Artificial Intelligence* 8 (1977): 15–45.

Table 12.1   Symbols used in flowcharts *(continued)*

Symbol	Meaning	Example
Oval box	Beginning or end of process	START
Arrows	Flow between boxes	What to do for each branch of a decision

If you're going to be drawing a lot of flowcharts, a software program like *Visio* can help. When you're drawing flowcharts during an interview with a domain expert, software might be too unwieldy, in which case a dime-store plastic drawing template and a sharp pencil might be a better choice.

12.1.1 *From flowcharts to rules*

Translating flowcharts into rules is fairly straightforward. In general, there is one rule for every action box, and there are additional rules for some of the oval boxes. A possible set of rules for the flowchart in figure 12.1 is shown in listing 12.1. The listing includes three rules: one each for the action boxes in the flowchart and one for the *END* oval. Note that each rule corresponds to a specific hypothesis about what might be wrong with the car. In a more complex flowchart, this last correspondence might no longer hold, but the matchup between rules and boxes still would.

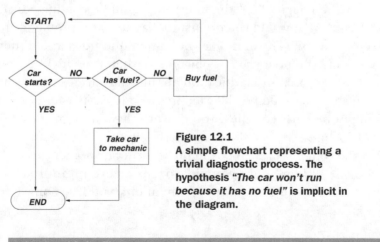

Figure 12.1
A simple flowchart representing a trivial diagnostic process. The hypothesis *"The car won't run because it has no fuel"* is implicit in the diagram.

Listing 12.1   Three rules that capture the logic from figure 12.1

```
(defrule no-fuel
    "This rule corresponds to the 'buy fuel' box"
    (car-starts no)
```

```
        (car-has-fuel no)
        =>
        (assert (buy fuel)))

(defrule faulty-engine
        "This rule is for the 'take car to mechanic' box"
        (car-starts no)
        (car-has-fuel yes)
        =>
        (assert (take car to mechanic)))

(defrule car-is-ok
        "This rule corresponds to the 'END' oval"
        (car-starts yes)
        =>
        (assert (car is ok)))
```

The program you are building will diagnose problems with computers, so you should be able to represent the knowledge you gather in a series of flowcharts. If you were gathering the knowledge by interviewing a computer repair technician, you could start by asking her to list some of the most common computer problems she deals with. For each of these problems, you'd develop a flowchart around the hypothesis that this particular problem was affecting the broken computer. Each of these flowcharts would show the series of tests the technician would perform to attempt to verify or disprove the hypothesis.

It should be easy to imagine how the interview would be conducted. For each flowchart, you'd ask, "What would you do first to diagnose this problem, and what are the possible outcomes?" The most likely follow-up questions would then be of the form, "What would you do if you saw outcome *X* when you did *Y*?" In between, of course, you'd need to ask for clarification about what various technical terms meant, and these answers would be collected in prose form. Because each step in the flowchart might be fairly complex, you'd probably want to give each box an identifier like *F10-3* (meaning the third numbered box on flowchart number 10) and then record the contents of each box in prose form on another piece of paper.

A real diagnostic system might contain dozens or even hundreds of these annotated flowcharts. Due to obvious space limitations, you'll see only a few simple ones here.

12.2 *The problem domain*

Of course, "problems with desktop computers" is a very broad domain, and you need to narrow it down a lot before you can get started. First, let's specialize desktop computers to x86-based desktop computers. We won't consider Macintosh machines or any other architectures—just those systems that are commonly referred to as PCs. You can formalize this specialization in a rule:

```
(defrule MAIN::right-architecture
    (declare (auto-focus TRUE))
    (answer (ident hardware) (text ~x86))
    =>
    (recommend-action "consult a human expert")
    (halt))
```

You'll write the function `recommend-action` later. Note that this rule, like many others in this system, calls `(halt)` to terminate execution. Although this isn't really necessary right now, you'll see why you need to do this in chapter 13 when you add a graphical interface to this application. The `auto-focus` declaration ensures that as soon as the system has a recommendation to make, it will be made—even if some other module has the focus at the time. You'll use this declaration in all the rules that make recommendations.

To further restrict the domain, the system you're writing diagnoses only hardware problems, not software issues. Broken power supplies, loose video cards, and faulty memory chips are typical of the class of problems that your program will diagnose. It won't be able to help with questions like, "Why can't I connect to the network?" and "What is a General Protection Fault?"

Finally, let's restrict the domain to include only computers that won't boot. This leaves out many hardware problems: You won't try to diagnose nonfunctional network cards, jammed CD-ROM drives, and other broken components not directly involved in booting the machine.

12.2.1 *Writing the first rules*

A simple top-level flowchart for the program is shown in figure 12.2. If the computer makes no sound at all, the presumed hypotheses are *The computer isn't getting any electricity* and *The power supply is faulty.* You can write these two hypotheses as rules in the MAIN module, as shown in listing 12.2. The rule `not-plugged-in` handles the case where the computer makes no sound and is not plugged in; the rule `power-supply-broken` handles the case where the silent computer *is* plugged in. The two versions of the first pattern in the two rules represent the two outcomes from the decision *Is there any sound?* in the center of figure 12.2.

Listing 12.2   *Rules to diagnose a computer that makes no sound*

```
(deffunction recommend-action (?action)
   "Give final instructions to the user"
   (printout t "I recommend that you " ?action crlf))

(defrule MAIN::not-plugged-in
   (declare (auto-focus TRUE))
   (answer (ident sound) (text no))
   (answer (ident plugged-in) (text no))
   =>
   (recommend-action "plug in the computer")
   (halt))

(defrule MAIN::power-supply-broken
   (declare (auto-focus TRUE))
   (answer (ident sound) (text no))
   (answer (ident plugged-in) (text yes))
   =>
   (recommend-action "repair or replace power supply")
   (halt))
```

Figure 12.2, and all the flowcharts you'll use to develop this application, are vastly simplified. The action *Check power supply* should ideally expand to a whole flowchart of its own, explaining the steps involved in diagnosing power-supply problems. Unfortunately, to present that flowchart and all the rules to support it and the dozens of others you'd need to collect, I'd fill another whole book. Because this is a programming book, not a PC repair manual, I'll keep things simple.

These rules assume something else is taking care of asking the user questions—the rules just depend on the answers. Whereas in the Tax Forms Advisor application from part 3 you had to explicitly write rules to ask the questions, in this application, the questions are asked automatically using backward chaining.

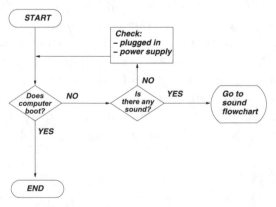

Figure 12.2
A simple top-level flowchart for diagnosing PC hardware problems. This flowchart can diagnose the problem *"The computer isn't getting any electricity."*

Let's see how this works. After that, we'll reexamine and extend the ask module from part 3 to meet the needs of the current project.

12.3 *Asking questions with backward chaining*

In the Tax Forms Advisor application, an entire module named interview was dedicated to picking out questions to ask the user. In general, there was one rule in interview specific to each question the application might ask, and another rule in the recommend module to use the answer. Because that application included only a dozen or so possible questions, this approach wasn't much of a problem; but it obviously wouldn't scale well to a system with hundreds of questions. You need something easier for the application you're writing now. Ideally, you'd like to have just a few generic rules that somehow know how to ask the appropriate questions at the right time. In this application, when a diagnostic rule is partially matched and needs a MAIN::answer fact to match it further, you'd like the appropriate question to be asked and the resulting answer fact to be asserted.

You'll use backward chaining, so your new program will automatically know when to ask each question. Recall from section 7.4 that in Jess, backward chaining works by creating special trigger facts based on partially matched rules. To make backward chaining work, you first have to turn it on with the do-backward-chaining function; then you write rules to match the trigger facts. The ask module asks questions based on the MAIN::ask facts it sees, so your backward-chaining rule (called supply-answers) can match MAIN::need-answer trigger facts and assert MAIN::ask facts in response; this process is shown in figure 12.3. The rule supply-answers is shown in listing 12.3. supply-answers has the auto-focus property and is in its own module; this is the same trick the ask module uses so that it can fire immediately whenever it is activated.

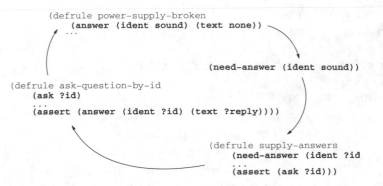

Figure 12.3   The cycle of rules that fire to get answers from the user in this application. The rule
`power-supply-broken` **needs an `answer` fact before it matches. Jess's backward-chaining
engine detects this requirement and asserts a `need-answer` fact. The rule `supply-answers`
detects this fact and asserts an `ask` fact in response. Finally, the `ask-question-by-id` rule fires
in response to the `ask` fact and supplies the `answer` fact needed by `power-supply-broken`.**

Listing 12.3   A rule to ask questions via backward chaining

```
(do-backward-chaining answer)

(defmodule trigger)

(defrule trigger::supply-answers
    (declare (auto-focus TRUE))
    (MAIN::need-answer (ident ?id))
    (not (MAIN::answer (ident ?id)))
    (not (MAIN::ask ?))
    =>
    (assert (MAIN::ask ?id))
    (return))
```

12.4 *Checking the answers*

The `ask` module developed in section 10.6 was a simple, general-purpose mechanism for asking questions. For this application, you need to extend it a little. In
particular, whereas the previous application only asked questions with yes/no and
numeric answers, this application needs to be able to validate three different
kinds of answers:

- *Multiple choice (multi)*—One of a set of allowed answers. Yes or no questions
  are a special case of this type.
- *Numeric*—Any integer value.
- *Text*—Any arbitrary text.

Furthermore, looking ahead to chapter 13, this application will have a graphical interface. The original version of the ask module depended on the fact that all answers were read from the console using the Jess (read) function. (read) interprets what it reads, which guarantees that something that looks like an integer is held internally as a jess.Value object of type RU.INTEGER. In the last application, then, the Jess parser figured out if something was a number before the ask module ever saw it. You can't make that assumption any longer, because you're going to use a GUI, not (read), to collect answers. Some numbers may arrive as text and need to be parsed.

12.4.1 *Modifying the ask module*

In general, then, you need to extend and enhance the ask module for this application. The first extension adds a multislot to the question template to hold the possible values for multiple-choice questions. The ask-question-by-id rule needs to match this multifield and pass it along to an extended version of the ask-user function. ask-user, in turn, needs to pass the multifield to an enhanced is-of-type function, which can validate questions of type multi, numeric, and text. The new template and rule are shown in listing 12.4, and the modified functions appear in listing 12.5.

Listing 12.4   Modifications to the question-asking rules

```
(deftemplate question
    "A question the application may ask"
    (slot text)         ;; The question itself
    (slot type)         ;; Can be multi, text, or numeric
    (multislot valid)   ;; The allowed answers for type multi
    (slot ident))       ;; The "name" of the question

(defrule ask::ask-question-by-id
    "Ask a question and assert the answer"
    (declare (auto-focus TRUE))
    (MAIN::question (ident ?id) (text ?text)
                    (valid $?valid) (type ?type))
    (not (MAIN::answer (ident ?id)))
    ?ask <- (MAIN::ask ?id)
    =>
    (retract ?ask)
    (bind ?answer (ask-user ?text ?type ?valid))
    (assert (answer (ident ?id) (text ?answer)))
    (return))
```

Listing 12.5   Modifications to the question-asking functions

```
(deffunction ask-user (?question ?type ?valid)
   "Ask a question, and return the answer"
   (bind ?answer "")
   (while (not (is-of-type ?answer ?type ?valid)) do
     (printout t ?question " ")
     (if (eq ?type multi) then
       (printout t crlf "Valid answers are ")
       (foreach ?item ?valid
         (printout t ?item " "))
       (printout t ":"))
     (bind ?answer (read)))
   (return ?answer))

(deffunction is-of-type (?answer ?type ?valid)
   "Check that the answer has the right form"
   (if (eq ?type multi) then
     (foreach ?item ?valid
       (if (eq (sym-cat ?answer) (sym-cat ?item)) then
         (return TRUE)))
     (return FALSE))

   (if (eq ?type number) then
     (return (is-a-number ?answer)))

   ;; plain text
   (return (> (str-length ?answer) 0)))

(deffunction is-a-number (?value)
   "Return TRUE if ?value is a number"
   (try
     (integer ?value)
     (return TRUE)
   catch
     (return FALSE)))
```

This version of the `is-of-type` function has to do more work than the version in section 10.6, because it needs to check three different kinds of questions and it can't assume the answers will arrive as Jess numbers and symbols; every answer might be in the form of a string and need to be parsed further. When checking multi answers, `is-of-type` therefore uses the `sym-cat` function to convert the answer to a symbol before comparing it to each possible result. When checking numeric answers, `is-of-type` calls another new function, `is-a-number`, to do the work.

The new `is-a-number` utility function uses Jess's built-in `integer` function, which either returns an integer version of its argument or throws an exception if the argument can't be interpreted as a number. The `is-a-number` function uses the Jess `try` function to catch that exception and return `FALSE`. (We looked at `try` in section 5.4.)

12.5 *The rest of the rules*

Now that the infrastructure is squared away, let's go back to looking at some rules. If the computer whirrs, beeps, or makes any other sounds when turned on, the top-level flowchart directs you to continue on to the next flowchart, shown in figure 12.4. Let's translate this into rules one piece at a time.

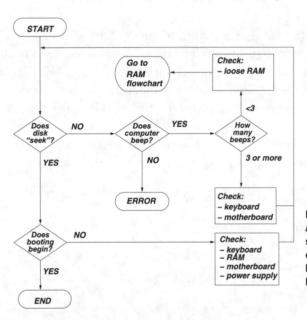

Figure 12.4
A simple flowchart for diagnosing some hardware problems in computers that make sound but don't boot. The *ERROR* state is supposed to be impossible to reach.

12.5.1 *Rules about sound*

The trigger to enter this flowchart in the first place occurs when the user answers "no" to the `sound` question; therefore all the rules begin with the pattern `(answer (ident sound) (text no))`. Any decisions made before this point are irrelevant to these rules. The first decision in the sound flowchart is whether the disk makes "seeking" sounds; so, similarly, all the rules in this flowchart include a pattern to match one of the possible answers to the `seek` question. From this point, the rules diverge; you can look at the path through the flowchart to each action box to see how to define each rule. For example, the *Check keyboard and motherboard* action is reached by passing through the seek, does-beep, and how-many-beeps decisions, so it looks like this:

```
(defrule MAIN::motherboard-or-keyboard
    (declare (auto-focus TRUE))
    (answer (ident sound) (text yes))
    (answer (ident seek) (text no))
    (answer (ident does-beep) (text yes))
    (answer (ident how-many-beeps) (text ?t))
    (test (>= (integer ?t) 3))
    =>
    (recommend-action "check keyboard and motherboard")
    (halt))
```

Note that you have to use the integer function to convert the answer to a number before checking if it's greater than or equal to three. You use a test conditional element instead of putting the test on ?t directly into the last answer pattern due to a limitation imposed by the backward-chaining machinery: Patterns that match backward-chaining reactive patterns can only contain simple tests—function calls aren't allowed.

The check-ram rule is similar, but with a twist. Besides recommending an action, this rule asserts a check fact, and does *not* call (halt):

```
(defrule MAIN::check-ram
    (declare (auto-focus TRUE))
    (answer (ident sound) (text yes))
    (answer (ident seek) (text no))
    (answer (ident does-beep) (text yes))
    (answer (ident how-many-beeps) (text ?t))
    (test (< (integer ?t) 3))
    =>
    (assert (check loose-ram))
    (recommend-action "check for loose RAM, then continue"))
```

You'll use the check fact as the trigger to enter the RAM flowchart, shown later in figure 12.5. This trick lets the system ask further questions based on the results of a recommended action. If you were writing a full diagnostic system with dozens of flowcharts, you'd use this trick many times.

12.5.2 *Degrading gracefully*

If the computer is making a sound, but the disk doesn't seek and there is no beeping, then the system has reached the limits of its knowledge, represented by the oval labeled *ERROR*. The unknown-sound rule expresses this end point:

```
(defrule MAIN::unknown-sound
    (declare (auto-focus TRUE))
    (answer (ident sound) (text yes))
```

```
(answer (ident seek) (text no))
(answer (ident does-beep) (text no))
=>
(recommend-action "consult a human expert")
(halt))
```

12.5.3 *To boot, or not to boot*

If the disk *does* make a seeking sound, then there is one more decision to make: Does the computer begin to boot into the operating system before failing? Two more rules cover the two possible answers:

```
(defrule MAIN::no-boot-start
    (declare (auto-focus TRUE))
    (answer (ident sound) (text yes))
    (answer (ident seek) (text yes))
    (answer (ident boot-begins) (text no))
    =>
    (recommend-action
        "check keyboard, RAM, motherboard, and power supply")
    (halt))

(defrule MAIN::boot-start
    (declare (auto-focus TRUE))
    (answer (ident sound) (text yes))
    (answer (ident seek) (text yes))
    (answer (ident boot-begins) (text yes))
    =>
    (recommend-action "consult a software expert")
    (halt))
```

12.5.4 *RAM problems*

The RAM flowchart shown in figure 12.5 is simple—it includes only two more rules. One handles the case where the RAM memory modules are loose in their sockets, and the other handles the case where they are not. These two rules are slightly different than all the others in that they will be asked *after* a recommended action has already been taken—the *Check RAM* recommendation from rule check-ram:

```
(defrule MAIN::loose-ram
    (declare (auto-focus TRUE))
    (check loose-ram)
    (answer (ident loose-ram) (text yes))
    =>
    (recommend-action "remove and reseat memory modules")
    (halt))

(defrule MAIN::faulty-ram
    (declare (auto-focus TRUE))
```

```
(check loose-ram)
(answer (ident loose-ram) (text no))
=>
(recommend-action
    "replace memory modules one by one and retest")
(halt))
```

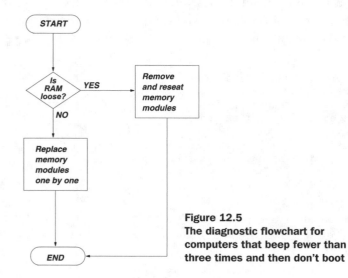

Figure 12.5
The diagnostic flowchart for
computers that beep fewer than
three times and then don't boot

12.5.5 *Questioning authority*

Now that you've written all the rules, you need the questions! Listing 12.6 shows
them collected in a deffacts.

Listing 12.6   Questions the hardware diagnostic system can ask

```
(deffacts MAIN::question-data
    (question (ident hardware)
      (type multi) (valid x86 Macintosh other)
      (text "What kind of hardware is it?"))
    (question
      (ident sound) (type multi) (valid yes no)
      (text "Does the computer make any sound?"))
    (question
      (ident plugged-in) (type multi) (valid yes no)
      (text "Is the computer plugged in?"))
    (question
      (ident seek) (type multi) (valid yes no)
```

```
           (text "Does the disk make \"seeking\" sounds?"))
       (question
           (ident does-beep) (type multi) (valid yes no)
           (text "Does the computer beep?"))
       (question
           (ident how-many-beeps) (type number) (valid)
           (text "How many times does it beep?"))
       (question
           (ident loose-ram) (type multi) (valid yes no)
           (text "Are any of the memory modules loose?"))
       (question
           (ident boot-begins) (type multi) (valid yes no)
           (text "Does the computer begin to boot?")))
```

You can now run the complete application by calling `reset` and `run-until-halt`.

12.6 *Testing*

I haven't mentioned testing so far in this chapter, but don't take this to mean I've forgotten about the test-first strategy I talked about in previous parts of this book. The larger and more complex the system, the more important it is to test each part in isolation. When I modified the `ask` module, for example, I reran all the tests for it that I developed in part 3, and I wrote several more. I confirmed that `ask` would only accept the allowed answers for multiple-choice questions.

Next I developed and tested the `trigger` module. `trigger` can and should be tested first in isolation—that is, without `ask` loaded in to complicate matters. To test `trigger`, I wrote one dummy rule with an `initial-fact` pattern and one answer pattern. Then I used `(watch all)` to confirm that executing the `(reset)` command made the `trigger` module come into focus, the `supply-answers` rule fire, and the appropriate `MAIN::ask` fact appear in working memory.

Then, as I translated each new flowchart into rules, I ran the application and answered questions based on a set of planned diagnostic scenarios, confirming that the diagnosis was correct in every case. As discussed in section 11.2.3, don't be discouraged by the thought that you should have 100% test coverage. Remember that *some* testing is infinitely better than none at all.

One issue that came up during this kind of testing was that the `hardware` question (which you want to be asked first) isn't asked until the end of the program. Paradoxically, this happens because you define the `right-architecture` question fact first. The `need-answer` trigger fact for this rule is generated as soon as the rule is defined, and under Jess's default `depth` conflict-resolution strategy, later activations fire before earlier ones. Thus, although the decision to ask the `hardware` question is made first, it is overridden by the need to ask other questions. You can fix this problem by telling the backward-chaining mechanism not to try to trigger the `right-architecture` rule, and then asserting the appropriate `MAIN::ask` fact at the right time. You can modify the `right-architecture` rule using the `explicit` conditional element, which cancels backward-chaining requests for a single pattern:

```
(defrule MAIN::right-architecture
    (declare (auto-focus TRUE))
    (explicit (answer (ident hardware) (text ~x86)))
    =>
    (recommend-action "consult a human expert")
    (halt))
```

Adding a `(MAIN::ask hardware)` fact at the end of `deffacts question-data` makes the `hardware` question come out first. Give the application a try and make sure the conclusions it reaches are the same that you'd arrive at by following the flowcharts.

12.7 Summary

In this chapter, you saw how backward chaining can be used to do something automatically, on demand; in this case, you used it to schedule questions to be asked using a single, generic rule. The combination of forward-chaining inference rules and backward-chaining infrastructure rules is a powerful and common pattern in Jess systems. Another common application of this idea is fetching needed facts automatically from a database.

Flowcharts are a reasonable way to represent some kinds of knowledge, and you used them to good effect in this chapter. The collection of inference rules in this chapter was more complex than you've seen before; most rules that fire can trigger the firing of multiple other rules. The modular and descriptive nature of individual rules makes a program like this easier to modify over time and easier to develop incrementally compared to a monolithic program without rules.

In the next chapter, you'll again tinker with the `ask` module. This time, you'll give it a graphical interface and free the user from the need to type answers like **yes** and **no** at the command line.

Adding a graphical interface

13

In this chapter you'll...

- Create a window
- Fill it with graphical components
- Write event handlers
- ... all from the Jess language

These days, virtually all computer applications come with a graphical user interface (GUI). Graphical interfaces make many users feel more comfortable than command lines. Furthermore, by providing a bounded set of commands (explicit in menus or implicit in radio buttons, checkboxes, and other controls), GUIs provide guidance that helps users use the application efficiently and correctly. One advantage of a GUI is perhaps less obvious: Because it limits user actions, it can make invalid user inputs impossible, thereby simplifying the application's internal error-checking code.

Your first real application, the Tax Forms Advisor, had only a command-line interface. The PC Repair Assistant you're developing now should have a friendlier GUI. You'll develop such an interface in this chapter using only Jess's Java reflection capabilities—that is, you'll write only Jess scripts, not Java code. In the process, we'll look at how Jess lets you develop software using the Java libraries in an iterative and interactive way.

The GUI you'll develop in this chapter will use Java's Swing library. I'll assume some basic knowledge of Swing (and Java GUIs in general) on your part. You might want to keep some documentation for the javax.swing package handy for reference.

Note that you'll be using an iterative approach to develop this GUI; you'll see the same Jess functions presented several times with various refinements applied each time. The final code for the completed application is available from this book's web site.

13.1 *Getting started*

You'll be using many of the classes in Java's javax.swing, java.awt, and java.awt.event packages. Although you could spell out these package names when you need them, it will be easier if you use Jess's import function to make this unnecessary. Jess's import function, like the Java keyword, makes it possible for you to refer to all the classes in a given Java package by using their class names, without spelling out the package name each time. Note how after importing javax.swing.*, you can create a javax.swing.JButton using just its class name:

```
Jess> (import javax.swing.*)
TRUE
Jess> (import java.awt.*)
TRUE
Jess> (import java.awt.event.*)
TRUE
Jess> (new JButton "Example Button")
<External-address:javax.swing.JButton>
```

The graphical components of the application will be accessed from different sections of Jess code. In particular, several functions need access to the application's top-level window component (a JFrame). You'll therefore store a reference to it in a defglobal. Unfortunately, the reset function by default resets the values of defglobals, and it would complicate the application if you had to worry about the possibility of your only reference to the JFrame disappearing. To deal with this situation, you use the set-reset-globals function to tell Jess to leave defglobals alone when reset is called:

```
Jess> (set-reset-globals FALSE)
FALSE
```

With these details taken care of, you can start coding the GUI.

13.2 *Displaying a window*

The first and most fundamental graphical element you need to create is a javax.swing.JFrame—a top-level window. Let's create one with an appropriate title, size it, make it visible, and keep a reference to it in a defglobal named ?*frame*:

```
Jess> (defglobal ?*frame* = (new JFrame "Diagnostic Assistant"))
TRUE
Jess> (?*frame* setSize 520 140)
Jess> (?*frame* setVisible TRUE)
```

I'm cheating a little here: I determined the appropriate size after the whole GUI was designed, and then came back here and typed it in. In your own programs, you will learn the dimensions necessary through experience or experimentation. When you enter the last line of code, an empty window appears on the screen, as shown in figure 13.1.

Figure 13.1   An empty JFrame created via a short Jess script as shown in the text

13.3 *Displaying questions*

Right now, the application you're developing displays questions and accepts answers from the command line. As a first step toward producing a real GUI, let's change the application to display the text of the questions in the window you've created (for the moment, you'll still accept input from the command line). You can use a JTextArea inside a JScrollPane to accomplish this. You need to access the JTextArea from the ask module, so you'll store a reference to it in a defglobal named qfield. Here's the code to create a JTextArea and add it to your JFrame:

```
Jess> (defglobal ?*qfield* = (new JTextArea 5 40))
TRUE
Jess> (bind ?scroll (new JScrollPane ?*qfield*))
<External-Address:javax.swing.JScrollPane>
Jess> ((?*frame* getContentPane) add ?scroll)
Jess> (?*qfield* setText "Please wait...")
Jess> (?*frame* repaint)
```

You set the text of the new text area to the string "Please wait...". Figure 13.2 shows what the window looks like now

As you'll recall from chapter 12, you used the ask module (as originally defined in chapter 10) to provide the temporary command-line interface to your application. In this chapter, you'll modify the ask module yet again to connect it to your GUI. In particular, you need to modify the function ask-user. Listing 13.1 is a new version of ask-user that displays the questions in the JTextArea instead of at the command line. If you run the whole application with this modified ask-user, you'll need to look at the JFrame to see the questions and at the command line to type your answers. You'll return to this function soon—the final version will no longer read from the command line:.

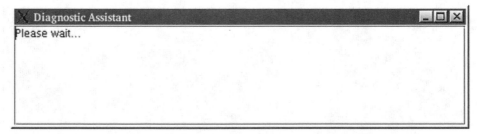

Figure 13.2   Application window with an added JTextArea for displaying questions

---

Listing 13.1 `ask-user` **function to display questions (changed lines in bold)**

```
(deffunction ask-user (?question ?type ?valid)
    "Ask a question, and return the answer"
    (bind ?answer "")
    (while (not (is-of-type ?answer ?type ?valid)) do
      (bind ?s ?question " ")
      (if (eq ?type multi) then
        (bind ?s (str-cat ?s ?*crlf*
                    "Valid answers are "))
        (foreach ?item ?valid
          (bind ?s (str-cat ?s ?item " "))))
      (bind ?s (str-cat ?s ":"))
      (?*qfield* setText ?s)
      (bind ?answer (read)))
    (return ?answer))
```

13.4 *Getting answers*

Now that your application displays questions to the user via its new GUI, it ought to collect answers the same way. Currently, the input routine `ask-user` reads answers as strings the user types at the command line. As a first step, you'll modify the ask module to use a simple text field to collect its answers for all question types. This will give you a framework to build on (later you'll replace this input field with a combo box and other more user-friendly components). First you'll build a panel containing a `JTextField` and a `JButton` labeled OK; then you'll add it to the bottom of the application window. Listing 13.2 shows the code to do this; the result looks like figure 13.3. I used `get-member` to obtain the value of the constant SOUTH in the `BorderLayout` class. The calls to `validate` and `repaint` are necessary whenever you modify the contents of a window that's already visible on the screen.

Listing 13.2 **Adding an input area to the application window**

```
;; Add a JTextField and an OK button to our application window
(defglobal ?*apanel* = (new JPanel))
(defglobal ?*afield* = (new JTextField 40))
(defglobal ?*afield-ok* = (new JButton OK))
(?*apanel* add ?*afield*)
(?*apanel* add ?*afield-ok*)
((?*frame* getContentPane) add ?*apanel*
    (get-member BorderLayout SOUTH))
(?*frame* validate)
(?*frame* repaint)

;; Now attach an event handler
(deffunction read-input (?EVENT)
```

```
        "An event handler for the user input field"
        (bind ?text (sym-cat (?*afield* getText)))
        (assert (ask::user-input ?text)))

    (bind ?handler
        (new jess.awt.ActionListener read-input (engine)))
    (?*afield* addActionListener ?handler)
    (?*afield-ok* addActionListener ?handler)
```

In Java programming, you add behaviors to components like buttons and text fields by writing *event handlers*. An event handler is an implementation of a special interface, with a member function that performs the desired behavior. The interface used for button clicks is java.awt.event.ActionListener. You *register* the event handlers you write by calling an appropriate method on the component; for ActionListener the method is called addActionListener. When some user input occurs, the component creates an *event object* and passes it as an argument to the appropriate method of all the event handlers that are registered with it. In the case of button clicks, the event object is an instance of the class java.awt.event.ActionEvent, and the method in the ActionListener interface is called actionPerformed.

The function read-input in listing 13.2 is an event handler written in Jess. The class jess.awt.ActionListener is an *event adapter* that lets you specify that a deffunction should be invoked when a Java ActionEvent occurs. Jess supplies a whole family of these event adapters, one for each event type defined by the Java APIs, and they all are used the same way. You can create one using the name of a deffunction and a jess.Rete object (see the next section) as constructor arguments. Then you use the matching Java method on an AWT or Swing component to register the listener, just as you would in Java. When the component sends an

Figure 13.3   Application window with both an area for displaying questions and a lower panel for collecting answers

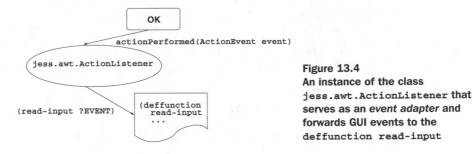

Figure 13.4
An instance of the class
`jess.awt.ActionListener` **that**
serves as an *event adapter* **and**
forwards GUI events to the
`deffunction read-input`

event, the event adapter invokes the `deffunction`, passing it the event object as the lone argument (the parameter `?EVENT` in the listing). This arrangement is shown in figure 13.4.

Now you have an input field that asserts a Jess fact in response to a button click or the user pressing Enter. Before you can modify the program to use this asserted fact, however, we need to look in a bit more depth at the architecture of a GUI-based application.

13.4.1 *The main thread vs. the event thread*

A *thread* is a single flow of control in a Java program. Individual streams of code can be, and often are, running in multiple separate threads simultaneously. You can create threads explicitly using the `java.lang.Thread` class, and Java creates some threads on its own—for example, the main thread from which the `main()` function is called.

Every Java program is a multithreaded program. Even in a "Hello, World" program, where the user's code clearly runs only in the main thread, the JVM creates a number of other threads to perform background duties like garbage collection.

In graphical programs, user code typically runs in several threads. Some of the code you write runs on the main thread (like the setup code you've written so far), while other code runs on the *event thread*. When a menu item is chosen or a button is clicked, the event handlers that are invoked run on the event thread. Sometimes this is unimportant, but when code on the event thread and code on the main thread need to coordinate their activities, you have to think clearly about what code is running where.

In the program you're developing, the `(run)` function will be called on the main thread, and so the code for all the rules that fire will execute on the main thread. On the other hand, you want the user to click the OK button on the GUI. This action will trigger some code to run on the event thread, and you want to have that affect the behavior of the rules. The situation is depicted in figure 13.5.

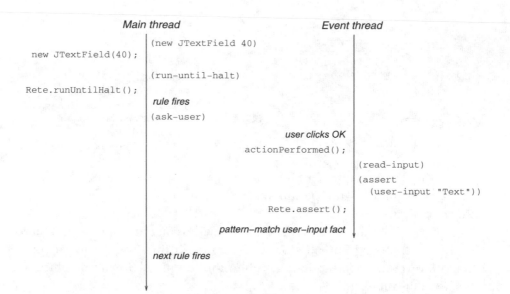

Figure 13.5   Some of the code in a GUI application runs on the main thread, and other code runs on the event thread. The separate threads can communicate by calling Jess functions. In the diagram, time flows down. Note how calling a Jess function like `(run)` results in a Java function like `Rete.run()` being called a short time later.

You'll adopt the following strategy to get the main thread and the event thread to cooperate:

1   The main thread sets up the GUI to display the question.

2   The main thread sleeps until a reply is available.

3   When the user presses Enter or clicks the OK button, the event thread asserts a fact containing a reply.

4   The main thread wakes up and processes the reply. If the reply is invalid, go back to step 1. If it is valid, assert the `answer` fact and return from the module.

Jess contains a mechanism that makes this process simple to implement. There is a function you can call to make the current thread sleep when no activated rules are on the agenda of the current module, and then wake up and continue once a new activation arrives. No Jess language function lets you access this mechanism directly, however—you have to call it as a Java method.

The class jess.Rete

Jess's rule engine is embodied in a class named `jess.Rete`. Many of the most important functions you've seen so far in the Jess language—`run`, `reset`, `clear`, assert—correspond to single Java method calls on instances of this class (`run()`, `reset()`, `clear()`, `assertFact()`). When you start `jess.Main` from the command line, a single instance of `jess.Rete` is created, and all of your program's rules and facts belong to it. You can get a reference to this `jess.Rete` object using the `engine` function in Jess. The code

```
((engine) run)
```

is therefore more or less equivalent to

```
(run)
```

Now let's return to our discussion of coordinating multiple threads in your application. The function you're interested in is called `waitForActivations`. If this method is called when the current module's agenda is empty, it doesn't return right away. Rather, it uses the `wait()` method from the `java.lang.Object` class to wait for new activations to arrive. Note that the only way `waitForActivations` can return is for code on some other thread to call a function that modifies working memory. You can call `waitForActivations` from Jess like this:

```
((engine) waitForActivations)
```

Listing 13.3 shows the changed parts of a new version of the `ask` module that implements this idea. Whereas the old version of `ask` contained just one rule that asked the question and returned the answer, this new version contains two rules: one that sets up the question (`ask-question-by-id`) and one that validates the answer and either returns the answer or asks the question again (`collect-user-input`).

Listing 13.3 *ask* module that expects GUI input as *user-input* facts

```
(deffunction ask-user (?question ?type ?valid)
    "Set up the GUI to ask a question"
    (bind ?s ?question " ")
    (if (eq ?type multi) then
      (bind ?s (str-cat ?s ?*crlf* "Valid answers are "))
      (foreach ?item ?valid
        (bind ?s (str-cat ?s ?item " "))))
    (bind ?s (str-cat ?s ":"))
    (?*qfield* setText ?s)
    (?*afield* setText ""))

(defrule ask::ask-question-by-id
    "Given the identifier of a question, ask it"
    (declare (auto-focus TRUE))
    (MAIN::question (ident ?id) (text ?text)
                    (type ?type) (valid $?valid))
```

```
        (not (MAIN::answer (ident ?id)))
        (MAIN::ask ?id)
        =>
        (ask-user ?text ?type ?valid)
        ((engine) waitForActivations))

(defrule ask::collect-user-input
    "Check and optionally return an answer from the GUI"
    (declare (auto-focus TRUE))
    (MAIN::question (ident ?id) (text ?text) (type ?type))
    (not (MAIN::answer (ident ?id)))
    ?user <- (user-input ?input)
    ?ask <- (MAIN::ask ?id)
    =>
    (if (is-of-type ?input ?type ?valid) then
        (assert (MAIN::answer (ident ?id) (text ?input)))
        (retract ?ask ?user)
        (return)
    else
        (retract ?ask ?user)
        (assert (MAIN::ask ?id))))
```

Here's what happens when the new ask module is used:

1 You assert a MAIN::ask fact giving the identifier for a question.

2 On the main thread, the rule ask-question-by-id is activated by the MAIN::ask fact and the MAIN::question fact with the given identifier. This rule has the auto-focus property, so the ask module immediately gets the focus.

3 ask-question-by-id calls the function ask-user and then uses waitForActivations to pause until another rule in this module is activated.

4 ask-user sets up the GUI to display the proper question, and clears the answer area.

5 Nothing happens until the user enters some text and presses Enter or clicks the OK button.

6 The event handler read-input, running on the event thread, asserts an ask::user-input fact containing the text entered by the user, as a symbol.

7 The ask::user-input fact, together with the MAIN::question fact and the MAIN::ask fact, activate the rule collect-user-input. The method waitForActivations finally returns due to this activation, and the right-hand side of ask-question-by-id completes.

8   Back on the main thread, `collect-user-input` asserts a `MAIN::answer` fact, retracts the `MAIN::ask` and `ask::user-input` facts, and returns from the `ask` module.

13.5 *Better input components*

As it stands, the user of your program has to answer questions by typing a reply into a `JTextField`. Of course, most GUIs don't work that way. For example, users aren't accustomed to typing **x86** or **Macintosh** into a GUI; they're used to selecting choices from a combo box. This application should work the same way.

Recall that the `question` fact template has a slot named `type`, indicating the kind of answer expected for each question. Your interface should display different user-input panels depending on the value of this `type` field. What panels will you need? Looking back at the questions defined in the previous chapter, you'll need only two:

- *Multiple choice*—A panel with a pop-up menu (a combo box) containing a list of choices.
- *Numeric*—A text field that accepts numeric input. You've essentially already done this one.

Once again, the `ask` module can be modified to accommodate this latest requirement. You can change the `ask-user` function so that it sets up the appropriate input component for each question based on the type of question being asked. For questions with numeric answers, you use the existing `JTextField`, and for multiple-choice questions, you use a new `JComboBox`.

Setting up the `JComboBox` and its associated OK button is similar to setting up the `JTextField`. After the components are created, the `JButton` needs an event handler to assert the selected item as an `answer` fact:

```
(defglobal ?*acombo* = (new JComboBox (create$ "yes" "no")))
(defglobal ?*acombo-ok* = (new JButton OK))

(deffunction combo-input (?EVENT)
    "An event handler for the combo box"
    (assert
      (ask::user-input (sym-cat (?*acombo* getSelectedItem)))))

(bind ?handler (new jess.awt.ActionListener combo-input (engine)))
(?*acombo-ok* addActionListener ?handler)
```

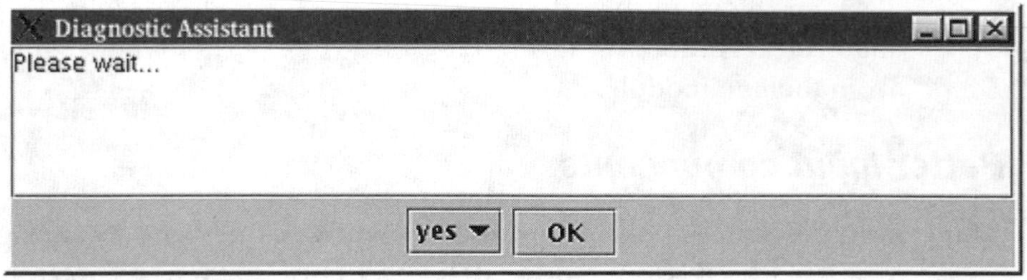

Figure 13.6   The multiple choice input panel displays a combo box and a button. The choices in the combo box are changed based on the question being displayed.

One interesting bit about this code snippet is the call to the JComboBox constructor. The constructor expects an array of Object as an argument. In this code, you pass a Jess list made by create$; Jess automatically converts it to the needed array.

With the JComboBox defined, you can modify ask-user one final time:

```
(deffunction ask-user (?question ?type ?valid)
    "Set up the GUI to ask a question"
    (?*qfield* setText ?question)
    (?*apanel* removeAll)
    (if (eq ?type multi) then
      (?*apanel* add ?*acombo*)
      (?*apanel* add ?*acombo-ok*)
      (?*acombo* removeAllItems)
      (foreach ?item ?valid
        (?*acombo* addItem ?item))
    else
      (?*apanel* add ?*afield*)
      (?*apanel* add ?*afield-ok*)
      (?*afield* setText ""))
    (?*frame* validate)
    (?*frame* repaint))
```

This version is somewhat simpler because it doesn't have to compose a complex prompt string. Instead, based on the question type, it installs one of two possible sets of components in the JPanel at the bottom of the window. Figure 13.6 shows what the application looks like with the combo box panel installed.

13.6 *Finishing touches*

The current version of the recommend-action function still prints its recommendations to the command line. Java offers the convenient JOptionPane class as a quick way to post a modal dialog box. You can easily modify recommend-action to use it:

```
(deffunction recommend-action (?action)
   "Give final instructions to the user"
   (call JOptionPane showMessageDialog ?*frame*
     (str-cat "I recommend that you " ?action)
     "Recommendation"
     (get-member JOptionPane INFORMATION_MESSAGE)))
```

The arguments to the static `showMessageDialog` method are, in order, the parent window, the message, the window title, and a constant that indicates what kind of icon to display.

Another limitation of the application is that there's no way to exit. You can tell the `JFrame` to call `System.exit` method when it is closed using `JFrame`'s `setDefaultCloseOperation` method:

```
(?*frame* setDefaultCloseOperation
   (get-member JFrame EXIT_ON_CLOSE))
```

Finally, during testing I noticed that it's a bit disorienting to have question text remain in the window after the application has finished. It would be nice to have the old question removed when the program is through. You can't put code to do this into `recommend-action`, because sometimes this function is called to make an intermediate recommendation, and more questions will follow. You certainly don't want to go back and change all the rules to add GUI-specific code. What can you do?

If you look at your rules, you'll recall that they call `halt` as appropriate to terminate execution of the system. You can therefore use the `defadvice` function to modify the behavior of `halt` (see section 4.5 to learn more about `defadvice`):

```
(defadvice before halt
   (?*qfield* setText "Close window to exit"))
```

Now, when a rule calls `halt` to halt execution, the contents of the question field will automatically change.

13.7 *Testing the interface*

Testing graphical applications automatically is difficult. There are commercial tools to help you do it, but most of them are fragile, hard to use, and expensive. The classic problem with automated GUI-testing tools is that they make your life harder rather than easier when you need to make changes to your interface, because changes to the GUI may force changes to the test. It's easy to write tests for a GUI that are so fragile that they must be rewritten any time the GUI layout changes even a little. Tests that expect particular GUI components to lie at specific screen coordinates are the most delicate in this respect. If you do use a GUI-testing tool, try not to write tests based on absolute screen coordinates. Tests that refer to components by name are much more robust.

You can use the Java class `java.awt.Robot` to write your own automated tests. This class lets you move the mouse pointer, press mouse buttons, and type text as if from the keyboard, all under programmatic control. I've personally found the combination of `java.awt.Robot` and Jess's scripting capabilities to be particularly powerful.

Besides automated testing, you can of course do manual testing. If (as was the case here) you wrote and tested the underlying logic of the application first, testing the GUI by hand isn't quite so bad. Rather than trying to test every path through the knowledge base, your GUI testing effort should be concentrated on trying every situation the GUI is meant to handle. For this application, you'd want to try both multiple-choice and numeric input, and some recommendations that call `(halt)` and some that don't. You can also run through some of the same test scenarios you used with the command-line version of the application, entering the data into the GUI instead.

13.8 *Summary*

In part 4 of this book, you've built a fairly sophisticated application in about 230 lines of Jess code. You collected knowledge in the form of flowcharts and then translated the flowcharts into rules. The flowcharts are a compact and useful form of documentation for the resulting knowledge base.

The PC Repair Assistant uses backward chaining to automatically form hypotheses about possible problems and ask the appropriate questions, based just on the antecedents of the rules in the knowledge base. This approach scales well to large systems, unlike the more unwieldy approach used by the Tax Forms Advisor in part 3. Because you used backward chaining to let Jess choose the questions automatically, you needed only half as many rules compared to the tax advisor.

Once the application logic was written, tested, and debugged, you wrapped it in a graphical user interface using only Jess code. Adding a GUI required you to make some changes to the `ask` module used for asking questions, but you didn't need to touch any of the rules. The final incarnation of the `ask` module uses Jess's `waitForActivations` Java API function to communicate between Java's event thread and the main thread where rules fire.

In this and the previous part, you developed complete, isolated applications from the ground up using Jess. In the real world, however, Jess usually needs to cooperate with Java code outside of itself. In the next part of this book, you will learn how to put Java objects into Jess's working memory so that Jess can reason about the outside world. You'll also learn how to extend the Jess language by writing functions in Java.

Part 5

Reasoning about reality: the HVAC Controller

The applications you've written so far have been written entirely as Jess scripts. In much real software, however, the rule engine has to be integrated with existing Java code. In part 5, you'll write some Java as well as Jess code, and in so doing, you'll begin to learn about Jess's Java APIs.

The *HVAC Controller* you'll write is a soft real-time control system for the heating and cooling systems in an office building. We'll look at how such a system can be interfaced to real hardware. You'll write rules that react not just to ordinary facts in Jess's working memory, but to shadow facts that are tied to JavaBeans; the JavaBeans will be wrappers around the HVAC interface software.

At the end of chapter 16 is a special essay by Bob Orchard, the author of the FuzzyJess extension that adds fuzzy logic capabilities to Jess. Bob looks at how the HVAC Controller can be extended and improved further by the application of fuzzy logic.

14

The reality connection

221

> *No man is an island, entire of itself; every man is a piece of the*
> *continent, a part of the main.*
>   —John Donne

These days, very little software is written to stand alone. Component architectures, application servers, and networking have made it easier than ever to assemble software out of disparate parts. It's becoming increasingly rare to code a completely self-contained application. After all, with so many high-quality libraries, components, tools, services, and containers available, why reinvent the wheel?

So far in this book, you've written two applications using Jess. In each case, you used Jess as a standalone system. You didn't write or use a single line of Java code except Jess itself. You'll occasionally write software this way, but for the remainder of the book, we'll look at more realistic systems that use Jess as a part of a larger whole. Jess was designed to be embedded in other Java software. You've already seen how Jess can call Java functions—now you'll see that outside Java code can just as easily call on Jess. Each of the remaining applications you build will include a component written in Java.

In the next few chapters, you'll develop the control software for the HVAC (heating, ventilation, and air conditioning) systems in a large building. Jess will receive real-time temperature data and, based on these readings, will send commands to the multiple heating and cooling units in the building. Although this is a specialized example, the same principles would apply to controlling chemical plants, intelligent traffic-light sequencing, monitoring automated assembly lines, and even implementing manufacturing resource planning (MRP) systems. In every case, Jess has to receive data from the outside world and try to take action to affect the readings.

The Tax Forms Advisor from part 3 of this book and the PC Repair Assistant from part 4 only reasoned about facts in working memory. Facts are `jess.Fact` objects, and they live entirely inside Jess. When Jess is being used to directly react to events in the real world, it only makes sense that Jess needs to be able to reason about objects outside of itself. Section 6.5 talked about using the `definstance` function to add JavaBeans to working memory. The application you're about to build uses this technique to interact with a collection of thermostats, geothermal heat pumps, and automated air vents.

Your first task, and the topic of this chapter, is to learn about the system you're going to control. You will build a set of JavaBeans to represent and interact with the hardware, and then begin to use them from Jess. You'll also build a software simulator so that you can test your application.

To complete the control rules cleanly, you need to extend the Jess language by adding some custom functions written in Java; this is the subject of chapter 15. We'll look at Jess's external function interface and learn something about how Jess's function call mechanism works under the hood. Finally, in chapter 16, you'll write the rules, and the application will come together.

14.1 The system

Imagine a tall building (figure 14.1). The building is heated and cooled by a number of *heat pumps*. A heat pump is both a heating and cooling device. At any time, it can be in one of three modes: heating, cooling, or off. In this building, each heat pump services three adjacent floors

Warm or cold air from the heat pumps enters the building through adjustable vents. Each vent can be either open or closed, and although there may be several vents on each floor, they are wired in such a way that they must open and close in concert—that is, they act like a single vent.

You probably know that warm air rises and cold air sinks—it's basic physics. This adds a bit of nonlinearity to the system, because each heat pump can affect not only the floors to which it directly sends heated or cooled air, but the floors above and below it as well..

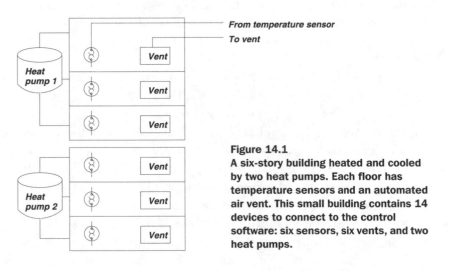

Figure 14.1
A six-story building heated and cooled by two heat pumps. Each floor has temperature sensors and an automated air vent. This small building contains 14 devices to connect to the control software: six sensors, six vents, and two heat pumps.

14.2 *Defining the hardware interface*

This system includes hardware and software components. This is a book about software, so perhaps we should get the hardware considerations out of the way first. Assume that the building's control systems, purchased from Acme HVAC Systems, Inc., include all the sensors and actuators you need. In fact, they're already connected to one master computer on which the control software will run. Acme HVAC Systems has provided a library of functions you can call from C language code to turn the heat pumps on and off, read the temperatures, and operate the vents. To make this concrete, imagine that this is a complete list of the available library functions:

```
int getHeatPumpState(int heatPump);
void setHeatPumpState(int heatPump, int state);

double getTemperature(int sensor);

int getVentState(int vent);
void setVentState(int vent, int state);
```

Note that these are C functions, so on and off values like the state of each vent must be represented as type int, because classic C doesn't have a boolean type like Java. The first argument to every function is an index; for example, you would pass the value 3 to getTemperature to get the temperature reading from sensor number 3. By convention, all these index numbers start at 1, not 0.

14.2.1 *Native methods*

Of course, you're writing the software in Java, so you need to make the connection between your Java code and the C library. This is easy enough to do using the *Java Native Interface* (JNI). A *native method* is a method of a Java class that happens to be written in some system-level language like C. Native methods use a special JNI library to bridge the gap between the Java virtual machine and the real machine outside. The knowledge that your program will be dealing with external hardware can be encapsulated inside a single Java class; that class will have one native method for each of the C library functions.

Writing native methods is outside the scope of this book. The best reference for writing them is probably Sun's web-based Java tutorial (http://java.sun.com/docs/books/tutorial/native1.1/index.html). For our purposes, all you need to know is that from the Java side, you declare a native method like this:

```
public native void myMethod(String myArgument);
```

A native method has no body (just like an abstract method) and includes the keyword `native` in its declaration; otherwise, there's nothing special about it. Java expects to find the definition of this method in an external library you must provide.

The important thing to realize here is that any Java code can call `myMethod` without knowing that it's a native method. From the caller's perspective, a native method looks like any other Java method. A subclass can override a normal parent method using a native method, and an implementation of an interface can provide a native method to satisfy the interface.

You can use this last fact to your advantage. You'll define a Java interface to represent the functions in the C library. Then you can write multiple implementations of the interface: one that uses native methods to access the real hardware, and one that implements a simulation of the hardware. You can then use the simulator to develop and test the software. When the software is ready, you could swap in the hardware implementation and try it out on the real system. For the purposes of this book, you'll only write the simulator.

The interface has one method for each of the C library functions, so it looks like this:

```
package control;
public interface Hardware {
    public final int OFF=0, HEATING=1, COOLING=2;

    int getHeatPumpState(int heatPump);
    void setHeatPumpState(int heatPump, int state);
    int getNumberOfHeatPumps();

    double getTemperature(int sensor);

    boolean getVentState(int vent);
    void setVentState(int vent, boolean state);
}
```

Note that you'll put all the Java code you write for this application into a package named `control`.

The methods in this interface look a lot like the C functions, with a few exceptions. Some of the `int` types are now `boolean`, because in Java, `boolean` is the best type to represent an on or off value. The heat pump state is still represented as an integer, though, and three constants represent the legal values (which presumably came from the C library manual).

14.2.2 *Writing a simulator*

The hardware simulator is fairly simple. The implementations of methods like `getVentState` and `setVentState` are trivial. The simulator object contains an array of `boolean` to record the state of each vent, and these two methods simply set and get the appropriate elements of that array. The only complicated method is `getTemperature`, because it must return a realistic temperature based on the complete state of the system. The simple part of the simulator is shown in listing 14.1; you'll work on `getTemperature` next. Note that the implementation shown here, like most published code, skimps on error handling. All the getter and setter methods should check that their first arguments are greater than zero and less than or equal to the number of devices, but we've omitted this code here to keep things short. This version of `Simulator` is an abstract class because we haven't implemented `getTemperature` yet.

Listing 14.1   The basic parts of the hardware simulator

```
package control;
public abstract class Simulator implements Hardware {
    private int[] m_heatpumps;
    private boolean[] m_vents, m_sensors;

    public Simulator(int numberOfFloors) {
        if (numberOfFloors % 3 != 0)
          throw new RuntimeException("Illegal value");

        m_heatpumps = new int[numberOfFloors/3];
        m_vents = new boolean[numberOfFloors];
        m_sensors = new boolean[numberOfFloors];
    }

    public int getHeatPumpState(int heatPump) {
        return m_heatpumps[heatPump-1];
    }

    public void setHeatPumpState(int heatPump, int state) {
        switch (state) {
        case OFF: case HEATING: case COOLING:
            m_heatpumps[heatPump-1] = state; break;
        default:
            throw new RuntimeException("Illegal value");
        }
    }

    public int getNumberOfHeatPumps() {
        return m_heatpumps.length;
    }

    public boolean getVentState(int vent) {
        return m_vents[vent-1];
    }

    public void setVentState(int vent, boolean state) {
        m_vents[vent-1] = state;
    }

}
```

14.2.3 *Simulating getTemperature*

The meat of the HVAC simulator is the `getTemperature` method, which returns a value based on the complete state of the system. Each time you call `getTemperature` with a given argument, you can get a different answer back, because the temperatures will constantly change based on many factors. At least four things go into the calculation of the temperature on each floor of the building:

- The current temperature on that floor
- Whether the floor is actively being heated or cooled
- Heat leakage from outside, through the walls
- Heat leakage from other floors

The simulator should take each of these factors into account. The current temperature on each floor can be held in an array of `double`, so that's easy. Whether a given floor is being heated or cooled depends on what the corresponding heat pump is doing and whether that floor's vent is open or closed. To account for heat leakage from outside, you need a variable to hold the outside temperature. Finally, the same array of current temperatures is all you need to compute the heat leakage from other floors.

The simplest way to write the simulator is so that it works in real time—it includes a loop that continuously recomputes the temperature. This loop runs in a separate thread, so the temperatures continue to update even if no calls to `getTemperature` are made. Therefore, all you need to do is to figure out an equation to calculate the current temperature from the temperature at the last time step and the changes due to the factors just listed.

A law of physics called *Newton's Law of Cooling*, simply put, states that the larger the temperature difference between two bodies, the faster heat flows between them. Therefore, a reasonable way to calculate the temperature change per second on a given floor is to calculate the difference between that floor's current temperature and some other body (such as the outside air or the hot air coming from the heat pump) and multiply this difference by some constant value giving the actual heat transfer rate. The constant varies depending on the materials involved; we'll arbitrarily choose the value 0.01. If you do this for each source of heat, for each floor, for each time step, you'll have a reasonable simulation of the temperatures in an office building. The code to do this is shown in listing 14.2. `HOT` and `COLD` represent the temperatures of the hot and cold air coming from the heat pump, and `m_outdoor` is the (variable) temperature of the outside air. The big `while` loop looks at each floor in turn, calculating the contribution of each of the factors listed earlier to the new temperature for that floor. `Simulator`'s constructor starts a background thread that periodically updates the temperature for each floor.

Listing 14.2 An implementation of `getTemperature`

```java
package control;
import java.util.Arrays;

public class Simulator implements Hardware {
    private final double RATE = 0.01;
    private final double HOT = 100, COLD=50;
    private double[] m_temperature;
    double m_outdoor = 90;

    public Simulator(int numberOfFloors) {
        //...
        m_temperature = new double[numberOfFloors];
        Arrays.fill(m_temperature, 70);
        new Thread(this).start();
    }
    //...
    public double getTemperature(int sensor) {
        return m_temperature[sensor-1];
    }

    public void run() {
        while (true) {
            for (int i=0; i<m_temperature.length; ++i) {
                double temp = m_temperature[i];

                // Heating and cooling, and heat rising
                switch (state(i)) {
                case HEATING:
                    temp += (HOT-temp)*RATE; break;
                case COOLING:
                    temp += (COLD-temp)*RATE; break;
                case OFF:
                    temp += (i+1)*0.005; break;
                }

                // Outdoor leakage
                temp += (m_outdoor-temp)*RATE/2;

                m_temperature[i] = temp;
            }
            try {Thread.sleep(1000);}
            catch (InterruptedException ie) { return;}
        }
    }
}
```

```
private int state(int floor) {
    if (getVentState(floor + 1))
        return getHeatPumpState(floor/3 + 1);
    else
        return OFF;
}
}
```

14.2.4 Adding a graphical interface

Now the simulator runs, but currently there's no way to see what it's doing. A graphical display that shows the full state of the building at a glance would be very helpful. A simple GUI could display a row of labels for each floor: one label each for heat pump state, vent state, and temperature. If you add a text field that lets you set the outdoor temperature, the simulator will be ready to test the HVAC Controller system. Figure 14.2 is a screen shot of this simple interface. I won't show the code here, but it's included in the sample code for this chapter. The SimulatorGUI class has a constructor that accepts a Simulator as a constructor argument and then uses a thread to poll the Simulator to determine its state over time.

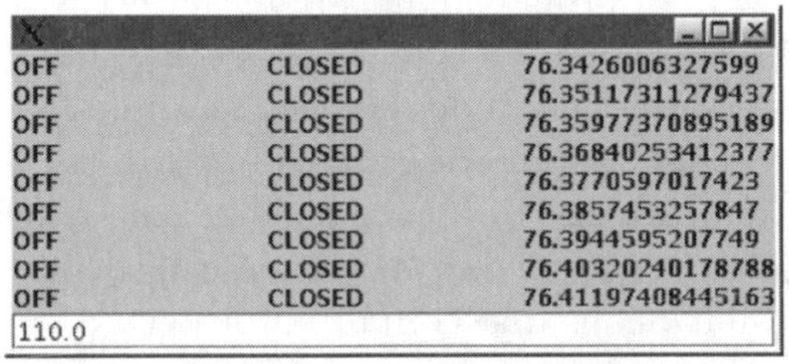

Figure 14.2
A GUI for the HVAC simulator. The three columns of labels represent the heat pump state, vent state, and temperature for each floor. The text field on the bottom shows the current outdoor temperature.

The simulator is now a reasonable stand-in for a real HVAC system. Next you need a way to connect the simulator—or, in its place, the HVAC system itself—to Jess. You'll do this by wrapping the simulator's interface in a set of JavaBeans.

14.3 *Writing the JavaBeans*

Jess's working memory can hold not only plain facts, but also *shadow facts*, which are placeholders for Java objects outside of Jess (see section 6.5 for the details). More specifically, they are placeholders for JavaBeans. From Jess's perspective, a JavaBean is just an instance of a Java class with one or more *properties*—specially named methods that let you read and/or write to a named characteristic of the object. A very simple JavaBean to represent a temperature sensor for the HVAC system could look like this:

```
package control;

public class Thermometer {
    private Hardware m_hardware;
    private int m_floor;
    public Thermometer(Hardware hw, int floor) {
        m_hardware = hw;
        m_floor = floor;
    }

    public double getReading() {
        return m_hardware.getTemperature(m_floor);
    }
}
```

This Bean has one read-only property named reading. If you used this as is, Jess could create shadow facts for Thermometer instances, and each Thermometer fact would have a reading slot—but if the value in that slot changed, Jess wouldn't know it. The shadow fact's reading slot would never change.

A more useful Bean includes a mechanism for notifying interested parties that the value of a property has changed. The standard JavaBeans mechanism for doing this is via PropertyChangeEvents. Jess works best with Beans that send one of these events whenever the value of any property changes. It's fairly easy to implement this behavior in your own Beans using the helper class PropertyChangeSupport in the java.beans package. Most of the code you need to write is boilerplate. A class that supports PropertyChangeListeners must include the methods addPropertyChangeListener and removePropertyChangeListener; they always look the same, but they still have to be included in every JavaBean you write. Many people create a base class for their Beans that contains a protected Property-ChangeSupport member and implementations of these two methods; you'll do this here. The helper class looks like this:

```
package control;

import java.beans.*;

public abstract class BeanSupport {
    protected PropertyChangeSupport m_pcs =
        new PropertyChangeSupport(this);

    public void
    addPropertyChangeListener(PropertyChangeListener p) {
        m_pcs.addPropertyChangeListener(p);
    }
    public void
    removePropertyChangeListener(PropertyChangeListener p) {
        m_pcs.removePropertyChangeListener(p);
    }
}
```

Note that `PropertyChangeSupport` itself includes the `addPropertyChangeLis-tener` and `removePropertyChangeListener` methods. It would be nice if you could use `PropertyChangeSupport` as a base class for your JavaBean—but you can't: `PropertyChangeSupport`'s only constructor accepts the source object (the JavaBean) as an argument, and `super(this)` is invalid Java. A default constructor that assumed the current object was the source would have been useful!

You can now add a `run` method to `Thermometer` that polls the temperature on a given floor, sending out `PropertyChangeEvents` to notify Jess when the temperature changes. You'll also add a read-only `floor` property to identify the individual `Thermometer`. The result is shown in listing 14.3.

Listing 14.3   The `Thermometer` class, including automated notification

```
package control;

public class Thermometer extends BeanSupport
    implements Runnable {
    private Hardware m_hardware;
    private int m_floor;
    private double m_oldReading;

    public Thermometer(Hardware hw, int floor) {
        m_hardware = hw;
        m_floor = floor;
        new Thread(this).start();
    }

    public int getFloor() {
        return m_floor;
    }

    public double getReading() {
        return m_hardware.getTemperature(m_floor);
    }

    public void run() {
        while (true) {
            double reading = getReading();
            m_pcs.firePropertyChange("reading",
                new Double(m_oldReading),
                new Double(reading));
            m_oldReading = reading;
            try { Thread.sleep(1000); }
            catch (InterruptedException ie) { return; }
        }
    }
}
```

The `PropertyChangeSupport` class needs the name of the property along with the old and new values to create the appropriate event. Note that `PropertyChangeSupport` is smart enough to send an event only if the old and new values are different, so you don't need to bother with that test yourself. There are a few overloaded versions of the `firePropertyChange` method to handle different properties of different types. For some types, though, like the `double` value here, you need to use wrapper objects to pass the old and new values.

14.3.1 *Rules about Thermometers*

Given this improved version of `Thermometer`, it's possible to write rules that react to temperatures. If this class and the `Simulator` class have been compiled and are available on the `CLASSPATH`, the following code will print a warning message after a short interval. Remember that all the code for the HVAC Controller is available from this book's web site:

```
;; Create a simulator
(bind ?hardware (new control.Simulator 3))

;; Monitor the temperature on the first floor
(defclass Thermometer control.Thermometer)
(definstance Thermometer
    (new control.Thermometer ?hardware 1))

;; Report when the temperature gets to be over 72
(defrule report-high-temperature
    (Thermometer (reading ?r&:(> ?r 72)))
    =>
    (printout t "It's getting warm on the first floor" crlf)
    (halt))

(run-until-halt)
(exit)
```

The `defclass` function (first discussed in section 6.5) tells Jess that you're going to define shadow facts for objects of a certain class (here `control.Thermometer`). The `definstance` function installs an object of that class into Jess. Finally, the rule here matches only `Thermometers` that are reading over 72 degrees. The temperatures in the simulator start at 70 and drift up quickly, so this rule fires after a short interval. Notice how once a JavaBean is installed into Jess, it looks just like an ordinary fact, and the `Thermometer` pattern that matches the Bean here is just an ordinary pattern. You use `(run-until-halt)` instead of `(run)` because you want Jess to wait for the rule to be activated—the agenda will be empty when you call `(run-until-halt)`, but when the temperature becomes high enough, the rule will activate and fire.

14.3.2 *Writing the other Beans*

The `Hardware` interface, like the C library it wraps, represents the state of a vent as a Boolean value and the state of a heat pump as an integer. Because symbols like `open` and `closed` would be easier to work with than the corresponding Boolean values `true` or `false`, it would be a good idea to write the `Vent` and `HeatPump` JavaBeans to use meaningful strings as property values. You need to convert both ways between these symbols and the underlying integer and Boolean values, and you'll need to do so in the code you write in the next chapter, too, so let's isolate the code to do these conversions in a single class named `State`. Part of the straightforward `State` class is shown in listing 14.4.

Listing 14.4   Converting between the `Hardware` states and convenient symbolic names

```
package control;

public class State {
    public static final String
        OPEN="open",
        CLOSED="closed",
        OFF="off",
        HEATING="heating",
        COOLING="cooling";

    public static String vent(boolean val) {
        return val ? OPEN : CLOSED;
    }

    public static boolean vent(String val) {
        if (val.equals(OPEN))
            return true;
        else if (val.equals(CLOSED))
            return false;
        else
            throw new IllegalArgumentException(val);
    }

    // Analagous heatpump() methods not shown
}
```

By collecting these conversions together in a single class and defining the symbols as constants in one place, you may avoid a lot of debugging.

The Vent bean

The other JavaBeans you need to write are a little different from the `Thermometer` class. Whereas the `Hardware` interface only has a method for reading the temperature, there are methods for both getting and setting the heat-pump and vent states. The corresponding `HeatPump` and `Vent` Beans therefore need both setting and getting methods. Calling `Vent.setState` (for example) should fire a `PropertyChangeEvent`. Of course, there should also be a background thread watching for changes from the outside. You can reuse the `BeanSupport` base class to help implement the event support. The `Vent` class is shown in listing 14.5. Note how it uses `State` to convert between Boolean values and the symbolic constants `open` and `closed`. The `HeatPump` class (not shown) is very similar.

Listing 14.5   A JavaBean to represent an automated vent

```
package control;

public class Vent extends BeanSupport
    implements Runnable {
    private Hardware m_hardware;
    private int m_floor;
    private boolean m_oldState;

    public Vent(Hardware hw, int floor) {
        m_hardware = hw;
        m_floor = floor;
        new Thread(this).start();
    }

    public int getFloor() {
        return m_floor;
    }

    public String getState() {
        return State.vent(m_hardware.getVentState(m_floor));
    }

    public void setState(String szState) {
        boolean state = State.vent(szState);
        m_hardware.setVentState(m_floor, state);
        m_pcs.firePropertyChange("state",
            new Boolean(m_oldState),
            new Boolean(state));
        m_oldState = state;
    }

    public void run() {
        while (true) {
            boolean state = m_hardware.getVentState(m_floor);
            m_pcs.firePropertyChange("state",
                new Boolean(m_oldState),
                new Boolean(state));
            m_oldState = state;
```

```
        try { Thread.sleep(1000); }
        catch (InterruptedException ie) { return; }
      }
    }
  }
```

14.4 JavaBeans and serialization

The notion of *pickling* is part of the JavaBeans concept. The state of an application made out of JavaBeans is fully specified by the values of all the properties of those Beans together with information about the connections between the Beans. A Java-Beans framework can create an instant application by storing the property values and connection information in a file and then later reconstituting the original Beans. Generally, Java's serialization API is used to do the pickling, so most Java-Beans implement the `java.io.Serializable` interface. It's easy to add this capability to your own JavaBeans: just declare that the class `implements Serializable`. There are no methods in the `Serializable` interface; it is a *tagging interface* used to signify to the Java virtual machine that it is OK to serialize the data from instances of the class.

Jess includes two built-in functions, `bload` and `bsave`, that can save and restore Jess's state on any Java input and output streams using Java's serialization API. If you intend to use these functions, be sure any Java objects you add to working memory implement `java.io.Serializable`, or these functions will fail. You won't be using `bload` or `bsave` in the HVAC Controller application, so it won't be necessary to make the Beans from this chapter implement this interface.

14.5 Summary

In this chapter, you began the work of using Jess to control the HVAC systems of an office building. You defined a Java interface to represent Acme HVAC Systems' C language library. You wrote a simulator in Java to test your control algorithms against that interface. You then wrote some JavaBeans, which you can inject into Jess's working memory so that Jess can monitor the state of the HVAC system in real time. The sample rule in section 14.3.1 suggests how these JavaBeans will be used.

In the next chapter, you will write additional Java functions to help control the HVAC systems. You will then use these Java functions to extend the Jess language by adding new commands. While we're at it, we'll look at Jess's extension facilities in general, and the `jess.Userfunction` interface in particular, and you'll learn how to write a range of different Jess extensions.

Armed with all the Java code developed in this and the next chapter, writing the rules to control the HVAC system will be straightforward. That will be the task of chapter 16.

15

Extending the Jess language

In this chapter you'll...

- Be introduced to the Userfunction interface
- Learn to extend the Jess language
- Write Jess functions to interface with HVAC hardware

The HVAC Controller system you're writing needs to be able to switch the various heat pumps and vents on and off in response to changing temperatures. Although it would be possible to do this just by using the (modify) function on the shadow facts representing the devices, that approach won't always be convenient. Furthermore, the rules need access to other functions in the Hardware interface that aren't used by the JavaBeans. It would be best to have a simple and consistent interface to all these capabilities.

To accomplish this, you'll add some new functions to the Jess language itself. You'll define these functions in Java, package them together, and provide a simple mechanism for getting them loaded into Jess. Once you've done this, the functions will be indistinguishable from any of Jess's built-in functions. In this chapter, I'll describe the general mechanism for adding new functions to the Jess language, and you'll apply it to the specific application.

15.1 *The Userfunction interface*

In previous chapters, you've seen many examples of calling Java functions from the Jess language. In chapter 13, you wrote an entire graphical interface this way. The Jess language is wonderfully expressive when you're writing logical conditions. For many routine tasks, though, Jess language code is more verbose than the equivalent Java code would be. There are even some things (in particular, manipulating multidimensional arrays) that you can't do from the Jess language. These tasks should be done in Java (the old proverb about using the right tool for the right job comes to mind).

For these cases where writing Jess code alone isn't enough, Jess includes the Userfunction interface. If you implement Userfunction in a Java class, Jess can invoke your class like any other Jess function. In fact, all of Jess's built-in functions are themselves implementations of Userfunction.

The Userfunction interface is quite simple—it contains only two Java method declarations:

```
package jess;

public interface Userfunction {
    String getName();
    Value call(ValueVector vv, Context context)
        throws JessException;
}
```

I'll discuss each of these methods quickly here, and then explore each of them at greater length in the following sections.

15.1.1   *The getName method*

The `getName` method should return the name Jess will use for the function. Any legal Jess symbol (see section 4.1.2) can be a function name, including weird ones like `<=` and `*` (of course, those are already taken). The only important thing to remember about implementing `getName` is that it should always return the same name for a given object: A `Userfunction` can't change its name over time. Jess keeps `Userfunction` objects in a hash table using the name as the key, so changing the name would corrupt this data structure.

A typical `getName` implementation looks like this:

```
public String getName() {
    return "kill";
}
```

Some implementations are more complex (see section 15.4.2). This `Userfunction` will be callable from Jess using the name *kill*—that is, `(kill)`.

15.1.2   *The call method*

The most important part of a `Userfunction` is its `call` method. Jess invokes the `call` method when your `Userfunction` is called from Jess language code. The first argument to the function is a list of the arguments your function was called with, and the second argument is an *execution context*—basically, your `Userfunction`'s handle to Jess itself. You'll learn about Jess's `ValueVector`, `Value`, and `Context` classes in the following sections.

A very simple implementation of `call` for `kill` might look like this:

```
public Value call(ValueVector vv, Context context) {
    System.exit(-1);
    return null;
}
```

The `kill` function kills the program and returns an error status to the operating system; it's similar to Jess's built-in `exit` function (which calls `System.exit(0)`). This `call` method doesn't really return a value to Jess, because the method never returns—although the Java compiler insists you return *something*, so I used `null`.

15.1.3   *Loading a Userfunction into Jess*

You've written a `Userfunction` of your own containing the two methods described so far, and you'd like to try it out. Let's say you've written a class named `org.me.Kill` that implements the `Userfunction` interface using the two methods. You can load it into Jess from the command prompt using the `load-function` function:

```
Jess> (load-function org.me.Kill)
TRUE
```

Then you can call it like any other Jess function:

```
Jess> (kill)
%
```

(The % symbol is a system prompt: kill exits to the operating system.) From Java, you can create an instance of your Userfunction class and install it using the addUserfunction() method in the jess.Rete class.

kill is OK for a first attempt, but it doesn't let you specify the status code to be passed to System.exit. You'll fix that in the next section.

15.2 *Handling arguments*

The first parameter to call is a jess.ValueVector. The jess.ValueVector class is Jess's internal representation of a list, and therefore it has a central role in programming with Jess in Java. The ValueVector class is used to represent plain lists, whereas specialized subclasses are used as function calls (jess.Funcall) and facts (jess.Fact). Other classes, like jess.Deftemplate, use ValueVectors internally.

Working with ValueVector is simple. Its API is reminiscent of standard container classes like java.util.Vector. Like that class, it is a self-extending array: When new elements are added, the ValueVector grows in size to accommodate them. Here is a bit of example Java code in which you create the Jess list (a b c):

```
ValueVector vv = new ValueVector();
vv.add(new Value("a", RU.ATOM));
vv.add(new Value("b", RU.ATOM));
vv.add(new Value("c", RU.ATOM));
```

The get method retrieves an element from the ValueVector using a zero-based index. Continuing the previous example:

```
// Prints "b"
System.out.println(vv.get(1));
```

When your Userfunction's call method is invoked, the first element of the ValueVector argument is the name of your function, and the subsequent elements are the arguments that were passed to your function.

15.2.1 *How many arguments?*

You can get the total length of the ValueVector using the size() method. It follows that any Userfunction can take a variable number of arguments, unless you take specific action to enforce a certain length for your argument list. If your

Userfunction accepts precisely one argument, you might begin your implementation of call like this:

```
public Value call(ValueVector vv, Context context)
    throws JessException {
    if (vv.size() != 2)
        throw new JessException("kill",
            "Wrong number of arguments", vv.size()-1);
    ...
}
```

On the other hand, a function that takes an arbitrary list of arguments could use size() as the upper limit of a processing loop.

15.2.2 *Using arguments*

Suppose that the one argument to kill is the value that should be passed to System.exit(). You might write the following:

```
public Value call(ValueVector vv, Context context) {
    if (vv.size() != 2)
        throw new JessException("kill",
            "Wrong number of arguments", vv.size()-1);
    System.exit(vv.get(1).intValue(context));
    return null;
}
```

The values returned by ValueVector.get() are always jess.Value objects. A jess.Value is a kind of generic wrapper for any Jess data object—something like a VARIANT in Microsoft COM programming, or an Any in CORBA programming. Once it is constructed, a Value's type and contents cannot be changed; it is *immutable*. (You might know that Java defines many such immutable classes; Integer and String are two well-known examples.) Value has a type() member function you can call to find out what kind of data a Value object contains; it returns one of the constants from the jess.RU class (see table 15.1). Many of these types are discussed in chapter 5.

For each type, table 15.1 also lists a method that tries to return a value appropriate for that type. You've already seen the intValue method, which tries to return a Java int based on the data held in the Value object. In general, a Value tries to automatically convert the data it holds to the type you request; for instance, if you call intValue() on a Value holding "1.0" as an RU.STRING, the string will be parsed and the method will return 1. There are limits to this capability, of course. If some data cannot be converted to the requested type, intValue (and all the other methods in table 14.1) will throw jess.JessException.

Table 15.1 `Value` types defined in the `jess.RU` class, and the methods used to retrieve each type

Name	Method	Meaning
ATOM	atomValue()	Jess symbol
STRING	stringValue()	Jess string
INTEGER	intValue()	Jess integer
VARIABLE	variableValue()	Jess variable
MULTIVARIABLE	variableValue()	Jess multifield
FACT	factValue()	Jess fact
FLOAT	floatValue()	Jess float
FUNCALL	funcallValue()	Jess function call
LIST	listValue()	Jess list
EXTERNAL_ADDRESS	externalAddressValue()	Java object
LONG	longValue()	Java long

15.2.3 *Resolving variable arguments*

If `kill` is called like this:

```
Jess> (kill ?errorCode)
%
```

then the type of the argument `Value` object is `RU.VARIABLE`. If you call `intValue` on such a `Value`, the variable is automatically *resolved*, and the return value is the value of the variable. This is why `intValue` and friends require a `jess.Context` as an argument. `Context` objects contain information about the situation in which your function was called, including a pointer to the `Rete` object and, more relevant here, the current values of all the variables that have been defined.

In many cases, the fact that each argument might be a variable is irrelevant—variables are resolved automatically. But because looking up the value of a variable is a more expensive operation than just fetching the data from a `Value`, if you're going to reference a `Value` more than once in your `Userfunction`, it may be more efficient to separate the value resolution from the data access using the `resolveValue` method. You can call `resolveValue` on any `Value`. For `Value` objects of most types, `resolveValue` is a very inexpensive operation that returns the `Value` object itself. But for some types, it returns a new "real" `Value`. For `RU.VARIABLE` and `RU.MULTIVARIABLE` types, this is the value of the variable. The following (admittedly contrived) example computes the fractional part of a real number; it uses `resolveValue` to avoid looking up the value of its argument twice:

```
public Value call(ValueVector vv, Context context) {
    Value num = vv.get(1).resolveValue(context);
    double frac =
        num.floatValue(context) - num.intValue(context);
    ...
}
```

Note that the `variableValue` method returns the name of the variable actually passed, and `Context` has a public method `setVariable` that you can use to set a variable's value by name. This suggests that Jess's built-in `bind` function could simply be written as follows:

```
package jess;

class Bind implements Userfunction {
    public String getName() { return "bind"; }

    public Value call(ValueVector vv, Context c)
        throws JessException {
        Value rv = vv.get(2).resolveValue(c);
        c.setVariable(vv.get(1).variableValue(c), rv);
        return rv;
    }
}
```

And in fact, it is. Note that because `ValueVector.get` will throw an exception if there aren't enough arguments, and `variableValue` will throw an exception if `vv.get(1)` isn't a variable, this function (like many `Userfunctions`) doesn't have to do any explicit error checking.

15.2.4 *Resolving function call arguments*

What happens if `kill` is called like this?

```
Jess> (kill (+ 1 1))
%
```

What is the type of the first argument in this case? It is an `RU.FUNCALL` value—a representation of the function call. In many languages (Java is just one example), all the arguments to a function are fully resolved before the function is invoked. Jess, however, works differently—*none* of the arguments is resolved before you see them. Just as for variables, function call arguments are resolved automatically by methods like `intValue`. But now you should see why using `resolveValue` is important—not using it could result in function call arguments being invoked multiple times!

A similar but subtler problem arises if you try to store an argument in a Java data structure, or otherwise arrange to have a Value object live longer than the body of your call method. If you do this with a value of a simple type, there are no problems. But if you store a value of type RU.VARIABLE or RU.FUNCALL, it often won't be possible to resolve the value later, because you can't resolve a variable without the relevant jess.Context object. If you look back at the implementation of bind in the previous section, you'll see that before using the second argument as an argument to setVariable, I was careful to call resolveValue to get the real value of the argument. That way, calling (bind ?x (+ ?y 1)) sets ?x equal to one greater than the current value of ?y. If bind didn't use resolveValue, ?x would hold the function call (+ ?y 1). Accessing ?x might give a value that changed over time as ?y changed, or it might give an error if ?y isn't defined when ?x is read.

Just as bind's implementation takes advantage of Jess's lazy resolution to allow it to set the value of a variable, control structures use it to allow them to call a function multiple times. You can take advantage of this functionality to write your own control structures. Here's an implementation of a Userfunction named n-times that evaluates its second argument a number of times specified by its first argument:

```
import jess.*;

public class NTimes implements Userfunction {
    public String getName() { return "n-times";}
    public Value call(ValueVector vv, Context c)
        throws JessException {
        int count = vv.get(1).intValue(c);
        Value expr = vv.get(2);
        for (int i=0; i<count; ++i)
            expr.resolveValue(c);
        return Funcall.TRUE;
    }
}
```

You can compile this class, load the function into Jess, and call it:

```
Jess> (load-function NTimes)
TRUE
Jess> (n-times 10 (printout t "*"))
**********TRUE
Jess>
```

Each time the Java method resolveValue is called, the Jess function in expr is evaluated, and so this line of code prints 10 asterisks. This is how Jess's built-in control structures like while and foreach are implemented.

15.3 *Returning a value*

The `call` method returns a `Value` object. You can return one of `call`'s arguments, return one of a handful of constants in the jess.`Funcall` class, or create a new `Value` of your own. You should never return one of `call`'s arguments directly; rather, evaluate the argument by calling `resolveValue` on it, and return the result instead. Failing to do this will result in undefined behavior.

The `Funcall` class contains a few constants you can use as function return values:

- `TRUE`—Boolean true
- `FALSE`—Boolean false
- `NIL`—No value
- `NILLLIST`—An empty list
- `EOF`—End of file

Many functions return `TRUE` when there is no other sensible return value. Java's `null` is *not* a legal return value for `call`. Jess's equivalent of `null` is the symbol `nil`; you can always therefore return `Funcall.NIL`. The function `printout` is one of the few built-ins that return `nil`. This value makes sense for `printout` because `nil` return values aren't displayed by the Jess command prompt.

15.3.1 *Constructing Value objects*

`Value` objects are constructed by specifying the data and (usually) the type. The type is one of the constants listed in table 15.1. Each overloaded constructor assures that the given data and the given type are compatible. Note that for each constructor, more than one value of the `type` parameter may be acceptable. It's usually obvious which types can be created using each constructor; for example, you can only construct `RU.FLOAT` objects using the constructor that takes a `double` argument. The available constructors in jess.`Value` are as follows:

- `public Value(Object o) throws JessException`
- `public Value(String s, int type) throws JessException`
- `public Value(Value v)`
- `public Value(ValueVector f, int type) throws JessException`
- `public Value(double d, int type) throws JessException`
- `public Value(int value, int type) throws JessException`

`Value` has a number of subclasses that are used to hold some specialized kinds of data. `Variable`, `FuncallValue`, `FactIDValue`, and `LongValue` are the four of most interest to us. When you want to create a value to represent a variable, a function call, a fact, or a Java `long`, you must use the appropriate subclass. Refer to the API documentation for more information about these classes.

15.4 Beyond simple examples

We've covered all that you need to know to write many useful Jess extension functions. In this section, we'll look at some subtle techniques that can make your `Userfunctions` even more powerful.

15.4.1 Holding state

A `Userfunction` is really just an ordinary Java class, and so it can do things that ordinary Java classes do. In particular, it can contain member variables. Many of Jess's built-in functions contain member variables that hold data for the functions to operate on. For instance, the class that implements the `bag` function (which lets you create, modify, and maintain collections of objects) includes a `Hashtable` member variable that is used to store all the collections you create. When you load a `Userfunction` into Jess, only a single object of your class is created; that single object is used every time the `Userfunction` is called, so the values of those member variables are preserved.

Note that the `Rete` class has a method `findUserfunction` that returns the object that implements a given function. If you know the class name of that function, you can retrieve the object, cast it to the known type, and retrieve any state it holds. This is a convenient way to write a collection of cooperating functions that must share state. Recall that a single Java program might contain multiple instances of the `jess.Rete` class. If you install a separate instance of your `Userfunction` into each one, then each one will maintain its own state, separately.

When you write the `Userfunctions` for the HVAC Controller system, the classes will include a member variable to point to the `Hardware` object on which they operate. The multiple classes will use `findUserfunction` to share this state.

15.4.2 Multiple personalities

Consider this trivial `Userfunction` class:

```
include jess.*;

public class AnyString implements Userfunction {
    private String m_name;
    public AnyString(String name) { m_name = name;}
    public String getName() return m_name;
```

```
public Value call(ValueVector vv, Context c) {
    return new Value(m_name, RU.STRING);
}
```
}

It can be constructed using any string; when it is registered with Jess, that string will be its name. It will return the same string as its result. You won't be able to use `load-function` to load this class into Jess, because `load-function` won't let you specify the constructor argument; instead you can call the `addUserfunction` method in the `Rete` class from Java.

Although this function isn't useful as is, it illustrates an important principle: One Java class can implement multiple `Userfunctions`. A `call` method can choose from among several possible actions depending on the name the function is invoked with. If several `Userfunction` implementations need to share code (as the HVAC functions surely will), packaging them into a single class this way makes sense. Some of Jess's built-in functions use this technique.

15.4.3 *Userfunctions and serialization*

As we discussed in section 14.4, Jess's `bload` and `bsave` functions use Java's serialization API to preserve and restore Jess's state from any storage medium: a file, a network pipe, and so forth. More formally, these functions save or restore all the member data of the active `jess.Rete` object. Therefore, all the Java objects that are part of the `Rete` object's state should implement the `java.io.Serializable` interface. This is a *tagging interface*, which means it contains no methods, and just serves as a signal to the Java virtual machine that serializing objects of the given class is OK. Because the `Userfunctions` registered with Jess become part of a `Rete` object's state, it is generally important that all your `Userfunction` classes implement this interface—unless you're sure you'll never use `bload` and `bsave` when they are registered.

Because the current program will be controlling hardware (which obviously can't be stored in a file!), it won't be necessary for the `Userfunction` classes to implement `Serializable`, either. It would not be reasonable to expect `bload` to be able to restore the control program to a consistent state from offline storage.

15.4.4 *Grouping functions with Userpackage*

If you've written a group of related `Userfunctions`—either in a single class or in a group of classes—it would be convenient to provide a way for them to be loaded together into Jess with a single function call. This is especially true if your `Userfunction` objects need constructor arguments, like the `AnyString` class earlier. The `jess.Userpackage` interface takes care of this for you. User-package has one method, `add`; you implement `add` to initialize and install any number of `Userfunction` objects. Here's a simple `Userpackage` to install a few `AnyString` functions:

```
import jess.*;

public class AnyStringPackage implements Userpackage {
    public void add(Rete engine) {
        engine.addUserfunction(new AnyString("fred"));
        engine.addUserfunction(new AnyString("george"));
        engine.addUserfunction(new AnyString("ron"));
        engine.addUserfunction(new AnyString("percy"));
    }
}
```

You can install a `Userpackage` into Jess using the `load-package` function or the `addUserpackage` method in the `Rete` class. In the next section, you will finally write the HVAC functions and collect them in a `Userpackage`.

15.5 *The HVAC functions*

You've learned everything you need to know to develop the `Userfunctions` for the HVAC system. You need to be able to:

- Create a simulator, including a GUI
- Get the number of floors and heat pumps
- Determine which heat pump goes with which floor
- Operate the heat pumps and vents

Let's tackle these tasks one at a time, in this order.

15.5.1 *Creating a simulator*

The first command you will write creates a hardware simulator, attaches a GUI to it, and stores it somewhere where the other functions can access it. If you assume that each individual instance of Jess (each individual `jess.Rete` object) controls only one building's systems at a time, then storing a reference to the simulator in the `Userfunction` object itself will work well. Name the Jess function `init-simulator`; here is the implementation:

```
package control;
import jess.*;

class InitSimulator implements Userfunction {
```

```
        static final String NAME = "init-simulator";
        private Simulator m_simulator;
        public static Simulator getSimulator(Context c) {
            Rete engine = c.getEngine();
            InitSimulator is =
                (InitSimulator) engine.findUserfunction(NAME);
            return is.m_simulator;
        }
        public String getName() { return NAME; }
        public Value call(ValueVector vv, Context c)
        throws JessException {
            int nFloors = vv.get(1).intValue(c);
            m_simulator = new Simulator(nFloors);
            new SimulatorGUI(m_simulator);
            return new Value(m_simulator);
        }
    }
```

This function is fairly straightforward. It accepts one argument: the number of floors in the simulated building. The Userfunction creates a simulator and returns it as an RU.EXTERNAL_ADDRESS, via the Value constructor that accepts a java.lang.Object argument. Note that this class, like all the Userfunction classes you will write, is not public; it is meant to be loaded only via the Userpackage you will define at the end of this section.

The static getSimulator method is an implementation of a technique mentioned in the previous section: It finds an InitSimulator object registered in a given Rete object and extracts and returns its state (here the m_simulator member variable). Several of the other Userfunctions will use getSimulator to find their associated InitSimulator object and retrieve the Simulator.

15.5.2 *Counting devices*

As you have seen, a single Userfunction class can have multiple personalities: It can behave differently depending on the name it was registered with. You'll use this trick to write one class to implement both a function to return the number of heat pumps and a second function to return the number of floors in the building:

```
package control;
import jess.*;

class CountDevices implements Userfunction {
    static final String N_HEATPUMPS = "n-heatpumps";
    static final String N_FLOORS = "n-floors";
    private String m_name;
    public CountDevices(String name) {
        m_name = name;
    }
```

```
public String getName() { return m_name; }
public Value call(ValueVector vv, Context c)
throws JessException {
    Rete engine = c.getEngine();

    Simulator sim = InitSimulator.getSimulator(c);
    int nHeatPumps = sim.getNumberOfHeatPumps();
    if (m_name.equals(N_HEATPUMPS))
        return new Value(nHeatPumps, RU.INTEGER);
    else
        return new Value(nHeatPumps/3, RU.INTEGER);
}
}
```

The `CountDevices` class retrieves its associated `InitSimulator` object from Jess to get access to the simulator; once it has that, the rest of the work is trivial. One thing worth noticing about this class and the previous one is that the function names are all defined as static final string variables like `InitSimulator.NAME` and `CountDevices.N_FLOORS`. Each of the function names is used several times: in `getName`; possibly as a constructor argument; and, as here, sometimes in the program logic, for those functions that decide what to do based on their name. It's important that every use of the name match exactly, so it's good programming practice to define each name as a constant in one place.

15.5.3 *Matching heat pumps and floors*

Given the number of a floor, which heat pump corresponds to it? Heat pump 1 services floors 1, 2, and 3, whereas heat pump 2 services floors 4, 5, and 6. One way to compute this relationship is to subtract 1 from the floor number, perform integer division by 3, and add 1 to the result. This is not a slow calculation, but it's a bit messy, so you implement it in Java:

```
package control;
import jess.*;

class WhichPump implements Userfunction {
    public String getName() { return "which-pump"; }
    public Value call(ValueVector vv, Context c)
    throws JessException {
        int floor = vv.get(1).intValue(c);
        int heatPump = (floor-1)/3 + 1;
        return new Value(heatPump, RU.INTEGER);
    }
}
```

This basic `Userfunction` should be familiar to you by now.

15.5.4 *Operating the hardware*

You need several `Userfunctions` to read and change the operating mode of each heat pump and to check, open, and close the vents. It would be nice if you could use symbolic names for the heat pump and vent states, something like this:

```
Jess> (get-hp-state 2)
cooling
Jess> (set-vent-state 4 open)
```

This is easy enough to implement: Because there are so few alternatives, the `call` methods can contain multiway branches or `switch` statements to handle each of the possible options. The function to read the heat pump state looks like this:

```
package control;
import jess.*;

class ReadHeatPump implements Userfunction {
    public String getName() { return "get-hp-state"; }
    public Value call(ValueVector vv, Context c)
    throws JessException {
        int heatPump = vv.get(1).intValue(c);
        Simulator sim = InitSimulator.getSimulator(c);
        int state = sim.getHeatPumpState(heatPump);
        try {
            return new Value(State.heatpump(state), RU.ATOM);
        } catch (IllegalArgumentException iae) {
            throw new JessException("get-hp-state",
                                    "Unexpected state",
                                     state);
        }
    }
}
```

This `Userfunction` returns symbols (values of type `RU.ATOM`) to represent the heat pump states. It uses the `getSimulator` method from `InitSimulator`; the next few classes will use this method, too.

The `Userfunction` for setting the heat pump state is similar, but it must do the mapping between state names and numeric states in the reverse order:

```
package control;
import jess.*;

class WriteHeatPump implements Userfunction {
    public String getName() { return "set-hp-state"; }
    public Value call(ValueVector vv, Context c)
    throws JessException {
        int heatPump = vv.get(1).intValue(c);
        Simulator sim = InitSimulator.getSimulator(c);
        String szState = vv.get(2).stringValue(c);
```

```
            try {
                int state = State.heatpump(szState);
                sim.setHeatPumpState(heatPump, state);
            } catch (IllegalArgumentException iae) {
                throw new JessException("set-hp-state",
                                        "Invalid state",
                                        szState);
            }
            return Funcall.TRUE;
        }
    }
```

Finally, you need two more `Userfunctions` to read and write the state of the vents. These are similar to the last two, but because the vent state is a Boolean value, they are a bit simpler; the function to read a vent's state can dispense with error handling altogether:

```
package control;
import jess.*;

class ReadVent implements Userfunction {
    public String getName() { return "get-vent-state"; }
    public Value call(ValueVector vv, Context c)
    throws JessException {
        int vent = vv.get(1).intValue(c);
        Simulator sim = InitSimulator.getSimulator(c);
        boolean state = sim.getVentState(vent);
        return new Value(State.vent(state), RU.ATOM);
    }
}

class WriteVent implements Userfunction {
    public String getName() { return "set-vent-state"; }
    public Value call(ValueVector vv, Context c)
    throws JessException {
        int vent = vv.get(1).intValue(c);
        Simulator sim = InitSimulator.getSimulator(c);
        String szState = vv.get(2).stringValue(c);
        try {
            boolean state = State.vent(szState);
            sim.setVentState(vent, state);
        } catch (IllegalArgumentException iae) {
            throw new JessException("set-vent-state",
                                    "Invalid state",
                                    szState);
        }
        return Funcall.TRUE;
    }
}
```

The functions `init-simulator`, `n-heatpumps`, `n-floors`, `which-pump`, `get-hp-state`, `set-hp-state`, `get-vent-state`, and `set-vent-state` considerably simplify the rules you'll write in the next chapter.

15.5.5 *Implementing a Userpackage*

Several of the functions you wrote in this section are implemented by classes that require constructor arguments, and most of them depend on the existence of an `InitSimulator` object. Therefore, it wouldn't make sense to allow them to be installed into Jess one at a time. Instead, they can all be installed together as a single *package* using the `Userpackage` interface. The `Userpackage` for the hardware functions is straightforward:

```
package control;
import jess.*;

public class HardwareFunctions implements Userpackage {
    public void add(Rete engine) {
        engine.addUserfunction(new InitSimulator());
        engine.addUserfunction(
            new CountDevices(CountDevices.N_HEATPUMPS));
        engine.addUserfunction(
            new CountDevices(CountDevices.N_FLOORS));
        engine.addUserfunction(new WhichPump());
        engine.addUserfunction(new ReadHeatPump());
        engine.addUserfunction(new WriteHeatPump());
        engine.addUserfunction(new ReadVent());
        engine.addUserfunction(new WriteVent());
    }
}
```

The Jess function call (`load-package control.HardwareFunctions`) now makes all the `Userfunctions` you've written available from Jess.

15.6 *Testing*

Testing these functions by hand using the simulator GUI is easy and actually kind of fun. Load the functions using `load-package`, and then call (`init-simulator 9`); the GUI from figure 14.2 appears. When you first see this window, all the heat pumps are in the OFF state, and all the vents are CLOSED. The temperatures in the right-hand column of the GUI are rising, because when the simulator is turned on, the outdoor temperature is a scorching 110 degrees F.

First, check that you can count devices properly using the `n-heatpumps` (should return 3) and `n-floors` (should return 9) functions. Make sure that `which-pump` returns the correct values for each floor of the building (should return 1 for arguments 1–3, 2 for 4–6, and 3 for 7–9). You can (and should) write automated tests for these functions, too (perhaps using the testing framework in Appendix C).

Now, turn on the heat pumps using `set-hp-state` and open the vents with `set-vent-state`. You should be able to reduce the temperature of every floor by putting each heat pump in the `cooling` state. Try closing individual vents to see what happens. Try to keep each floor at 72 degrees by operating the controls yourself; it's quite difficult.

Change the outdoor temperature to 50 degrees by typing into the GUI's text field. The temperatures should begin to drop. Switch all the heat pumps into the `heating` state and try to stabilize the temperatures at 68 degrees. Not only is this exercise a useful way to test the code you've written, but it may give you some insights into the system's behavior that will be helpful when, in the next chapter, you write the rules to control it.

15.7 *Summary*

It is easy to extend the Jess language with functions written in Java. Any class that implements the `jess.Userfunction` interface can act as a Jess extension function. Extensions can be loaded from Jess using `load-function` or from Java code using `Rete.addUserfunction`. Extensions can be grouped into packages and loaded with a single call to `load-package`.

Every function built into Jess is itself a `Userfunction`. By implication, anything a Jess built-in function can do, you can do in your own extension functions. By way of example, you saw how you can manipulate variables and write your own Jess control structures in Java. For more useful tools for doing this kind of coding, look at the API for `jess.Context` class.

In the next chapter, you will write the Jess rules for controlling the Acme HVAC Systems devices. The rules will pattern-match the JavaBeans you developed in chapter 14 and call the functions you wrote in this chapter. Then you'll assemble and test the complete application.

Writing the rules

16

In this chapter you'll...

- Write real-time control rules
- Learn about fuzzy logic
- Write a fuzzy version of the HVAC Controller

You've spent the last two chapters programming in Java, developing the infrastructure for an HVAC Controller application. In this chapter, you'll assemble all the pieces and write the Jess rules to regulate the system. In fact, you'll write the rules *twice*.

First, you'll write a set of rules that use simple logic and the Boolean vent states you programmed in chapter 15 (they're "Boolean" because they're either open or closed). If a given floor of the building gets too cold, its heat pump will be turned on; when it gets too warm, its heat will be turned off. This system will work much like a network of traditional mechanical thermostats, and it will keep the temperature stable to within plus or minus one or two degrees.

Next, you'll improve the control program using *fuzzy logic* and continuously variable vent controls. The fuzzy rules will be able to adjust the vents to provide optimal air flow for each floor; as a result, this second system will control the temperature to within a small fraction of a degree.

Let's get started by developing a simple control algorithm for the HVAC system.

16.1 *The control algorithm*

You can get an advanced degree in the engineering of control systems. It's a vast and complex discipline, and we can't hope to cover it all here. Instead, I'll state some commonsense principles to which your system should adhere, and then we'll come up with a simple, ad hoc control algorithm to satisfy these requirements.

16.1.1 *Knowledge engineering with truth tables*

The best expert to interview for this project would be a control systems engineer. Ideally, he'd already be familiar with heat pumps and have experience building control systems for them. A certified Acme HVAC Systems engineer would of course be perfect! The world is rarely perfect, however, and most likely you'd talk to an engineer whose specialty wasn't HVAC control. In that case, you'd combine knowledge from the expert with information gleaned from the *Acme HVAC Systems Installation Guide*, the *Acme User's Manual*, and any other documentation you could get your hands on.

Flowcharts are ideal for describing diagnostic systems, but they would not be the best way to capture the collected knowledge here. A better alternative is to use *truth tables*. A truth table is a chart with rows and columns that correspond to some combination of inputs to the system. The individual entries in the table describe the desired output of the system given those inputs. A vastly simplified truth table for the HVAC Controller system might look like table 16.1. In the following sections, you'll fill in the details.

Table 16.1 **Oversimplified truth table for the HVAC Controller system. Each row represents one possible current heat-pump setting; each column represents one possible temperature reading.**

	Too Cold	Just Right	Too Hot
Off	Start Heating	Do Nothing	Start Cooling
Heating	Do Nothing	Turn Off	Turn Off
Cooling	Turn Off	Turn Off	Do Nothing

16.1.2 *How heat pumps work*

You may know how an air conditioner works. A *working fluid* (historically, often the gas Freon) is compressed by a pump outside your house. Compressing a fluid creates heat, so a fan dissipates this heat outside. The compressed, somewhat cooled fluid is then circulated inside the house, where it is allowed to expand quickly. Just as compressing a fluid creates heat, an expanding gas absorbs heat. This process cools a radiator inside the house, and a fan blows through the radiator to create a nice cool breeze. The expanded fluid is pumped back outside to be compressed again.

A heat pump is basically an air conditioner that can run in either direction. It can either cool the inside of a building and expel hot air outside, or cool the outside air and expel the waste heat inside, heating the building.

16.1.3 *Using guard lines*

The number one rule of operating a heat pump is that you can't quickly or repeatedly switch it between heating and cooling. If you do, the heat pump may be damaged, if condensation forms and then freezes inside the pump. Industrial-grade heat pumps can cost thousands of dollars, so this can be an expensive mistake.

Your control system must respect this rule. One easy way to do this is to use *guard lines*. There will always be some target temperature—for example, 70 degrees. If you defined your rules to heat or cool the building whenever the temperature was different from precisely 70 degrees, then your system would be constantly switching between heating and cooling mode, trying to get the temperature exactly right. Instead, you'll define a range of acceptable temperatures delimited by upper and lower guard lines (which may move up or down depending on conditions). As long as the temperature is within the valid range, the system will be turned off. The guard lines therefore serve as a kind of buffer, so the system can't be rapidly cycled between operating modes. Table 16.2 is an update truth table that includes guard lines.

Table 16.2 Truth table for the HVAC Controller system, including guard lines. The two added columns represent the regions between the set point and each guard line.

	Too Cold	Lower Guard	Just Right	Upper Guard	Too Hot
Off	Start Heating	Do Nothing	Do Nothing	Do Nothing	Start Cooling
Heating	Do Nothing	Do Nothing	Do Nothing	Turn Off	Turn Off
Cooling	Turn Off	Turn Off	Do Nothing	Do Nothing	Do Nothing

16.1.4 Saving energy

There are two ways to shut off the air to a given floor: You can close the vent for that floor or shut off the heat pump that services it. If any floor serviced by a heat pump needs to be heated or cooled, then of course that heat pump needs to be turned on. If a heat pump is on, and none of its floors needs service, then you must be sure to shut off the heat pump, rather than simply closing all the vents.

16.2 Setting up

It's time to begin writing the Jess code for the HVAC Controller. Before you do anything else, load the `Userfunctions` you wrote in chapter 15:

```
(load-package control.HardwareFunctions)
```

Next you need to create a `Simulator` object and make it available to Jess. You can store a reference to it in a `defglobal` using code like this:

```
(defglobal ?*hw* = (init-simulator 9))
(set-reset-globals FALSE)
```

The graphical monitor for the simulator will appear as soon as the first line is executed. The call to `set-reset-globals` tells Jess not to reinitialize `?*hw*` when `reset` is called. If you didn't call `set-reset-globals`, you could end up with multiple simulator GUIs on the screen, and the connections between the JavaBeans and the simulator would be broken.

Next you need to use `defclass` to tell Jess about your JavaBean classes, and then create all the necessary JavaBeans and use `definstance` to connect the hardware to Jess. You need `control.Vent` and `control.Thermometer` objects for each floor and a `control.HeatPump` for every three floors. Because Jess doesn't have a built-in function that works like Java's `for` loop, you use Jess's `while` instead:

```
;; Tell Jess about the JavaBean classes
(defclass Thermometer control.Thermometer)
```

```
(defclass Vent control.Vent)
(defclass HeatPump control.HeatPump)

;; Create the Vent and Thermometer Beans
(bind ?n (n-floors))
(while (> ?n 0) do
    (definstance Thermometer
        (new control.Thermometer ?*hw* ?n))
    (definstance Vent (new control.Vent ?*hw* ?n))
    (bind ?n (- ?n 1)))

;; Create the HeatPump Beans
(bind ?n (n-heatpumps))
(while (> ?n 0) do
    (definstance HeatPump (new control.HeatPump ?*hw* ?n))
    (bind ?n (- ?n 1)))
```

If you use the `batch` command to execute what you've written so far, you can then use the `facts` command to check that all the shadow facts exist. If you check them repeatedly, you'll see that the temperature data changes over time and stays in sync with the readings in the simulator GUI. If you're using the Jess-Win IDE (http://herzberg.ca.sandia.gov/jess/user.shtml), you can watch the facts change in real time.

16.3 *Controlling the heat pumps*

The heat pumps are controlled by a small cluster of rules. You control the vents from a separate set of rules, for clarity's sake. First, if a floor is outside the acceptable temperature range and its heat pump is off, its corresponding heat pump needs to be turned on and put in the correct mode. This corresponds to the behavior in truth table 16.2. The rule `floor-too-cold-pump-off` handles the case where a floor is too cold; a separate `floor-too-hot-pump-off` rule (not shown) is also needed:

```
;; Temperature set point
(defglobal ?*set-point* = 70)

;; Deffunctions
(deffunction too-cold (?t)
    (return (< ?t (- ?*set-point* 2))))

;; Rules
(defrule floor-too-cold-pump-off
    (Thermometer (floor ?f) (reading ?t&:(too-cold ?t)))
    (HeatPump (state "off") (number ?p&=(which-pump ?f)))
    =>
    (set-hp-state ?p heating))
```

There are a few things to notice about this rule. We used several of the Userfunc-tions defined in the last chapter to keep this rule simple. The test (number ?p&=(which-pump ?f)) means "if this heat pump is the one that services floor ?f." You define a deffunction named too-cold that deals with the guard line con-cept; here, the lower guard line is defined as 2 degrees below the temperature set point (in the defglobal ?*set-point*). Finally, you're able to use symbolic names for the state of the heat pump. Words like *off* and *heating* make the rule eas-ier to understand. Note that in the test (state "off") you have to enclose the name of the state in quotes, so that it's a string rather than a symbol. Doing so is necessary because you're matching a JavaBean property, and JavaBeans can't have symbols as property values—only strings.

16.3.1 *Enough is enough*

If all the floors serviced by a heat pump are within the acceptable temperature range, the heat pump should be shut off. Exactly what should be the criteria for shutting off the pumps? If the heat pump is in cooling mode, there are three pos-sible criteria:

- You run the heat pump until too-hot is not true for any floor.
- You run the heat pump until the temperature on each floor is below the set point.
- You run the heat pump until too-cold is true for each floor.

The first case would lead to rapid cycling of the heat pump, because when the temperatures went below the upper guard line, the pump would be turned off, and when they went above the upper guard line, the pump would be turned on. As I've said, rapid mode switching is bad for heat pumps, so you don't want to do this. In addition, the average temperature would be the temperature at the guard line, not near the actual set point.

The third case would lead to nice, slow switching between the cooling and off states and an average temperature (the midpoint between the lowest and highest operating temperatures) equal to the set point. The temperature would cycle between the upper and lower guard lines. Unfortunately, this means that at the moment the heat pump was switched off, all the floors connected to it might be too cold. As soon as the pump was switched off, the state of the system would be indistinguishable from the case where the building needed to be heated, so the heating rules would switch the heat pump into heating mode. Switching back and forth between heating and cooling mode is bad for a heat pump, so this alterna-tive is also unacceptable.

The second case, running until the temperature dips below the set point, leads to gradual switching, because a range of temperatures is allowed. The average temperature is then above the set point—most of the time, the room is warmer than the set temperature, but not by much. Most importantly, though, the heat pump cycles between cooling mode and off mode without any danger of being switched into heating mode, which is exactly what you want. Therefore, your rule will use the actual set point as the shut-off criterion. If the heat pump is in cooling mode and the temperature of all connected floors is below the set point, then the heat pump will be shut off. This behavior corresponds to what is shown in the Cooling row in table 16.2. A similar argument would let you substitute *heating* and *above* for *cooling* and *below.*

Again, you'll write this as two rules, and I'll just show the cooling version here:

```
(defrule floors-cool-enough
    (HeatPump (state "cooling") (number ?p))
    (not (Thermometer (floor ?f&:(= ?p (which-pump ?f)))
    (reading ?t&:(> ?t ?*set-point*))))
    =>
    (set-hp-state ?p off))
```

This rule could be rendered in English as "if there is a heat pump in the cooling state, and there are no floors serviced by this pump with temperature above the set point, then turn the heat pump off."

16.3.2 *The moment of truth*

These four rules are enough to regulate the temperatures of the HVAC simulator. Adding the vent control rules will refine the behavior, but the basic heating and cooling control is already in place. To make the program work, you need to add calls to set-vent-state to open all the vents manually, of course.

Testing the system at this stage shows that the rules defined so far suffice to turn the heat pumps on and off. Without the vent-control rules, however, the temperature differential between floors has a tendency to force the system to overshoot. When the system is in cooling mode, some floors are cooled below the lower guard line, while others are still in the comfort zone. Unfortunately, this set of rules turns the heat pump off and then immediately puts it into heating mode under these conditions. You need to add rules to equalize the temperature between floors so this won't happen.

16.4 *Controlling the vents*

Although this may seem obvious, it's worth stating for the record; the vents have two purposes:

- To let the hot or cold air in, when needed
- To keep it out when it's not

Therefore, you need two different sets of rules to control the vents: rules that open the vent when a floor needs service, and rules that close it when the floor's temperature is acceptable. The only thing you need to decide is where the important temperatures are. Because you want the vents to help moderate the system, you'll switch them based on the set point temperature. Note that because a vent doesn't accomplish anything unless the heat pump is on, you need to include the state of the heat pump in each rule. Table 16.3 is a truth table for what to do when the heat pump for a floor is in cooling mode.

Table 16.3   The truth table for vent operation when the heat pump for a floor is in cooling mode. The rows correspond to the current vent state.

	Too Cold	Lower Guard	Just Right	Upper Guard	Too Hot
Open	Close Vent	Close Vent	Do Nothing	Do Nothing	Do Nothing
Closed	Do Nothing	Do Nothing	Do Nothing	Open Vent	Open Vent

This truth table could lead to oscillations of the vents. If the temperature were hovering right at the set point, the vents might open and close rapidly. If this oscillation became a problem (and in a real system, it would, because the vents would be noisy), then you could establish a second set of guard lines, closer together than the ones you're using for the heat pump. The vents could then be opened or closed only when the temperature passed these guard lines. We won't complicate the HVAC Controller system with this detail, but you should keep an eye out for the problem during testing.

16.4.1 *The vent rules*

Now you're ready to write the vent rules. The following rule says that if the heat pump for a floor is in cooling mode, the vent is closed, and the temperature is above the set point, then the vent should be opened:

```
(defrule floor-too-hot-vent-closed
    (HeatPump (state "cooling") (number ?p))
```

```
(Vent (state "closed") (floor ?f&:(eq ?p (which-pump ?f))))
(Thermometer (floor ?f)
(reading ?t&:(> ?t ?*set-point*)))
=>
(set-vent-state ?f open))
```

Similarly, if the heat pump for a floor is cooling, the floor is too cold, and the vent is open, then the vent should be closed:

```
(defrule floor-too-cold-vent-open
    (HeatPump (state "cooling") (number ?p))
    (Vent (state "open") (floor ?f&:(eq ?p (which-pump ?f))))
    (Thermometer (floor ?f)
    (reading ?t&:(< ?t ?*set-point*)))
    =>
    (set-vent-state ?f closed))
```

You need analogous rules `floor-too-cold-vent-closed` and `floor-too-hot-vent-open`, dictating what to do when the heat pump is in heating mode; these aren't shown here, but they're very similar to the other pair. The four rules correspond to the four cells in table 16.3 that have an entry other than Do Nothing.

16.5 *Testing the whole system*

The first version of the HVAC Controller system is now essentially complete. All that remains is to clean things up a bit and test it in operation. You can delete any top-level function calls to `set-vent-state` that were used for testing the last time around.

You should find that this set of rules controls the temperature of every floor to within 2 degrees of the set point. While testing, keep an eye out for heat pumps that are turned on and off quickly, or that rapidly move between the heating and cooling state. This set of rules should avoid both of these problems.

If you're using the version of the code downloaded from this book's web site, then when the simulator starts, the outdoor temperature is 90 degrees F and the set point is 70, so the heat pumps are in cooling mode. Notice how the heat pump for the highest floors turns on first and runs the most; this is a consequence of the "heat rises" property you built into the simulator. The vents open and close frequently to keep the temperatures of the three floors connected to each heat pump as close together as possible. Once the system reaches equilibrium, each heat pump spends some of its time turned off. Watch the temperatures and make sure they all stay in the range between the set point and the upper guard line (between 70 and 72 degrees).

Now set the outdoor temperature to 50 degrees. As the temperature of each floor drifts down, most of the heat pumps will shut off. Eventually the lower floors will need to be heated, and those heat pumps should move into heating mode. The upper floors will still be hotter than the rest and will need cooling instead. Make sure the floors that need heating stay between 68 and 70 degrees, while the upper floors stay between 70 and 72.

Next try an outdoor temperature of 20 degrees. The upper floors will lose enough heat to the outside that they too will require heating.

Finally, try outdoor temperatures very close to the set point. Try several temperatures from 67 to 73, watching carefully for illegal transitions from heating to cooling.

You can experiment with different numbers of floors by specifying larger or smaller numbers in the call to `init-simulator` (the number of floors should be divisible by 3). You should find that the HVAC Controller system has no problem handling a building with 99 floors or more. Remember that 99 floors corresponds to 99 `Thermometers`, 99 `Vents`, and 33 `HeatPumps`, for a total of 231 constantly changing inputs—a reasonably complex system! Each Bean runs in its own Java thread, demonstrating Jess's ability to run well in a multithreaded environment; with 99 floors, Jess is receiving asynchronous property change events from 231 different threads.

The system you've built works fairly well, although because the vents can only be completely open or completely closed, the temperature at each floor fluctuates by as much as +/– one or two degrees. If the vents were continuously variable, the temperature could be controlled more closely. In the next section, we'll look at one way to incorporate this new feature using *fuzzy logic*.

16.6 *Controlling with fuzzy rules*

This section was written with Bob Orchard

The first HVAC Controller system was based on traditional *Boolean logic*. In Boolean logic, the state of a system is *crisp*, meaning it has distinct, well-defined values. For example, in the system you've developed, the temperature of a floor is always in one of three distinct states: too hot, too cold, or just right. The decisions a Boolean system can make are equally sharp: a heat pump should be turned on or off, and a vent should be open or closed.

Many modern control systems are based on *fuzzy logic*. In fuzzy logic, the same set of states can be used, but the transitions between them are not sharp. For example, although temperatures above 72 degrees will still be considered too hot, a fuzzy control system will consider 72.5 degrees to be "slightly too hot" and

80 degrees to be "very too hot." A fuzzy control system can then make somewhat more subjective decisions. Whereas the system you've developed here only knows how to open or close the vent at each floor, a fuzzy control system can continuously vary the vent openings. A fuzzy system will be able to control the temperature much more closely. As an added benefit, there will be less abrupt cycling of the heat pumps, so they will have a longer useful life.

More generally, fuzzy systems are subtler than Boolean systems. This makes fuzzy rules a good choice whenever you need to make distinctions that aren't clearly drawn—for example, in systems that have to classify items into indistinct categories.

FuzzyJess, written by Bob Orchard at the National Research Council of Canada's Institute for Information Technology, is a set of Jess extensions that gives you the ability to write fuzzy rules in Jess.[1] FuzzyJess is part of the FuzzyJ Toolkit, a powerful set of fuzzy logic tools written in Java. In the remainder of this chapter, we'll show how to use FuzzyJ and FuzzyJess to write a fuzzy-logic version of the HVAC Controller system.[2]

16.6.1 *Fuzzy logic, briefly*

In the real world, there exists much fuzzy knowledge—knowledge that is vague, imprecise, uncertain, ambiguous, inexact, or probabilistic in nature. Human thinking and reasoning frequently involve fuzzy information, possibly originating from inherently inexact human concepts and matching of similar rather then identical experiences. In systems based on a classical set theory and two-valued logic, it is very difficult to answer some questions because they do not have completely true or false answers. Humans, however, can often give satisfactory answers to these questions.

Fuzziness

Fuzziness occurs when the boundary of a piece of information is not clear-cut. For example, words such as *young, tall, good,* and *high* are fuzzy. No single quantitative

---

[1] You can get FuzzyJess and the FuzzyJ Toolkit from http://www.iit.nrc.ca/IR_public/fuzzy/fuzzyJToolkit.html.

[2] There isn't space here to provide a full tutorial on the topic of fuzzy logic or FuzzyJess and the FuzzyJ Toolkit. For that, you need to refer to other sources of information, such as Bart Kosko, *Fuzzy Engineering* (Upper Saddle River, NJ: Prentice Hall, 1997); Leferi Tsoukalas and Robert Uhrig, *Fuzzy and Neural Approaches in Engineering* (New York: John Wiley & Sons, 1997); or the documentation provided with the FuzzyJ Toolkit.

value defines the term *young* when describing a fuzzy concept (or fuzzy variable) such as age. For some people, age 25 is young; for others, age 35 is young. The concept *young* has no clean boundary. In most situations, you could say that age 1 is definitely young and age 100 is definitely not young. However, age 35 has some possibility of being young; its status usually depends on the context in which it is being considered. In fact, an age can have some possibility of being young and also some possibility of being old. It belongs to more than one set at the same time with different *degrees of membership* in the sets. The representation of this kind of information is handled by fuzzy set theory.

Unlike classical set theory, which deals with objects whose membership to a set can be clearly described, in fuzzy set theory, membership of an element in a set can be partial—that is, an element belongs to a set with a certain grade (or degree, or possibility) of membership. This grade of membership in the fuzzy set is usually represented by values from 0 to 1 (with 0 meaning definitely not a member of the set and 1 meaning definitely is a member of the set). For example, the fuzzy term *young* might be defined and shown graphically as in figure 16.1. There you can see that between 0 and 25 years of age, the membership value is 1 (definitely young), above 50 it is 0 (definitely not young), and between 25 and 50 the membership value decreases (partial membership in the set).

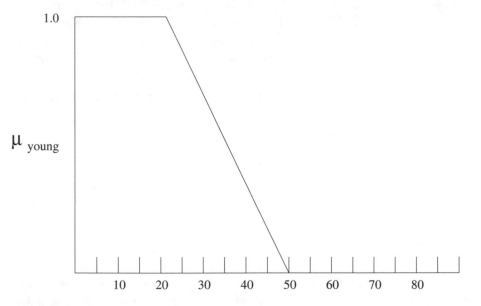

Figure 16.1 Possibility distribution of young

Representing fuzziness in FuzzyJ: FuzzyVariable, FuzzySet, and FuzzyValue

Fuzzy concepts are represented using fuzzy variables, fuzzy sets, and fuzzy values in the FuzzyJ Toolkit. A `FuzzyVariable` defines the basic components used to describe a fuzzy concept. It consists of a name for the variable (for example, air temperature), the units of the variable if required (for example, degrees C), a range of valid values (from 0 to 100), and a set of fuzzy terms that can be used to describe the particular fuzzy concepts for this variable. The fuzzy terms are described using a term name, such as *cold*, along with a `FuzzySet` representing that term.

A `FuzzyValue` is normally created by specifying a `FuzzyVariable` and a fuzzy expression. The following example shows how this is done in Java code using classes from the FuzzyJ Toolkit:

```
//definition of fuzzy variable 'Temperature'
//with terms 'cold', 'OK' and 'hot'
FuzzyVariable temperature =
  new FuzzyVariable("Temperature", 0, 100, "degrees C");
temperature.addTerm("cold", new ZFuzzySet(8, 15));
temperature.addTerm("OK", new triangleFuzzySet(8, 15,
  25));temperature.addTerm("hot", new SFuzzySet(15, 25));

// definition of FuzzyValue for concept 'temperature is hot'
FuzzyValue tempHotFVal = new FuzzyValue(temperature, "hot");

// 'fuzzifying' the current 'crisp' temperature
// (various ways to do this; here we represent an imprecison
// in the temperature sensor of +/- 0.1 degree)
FuzzyValue currentTempFVal =
  FuzzyValue(temperature, new PIFuzzySet(35.0, 0.1));
```

Without getting into too much detail, this code creates a `FuzzyVariable`, temperature, that provides the basis for building fuzzy concepts about temperature. The domain for the variable is from 0 to 100 degrees C, and the code defines three terms—*cold, OK,* and *hot*—that you can now use to represent specific temperature concepts. The terms are defined using `FuzzySets`. In this case, *cold* is represented by a subclass of `FuzzySet`, `ZFuzzySet`, which defines a Z-shaped fuzzy set like the one shown in figure 16.1.

Once the `FuzzyVariable` and the terms that are to be used to describe concepts about that variable are ready, you can create `FuzzyValues`. The example creates an object, tempHot. Ultimately the `FuzzyValue` is just a `FuzzySet` (or at least it contains a `FuzzySet`), but it also has a context: the `FuzzyVariable` it is associated with. You can perform operations on `FuzzyValues`. For example, the *union* and *intersection* of two `FuzzyValues` are defined, but only between `FuzzyValues` that share the same `FuzzyVariable`. This is reasonable because doing the intersection of "hot temperature" and "low pressure" makes no sense—it's like adding 5 apples to 6 oranges.

FuzzyRules

Let's continue the example and add two simple *FuzzyRules,* which can be expressed in pseudo-English as follows:

```
IF the temperature is warm
THEN set the vent position to mostly open

IF the temperature is hot
THEN set the vent position to fully open
```

The rules in FuzzyJess might appear like this:

```
(defrule temp-warm-set-vent-mostly-open
    (temperature ?t&:(fuzzy-match ?t "warm"))
  =>
    (assert (vent (new FuzzyValue ?*ventFVar* "mostlyOpen"))))

(defrule temp-hot-set-vent-fully-open
    (temperature ?t&:(fuzzy-match ?t "hot"))
  =>
    (assert (vent (new FuzzyValue ?*ventFVar* "fullyOpen")))
```

The FuzzyJess function `fuzzy-match` compares two `FuzzyValues` to see how well they match. In this case, the `temperature` fact has a `FuzzyValue` that is a fuzzified version of the current crisp temperature; it is compared to the `warm` `FuzzyValue`. If there is some degree of matching (this level can be set by the user), then the `temp-warm-set-vent-mostly-open` rule will fire, and a `vent` fact will be asserted with a `mostlyOpen` `FuzzyValue` (scaled by the degree of matching of the temperature `FuzzyValue`).

In a complete system, you normally have a number of rules that cover the range of decisions to be made. Here, for example, the temperature might also match the `FuzzyValue` `hot` to some degree, which would produce a vent fact with the `FuzzyValue` `fullyOpen` as an output (again, suitably scaled to represent the degree of matching). These output facts would be combined into a single fuzzy output fact to represent the *global decision* of the system.

You can leave this combined output as a `FuzzyValue`; but, in general, you'll go through a process of *defuzzification* of the output, transforming the `FuzzyValue` to get a *crisp* value. Doing so allows the system to take some real-world action, such as moving a vent by some real-valued amount. There are a number of ways to defuzzify a `FuzzySet`. One of the more common is to look at the area under the graph of the `FuzzySet` and find the center of gravity (or center of mass). Details of this and other types of defuzzification are found in the FuzzyJ documentation.

To wrap up and review, here are the steps normally taken in a fuzzy control application:

1   Collect the system inputs.

2   Fuzzify the inputs (make them appropriate fuzzy values, usually representing the imprecision in the input value).

3   Apply the fuzzy inputs to all the rules in the system, executing the rules one at a time and performing a global accumulation of the outputs. (FuzzyJess does this for you.)

4   Defuzzify the outputs (create crisp numbers from the output fuzzy values).

5   Apply the crisp outputs to the system.

6   Repeat all the steps until the system is in a controlled state.

16.6.2 *The Fuzzy HVAC Controller*

With this brief introduction to fuzzy logic and FuzzyJ/FuzzyJess we can now return to the HVAC Controller example. Recall that the decisions and actions (in the rules) used to control the heat pumps and vents are all binary (set the vent to the open state) or crisp (if the thermometer reading is less than the desired set point …). In the two versions of the fuzzy controller described next, you will define fuzzy terms for the temperature and for setting the vent positions. This indicates that you are going to extend the functionality of the system a little and not restrict the vents to a fully open or fully closed position; you will allow them to be partially open as well. The code for both versions of the fuzzy HVAC Controller (along with all the other code from this book) is available from the book's web site.

Version 1: absolute vent positions

In your first attempt at controlling the temperature in the building, you will define fuzzy terms for describing the temperature and some terms for controlling the vent opening. You'll first modify the Thermometer bean class to make it work with fuzzy temperatures. You must import the nrc.fuzzy package; store the fuzzy reading of the temperature; define a fuzzy variable for the thermometer so you can add the terms cold, cool, OK, warm, and hot; and notify Jess whenever the FuzzyValue for the temperature reading changes. The code for this functionality is shown in listing 16.1 with the major changes highlighted in bold. Because not every Thermometer object needs to define the FuzzyVariable, you make it static. Figure 16.2 shows the fuzzy sets that represent the terms for describing temperature.

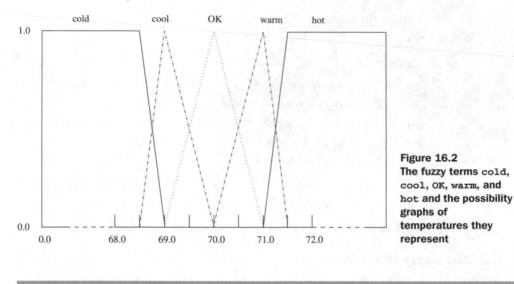

cold   cool   OK   warm   hot

Figure 16.2
The fuzzy terms cold, cool, OK, warm, and hot and the possibility graphs of temperatures they represent

---

Listing 16.1 Thermometer class with a new fuzzy reading property

```java
package fuzzy;
import nrc.fuzzy.*;
public class Thermometer extends BeanSupport
  implements Runnable {

  private Hardware m_hardware;
  private int m_floor;
  private double m_oldReading;
  private FuzzyValue m_fuzzyReading;

  private static FuzzyVariable m_thermometerFV = null;

  static {
    try {
      m_thermometerFV = new FuzzyVariable("thermometer", 0, 120);
    } catch (InvalidFuzzyVariableNameException nameEx) {
      /* NOTHING */
    } catch (InvalidUODRangeException rangeEx) {
      /* NOTHING */
    }

    try {
      m_thermometerFV.addTerm("cold", new RFuzzySet(68.5,69,
                              new RightLinearFunction()));
      m_thermometerFV.addTerm("cool",
                              new TriangleFuzzySet(68.5,69,70));
      m_thermometerFV.addTerm("OK",
                              new TriangleFuzzySet(69,70,71));
      m_thermometerFV.addTerm("warm",
                              new TriangleFuzzySet(70,71,71.5));
```

Create FuzzyVariable to represent temperature ❶

```
        m_thermometerFV.addTerm("hot",  new LFuzzySet(71,71.5,
                              new LeftLinearFunction())));
  } catch (XValuesOutOfOrderException outOfOrderEx) {
    /* NOTHING */
  } catch (XValueOutsideUODException outsideOUD) {
    /* NOTHING */
  }
}

public Thermometer(Hardware hw, int floor) {
  m_hardware = hw;
  m_floor = floor;
  new Thread(this).start();
}

public int getFloor() {
  return m_floor;

}
public double getReading() {
  return m_hardware.getTemperature(m_floor);
}

public FuzzyValue getFuzzyReading() {
  return m_fuzzyReading;
}

public void run() {
  while (true) {
    double reading = getReading();
    boolean readingChanged = (reading != m_oldReading);
    m_pcs.firePropertyChange("reading",
                              new Double(m_oldReading),
                              new Double(reading));
    m_oldReading = reading;
    if (readingChanged) {
      try {
        m_fuzzyReading = new FuzzyValue(m_thermometerFV,
                          new SingletonFuzzySet(reading));
      } catch (XValuesOutOfOrderException xvorder)  {
        System.out.println("Error: " + xvorder); return;
      } catch (XValueOutsideUODException xvuod) {
        System.out.println("Error: " + xvuod); return;
      }
      // do NOT use an old value when notifying of changes
      // to FuzzyValues. firePropertyChange will not pass it
      // on since FuzzyValues with the same FuzzyVariable
      // are considered to be EQUAL ... even if they have
      // different FuzzySets!
      m_pcs.firePropertyChange("fuzzyReading",
                              null,(Object)m_fuzzyReading);
    }
```

2 **Fuzzy reading value**

Send property change notification **3**

```
        try {
          Thread.sleep(1000);
        } catch (InterruptedException ie) {
          return;
        }
      }
    }
  }
```

❶ This part of the code creates a FuzzyVariable to represent the temperature and loads it with appropriate fuzzy terms like *cool, warm,* and so on.

❷ The *fuzzy reading* is the value you match in your new set of rules, so it needs to be available as a JavaBeans property.

❸ This block of code sends out a property change notification for the fuzzy temperature reading whenever a change is detected in the crisp temperature reading.

Next you augment the Vent bean in a similar fashion to define the terms for controlling the vent openings (fullyClosed, slightlyOpen, halfOpen, mostlyOpen, and fullyOpen) and also to notify Jess when the FuzzyValues change. Again, the modified code (see listing 16.2) is highlighted in bold; figure 16.3 shows the fuzzy sets for the new terms.]

Listing 16.2   Vent class modifed to support a fuzzy vent position description

```
package fuzzy;
import nrc.fuzzy.*;

public class Vent extends BeanSupport {

  private Hardware m_hardware;                 Create FuzzyVariable to
  private int m_floor;                         represent vent position  ❶
  private double m_oldState;
  private static FuzzyVariable m_ventFV = null;

  static {
    try {
      m_ventFV = new FuzzyVariable("vent", 0, 1);
    } catch (InvalidFuzzyVariableNameException nameEx) {
      /* NOTHING */
    } catch (InvalidUODRangeException rangeEx) {
      /* NOTHING */
    }

    try {
      m_ventFV.addTerm("fullyClosed", new SingletonFuzzySet(0.0));
      m_ventFV.addTerm("slightlyOpen",
                        new SingletonFuzzySet(0.25));
```

```
      m_ventFV.addTerm("halfOpen",   new SingletonFuzzySet(0.5));
      m_ventFV.addTerm("mostlyOpen", new SingletonFuzzySet(0.75));
      m_ventFV.addTerm("fullyOpen",  new SingletonFuzzySet(1.0));
    } catch (XValuesOutOfOrderException outOfOrderEx) {
      /* NOTHING */
    } catch (XValueOutsideUODException outsideOUD) {
      /* NOTHING */
    }
  }

  public Vent(Hardware hw, int floor) {
    m_hardware = hw;
    m_floor = floor;
  }

  public static FuzzyVariable getVentFuzzyVariable() {
    return m_ventFV;
  }

  public int getFloor() {
    return m_floor;
  }

  public double getState() {
    return m_hardware.getVentState(m_floor);
  }

  public void setState(double state) {
    m_hardware.setVentState(m_floor, state);
  }
}
```

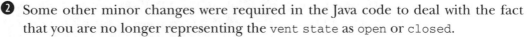 ❷ Modify method to return numeric value

❶ This part of the code creates a new FuzzyVariable to represent the vent position and loads the linguistic terms into the variable. Note that you no longer define the Vent Bean to implement Runnable, because you do not need to provide Jess with updated values of the vent state (manual vent adjustments will no longer be allowed).[3]

❷ Some other minor changes were required in the Java code to deal with the fact that you are no longer representing the vent state as open or closed.

---

[3] If you already have some knowledge of FuzzyJ and fuzzy rules in general, you might notice that the FuzzyValues for the vent terms are created with singleton FuzzySets. These specialized FuzzySets have a value of 1.0 at the single point specified and a value of 0.0 everywhere else. Using this type of set in your fuzzy conclusions together with a defuzzification method that takes the weighted average of these singleton outputs, you are implementing zero-order Takagi-Sugeno-Kang (TSK) rules. Zero-order TSK rules have fuzzy inputs, but they have crisp, constant outputs. See the FuzzyJ Toolkit User's Guide for more information about TSK rules.

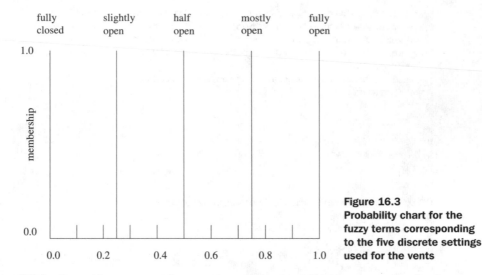

fully closed   slightly open   half open   mostly open   fully open

membership

1.0

0.0

0.0   0.2   0.4   0.6   0.8   1.0

**Figure 16.3
Probability chart for the
fuzzy terms corresponding
to the five discrete settings
used for the vents**

With these changes made, you can now consider the new set of rules needed to control the vents. Because you are not changing the way you determine when the heat pump should be cooling, heating, or off, you will essentially leave the rules that determine the heat pump state as they are. However, to allow the temperature to fluctuate close to the set point without turning off the heat pump, you need to make a minor change to the rules `floor-hot-enough` and `floor-cool-enough`. In these two rules, rather than turn off the heat pump as soon as all the floors have passed the set point, you allow a 0.25-degree overshoot or undershoot of the set point before making the decision to turn off the heat pump. Why do this, and why 0.25 degrees? Consider the following situation. If the heat pump is cooling, then the situation is normally that the outside temperature is above the set point temperature. If the temperature cools to the set point and you shut the heat pump down as soon as this happens, then the heat pump cannot be turned on again until it reaches the guard limit (in this situation, the set point temperature + 2.0 degrees). In the non-fuzzy case where you can only have the cooling either fully on or fully off, this makes some sense. But now that you can change the amount of cooling by controlling the vents, you want to give the system an opportunity to adjust the amount of cooling. Allowing an overshoot (or undershoot) of the set point gives the system an opportunity to find a vent opening that provides just enough cooling to match the heat that is warming the system. The 0.25 value was an initial guess, and it turned out to provide quite good behavior. A bit of experimentation might allow you to reduce it, thus keeping the guard temperature far enough away to avoid too rapid cycling from cooling to heating (you could also consider adjusting the guard temperatures or implementing a timer to make sure the heat pump does not cycle in less than some certain time).

The vent control rules used in this first fuzzy version are simple. You have two basic situations to consider: when the heat pump is cooling and when it is heating. If it is off, then it won't matter where the vents are set. So, when the heat pump is heating, you define five rules that are related to the temperature and the terms defined for the temperature. These rules should make some sense to you. This is one of the useful features of fuzzy systems; with a suitable set of concepts defined, you can often express decisions in a simple and understandable way. In pseudo-English, they look like this:

```
IF we are heating and the floor temperature is hot
THEN set the vent to fullyClosed

IF we are heating and the floor temperature is warm
Then set the vent to slightlyOpen

IF we are heating and the floor temperature is OK
THEN set the vent to halfOpen

IF we are heating and the floor temperature is cool
THEN set the vent to mostlyOpen

IF we are heating and the floor temperature is cold
THEN set the vent to fullyOpen
```

A similar set of five additional rules, not shown here, is defined for the situation where the heat pump is in a cooling state. In FuzzyJess, the code for one of the previous rules is written as follows:

```
(defrule heating-and-temp-cool
   (HeatPump (state "heating") (number ?p))
   (Thermometer (floor ?f&:(eq ?p (which-pump ?f)))
               (fuzzyReading ?t&:(fuzzy-match ?t "cool")))
   =>
   (assert
     (fuzzy-vent (floor ?f)
     (fuzzy-state (new FuzzyValue ?*ventFVar* "mostlyOpen")))))
)
```

There is just one thing left to do. In order to set the vent position, you need to define a rule that takes the combined output of all the rules and defuzzifies the result, giving the required new setting for the vent. Because the rule must wait until all the other fuzzy rules have fired, to allow Jess to combine the outputs, it is set at a lower priority (salience) than these rules. The `FuzzyValue` method `weightedAverageDefuzzify` transforms the `FuzzyValue` into a crisp value; this value is sent to the simulator to make the adjustment. This final rule is coded as follows:

```
(defrule set-vent-state
   (declare (salience -100))
   ?fv <- (fuzzy-vent (floor ?f) (fuzzy-state ?fs))
  =>
   (bind ?vent-state (?fs weightedAverageDefuzzify))
   (set-vent-state ?f ?vent-state)
   (retract ?fv))
```

When you run this example (a sample batch file is provided to help, and you will need the FuzzyJ Toolkit version 1.3 or later with FuzzyJess and Jess version 6.1 or later), it will do a very good job of controlling the system. With an outside temperature of 90 and a set point temperature of 70, the system quickly settles close to 70 degrees with each vent close to 0.5 open. If the outside temperature is set to 100, then the system again settles at a temperature close to 70.8 with the vents opened at about 0.7. With an outside temperature of 110, the system settles at a temperature near 71.3. This is quite good, in that the temperature does not fluctuate much and stays within the guard temperatures. However, the application only works extremely well (getting to 70 degrees and staying there) for a small set of conditions.

The rules do not handle a widely varying set of initial conditions, and the shape of the fuzzy sets should probably be changed to suit these situations. In particular, the definitions of hot, cold, and so on for temperature need to be adjusted for the current set point. One option would be to modify the sets according to the new set point; another would be to define the sets as a temperature difference from the set point. This option is addressed in the next example. It results in far less movement of the valves and less fluctuation of the temperature than the non-fuzzy approach.

Version 2: relative vent positions

Often, control systems use not only the difference in the value from its set point but also the rate at which the change is taking place to determine how to adjust the control parameters. In this case, this behavior means monitoring not only the temperature but also the rate of change of the temperature over time. In the first version of the fuzzy controller, you defined the terms to describe the temperature based on a fixed temperature (70 degrees). This definition causes some difficulty if you change the set point from 70 degrees. So, in this new version you'll provide a method in the Thermometer class to allow the definitions of cold, cool, OK, warm, and hot to be redefined when the set point value changes. You'll also prepare the Thermometer class to determine the rate of change of the temperature and define three fuzzy terms to describe the rate of change: *decreasing, zero,* and *increasing.* The new Thermometer class is defined in listing 16.3.

Listing 16.3 Final version of the `Thermometer` class

```
package fuzzy;
import nrc.fuzzy;

public class Thermometer extends BeanSupport
  implements Runnable {

  private Hardware m_hardware;
  private int m_floor;
  private double m_oldReading;
  private FuzzyValue m_fuzzyReading;
  private FuzzyValue m_fuzzyReadingRateOfChange;

  private static FuzzyVariable m_thermometerFV = null;
  private static FuzzyVariable m_thermometerRateOfChangeFV = null;

  static {
    try {
      m_thermometerFV = new FuzzyVariable("thermometer", 0, 120);
    } catch (InvalidFuzzyVariableNameException nameEx) {
      /* NOTHING */
    } catch (InvalidUODRangeException rangeEx) {
      /* NOTHING */
    }

    SetThermometerFVTerms(70.0);

    try {
      m_thermometerRateOfChangeFV =
        new FuzzyVariable("thermometerRateofChange", -10, 10);
    } catch (InvalidFuzzyVariableNameException nameEx) {
      /* NOTHING */
    } catch (InvalidUODRangeException rangeEx) {
      /* NOTHING */
    }

    try {
      m_thermometerRateOfChangeFV.addTerm("decreasing",
        new RFuzzySet(-0.10, 0.0, new RightLinearFunction()));
      m_thermometerRateOfChangeFV.addTerm("zero",
        new TriangleFuzzySet(-0.10, 0, 0.10));
      m_thermometerRateOfChangeFV.addTerm("increasing",
        new LFuzzySet(0.0, 0.10, new LeftLinearFunction()));
    } catch (XValuesOutOfOrderException outOfOrderEx) {
      /* NOTHING */
    } catch (XValueOutsideUODException outsideOUD) {
      /* NOTHING */
    }
  }

  public FuzzyValue getFuzzyReadingRateOfChange() {
    return m_fuzzyReadingRateOfChange;
  }
```

Set up FuzzyVariable ❶

JavaBeans property for temperature change rate ❷

```
public static void SetThermometerFVTerms( double setPoint) {
  try {
    m_thermometerFV.addTerm("cold",
      new RFuzzySet(setPoint-1.5,setPoint-1,
                    new RightLinearFunction()));
    m_thermometerFV.addTerm("cool",
      new TriangleFuzzySet(setPoint-1.5,setPoint-1,setPoint));
    m_thermometerFV.addTerm("OK",
      new TriangleFuzzySet(setPoint-1,setPoint,setPoint+1));
    m_thermometerFV.addTerm("warm",
      new TriangleFuzzySet(setPoint,setPoint+1,setPoint+1.5));
    m_thermometerFV.addTerm("hot",
      new LFuzzySet(setPoint+1,setPoint+1.5,
                    new LeftLinearFunction()));
  } catch (XValuesOutOfOrderException outOfOrderEx) {
    /* NOTHING */
  } catch (XValueOutsideUODException outsideOUD) {
    /* NOTHING */
  }
}

public void run() {
  boolean firstLoopDone = false;
  while (true) {
    double reading = getReading();
    double rateOfChange =
      firstLoopDone ? reading-m_oldReading : 0.0;
    boolean readingChanged = (reading != m_oldReading);
    m_pcs.firePropertyChange("reading",
                             new Double(m_oldReading),
                             new Double(reading));
    m_oldReading = reading;
    if (readingChanged) {
      try {
        m_fuzzyReading = new FuzzyValue(m_thermometerFV,
          new SingletonFuzzySet(reading));
      } catch (XValuesOutOfOrderException xvorder) {
        System.out.println("Error: " + xvorder); return;
      } catch (XValueOutsideUODException xvuod) {
        System.out.println("Error: " + xvuod); return;
      }
      m_pcs.firePropertyChange("fuzzyReading",
                               null, m_fuzzyReading);
    }
    try {
      m_fuzzyReadingRateOfChange =
        new FuzzyValue(m_thermometerRateOfChangeFV,
          new SingletonFuzzySet(rateOfChange));
    } catch (XValuesOutOfOrderException xvorder) {
      System.out.println("Error: " + xvorder); return;
    } catch (XValueOutsideUODException xvuod) {
```

Method to move temperature set point ③

Update variable representing rate of temperature change ④

```
        System.out.println("Error: " + xvuod); return;
    }
    m_pcs.firePropertyChange("fuzzyReadingRateOfChange",null,
                        m_fuzzyReadingRateOfChange);

    firstLoopDone = true;

    try {
      Thread.sleep(1000);
    } catch (InterruptedException ie) {
      return;
    }
  }
 }
}
```

❶ The code sets up a FuzzyVariable to represent the rate of change of temperature readings, with the three values decreasing, increasing, and zero.

❷ You make the temperature change-rate variable available as a JavaBeans property.

❸ This new method lets you move the temperature set point and redefine the temperature FuzzySet.

❹ Each time through the loop, you update the variable that represents the rate of temperature change.

You also need to change the way in which you set the vent position. Instead of trying to set an absolute value for the valve position, you'll determine how much to change the valve position from its current position. To do so, you define the seven terms NB, NM, NS, Z, PS, PM, and PB, representing a Negative Big change, a Negative Medium change, a Negative Small change, a Zero change, a Positive Small change, and so on. The final changes to the Vent class are shown in listing 16.4; the new fuzzy variable represents the magnitude of the desired change to the vent position.

Listing 16.4   Final modifications to the Vent class

```
package fuzzy;
import nrc.fuzzy.*;

public class Vent extends BeanSupport {
  private Hardware m_hardware;
  private int m_floor;
  private static FuzzyVariable m_ventChangeFV = null;

  static {
    try {
      m_ventChangeFV = new FuzzyVariable("ventChange", -1, 1);
    } catch (InvalidFuzzyVariableNameException nameEx) {
```

```
      /* NOTHING */
    } catch (InvalidUODRangeException rangeEx) {
      /* NOTHING */
    }

    try {
      m_ventChangeFV.addTerm("NB", new SingletonFuzzySet(-0.3));
      m_ventChangeFV.addTerm("NM", new SingletonFuzzySet(-0.15));
      m_ventChangeFV.addTerm("NS", new SingletonFuzzySet(-0.06));
      m_ventChangeFV.addTerm("Z",  new SingletonFuzzySet(0.0));
      m_ventChangeFV.addTerm("PS", new SingletonFuzzySet(0.06));
      m_ventChangeFV.addTerm("PM", new SingletonFuzzySet(0.15));
      m_ventChangeFV.addTerm("PB", new SingletonFuzzySet(0.3));
    } catch (XValuesOutOfOrderException outOfOrderEx) {
      /* NOTHING */
    } catch (XValueOutsideUODException outsideOUD) {
      /* NOTHING */
    }
  }

  public Vent(Hardware hw, int floor) {
    m_hardware = hw;
    m_floor = floor;
  }

  ...
}
```

The rules for controlling the heat pump are the same as in the first fuzzy control example. The rules to change the state of the vents now depend on the state of the heat pump, the temperature on the floor, and the rate of change of the temperature. You can build a pair of truth tables to show the correct vent changes for a temperature and rate of change. Table 16.4 shows for the situation when the heat pump is cooling; the table for the heating situation is similar.

Table 16.4 The recommended change to a vent for a given temperature and rate of temperature change

	Cold	Cool	OK	Warm	Hot
Decreasing	NB	NM	NS	Z	PS
Zero	NM	**NS**	Z	PS	PM
Increasing	NS	Z	PS	PM	PB

The highlighted value NS in the middle row of the second column of table 16.4 represents this pseudo-English rule:

```
If the heat pump is cooling
and the temperature is cool
and the rate of change of temperature is zero
Then adjust the vent position by a negative small amount
```

In Jess, you can write this rule like so:

```
(defrule cooling-and-temp-cool-rate-zero
    (HeatPump (state "cooling") (number ?p))
    (Thermometer
        (floor ?f&:(eq ?p (which-pump ?f)))
        (fuzzyReading ?t&:(fuzzy-match ?t "cool"))
        (fuzzyReadingRateOfChange ?tr&:(fuzzy-match ?tr "zero")))
    =>
    (assert (fuzzy-vent (floor ?f)
            (fuzzy-change-state (new FuzzyValue ?*ventFVar* "NS")))))
```

There will be one rule like this for each cell in table 16.4. Now you have 30 rules that determine how the vent should be changed. You might need to think about these rules to see if they make sense to you; but with a bit of analysis of the various situations, the rules should be similar to what your intuition would lead you to. As in the last example, a single rule is defined with a lower priority so that it may take the combined output of all the rules and defuzzify the result, giving the required change for the vent. This rule in this second fuzzy controller is as follows:

```
(defrule perform-vent-change
    (declare (salience -100))
    ?fv <- (fuzzy-vent (floor ?f) (fuzzy-change-state ?fs))
    =>
    (bind ?vent-change-amount (?fs weightedAverageDefuzzify))
    (change-vent-state ?f ?vent-change-amount)
    (retract ?fv))
```

The only other major change is to the `WriteVent` class and the `Simulator` class to support the ability to change the vent state by the specified amount. The function `change-vent-state` is a `Userfunction` defined in `WriteVent.java`; it in turn calls the simulator to calculate the new position for the vent and set it to that value. You also modify the `init-simulator` function to allow you to specify the initial temperature set-point value.

This fuzzy controller behaves very well at all realistic outside temperatures and keeps the temperature extremely close to the set point. As you can guess, getting the right fuzzy values and the right rules can be complicated. Should you have defined more fuzzy values for the rate of change? Should the shape and position of the fuzzy set be adjusted to get the best performance (moves quickly to the set point, reduces overshoot of the set point, and so forth)? A large body of work is devoted to determining these fuzzy control parameters and how they should change as the system changes dynamically. Yet, with a little common sense and the tools to describe your thoughts in an English-like manner, you have been able to construct a system that is robust to changes in outside temperature and set point and does an adequate job of keeping the temperature in a comfortable zone.

16.6.3 *Exploring the fuzzy controller*

You might want to modify the second fuzzy controller to allow the set point as well as the outside temperature to be changed in the user interface. Doing so should be relatively simple, because the required hooks are already included in the code (the method `SetThermometerFVTerms` in the `Thermometer` class).

You could make a number of other explorations:

- Would defining more terms for the temperature's rate of change improve the control? What would the new set of rules look like?

- How do the shape and position of the fuzzy sets you have used affect the control? Change them and explore. Perhaps you can devise some techniques to determine the "best" definitions for these fuzzy sets. You did not use the outside temperature in any of your reasoning—perhaps it would be useful in dynamically modifying the sets to get better control.

- When the system reaches a controlled state, the valve positions are still being modified at each cycle (perhaps by small amounts). Can you think of some techniques to stop moving the valves when you are "close enough" to the set point?

- Could you make the simulation itself more realistic? For example, when the heat pump is heating and all valves are fully open, x units of heat are delivered to each floor. When one of the valves is closed, the others still get x units of heat. A real system would not work this way; closing off one floor would increase the heat flow to the others. How could the system be modified to better implement what might actually happen? Would the control logic have to be altered to accommodate this change?

This has been a brief introduction to fuzzy systems, and the simulation is much simplified from the real world. However, I hope it has piqued your interest in the topic and that you will want to learn more and apply the techniques to your own applications.

16.7 *What's next?*

Now that you have built the HVAC Control system, you may have decided that it's overkill. After all, mechanical thermostats do a perfectly good job of controlling the temperature of most houses, and many larger buildings, too. The beauty of the rule-based controller is that it is easily extensible to cover many complicated situations. Do you want the set point to be lower on winter weekends and higher on summer weekends? Should the temperature be lower (or higher) at night to save energy, or should the system simply be turned off in the temperate spring and autumn? It would be easy to add a fancy rule-based timer to the program; a `Date` JavaBean that broadcasts regular time and date updates would be all the infrastructure you would need. Rules to change the set point based on the date and time would then be trivial.

Would you like the occupants of the building to be able to set the temperature of their own floor? Again, the modifications would be simple. You might use `(set-point)` facts instead of a single `defglobal` to track the separate set points, and modify the rules to match these facts instead of referencing `?*set-point*`.

Although a rule-based solution to this control problem may seem more complex than traditional alternatives, the complexity is accompanied by greatly increased features and flexibility.

16.8 Summary

In part 5 of this book, you've written a powerful system capable of controlling the heating, ventilation, and air-conditioning systems in a large office building. For the first time, you wrote an application that integrates code written in Java with code written in the Jess language.

You wrote a simulator to model the hardware your application is intended to control. The simulator runs in its own thread. You wrote JavaBeans and used them as working memory elements, and each Bean also includes its own thread for polling the state of the hardware device it stands in for. You saw how Jess works well in this multithreaded environment.

You learned how to extend the Jess language by writing `Userfunctions` and `Userpackages`. Many people have written Jess extensions and then made them publicly available. Examples include extensions for working with databases, with XML, and with fuzzy logic. See the Jess web site for details on obtaining these and other Jess extensions.

You developed several different sets of control rules: one conventional set, and one using fuzzy rules. The fuzzy rules, although more complex, controlled the temperature more tightly.

Although much of the HVAC Controller system application was written in Java, the main application code is written as a Jess script and runs with `jess.Main`. In the next part of this book, you'll integrate rules into a web-based application where Jess will run as part of a Java servlet. You won't use the `jess.Main` class, and so you'll need to learn how to embed the Jess rule engine into another application.

## Part 6

TekMart.com: rule-based applications for the Web

Given the ability of rule engines to cope with incomplete information and unpredictable events, rules and the World Wide Web are a perfect match. Rule-based systems are a part of most major web sites, where they are used for order processing, user preferences, data mining, and recommendations. In part 6, you'll develop a *Recommendations Agent* as part of an e-commerce web site based on servlets and JavaServer Pages.

Whereas in each of the previous applications you ran Jess as a free-standing application, in this case, you'll use Jess as a library embedded in the Tomcat servlet engine. Therefore, you need to learn more about Jess's Java APIs. In addition, the rules you'll write for this application will be the longest you've written so far—in fact, they approach the size of the rule that solved Mrs. Rosencrantz's word problem in chapter 1.

Jess on the Web

## 17

In this chapter you'll...

- Look at alternative Java web architectures
- Collect knowledge for a smart e-commerce application
- Write rules and queries for a web application

A sizeable and still-growing fraction of all software written today is deployed on intranets or the Internet. The rise of electronic commerce, enterprise applications, and web-based entertainment is a visible indicator of this trend.

Rule-based systems are commonly used in web-based applications. A Java rule engine can run on a client machine (as an applet) or, more commonly, on the server (in a J2EE application server). Rules can be used for order configuration, inventory management, human resources, manufacturing resource planning, games, and more.

In part 6 of this book, you'll develop a Recommendations Agent for an online store. The Recommendations Agent will look at the items a customer is buying and has bought in the past, and make recommendations for additional purchases. In this chapter, we'll look at an overview of web architectures and then develop the data structures and rules for the agent. In chapter 18, you'll learn how to embed Jess as a library in a larger application, and we'll study techniques for interacting with Jess through its Java API. In chapter 19, you'll package the Recommendations Agent as a web application deployed in a standard J2EE container. The application will be built from servlets and JavaServer Pages (see section 17.1.2 for definitions). You'll build a complete e-commerce web site in miniature to serve as an example platform for the Recommendations Agent, although you'll leave out the bits that are entirely unrelated to the agent (such as credit-card validation).

17.1 Java architectures for the Web

There are many different ways to deploy applications on the Web. (In this part of this book, I'll use the phrase *the Web* to refer to applications that use the HTTP and HTTPS protocols, either over corporate intranets or over the Internet as a whole.) In fact, new methods are being developed all the time, and many of these methods blur the traditional categories, making it hard to use any absolute terms to describe what is possible on the Web. For our purposes, though, web-based software can be divided into two broad categories: *fat-client* and *thin-client* applications.

17.1.1 Fat-client applications

A *fat-client* web application is most similar to a traditional client-server application: The code is divided more or less equally between a *client* (desktop) machine and a *server* (remote) machine. Fat-client solutions can automatically download and install the client software to the desktop machine, or they may use fixed clients (desktop applications) installed using physical media or manual network downloads. The client software might include an elaborate graphical interface, as well as some fraction of the business logic for the application.

There are two ways to build Java-based fat-client solutions that can be automatically downloaded to the client: using an applet or using Java Web Start.

Applets

The Java Applet API was included in the first release of the Java Developer's Kit (JDK). A Java *applet* is just a class that extends `java.applet.Applet` and provides implementations for one or more of the `Applet` methods `init`, `start`, `stop`, and `destroy`. These methods are called at well-defined times by the Java environment that hosts the applet—invariably a web browser.

Writing applets that can work effectively inside a browser can be challenging, because the user can browse away from the page containing an applet at any time, only to return later. An applet may or may not be destroyed during this time, and on returning to the original page the user may find a new instance of the applet. This lifecycle issue makes maintaining a consistent user session difficult.

To compound the problem, web browsers vary widely in their level of Java support. The major browsers include very old JVMs as standard equipment; in fact, some Internet Explorer users have no JVM installed. JavaSoft offers a Java Plug-in that provides a standard Java environment for browsers that use Netscape-style plug-ins, and targeting this platform can be a good solution, especially on an intranet. But the Java Plug-in is a large download, and many Internet users won't have it and won't want to download it. Dealing with the JVM support issue is the biggest obstacle to deploying substantial applets.

Jess supplies a simple example applet in the `jess.ConsoleApplet` class. `ConsoleApplet` presents the same GUI as `jess.Console`, so it's useful only in limited situations—applications that involve interview-style interaction with a user.

Java Web Start

The Java Web Start system lets a client click a link on a web page to download and automatically install what amounts to a normal desktop application written in Java. Java Web Start applications don't have the same kind of lifecycle problems that applets do; they can be launched, used, and exited like a normal application. Java Web Start is relatively new but is rapidly gaining acceptance. Like applets, Java Web Start applications rely on users having a properly configured JVM on their desktop. Again, it's easier to make this assumption on an intranet than on the Internet.

Pros and cons of fat clients

Fat-client architectures have both advantages and (mostly) disadvantages. The advantages are as follows:

- Little processing power is required on the server, because much of the code executes on the client.

- The programmer has maximum control over user interface, because it can be written using all of Java's APIs.

These are the disadvantages:

- It's hard to write complex client software that will work in a wide range of desktop environments.

- Downloading the client software may be intolerably slow for many users, especially on the Internet.

- If the client software is installed persistently on the desktop, backward compatibility becomes an issue; forcing all users to update software can be difficult.

The first disadvantage is enough of a problem that fat-client architectures are not used very often. This problem is most acute for applets, because web browser behavior varies widely between brands, or even between releases of a single browser. The Java Plug-in was designed to mitigate this problem, but getting potential users to install this hefty download is still an issue, especially on the Internet.

17.1.2 *Thin-client applications*

In a *thin-client* architecture, most of the application-specific code runs on the server. A web-based thin client is usually just HTML in a browser. There are many ways to write thin-client web applications in Java. Although I will describe them here one by one, they are often used in combination.

Servlets

Servlets, the server-side analogue of applets, are small modules that a web server or other container invokes in response to browser requests. Just as an applet is a subclass of `java.applet.Applet`, a servlet is an implementation of the `javax.servlet.Servlet` interface, or most commonly a subclass of the class `javax.servlet.http.HttpServlet`. Whereas applets run inside a browser on the user's desktop, servlets run in a *container* on a server machine. The Java 2 Enterprise Edition (J2EE) is a standard for deploying applications on a server; it includes, among other things, a servlet container.

The `HttpServlet` class includes methods you can override to process client requests that come in over the Web. It also provides methods the container invokes to initialize and destroy the servlet. You'll develop several servlets in chapter 19.

JavaServer Pages

Another way to deploy server-side Java applications is via *JavaServer Pages* (JSPs). A JSP is an HTML page with embedded Java code. In a way, a JSP is an inside-out version of a servlet: A servlet is Java code that often includes statements that print HTML. JSPs are compiled by a special program on the web server, generally into servlets, and then executed in response to browser requests. Whereas servlets are ideal when a server-side component needs to do a nontrivial amount of work and produce only a small amount of HTML, JSPs are perfect when a large HTML page needs to embed a small amount of computed information. Servlets and JSPs are often used together, with the JSPs providing the interface and the servlets providing the logic.[1] You'll use JSPs to provide the user interface for the Recommendations Agent in chapter 19.

Perhaps the best thing about JSPs is that they can be written in a regular HTML editor. Servlets must be written by experienced Java programmers, but JSPs can be written by web designers, perhaps with the use of some boilerplate provided by a Java guru. It's difficult to maintain a web page created by a servlet using a series of `println` calls, especially for a nonprogrammer, but maintaining a JSP-based site is not very different than maintaining a site built from static HTML pages.

Web services

Servlets and JSPs are designed to deliver HTML interfaces to human users. *Web services*, on the other hand, are designed to provide an interface that other software can use. The term *web service* generally refers to an application that can be sent commands using XML-based Simple Object Access Protocol (SOAP) messages. Web services can be used to build web applications with regular user interfaces, but they are also used as components of larger software systems.

Deploying an application as a web service lets people and companies around the world interact with it. For example, if company A deploys its order-configuration application as a web service, then company B's purchasing department can develop software to automatically purchase A's product. JavaSoft offers the Java Web Services Development Pack (JWSDP), an add-on for the J2EE application server, as a platform for web-service development.

---

[1] Bruce A. Tate, *Bitter Java* (Greenwich, CT: Manning, 2002).

Pros and cons of thin clients

Thin-client architectures have both good and bad points. The advantages are as follows:

- Little processing power is required on the client, because much of the code executes on the server.
- There are few or no client configuration problems. Few requirements are placed on the client, so compatibility isn't usually an issue.
- Upgrades are easy, because they happen at the server.

Here are the disadvantages:

- HTML user interfaces are not as interactive as Java GUIs. JavaScript can help, but at the cost of reintroducing potential compatibility problems.
- Powerful servers may be needed to meet demand.

Because the configuration and maintenance issues are much simpler, thin-client architectures are usually the preferred way to deploy an application on the Web. In chapter 19, you will develop the Recommendations Agent using a thin-client architecture.

17.2 *A Jess application for the Web*

One of the first and most famous rule-based applications was Digital Equipment Corporation's XCON order configuration system (see section 1.2.2). XCON helped sales consultants configure orders for DEC mainframe computers, making sure the order included all the accessories the customer needed.

The grandchildren of XCON are now on display all over the Web. Every web site that helps you select compatible options when you buy a computer online owes an obvious tip of the hat to XCON. Not quite so obvious, perhaps, are sites that recommend additional purchases the way a good sales clerk might ("This top would look cute with those pants!").

Rule-based order configuration and recommendation systems are common today. In this chapter and the next two, you'll build a system that combines both of these tasks: It will recommend items the customer probably needs, as well as items it thinks the customer might just enjoy.

17.3 *Knowledge engineering*

You're going to write a fairly general system to look at what a customer is ordering and suggest other things they might want to buy. Two kinds of "experts" might have knowledge you could add to such a system: technical folks and marketing folks. The technical knowledge will let the system tell the customer how to assemble a working system from individual components. The marketing knowledge can be used to try to convince the customer to buy more stuff.

For the current system, you'll base technical recommendations on the concept of *categories*. Every product will belong to one category; to use it, products from other categories may be required or desirable. For instance, the product Univac 2000 belongs to the category *computer*; to use it, you might need a video monitor (category *monitor*), because the monitor is not included. A monitor is therefore a *requirement* for computer customers. If the user of your system buys a Univac 2000, the system should recommend that she buy a monitor, too. Other accessories might also be nice: speakers and software, for example. These should also be recommended, and for the purposes of this system, you'll also call them *requirements*.

The marketing-derived rules that you'll include will be designed to help sell videotapes and video discs (DVDs). Assume that the marketing folks have identified four opportunities in this area:

- If a customer is buying a VCR or DVD player, recommend the appropriate media.
- If a customer has bought a VCR or DVD player on a previous visit, recommend more media for it.
- If a customer is buying a videotape or DVD, recommend another one.
- If a customer has bought a videotape or DVD in the past, recommend another one.

In every case, you should keep track of previous purchases, so you don't recommend a videotape or DVD the customer has already bought from you.

17.4 *Designing data structures*

After talking with the experts, you find that the important entities in the system include the following:

- *Products*—Things that are for sale
- *Customers*—Current and past users of the system
- *Orders*—Current and past customer purchases
- *Line items*—A collection of items that form an order
- *Recommendations*—What the system produces as output

You can define a `deftemplate` for each item in this list. The `product` template should include slots for the name, catalog number, and price of the product, of course. It also should include a slot to specify the category the product belongs to and the categories of other products required by this product:

```
(deftemplate product
    (slot name)
    (slot category)
    (slot part-number)
    (slot price)
    (multislot requires))
```

For example, a product named TekMart 19 TV might have the `category tv`, and the `requires` slot could contain `batteries` (for the remote control).

A customer is just a person with a name, address, and customer ID:

```
(deftemplate customer
    (multislot name)
    (multislot address)
    (slot customer-id))
```

An order is a collection of line items. Each line item knows which order it belongs to, what product is being ordered, and in what quantity. Although it's not strictly necessary, you'll find later that including the customer ID in each line item simplifies your rules considerably:

```
(deftemplate order
    (slot customer-id)
    (slot order-number))

(deftemplate line-item
    (slot order-number)
    (slot part-number)
    (slot customer-id)
    (slot quantity (default 1)))
```

Finally, recommendations link an order to a recommended product. The `because` multislot lists other products that triggered this recommendation, and the `type` slot distinguishes between product requirements (XCON's kind of recommendations) and marketing recommendations:

```
(deftemplate recommend
    (slot order-number)
    (multislot because)
    (slot type)
    (slot part-number))
```

With these basic data structures put together, you're ready to begin writing the rules for the order-configuration system.

17.5   *Writing the rules*

The rules you will write in this chapter examine facts and assert recommendations, but they won't display anything or otherwise interact with a user. You'll write the user interfaces for the web-based applications in HTML as JSPs, and you won't do that until chapter 19. For now, to see the effects of the rules you write, you'll have to use debugging commands like (watch) and (facts) (you learned about these in section 6.1.1).

As you write these rules, remember that Jess will be simultaneously processing many line items, belonging to many orders, placed by many different customers. There's nothing wrong with this scenario, and Jess will handle it very well. However, it will be important to make sure that all the rules identify the specific customer and order they are processing—that is, you can't accidentally recommend products one customer might like to some second unrelated customer. It will be easy to do this, but it is important to keep in mind.

17.5.1   *About testing*

The rules you're about to write will eventually be embedded in a web application. When they are, they won't have any command-line or GUI access, so it will be hard to debug them at that point. Therefore, it's important to test these rules as you write them. You can put some product, order, and line-item facts in a separate file, and load them using load-facts when you need to use them as test cases. Try to design test facts to probe each individual rule, and think about what the correct results should be before you run a test. For example, imagine you've written a rule like this one:

```
(defrule recommend-rubber-duck
    (customer (customer-id ?id))
    (not (and (order (order-number ?order) (customer-id ?id))
              (line-item (order-number ?order) (part-number ?part))
              (product (part-number ?part) (name "Rubber duck"))))
    =>
    (assert (recommend (order-number ?order) (part-number ?part))))
```

This rule says, "If there's a customer, and they've never bought a rubber duck from us, then recommend that they do so." To test this rule, you need several sets of facts: one set with a customer who has bought a rubber duck and another set with a customer who has not. You may also want to test a customer who has bought multiple rubber ducks. You should also test using customers who have placed multiple orders in the past, and customers who are new to the web site—both duck-buying customers and duckless ones.

17.5.2 *The recommend-requirements rule*

Perhaps the most important rule in the Recommendations Agent is the one that creates recommendations for products that are explicitly required by other products (like the batteries for the television set, mentioned earlier). Because you're interested in using the Recommendations Agent to maximize revenue, you won't recommend just *any* batteries for the television set: You'll recommend the *most expensive* package in the catalog. This rule is the longest one you've written, so let's break it down a little at a time:

The first two patterns match an order such that no other order with the same `customer-id` has a higher `order-number`—that is, it matches only the current order for any given customer.

```
(defrule recommend-requirements
    (order (customer-id ?id) (order-number ?currentOrder))
    (not (order (customer-id ?id)
                (order-number ?order2&:(> ?order2 ?currentOrder))))
```

The next pattern matches a line item in this customer's current order. The pattern after that matches the product represented by this line item, but only if that product requires some other category of product. This second pattern therefore identifies a case where you can make a recommendation:

```
(line-item (order-number ?currentOrder) (part-number ?part))
(product (part-number ?part) (name ?product)
        (requires $? ?category $?))
```

The fifth, positive pattern matches some other product, belonging to the category required by the first product. The sixth, negated pattern matches another product in this category that costs more than the first. Because it's negated, it means there's no such product—these two patterns together identify the most expensive product you could recommend:

```
(product (category ?category) (price ?price)
            (part-number ?second-part))
(not (product (category ?category) (price ?p&:(> ?p ?price))))
```

Now that you've identified the product to recommend, you can assert a recommend fact for it:

```
=>

(assert (recommend (order-number ?currentOrder)
                (type requirement)
                (part-number ?second-part)
                (because ?product))))
```

This one long rule will be a workhorse in your system.

17.5.3 *Recommending videos and DVDs*

You'll recall that the folks in marketing are interested in selling customers some extra videotapes and DVDs. There are four situations in which you should recommend some kind of media: when the customer is buying, or has bought in the past, a VCR or DVD player; and when the customer is buying, or has bought in the past, a videotape or DVD. You can handle the first case—recommending a tape or disk to go with a new player—by adding the appropriate category to the `requires` multislot of each player in the catalog. The other three cases require adding specific rules. First, let's look at the rule that recommends new media to anyone who has ever bought a player in the past:

```
(defrule recommend-media-for-player
    "If customer has bought a VCR or DVD player in the
    past, recommend some media for it."
    (product (part-number ?media) (category ?c&dvd-disk|videotape))

    (product (name ?name) (part-number ?player)
             (category =(if (eq ?c dvd-disk) then dvd else vcr)))
```

The first pattern matches any DVD or videotape, and the second pattern matches all the players that can play it. These two patterns include some fancy matching: The first pattern uses the | (or) connective constraint to match either `dvd-disk` or `videotape` in the `category` slot. The second pattern uses the = return value constraint and a conditional expression to select a value for the `category` slot that goes with the media category: `vcr` for `videotape` and `dvd` for `dvd-disk`.

We've deliberately put these two patterns at the beginning of this rule, because they match only things from the catalog and therefore will never change while the program is running. It's generally good to put the patterns that match fixed, unchanging facts at the top of a rule, so they won't need to be evaluated more than once. In general, ordering patterns is a balancing act, with at least three important, interacting factors:

- *Clarity*—You wrote the patterns in a rule in a specific order because that's the way they made sense.

- *Performance*—You certainly want to avoid doing repetitive work; ordering patterns to put the static ones at the top of the rule, as you've done here, helps you achieve this goal.

- *Memory use*—If you put patterns that match fewer facts toward the beginning of a rule, you'll reduce the number of partial matches and limit memory consumption.

Often, these three considerations conflict, and you have to make a judgment call. In this chapter, I've ordered the patterns placing the most emphasis on readability. In general, this is a good idea at first; you can always go back and reorder the patterns to increase performance and reduce memory usage later, if it turns out to be necessary.

The following three patterns identify a customer who has bought a player in the past and is placing a new order. The `line-item` pattern identifies a purchase of a player matched in the first part of the rule. The next two patterns identify the customer whose past order contained that line item, and who is placing a new order:

```
(line-item (customer-id ?id) (order-number ?order1)
           (part-number ?player))
(order (customer-id ?id)
       (order-number ?currentOrder&:(> ?currentOrder ?order1)))
(not (order (customer-id ?id)
            (order-number ?order3&:(> ?order3 ?currentOrder))))
```

The last two patterns narrow the matches a bit. The first pattern eliminates videotapes or DVDs the customer has purchased or is currently purchasing, and the final pattern ensures that you only recommend one videotape or one DVD per order:

```
(not (line-item (customer-id ?id) (part-number ?media)))
(not (recommend (order-number ?currentOrder)
                (type =(sym-cat discretionary- ?c))))
```

In the previous section, all the recommendations were of type `requirement`. The recommendations you're creating here are `discretionary-videotape` and `discretionary-dvd-disk`. Other parts of the system will therefore be able to tell the difference between true requirements and mere sales pitches. You compose the correct category name using the `sym-cat` function.

Finally, if all the patterns match, you've identified a videotape you can recommend to the customer:

```
=>
(assert (recommend (order-number ?currentOrder)
                   (because ?name)
                   (part-number ?media)
                   (type =(sym-cat discretionary- ?c)))))
```

This rule simply asserts a `recommend` fact, as `recommend-requirements` did, and leaves it up to other software to communicate with the user.

17.5.4 *Conspicuous consumption*

If one DVD or videotape is good, more must be even better. The rule `recommend-more-media` asks the customer if they'd like to buy a second videotape or DVD whenever they pick one out themselves. Although this version of the Recommendations Agent doesn't do it, a more fleshed-out version could offer a discount on purchases of multiples ("Buy one, get a second for half price!").

These first three patterns identify all pairs of videotapes and DVDs; the third pattern ensures that you consider only pairs of two different items:

```
(defrule recommend-more-media
    "If customer buys a disk or tape, recommend a random
    other item of the same category."
    ?p1 <- (product (part-number ?part1)
                    (category ?c&dvd-disk|videotape) (name ?name))
    ?p2 <- (product (part-number ?part2) (category ?c))
    (test (neq ?p1 ?p2))
```

The `test` pattern compares the `fact-ids` of the matched facts for inequality; this is a common idiom in Jess.

The `line-item` pattern identifies orders that include one member of a pair of media, and then the negated pattern eliminates orders that already include a discretionary media recommendation for this media type:

```
(line-item (order-number ?order) (part-number ?part1))
(not (recommend (order-number ?order)
                (type =(sym-cat discretionary- ?c))))
```

Because the customer is buying the first member of a pair of items, this rule recommends the second member:

```
    =>

    (assert (recommend (order-number ?order)
                       (because ?name)
                       (part-number ?part2)
                       (type =(sym-cat discretionary- ?c)))))
```

17.5.5 *More media rules*

There's one more marketing rule you haven't written yet: the rule `recommend-same-type-of-media`, which tries to get a past media customer to buy more media on every return visit. It's really just a combination of `recommend-more-media` and `recommend-media-for-player`, so I'll present it here without any narration:

```
(defrule recommend-same-type-of-media
    "If customer has bought a disk or tape in the past,
    recommend a random other item of the same category."
    ;; There are two recordings of the same type
    ?p1 <- (product (part-number ?part1)
                    (category ?c&dvd-disk|videotape) (name ?name))
    ?p2 <- (product (part-number ?part2) (category ?c))
    (test (neq ?p1 ?p2))
```

```
;; This customer has bought one of them in a past order
(line-item (customer-id ?id)
           (order-number ?order1) (part-number ?part1))
(order (customer-id ?id)
       (order-number ?currentOrder&:(> ?currentOrder ?order1)))
(not (order (customer-id ?id)
     (order-number ?order3&:(> ?order3 ?currentOrder))))

;; But not the other
(not (line-item (customer-id ?id) (part-number ?part2)))

;; and we haven't recommended any media of this type yet
(not (recommend (order-number ?currentOrder)
                (type =(sym-cat discretionary- ?c))))
=>

;; Recommend the other one.
(assert (recommend (order-number ?currentOrder)
                   (because ?name)
                   (part-number ?part2)
                   (type =(sym-cat discretionary- ?c)))))
```

17.6 *Refining the recommendations*

The rules you've written so far can sometimes generate multiple recommendations for the same product. You could complicate all the previous rules such that they won't generate the duplicate recommendations, or you could simply allow them to be created and then clean them up at the end. I've chosen to take the latter route. A single rule `coalesce-recommendations` combines multiple recommendations for the same product:

```
(defrule coalesce-recommendations
    "If there are multiple recommendations for the same product,
    coalesce them."
    ?r1 <- (recommend (order-number ?order) (type ?type)
                      (because ?product) (part-number ?part))
    ?r2 <- (recommend (order-number ?order) (part-number ?part)
                      (because $?products&
                               :(not (member$
                                          ?product
                                          $?products))))
    =>
    (retract ?r1 ?r2)
    (assert (recommend (order-number ?order) (type ?type)
                       (because (create$ ?product $?products))
                       (part-number ?part))))
```

The rule `recommend-requirements` can generate another kind of invalid recommendation: It may recommend a product as a requirement even though the customer is already buying another product in that same category. If the customer is buying cheap batteries, it would be pointless to recommend the expensive ones. Again, you could complicate the original rule to account for this situation, or you could write a cleanup rule. The rule `remove-satisfied-recommendations` retracts recommendations that are satisfied by other purchases in the same order:

```
(defrule remove-satisfied-recommendations
    "If there are two products in the same category, and
    one is part of an order, and there is a recommendation
    of type 'requirement' for the other part, then remove
    the recommendation, as the customer is
    already buying something in that category."
    (product (part-number ?part1) (category ?category))
    (product (part-number ?part2) (category ?category))
    (line-item (order-number ?order) (part-number ?part2))
    ?r <- (recommend (order-number ?order)
                     (part-number ?part1) (type requirement))
    =>
    (retract ?r))
```

You're finished writing the rules for the Recommendations Agent. Recall that you're going to integrate these rules into a web application, and that the web application will need access to the list of items in the current order, the list of recommendations, and the list of products in the catalog. The web application can use *queries* to get access to this information. In the next section, you'll write some queries for the web application to call.

17.7 *Some useful queries*

Queries let you efficiently access specified elements in Jess's working memory. In this way, they turn Jess into a relational database—albeit a slightly strange one that doesn't use SQL. When you build your web application, you won't use a traditional database: You'll use Jess to store all the application data, instead.

Recall from section 7.7 that a `defquery` is like a rule without a right-hand side. It includes a set of patterns that match facts the same way a rule's patterns do. The difference is that a rule is matched automatically, whereas a query is triggered by calling the function `run-query`. This function returns a `java.util.Iterator` that represents the list of matches for the query's patterns. The query `all-products` is the simplest possible example; it matches every product in the catalog:

```
(defquery all-products
    (product))
```

The web application will be able to get a list of all the products in the catalog by calling the Jess function `(run-query all-products)`. You'll need this to build an order form.

Queries can also contain a *variables declaration*. The variables declaration lists the arguments to the query. The arguments you supply to the run-query function are bound to the variables of the same names in the patterns, so you can specify at runtime the specific values the query's patterns should match. A query to list all the items in an order is a good example: It should take one argument, ?order, which specifies the order number of interest:

```
(defquery items-for-order
    (declare (variables ?order))
    (line-item (order-number ?order) (part-number ?part))
    (product (part-number ?part)))
```

Each match returned by this query will contain an item-number fact and the associated product fact. You'd need this information to compute an order total, print a shipping list, and so on. The recommendations-for-order query is similar:

```
(defquery recommendations-for-order
    (declare (variables ?order))
    (recommend (order-number ?order) (part-number ?part))
    (product (part-number ?part)))
```

This query lists all the recommendations associated with a given order. In this query and the last one, ?part is an *internal variable*: an undeclared variable used only to perform matching within the patterns of the query.

17.7.1 *Maintaining the order number*

The web application you're going to build needs to give each order a unique number. Traditionally, this task is handled using a stored procedure in a database: A tiny database table holds a single number, and a stored procedure increments the value in the table and returns it. Using a database makes this process safe for multiple concurrent instances of the web application; the database allows only one instance at a time to be updating the order number. In this application, you'll use the same technique, implemented in Jess using a deftemplate with a single slot to represent the tiny table, and a deffunction instead of a stored procedure. Jess will automatically supply the concurrency control (as you'll see in the next chapter). Here's the deftemplate:

```
(deftemplate next-order-number
    (slot value))
```

Here's a query to retrieve the single fact you expect to be using this template:

```
(defquery order-number
    (next-order-number))
```

And finally, here's a `deffunction` to return the next order number. If there's no next-order-number fact, this function creates one and returns the lowest possible order number (which you've arbitrarily specified as 1001). If there is such a fact, this function increments the value, modifies the fact, and returns the unincremented order number. `get-new-order-number` uses the `order-number` query to get hold of the fact it needs:

```
(deffunction get-new-order-number ()
    (bind ?it (run-query order-number))
    (if (not (?it hasNext)) then
        (assert (next-order-number (value 1002)))
        (return 1001)
    else
        (bind ?token (?it next))
        (bind ?fact (?token fact 1))
        (bind ?number (?fact getSlotValue value))
        (modify ?fact (value (+ ?number 1)))
        (return ?number)))
```

Before we move on to writing the Java code for the Recommendations Agent, you need to assemble one more chunk of Jess code: a module dedicated to initializing new orders.

17.8 *Cleaning up*

Web users are notoriously unpredictable. They'll click Stop to cancel transactions; they'll click Back right in the middle of a series of screens. As a result, your web application needs a way to reinitialize an order that's been partially filled out. Removing all the `line-items`, all the `recommends`, and the `order` fact from working memory should do it, because the web application will be able to reassert these facts based on other state information. You can use a `defmodule` containing a few auto-focus rules to do the cleanup (see section 7.6 for information about modules). Asserting the fact `(clean-up-order ?order)` will then clean up the order number `?order`:

```
(defmodule CLEANUP)

(defrule CLEANUP::initialize-order-1
    (declare (auto-focus TRUE))
    (MAIN::initialize-order ?number)
    ?item <- (line-item (order-number ?number))
    =>
    (retract ?item))

(defrule CLEANUP::initialize-order-2
    (declare (auto-focus TRUE))
```

```
            (MAIN::initialize-order ?number)
            ?rec <- (recommend (order-number ?number))
            =>
            (retract ?rec))
    (defrule CLEANUP::initialize-order-3
        (declare (auto-focus TRUE))
        ?init <- (MAIN::initialize-order ?number)
        (not (line-item (order-number ?number)))
        (not (recommend (order-number ?number)))
        =>
        (retract ?init))
    (defrule CLEANUP::clean-up-order
        (declare (auto-focus TRUE))
        ?clean <- (MAIN::clean-up-order ?number)
        ?order <- (order (order-number ?number))
        =>
        (assert (initialize-order ?number))
        (retract ?clean ?order))
```

The rule initialize-order-1 deletes all the line-item facts when it sees an initialize-order fact, and initialize-order-2 deletes all the recommend facts. initialize-order-3 deletes the initialize-order fact when no more line items or recommendations are left. Finally, clean-up-order serves as the entry point; it retracts the order fact, and then runs the other rules by asserting the initialize-order fact.

TIP   It's important that these rules be auto-focus rules in their own module. Because they delete individual recommendations, these rules could otherwise thrash back and forth with the recommendation rules: Each time a recommend fact was deleted, one of the recommendation rules could activate and fire, putting the same fact back into working memory, only to have it be deleted again, in an endless chain reaction. This kind of problem is sometimes called an *assertion storm*. You can stop an assertion storm either by removing all the requisite facts or by calling the Rete.halt() method, which forces that Rete object to halt immediately.

17.9 *Summary*

In this chapter, you've developed a basic set of rules for a Recommendations Agent. It's important to realize that you could add many other rules to this system without changing any of the data structures. With minor changes, you could add rules to support sale prices and two-for-one deals. However, this small core of rules is enough to support the goal here, which is to see how Jess can be embedded in web applications.

You've also seen your first practical examples of using the `defquery` construct. You wrote several queries, which the web application implementation code will need to use.

In chapter 19, you'll build a web application around the Recommendations Agent rule base. Before you can do that, however, you need to learn about using Jess from Java code. This is the subject we'll tackle in chapter 18.

18
Embedding Jess
in Java applications

In this chapter you'll...

- Learn about the `jess.Rete` class
- Create and manipulate facts from Java
- Work with Jess exceptions
- Learn to reroute Jess's I/O channels

Every application you've written so far has been based on the command-line interface tool `jess.Main`. The Tax Forms Advisor and PC Repair Assistant each consisted entirely of a single Jess script, whereas the HVAC Controller also included some Java classes. Each of these three programs could be launched by starting `jess.Main` and telling it the filename of a script from the command line.

It might look as though `jess.Main` is Jess's central class. In fact, `jess.Main` is just a command-line wrapper around the *Jess library*. With the library, you can create any number of individual Jess inference engines. You can define rules for them, add data to their working memories, run them in separate threads, and collect generated results—all from Java code, without using `jess.Main`.

The Jess library is obviously what you need to use to deploy rule-based web applications. Jess must be embedded inside some larger application: a web server, an application server, or even a browser. In this chapter, you'll learn general techniques for embedding Jess in Java software. In the next chapter, you'll put these techniques into practice and create a servlet-based web application around the Recommendations Agent rules you developed in chapter 17.

18.1 Getting started with the Jess library

Let's begin at the beginning. The core of the Jess library is the `jess.Rete` class (see section 13.4.1). An instance of `jess.Rete` is, in a sense, an instance of Jess. Every `jess.Rete` object has its own independent working memory, its own list of rules, and its own set of functions. The `Rete` class exports methods for adding, finding, and removing facts, rules, functions, and other constructs. The `Rete` class is a *facade*[1] for the Jess library: Although there are many other classes in the library, `jess.Rete` provides a convenient central access point.

It's easy to create a `jess.Rete` object. There is a default constructor (one that accepts no arguments):

```
import jess.*;
    ...
    Rete engine = new Rete();
```

The most commonly used constructor, however, accepts a `java.lang.Object` argument. The `Rete` object stores this `Object`, and whenever it needs to load a Java class (for instance, because of a call to Jess's `new` function), that `Object`'s class loader is used to find it. In some Java applications—especially in application

---

[1] E. Gamma, R. Helm, R. Johnson, and J. Vlissides, *Design Patterns: Elements of Reusable Object-Oriented Software* (Reading, MA: Addison-Wesley, 1995).

server environments—there can be multiple class loaders, and using the correct one is important. By supplying an object from your application as an argument to the Rete constructor, you tell Jess how to find the other classes in your application. This will be important when you build a web application in the next chapter.

18.1.1 *The executeCommand method*

Once your Java program creates a Rete object, what's next? One of the simplest and most powerful ways to manipulate Jess from Java is to use the executeCommand method. executeCommand accepts a String argument and returns a jess.Value (see section 4.1.3 and chapter 15 to learn about this class). The String is interpreted as an expression in the Jess language, and the return value is the result of evaluating the expression. So, for example, to add a fact to Jess's working memory and get access to the jess.Fact object, you might do the following:

```
import jess.*;
...
    Rete engine = new Rete();
    Value v = engine.executeCommand("(assert (color red))");
    Fact f = v.factValue(engine.getGlobalContext());
```

Section 15.2.2 describes *value resolution*—how to get information out of a jess.Value object. To resolve a jess.Value, you need a jess.Context object. The method getGlobalContext in jess.Rete is a convenient way to obtain one. Commands executed via executeCommand may refer to Jess variables; they are interpreted in this same global context.

Using executeCommand to interact with Jess has one other advantage: It is thread-safe. Only a single call to executeCommand can be simultaneously executing on a given instance of jess.Rete. The lock object is internal to the Rete instance, so executeCommand is synchronized independently of any other concurrency controls. This means that if your web application uses executeCommand to call the get-new-order-number function (see section 17.7.1), it needn't worry about interference between multiple threads.

18.1.2 *Exchanging Java objects*

Probably the most frequently asked question on the Jess email discussion list is some variation on, "How can I send my Java variable to my Jess program?" This section provides one easy answer to this important question. We'll discuss the following functions:

- Rete.store(String, Object)—Stores any object in a special hash table, from Java

- `Rete.store(String, Value)`—Stores a `jess.Value` in the table, from Java
- `Rete.fetch(String)`—Retrieves a `jess.Value`, from Java
- `(store symbol value)`—Stores a value in a hash table, from Jess
- `(fetch symbol)`—Retrieves a value from the hash table, from Jess

In the previous section, you asserted a fact `(color red)` into Jess's working memory from Java. What if instead of the symbol `red`, you wanted the fact to hold a `java.awt.Color` object representing a particular shade of red? It's not possible to construct a `String` argument for `executeCommand` that directly contains the `Color` object. This general problem—how to move objects in both directions between Jess and Java—is solved by the `store` and `fetch` functions. To send a Java object to Jess:

1 Choose a unique identifier.

2 In Java, call `Rete.store`, passing the identifier and the object as arguments.

3 In Jess, call `(fetch)`, using the same identifier to retrieve the object.

The color example would look like this:

```
import jess.*;
import java.awt.Color;
...
    Rete engine = new Rete();
    Color pink = new Color(255, 200, 200);
    engine.store("PINK", pink);
    Value v =
        engine.executeCommand("(assert (color (fetch PINK)))");
    Fact f = v.factValue(engine.getGlobalContext());
```

The `store` method saves the `Color` object in a hash table, using the string `"PINK"` as the key. The `fetch` function retrieves the object from the same hash table. Note that the `store` method is overloaded to accept either a `jess.Value` or a generic `java.lang.Object` as its second argument. The second version (the one used here) automatically wraps the `Object` in a `jess.Value` of type `RU.EXTERNAL_ADDRESS` before storing it.

Getting results

If sending Java variables to Jess is the topic of the most frequently asked Jess question, the second most popular question surely concerns retrieving values from Jess back into Java. Store/fetch works in the other direction, too. It's a handy way of returning results from Jess to Java. Here, a value computed on the right-hand side of a rule is retrieved from Java:

```
import jess.*;
...
    Rete engine = new Rete();
    engine.executeCommand("(assert (numbers 2 2))");
    String rule = "(defrule add-numbers" +
        "(numbers ?n1 ?n2)" +
        "=>" +
        "(store SUM (+ ?n1 ?n2)))";
    // Use executeCommand to define a rule
    engine.executeCommand(rule);
    // The rule fires and stores the result
    engine.executeCommand("(run)");
    Value sumValue = engine.fetch("SUM");
    int sum = sumValue.intValue(engine.getGlobalContext());
```

The Java variable `sum` is initialized to 4. This is a long-winded way of adding two numbers, of course, but the same technique works with more complex rules.

18.1.3 Beyond executeCommand

As you've seen, you can use the `executeCommand` method to do just about anything in Jess from Java. This approach has some problems, though:

- *It's verbose.* Beside typing the whole Jess command, you have to type `executeCommand`, and possibly some `store` and `fetch` calls.

- *It's potentially inefficient, because Jess has to parse the argument.* If the script passed to `executeCommand` is something that will take a while to run, this issue doesn't matter; but for a single short command, it could be a lot of overhead.

- *It's error-prone.* If the Jess script contains a syntax error, the Java compiler won't catch it—you won't find the error until you run your program.

The `executeCommand` method is very convenient, then, but it has some important disadvantages. Whenever possible, you should consider using Jess's direct Java APIs instead. Table 18.1 lists some Jess functions and the equivalent `Rete` methods.

Table 18.1 Some simple methods in the `jess.Rete` class

Rete method	Jess equivalent
reset()	(reset)
run()	(run)
run(int)	(run *number*)
clear()	(clear)

For example, in a code listing in the previous section, you had

```
engine.executeCommand("(run)");
```

Instead, you can write this code as follows:

```
engine.run();
```

The `Rete` class also includes direct Java equivalents of `(clear)`, `(reset)`, and many other important Jess functions. In the following sections, we'll look at what you can do with some more of these `Rete` methods.

18.2 *Working with Fact objects in Java*

Rather than using `executeCommand`, `store`, and `fetch` to assemble and assert facts from Java, you can construct `jess.Fact` objects directly. If a single fact is going to hold objects in several slots, this method will be more convenient, and it will always be more efficient. Table 18.2 lists some of the Java methods that will help you work with Fact objects.

Table 18.2 Some `jess.Rete` methods for working with facts

Rete method	Jess equivalent
addDeftemplate(Deftemplate)	(deftemplate)
assertFact(Fact)	(assert fact)
findDeftemplate(String)	None
findFactByFact(Fact)	None
findFactById(int)	(fact-id number)
retract(Fact)	(retract fact-id)

The `jess.Fact` class is a subclass of `ValueVector` (you met `ValueVector` in section 15.2). All the entries in the `ValueVector` correspond to slots of the `Fact`; the data for the first slot is the item at index 0. The *head* or name of the fact is stored in a separate variable and is accessible via the `getName` method.

Every `jess.Fact` has an associated `jess.Deftemplate` object that describes the slots the fact can have. All Facts with a given head should share the same `Deftemplate`. When you're programming in Java, it's up to you to enforce this requirement. If the `Deftemplate` you need has already been defined, you can use the `findDeftemplate` method in `Rete` to get a reference to it; otherwise, you'll have to construct it yourself. Once you've built a `Deftemplate`, you can reuse it for all the other `Fact`s of the same type that you create.

Listing 18.1 shows how to create a `Deftemplate` with two slots and then assert several facts that use it. `Deftemplate`'s first two constructor arguments are the name of the template and the documentation string for the template. The arguments to `addSlot` are a name for the slot, a default value for the slot, and the name of the data type of the slot, respectively. Jess doesn't do anything with the data type argument—it's reserved for future use.

Listing 18.1   Creating a `Deftemplate` and asserting `Fact` objects from Java

```
import jess.*;
public class CreateFacts {
    public static void main(String[] unused)
    throws JessException {
        Rete engine = new Rete();
        Deftemplate d =
            new Deftemplate("person", "A person", engine);
        d.addSlot("name", Funcall.NIL, "STRING");
        d.addSlot("address", Funcall.NIL, "STRING");
        engine.addDeftemplate(d);

        String[][] data = {
            {"Joe Smith", "123 Main Street"},
            {"Fred Jones", "333 Elm Circle"},
            {"Bob Weasley", "211 Planet Way"},
        };

        for (int i=0; i<data.length; ++i) {
            Fact f = new Fact("person", engine);
            f.setSlotValue("name",
                           new Value(data[i][0], RU.STRING));
            f.setSlotValue("address",
                           new Value(data[i][1], RU.STRING));
            engine.assertFact(f);
        }
        engine.executeCommand("(facts)");
    }
}
```

In listing 18.1, you specify a value for every slot in each `Fact`, but doing so is not required. If you don't specify a value for a slot, the default value is used when the `Fact` is asserted.

Once you assert a `Fact` object, you no longer "own" it—it becomes part of the `Rete` object's internal data structures. As such, you must not change the values of any of the `Fact`'s slots. If you retract the fact, the `Fact` object is released and you are free to alter it as you wish. You can retract your fact from the engine using the `retract` method.

18.2.1 *Multislots*

Jess facts can contain *multislots*—single slots that hold multiple data items. You can add a multislot to a `Deftemplate` using the `addMultiSlot` method. You can then set the value of that slot in a fact as usual, but the slot value must be a `jess.Value` of type `RU.LIST`. A `LIST` value contains a `ValueVector`; the elements of the `ValueVector` are then the contents of the multislot:

```
Rete engine = new Rete();
Deftemplate d =
    new Deftemplate("student", "A student", engine);
d.addSlot("name", Funcall.NIL, "STRING");
d.addMultiSlot("courses", Funcall.NILLIST);
engine.addDeftemplate(d);

Fact f = new Fact("student", engine);
f.setSlotValue("name", new Value("Fred Smith", RU.STRING));
ValueVector courses = new ValueVector();
courses.add(new Value("COMP 101", RU.STRING));
courses.add(new Value("HISTORY 202", RU.STRING));
f.setSlotValue("courses", new Value(courses, RU.LIST));
```

Note that even if a multislot contains only one value, you have to put it in a `ValueVector`. When you're programming in Java, it's up to you to follow this rule. The results of breaking it are undefined.

18.2.2 *Ordered facts*

As you saw in section 6.4, ordered facts like

```
(shopping-list bread milk jam)
(point 20 10)
(power off)
```

are represented as if they were unordered facts with a single multislot named `__data`, like this:

```
(shopping-list (__data bread milk jam))
(point (__data 20 10))
(power (__data off))
```

If you assert an ordered fact from the Jess language, the `deftemplate` is created automatically if it doesn't already exist. The same thing happens if you create the fact from Java. The `deftemplate` is created during the call to the `Fact` object's constructor:

```
Fact f = new Fact("shopping-list", engine);
f.setSlotValue("__data", new Value(new ValueVector().
    add(new Value("bread", RU.ATOM)).
    add(new Value("milk", RU.ATOM)).
    add(new Value("jam", RU.ATOM)), RU.LIST));
engine.assertFact(f);
```

This code uses an interesting shortcut: The `add` method in `ValueVector` returns the `ValueVector` you call it on. This means you can chain calls to this method, as we've done here. Some people like this technique, and some people hate it; I think it's a fine thing to do when you're building up a list of items.

18.2.3 Removing facts

The `retract` method in the `Rete` class lets you remove facts from working memory:

```
Fact f = …
engine.retract(f);
```

`retract` takes a `Fact` object as an argument. If you asserted the fact from Java, then it's easy to use it as an argument to `retract`. If you didn't, then you need to get hold of a `Fact` object somehow. There are two approaches: Either you can use the fact number of the `Fact` as an argument to the `findFactById` method in `Rete`, or you can construct a `Fact` just like the one you want to retract and use that as the argument to `retract` (it turns out that `retract` doesn't need you to pass in a `Fact` object that's really in working memory—it can instead be a `Fact` that's *identical* to one in working memory).

The working memory is stored as a hash table, with the `Fact` objects as the keys. That means finding out whether a `Fact` is in working memory already is a fast operation, but finding the `Fact` with a particular numeric identifier is slow (because Jess has to examine each `Fact` in working memory until it finds the right one). Therefore, there's no cheap way to remove a fact from working memory if you don't already have a reference to the `Fact` object: Either Jess has to do a slow lookup, or you have to do the work of constructing a duplicate `Fact` object. If you assert `Fact`s from Java and intend to retract them later in your application, be sure to keep references to the `Fact` objects you create.

18.3 Working with JavaBeans

Adding JavaBeans to Jess's working memory from Java is simple, and it works pretty much the same way as it does from the Jess language. Table 18.3 shows the correspondence between methods in the `Rete` class and the Jess functions you've already learned about.

Table 18.3 `jess.Rete` methods for working with JavaBeans

Rete method	Jess equivalent
`defclass(tag, class-name, parent)`	`(defclass tag class-name [parent])`
`definstance(tag, object, boolean)`	`(definstance tag object` `[static|dynamic])`
`undefinstance(object)`	`(undefinstance object)`

You use the `Rete.defclass` method to register a class with Jess, and then you use `Rete.definstance` to add individual instances to working memory. You can remove the objects using `Rete.undefinstance`. As an example, you can add a `java.awt.Button` to Jess's working memory like this:

```
Rete engine = ...
engine.defclass("button", "java.awt.Button", null);
Button b = new Button("OK");
engine.definstance("button", b, true);
```

You don't want this `defclass` to extend another one, so you pass `null` as the last argument to the `defclass` function. Because `java.awt.Button` sends `Property-ChangeEvents`, you can pass `true` as the last argument to `definstance`, making this a dynamic instance.

18.4 *Calling Jess functions from Java*

As you've seen, the `Rete` class exposes many Jess functions as public Java methods—many, but not all. Some Jess functions show up as Java methods in other classes: For example, the Jess `gensym*` function is available as the static `gensym` function in the `jess.RU` class. The `Userfunction` class that implements `gensym*` is just a thin wrapper around this static Java method.

Other Jess functions, however, are implemented directly in the `Userfunction` class. To call them from Java, you have to use an instance of the appropriate `Userfunction` class. The helper class `jess.Funcall` can make this process a little simpler. As an example, there's no specific Java API for the `watch` function. To turn on all the `watch` diagnostics from Java code (the equivalent of `(watch all)` in Jess), you can do this:

```
Rete engine = …
Context context = engine.getGlobalContext();
Funcall f = new Funcall("watch", engine);
f.arg("all");
f.execute(context);
```

Once you've created a `Funcall` object, you can save it and call `execute` on it any number of times. Alternatively, you can use the compressed form:

```
new Funcall("watch", engine).arg("all").execute(context);
```

Some Jess functions can fail, due to either programmer error or a runtime condition. In the next section, you'll learn how to deal with errors during execution.

18.5 *Working with JessException*

Jess's Java API reports errors by throwing instances of `jess.JessException`. Therefore, whenever you work with Jess in Java, you need to catch this exception. Working with `JessExceptions` can be a little tricky, as exception classes go, but using them correctly can save you a lot of head scratching when you're debugging your programs.

Here are some useful methods in `jess.JessException`:

- `getContext()`—Returns a Jess stack trace
- `getLineNumber()`—Returns the offending line number in Jess language code
- `getNextException()`—Returns a nested exception
- `getProgramText()`—Returns the offending Jess code itself
- `getRoutine()`—Returns the name of the Jess function or Java method

An instance of `JessException` can of course provide an error message and a Java stack trace, like all Java `Throwables`. If the error comes from executing code in the Jess language, the `JessException` can provide additional information about what went wrong. The `getContext` method, for example, returns a kind of Jess language stack trace, showing what functions and constructs were executing when an error occurred. The `getRoutine` method tells you what Jess function was executing, and the `getLineNumber` method points to a specific line in your script. `getProgramText` returns the actual snippet of Jess code that caused the error. The code in this example provokes a `JessException` by trying to multiply two symbols, and then demonstrates how to use some of these methods:

```
import jess.*;

public class CatchJessException {
    public static void main(String[] argv) {
        try {
            Rete r = new Rete();
            r.executeCommand("(* 1 2)\n(* 3 4)\n(* a b)");
        } catch (JessException je) {
            System.out.print("An error occurred at line " +
```

```
                                        je.getLineNumber());
              System.out.println(" which looks like " +
                                        je.getProgramText ());
              System.out.println("Message: " + je.getMessage());
          }
      }
  }
```

Running this program produces the following:

```
An error occurred at line 3 which looks like ( * a b )
Message: Not a number: "a"
```

The most important thing to remember about working with `JessExceptions` is never to ignore them. A truly remarkable number of people write code like this:

```
try {
    Rete r = new Rete();
    r.executeCommand("(* 1 2)\n(* 3 4)\n(* a b)");
} catch (JessException je) {
    /* NOTHING */
}
```

and then wonder why their program doesn't work. Don't be one of them! Always at least print the exception object itself to `System.out` or to a log file. `JessException`'s `toString` method produces the by-now-familiar exception display you see from the Jess command prompt. Printing the object `je` would give the following:

```
Jess reported an error in routine Value.numericValue
    while executing (+ a b).
    Message: Not a number: "a" (type = ATOM).
    Program text: ( + a b ) at line 3.
```

This is more information than the end user of your application probably needs to see, but it's better than no information at all.

18.5.1 *Nested exceptions*

The Jess function `call` can invoke any Java method. If the invoked Java method throws an exception, `call` creates a `JessException` object as a wrapper for the real exception and throws the wrapper instead. Therefore, when you catch a `Jess-Exception`, you may need to check it for a nested exception object using the `get-Cause` method. If `getCause` returns non-null, the returned exception is almost always more interesting than the `JessException` itself:

```
import jess.*;

public class CheckNextException {
    public static void main(String[] argv) {
        try {
            Rete r = new Rete();
```

```
            r.executeCommand("(new java.net.URL foo://bar)");
        } catch (JessException je) {
            System.out.println(je.getMessage());
            System.out.println(je.getCause().getMessage());
        }
    }
}
```

This code prints the following:

```
Constructor threw an exception
unknown protocol: foo
```

Note that the `toString` method of `JessException` does *not* display nested exceptions, so you need to check for and report them explicitly.

18.5.2 *Rolling your own*

The `call` method of the `Userfunction` interface can throw `JessException`, so if you're writing your own Jess commands, you may want to create your own `Jess-Exception` objects to report errors. The good news is that Jess automatically takes care of setting the line number, program text, and Jess stack trace information after your `JessException` is thrown; all you need to worry about are the routine name, error message, and possibly a nested exception.

`JessException` has three constructors, which differ only in their last argument. The first two arguments are always a routine name and a message. The routine name indicates where the exception was created. It can be either the name of a Java class and method, or the name of a Jess language function; use your best judgment. The routine name you use is displayed on the first line of the message returned by `JessException.toString()`.

The second argument to each `JessException` constructor is the error message—a short description of what went wrong, perhaps five words at most. For two of the three constructors, the third argument is simply more data to be appended to the message, with a space in between. One of the constructors accepts an `int`, which is handy for reporting number-related errors, and the other accepts a second `String`. For the third constructor, the last argument is a nested exception.

This code snippet is from an imaginary `Userfunction` that implements a `google` function in Jess. It tries to connect to the Google web site and reports any failure via a `JessException`:

```
try {
    Socket s = new Socket("www.google.com", 80);
    // use the socket ...
} catch (Exception ex) {
    throw new JessException("google", "Network error", ex);
}
```

Any exceptions thrown by the `Socket` constructor result in a `JessException` being thrown; the original exception is available via `getNextException`.

18.6 *Input and output*

The function `printout` was the first Jess function you learned. Until now, the first argument to printout has always been `t`, but I've never explained why. The time has come to break this silence and explain the topic of I/O routers. The following methods in the Rete class deal with these beasts:

- `addInputRouter(String name, Reader r, boolean mode)`—Defines or redefines an input router
- `getInputRouter(String name)`—Returns the named input router
- `removeInputRouter(String name)`—Undefines an input router
- `getInputMode(String name)`—Determines whether the named input router is console-like
- `addOutputRouter(String name, Writer w)`—Defines or redefines an output router
- `getOutputRouter(String name)`—Returns the named output router
- `removeOutputRouter(String name)`—Undefines an output router
- `getOutStream()`—Returns the standard output router
- `getErrStream()`—Returns the standard error router

You can use the `readline` and `printout` functions to collect input and display output from Jess:

```
(printout t "Enter 'y' or 'n': ")
(bind ?response (readline t))
```

The first argument to `printout` or `readline` is a *router*, a symbol that tells Jess where to send the output. Several routers are built into Jess, and they're all initially connected to standard input and output: text sent to `t`, `WSTDOUT` or `WSTDERR` all goes to `System.out` by default, and data read from `t` or `WSTDIN` comes from `System.in`. The `W*` routers are used internally by Jess. `WSTDOUT` is where Jess sends the `Jess>` prompt and the result of evaluating an expression you type at the prompt. `WSTDERR` is used for internal error messages. `WSTDIN` exists only for symmetry; Jess doesn't use it for anything.

A router is really just a symbolic name for a `java.io.Reader` (for input) or a `java.io.Writer` (for output). The defaults for the built-in routers are wrappers around `System.in` and `System.out`. Each `jess.Rete` object keeps its own table of routers (there are separate tables for input and output routers, so an input/output pair with the same name, like t, are separate, unconnected objects).

You can retrieve routers from this table by name with the getInputRouter and getOutputRouter methods. If you're writing a Userfunction or other Java code that wants to intersperse its output with Jess's other output, you can use getOutputRouter("WSTDOUT") to get an appropriate Writer object. The method getOutStream() is a special shortcut for this common operation.

Note that Jess's routers are not general I/O channels. Jess always interprets data from an input router as a sequence of Jess language tokens (symbols, numbers, and strings). As a result, you can't do binary I/O through a router. If you need to do binary I/O, you can use Jess's reflection capabilities to call read and write directly on appropriate Java streams.

18.6.1 *Using custom routers*

In the command-line client jess.Main, the default values for the built-in routers are fine; but if Jess is embedded in software with a GUI, it's likely that printing to standard output is inappropriate. If you want to be able to use readline, printout, and friends from an application that won't be used from the command line, you may need to set the standard routers to refer to Reader and Writer objects that are more appropriate for the situation. For example, if Jess was to be embedded in a web application, printout wouldn't be useful unless a new router were defined that sent its output to someplace other than System.out. You might define a new router using a java.io.StringWriter; printout could then send information to a string, which could then be retrieved when appropriate by the application. To define such a router named out, you could do the following:

```
StringWriter sw = new StringWriter();
Engine.addOutputRouter("out", sw);
```

If you then executed the Jess statement (printout out 12345 crlf), a subsequent call to sw.toString() would return the string "12345\n".

Sometimes, coming up with appropriate Readers and Writers is tricky. In the jess.Console graphical console application, for example, the output from (printout t) goes to one graphical text component in the GUI, and (readline t) takes input from a second text component. To make this work, Jess includes two adapter classes named jess.awt.TextAreaWriter and jess.awt.TextReader. TextAreaWriter is a subclass of Writer that takes a TextArea as a constructor argument. The abstract write method is implemented to call append on the java.awt.TextArea, accumulating text as it arrives. The jess.Console applica-

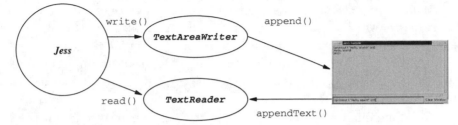

Figure 18.1 Usage diagram for `TextAreaWriter` and `TextReader`

tion installs a single instance of this class as the routers t, WSTDOUT, and WSTDERR. As a result, all of Jess's regular output goes to the TextArea (see figure 18.1).

The TextReader class is similarly used to collect user input from the GUI. Text-Reader is a subclass of Reader with read methods that return data from an internal buffer. TextReader also has a method appendText that lets you add text to this internal buffer. jess.Console connects a java.awt.TextField in its GUI to an instance of TextReader using an event handler: Whenever the user presses Enter in the TextField, the event handler calls appendText on the TextReader, making the text entered in the TextField available to be read from the Text-Reader's internal buffer. The connected TextReader object is installed as the t and WSTDIN input routers.

18.7 *Summary*

Jess is designed as a library that can be embedded into many different kinds of software. It has an extensive Java API to help you accomplish this functionality, and we have covered only some of it in this chapter.

The jess.Rete class plays a central role. Its methods let you define and retrieve constructs like rules and templates. You can use store and fetch to pass values between Jess and Java code. jess.Rete also manages a set of I/O routers that control how Jess prints output and reads input.

You can work with jess.Fact objects from Java whenever you need more control over the creation or manipulation of facts than you can get from the Jess language. Working with facts often involves manipulating the jess.Deftemplate objects that define the structure of the facts. You can also add JavaBeans to Jess's working memory from Java code using the defclass and definstance methods of the Rete class.

Jess uses the `jess.JessException` class to report errors, and you can use it to report errors when you write `Userfunctions`. A `JessException` often carries a wealth of useful information about the error it represents.

Jess's I/O functions read input from, and write input to, objects called *routers*. You can install your own routers, redirect the predefined routers, and even create your own router types.

In the next chapter, you'll use what you've just learned to deploy the Recommendations Agent you developed in chapter 17 as a web application.

19

Deploying
web-based applications

In this chapter you'll...

- Learn about the Tomcat servlet engine
- Develop servlets that embed Jess
- Write JavaServer Pages that use Jess
- Assemble the Recommendations Agent from these components

In chapter 17, you developed the rule base for a Recommendations Agent. The agent can recommend further items to a customer based on their past and present purchases, much as a good sales clerk working on commission might do. In this chapter, you'll build a web application around the Recommendations Agent. In the first few sections, I'll briefly describe some of the APIs and tools you'll be using, and then you'll begin to incrementally develop the application.

You're going to deploy this application using the *Java 2 Enterprise Edition* environment. J2EE is a standardized deployment platform for networked Java applications. Although you'll use specific software to make the examples concrete (in particular, the Tomcat servlet engine), the application you'll develop is completely general and can be installed in any J2EE-compliant application server. Using Jess for this application gives you the ability to use a rule engine while writing only portable code that won't tie you to a particular J2EE implementation. Tomcat is open source; you can download it from http://jakarta.apache.org/tomcat/.

Although I'll explain important things as I go along, I've written this chapter with a fairly experienced Java programmer in mind. Building a full web application from scratch requires a range of knowledge and technical skills, and there simply isn't enough room in this book to teach all of what you need to know. Beside basic Java programming, there's web browsing in general, the Java Servlet API, HTML, and the HTTP protocol. I have to assume you know at least a little about all these things.

If you've been working with Java for a while, this material should be easy for you to use. If you're new to Java or the Web, you may have a steeper learning curve. In that case, try not to get bogged down in the details; read through it, go off and hone your Java and web programming skills, and then come back and read it again.

One more thing: This is the largest application you've built so far in this book, and building and deploying it, while not rocket science, is more complicated than just typing `java jess.Main something.clp`. Therefore, I refer to some tools and software outside of Jess and Java. The choices I've made reflect my actual working environment: the Linux operating system, GNU `make` as a build tool, and the Tomcat servlet container as an application server. Your choices may be different: You may use a Microsoft operating system or the Jakarta project's Ant build manager, or you may have a commercial J2EE implementation. That's fine—but you may need to adjust file paths and command lines to suit your environment. I assume you understand your tools well enough to do this.

19.1 *The Java Servlet API*

You're going to build this application using the Java Servlet API (http://java.sun.com/products/servlet/index.html). We talked briefly about servlets in chapter 17. A servlet is a bit like a device driver: It's a chunk of code that implements a service and provides a small number of entry points through which the host system can access that service. A servlet is, of course, written in Java, and the most common variety of servlet is hosted by a web server and accessed via the web using the HTTP or HTTPS protocol. Here's a simple but complete servlet:

```java
import java.io.*;
import javax.servlet.http.*;

public class Hello extends HttpServlet {
    public void doGet(HttpServletRequest request,
                      HttpServletResponse response)
    throws IOException {
        response.setContentType("text/html");
        PrintWriter out = response.getWriter();
        out.println("<html>");
        out.println(" <head>");
        out.println("    <title>Hello World!</title>");
        out.println(" </head>");
        out.println(" <body>");
        out.println("    <h1>Hello World!</h1>");
        out.println(" </body>");
        out.println("</html>");
    }
}
```

This servlet does nothing but display "Hello World!" on an HTML page, but obviously the page could be far more complex; it could also contain data computed on the fly, so that the page was different each time. Servlets can contain other methods and other classes, so the sky's the limit as far as the content of the generated page goes.

Beside merely displaying a page, servlets can receive query data from the user and react to it. They can also load configuration data and base their behavior on that. They can be invoked by other servlets, and invoke still other servlets in turn. I'll describe how all this works as it comes up in this chapter.

The `HttpServletRequest` object provides input to the servlet, like the aforementioned query data (usually from HTML forms). The `HttpServletResponse` object represents the page that's being generated. This example only uses the `setContentType` and `getWriter` methods. The method `setContentType` specifies the MIME type of the data you're sending back from the servlet (often `text/`

html to indicate an HTML document). The method getWriter returns a Print-Writer to which you can send the text that makes up the HTML page.

19.2 *J2EE and the Tomcat engine*

Now that you have a simple servlet, how can you set things up so it can be accessed on the Web? You need to compile it and then *deploy* it into a *servlet container*. A servlet container is to a servlet what an operating system is to a device driver: the framework to which servlets are attached. The container provides essential services to the servlet, such as pipes to and from the network, methods to retrieve query data and configuration information, and a mechanism for communication with other servlets in the same container. Modern servlet containers are powerful things. The J2EE environment (of which they are a large part) and its standardized procedures for configuring, installing, and managing applications are a far cry from the early days of ad hoc web applications. Developing and deploying web applications is easier than it has ever been.

Tomcat is a servlet engine from the Apache project (http://jakarta.apache.org/tomcat/index.html). Tomcat is the reference implementation for the Java Servlet and JavaServer Pages specifications, and it's one component of JavaSoft's implementation of the Java 2 Enterprise Edition (J2EE). You can download and use Tomcat free of charge under the terms of the Apache Software License. All the APIs and techniques you will use are general, but I'll describe them in terms of Tomcat. I'll assume, for the sake of clarity, that you're using a Linux computer with a standalone Tomcat installation. The path to the root of the Tomcat installation is in an environment variable named TOMCAT. If your computer is running Windows instead of Linux, you'll need to adjust the paths a bit, but everything else should be the same.

19.2.1 *Deploying the Hello servlet*

Deploying the Hello servlet is a five-step process:

1 Compile the servlet.
2 Create a *deployment descriptor*.
3 Create the directory structure for your web application.
4 Copy the files into the right locations.
5 Restart (or start) Tomcat.

Compile the servlet

To compile the servlet, you need to include the file $(TOMCAT)/common/lib/servlet.jar in your class path. The following command line should do the trick:

```
javac -classpath $(TOMCAT)/common/lib/servlet.jar Hello.java
```

Create a deployment descriptor

A *deployment descriptor* is a short XML file named web.xml that describes how the container should configure your servlet. If you've never worked with XML before, the most important things to know are that first, XML files are plain text, just like Java source; and second, XML files have a picky syntax, which is less forgiving than HTML (to which XML has a strong family resemblance). Here's a basic web.xml file:

```
<?xml version="1.0" encoding="ISO-8859-1"?>

<!DOCTYPE web-app
    PUBLIC "-//Sun Microsystems, Inc.//DTD Web Application 2.3//EN"
    "http://java.sun.com/dtd/web-app_2_3.dtd">

<web-app>
    <servlet>
        <servlet-name>Hello</servlet-name>
        <servlet-class>Hello</servlet-class>
    </servlet>
</web-app>
```

Many other possible options can be included, but you'll worry about them when you need them.

Create the directory structure

Each web application should have its own subdirectory in $(TOMCAT)/webapps. This application directory should, in turn, have a subdirectory WEB-INF, and WEB-INF should have a classes subdirectory. You might create more subdirectories, but this small set is enough for now.

Copy the files

The web.xml file goes into the WEB-INF directory. The Hello.class file goes into classes. The resulting structure looks like this:

```
$(TOMCAT)/
    webapps/
        Hello/
            WEB-INF/
                web.xml
                classes/
                    Hello.class
```

It's not complicated, but you do have to get it right. During development, you must do this many, many times, so you should write a small script (or batch file, or Ant task, or `Makefile` target) to do this automatically. My `Makefile` for this servlet looks like this:

```
.SUFFIXES: .java .class

JAVA_HOME=/usr/java/j2sdk1.4.0
TOMCAT=/usr/local/jakarta-tomcat
APPNAME=Hello

SRC=$(shell find . -name '*.java' -print )
OBJ=$(SRC:.java=.class)

build: $(OBJ)

.java.class:
    javac \
        -classpath .:$(TOMCAT)/common/lib/servlet.jar $<

install: build
    rm -rf $(TOMCAT)/webapps/$(APPNAME)/*
    mkdir -p $(TOMCAT)/webapps/$(APPNAME)/WEB-INF
    cp web.xml $(TOMCAT)/webapps/$(APPNAME)/WEB-INF
    mkdir -p $(TOMCAT)/webapps/$(APPNAME)/WEB-INF/classes
    cp *.class $(TOMCAT)/webapps/$(APPNAME)/WEB-INF/classes

clean:
    rm -f *~ *.class
```

If you're new to `make`, note that the indented lines must start with real `tab` characters, not spaces! The `install` target in the `Makefile` compiles the application, re-creates the directory structure, and installs all the necessary files. This `Makefile` makes a good template for general servlet development—you'll expand it and use it for the Recommendations Agent application later in this chapter.

Restart Tomcat

The easiest and most reliable way to get Tomcat to load your new application—or reload it after a change—is to shut down Tomcat and start it up again. You can use the `startup` and `shutdown` scripts in `$(TOMCAT)/bin`, or you can do what I do, and write a third script named `restart` that combines the two functions. (Look at the `startup` and `shutdown` scripts and create `restart` by analogy.)

A properly laid-out web application will be detected automatically by Tomcat. The first time a browser request comes in for the `Hello` application, Tomcat will load the `web.xml` file to learn about the application, and find out that a servlet named `Hello` is implemented in a class named `Hello`. The first time the servlet is requested, Tomcat loads it in and calls the `doGet` method you implemented to satisfy the request. The generated page is returned to the browser.

Seeing the results

The default standalone Tomcat installation starts its own mini–web server on port 8080. Fire up your favorite web browser and visit the URL http://127.0.0.1:8080/Hello/servlet/Hello to see your first servlet in action. The result is shown in figure 19.1.

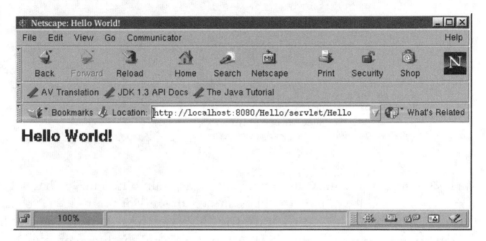

Figure 19.1 **The result of viewing the** `Hello` **servlet in Netscape**

19.3 *Your first Jess servlet*

Now that you've built a simple servlet, it's time to begin developing the Recommendations Agent web application. The first small step is to write a servlet that embeds Jess, however simply. Why not modify `Hello` to create `HelloJess`, which uses `printout` to create the same simple web page?

```
import jess.*;
import java.io.*;
import javax.servlet.*;
import javax.servlet.http.*;

public class HelloJess extends HttpServlet {

    public void doGet(HttpServletRequest request,
                      HttpServletResponse response)
    throws IOException, ServletException {
        response.setContentType("text/html");
        PrintWriter out = response.getWriter();
        Rete engine = new Rete();
        engine.addOutputRouter("page", out);
```

```
    try {
            print("<html>", engine);
            print("<head>", engine);
            print("<title>Hello World!</title>", engine);
            print("</head>", engine);
            print("<body>", engine);
            print("<h1>Hello World from Jess!</h1>", engine);
            print("</body>", engine);
            print("</html>", engine);
        } catch (JessException je) {
            throw new ServletException(je);
        }
    }

    private void print(String message, Rete engine)
    throws JessException {
        engine.executeCommand("(printout page \"" + message +
                              "\" crlf)");
    }
}
```

This servlet is very similar to the first one. The main difference is that `HelloJess` creates an instance of the `Rete` class, installs the servlet's output `Writer` as a Jess router named `page`, and then uses Jess's `printout` function (via the helper method `print`) to generate the HTML page. There's nothing complex here, but this example illustrates how simple it is to embed Jess in a Java application.

19.3.1 *Deploying the Jess servlet*

The `HelloJess` servlet needs to have access to the Jess library to run, so you must install Jess under Tomcat. This is easy enough to do: JAR files in the `$(TOMCAT)/lib` directory are automatically accessible to all installed web applications, so you'll package Jess as a JAR file and put it there. The binary Jess distribution already includes the JAR file `jess.jar`. If you have compiled your own copy of Jess from source, you can build a JAR file like this on Linux:

```
jar cf jess.jar `find jess -name '*.class' -print` jess/*.clp
```

Then copy `jess.jar` to the `$(TOMCAT)/lib` directory. In your `Makefile` (or Ant `build.xml` file, and so on), you may want to include a line that copies the `jess.jar` file.

Modify the `web.xml` file you used for the last servlet to account for the new servlet and application names, install the application as `HelloJess`, and restart Tomcat. If you then visit the URL http://127.0.0.1:8080/HelloJess/servlet/HelloJess you should see much the same web page as before—except this time, it is generated by Jess.

19.3.2 *Cleaning up the URL*

The URL you've been typing to see the servlets is quite verbose. By modifying the web.xml file slightly, you can tell Tomcat to shorten the URL considerably. Specifically, you can tell Tomcat that a request for any URL starting with http://127.0.0.1:8080/HelloJess should be routed to the HelloJess servlet—including, for instance, http://127.0.0.1:8080/HelloJess/index.html. Before the closing </webapp> tag, add the following block:

```
<servlet-mapping>
    <servlet-name>
        HelloJess
    </servlet-name>
    <url-pattern>
    /*
    </url-pattern>
</servlet-mapping>
```

After reinstalling the application and restarting Tomcat, you can see the Jess servlet by visiting http://127.0.0.1:8080/HelloJess. Note that now it's pretty much impossible to tell that the page is being generated by a servlet—both the page itself and the URL look perfectly normal, as if the page were a static HTML document.

19.4 *Application architecture: take one*

Now that the preliminaries are taken care of and you know how to write simple servlets that embed Jess, it's time to design and implement the Recommendations Agent. As a first stab at a design for the application, let's assume it will include four screens:

- A *login* screen, where the customer supplies her username
- A *catalog* screen, where the customer chooses products to purchase
- A *recommend* screen, where the customer selects additional recommended items to purchase
- A *purchase* screen, where the customer checks out

We're most interested in the catalog and recommend screens. The Recommendations Agent won't be able to recommend anything until the customer has selected some items, so you'll work on the catalog screen first.

Behind each of the screens is a servlet. You'll develop the servlets one at a time, and as we go along, I'll explain the pieces of the Servlet API and J2EE as necessary.

19.5 *Starting the Catalog servlet*

The Catalog servlet should perform the following steps:

1 Get the login name (previously stored by the Login servlet)
2 Call get-new-order-number to get a unique order number
3 Create a new user session with this login name and order number
4 Use the all-products query to get a list of product facts
5 Display an HTML form to let the customer purchase products

The last item should make you a little uncomfortable, especially if you've done web development in the past. The code for HelloJess was, to put it delicately, ugly. Java code to generate HTML is clumsy and verbose. Worse, if HTML is generated by Java, then a Java programmer is required if it becomes necessary to make any changes to the HTML. And changes *will* be necessary—you can bet on that. Web sites are redesigned frequently, and if a Java programmer needs to sit down, edit the code, and recompile the servlets every time management wants to change the layout of the tables, you've got a big maintenance problem on your hands.

You may have heard of the model-view-controller (MVC) paradigm for programming user interfaces. In an MVC design, the data (or *model*) is separated from the logic (or *controller*) and the GUI (or *view*), all in well-separated modules. If you broke the Catalog servlet into pieces this way, you could make the web site much easier to maintain. The controller logic would go in the Catalog servlet, and the view would be built directly in HTML (the data will be held in a Rete object, so the model is already nicely encapsulated). The HTML pages could be modified by web designers, the servlets could be modified (when necessary) by Java programmers, and maintaining the web site suddenly becomes much easier.

The only problem is that the HTML won't be static. The page produced by the Catalog servlet will change based on many pieces of data. For example, the customer's name will surely appear on the page. The list of products and prices will change from day to day, as well. How can you write HTML pages that can change in response to data in your servlets? The answer is to use JavaServer Pages, as you'll see in the next section.

19.5.1 *JavaServer Pages*

JavaServer Pages (JSPs) are HTML documents that contain bits of Java code. A J2EE container knows how to extract that Java code, translate the HTML into more Java code, and compile the JSP into a servlet that emits the original HTML plus the results of evaluating the Java code. Thus, a JSP is like the `Hello` servlet turned inside out: Instead of being Java code with embedded HTML, it's an HTML document with embedded Java code.

Unlike servlets, JSPs are easy for web designers to edit. Using JavaServer Pages as the interface to a web application while using servlets for the logic is an example of using the right tool for the right job.[1]

Here's a contrived example, `hello.jsp`, that uses a `Rete` object to print the now-familiar message `"Hello World from Jess!"`:

```
<html>
    <%@ page import="jess.*" %>
    <head>
        <title>Hello World!</title>
    </head>
    <body>
        <H1><%
            Rete engine = new Rete();
            engine.addOutputRouter("page", out);
            engine.executeCommand("(printout page " +
            "\"Hello World from Jess!\" crlf)");
        %></H1>
    </body>
</html>
```

The variable `out` is the same as the return value of `response.getWriter()` from the `Hello` servlet, and it's automatically available to all JSPs. The important thing about `hello.jsp` is that most of the file is plain, vanilla HTML. All the tags could be changed using just an HTML editor; no Java programmer need be involved.

To install a JSP in Tomcat, all you have to do is copy the source code into the top level of a web application's directory. Tomcat recognizes the JSP extension, and the first time the file is requested, it is compiled into a servlet and executed.

19.5.2 *Forwarding to a JSP*

A servlet and a JSP can collaborate easily. Generally, the servlet performs a computation, stores the result in the `HttpServletRequest` object, and then forwards the augmented request object to the JSP. The JSP finds the data it needs in the `HttpServletRequest` and generates the HTML page. For example, suppose you wanted to let a servlet create the `Rete` object used in the previous section and then pass it to the JSP. The relevant part of the servlet would look like this:

---

[1] For more information about designing applications with servlets and JSPs, see Bruce A. Tate, *Bitter Java* (Greenwich, CT: Manning, 2002).

```
Rete engine = new Rete();
request.setAttribute("engine", engine);
ServletContext servletContext = getServletContext();
RequestDispatcher dispatcher =
    servletContext.getRequestDispatcher("/hello.jsp");
dispatcher.forward(request, response);
return;
```

The JSP would be rewritten like this:

```
<html>
    <%@ page import="jess.*" %>
    <jsp:useBean id="engine" class="jess.Rete" scope="request"/>
    <head>
        <title>Hello World!</title>
    </head>
    <body>
        <H1><%
            engine.addOutputRouter("page", out);
            engine.executeCommand("(printout page " +
            "\"Hello World from Jess!\" crlf)");
        %></H1>
    </body>
</html>
```

The `jsp:useBean` tag automatically extracts the `Rete` object from the `HttpServletRequest` and assigns it to a variable of the correct type.

You can put the JSP-forwarding machinery into a method so it can be called with one line of code. You'll need such a method when you begin writing servlets; it looks like this:

```
protected void dispatch(HttpServletRequest request,
                        HttpServletResponse response,
                        String page)
throws IOException, ServletException {

    ServletContext servletContext = getServletContext();
    RequestDispatcher dispatcher =
        servletContext.getRequestDispatcher(page);
    dispatcher.forward(request, response);
}
```

With `dispatch`, the previous servlet body becomes the following:

```
Rete engine = new Rete();
request.setAttribute("engine", engine);
dispatch(request, response, "/hello.jsp");
return;
```

You'll see `dispatch` in all the servlets you'll write from now on.

19.6 *Application architecture, take two*

Let's reexamine the application architecture before you begin the implementation. There are so many pieces now that it makes sense to summarize them in a table; see table 19.1. Note that the order in which the files are listed is the order in which they'll execute during normal operation of the final application.

Table 19.1 The HTML files, JSPs, and servlets that make up the Recommendations Agent application

Source file	Description
index.html	Simple login screen
Catalog.java	Servlet to create the order object and list products
catalog.jsp	JSP to display the product table and a form for ordering
Recommend.java	Servlet that accepts the submitted order form and runs the Recommendations Agent
recommend.jsp	JSP to display recommendations and a form for adding them to the order
Purchase.java	Servlet to accept the completed order
purchase.jsp	Final screen

We'll concentrate on the Java code, in both the servlets and the Java parts of the JSPs. The HTML in the JSPs is simple, minimalist, and maybe even ugly. This is typical: The programmers produce stub JSPs with minimal HTML content, and the web designers then flesh them out, modifying the HTML parts and leaving the Java parts alone.

The index.html login screen and the purchase servlet and JSP are fairly trivial in this implementation (you won't collect credit card and shipping information). The Catalog and Recommend servlets and JSPs are the interesting parts—and now, finally, you can get started.

19.7 *The login screen*

The first page the customer sees is a login screen. A real login screen might collect a password as well as a username, but you'll leave that aside for now. All you need for the login screen is a simple HTML form that lets the customer enter a single string:

```
<HTML>
    <HEAD>
        <TITLE>Welcome to TekMart.com!</TITLE>
    </HEAD>
```

```
<BODY>
    <H1>Welcome to TekMart.com</H1>
    Welcome to the TekMart.com online store!
    <P>
    To get started, please enter your customer id:
    <FORM action="/Order/catalog" method="POST">
        <INPUT name="customerId">
        <INPUT type="submit" value="Log in">
    </FORM>
    </P>
</BODY>
</HTML>
```

There's not much to see here, assuming you're familiar with HTML forms. The customer sees an input field and a button labeled Log In, and can enter his login name and click the button. Figure 19.2 shows what the form looks like. The `action="/Order/catalog"` line gives the URL to which the result of submitting this form will be sent; you'll name this application Order, and `catalog` is the first servlet. The host name, port number, and other details are assumed (by the web browser that submits the form) to be the same as for the JSP.

Figure 19.2 The TekMart login screen, as implemented in the file `index.html`. The customer ID will be used by the servlets in the Recommendations Agent.

19.8 *The Catalog servlet*

The tasks the `Catalog` servlet has to do were listed in section 19.5. I'll repeat them here, slightly refined:

1 Get the login name as entered on the login screen; if none, return to the login screen

2 Call `get-new-order-number` to get a unique order number

3 Create a new user session with this login name and number

4 Use the `all-products` query to get a list of `product` facts

5 Forward the results to the JSP for display

Let's look at the `Catalog` servlet to see how these steps are implemented. I'll show the source code for `Catalog` a little at a time; if you find this confusing, the full source code is available on this book's web site.

19.8.1 *Initializing Jess*

The `Catalog` servlet gets right down to business with its `doGet` method:

```
public class Catalog extends BaseServlet {
    public void doGet(HttpServletRequest request,
                      HttpServletResponse response)
    throws IOException, ServletException {
        checkInitialized();
```

The web application uses a `Rete` object as its product database. Where does the `Rete` object come from? For efficiency, all customers will share a single `Rete` object (you can keep their data separate by using distinct order numbers). You want the `Rete` object to be initialized when the web application is first started, and you want it to persist as long as the web server is running. You can write a single method that checks whether the `Rete` object has been initialized and creates and initializes a new one if not. The `Rete` object should be stored in a location that is shared among all the servlets in the application. You can then call this method—call it `checkInitialized`—from the `doGet` method of each servlet you write. To make it easy to call, you can put it in a base class `BaseServlet` and let all your servlets extend `BaseServlet`. You'll be able to put other common behavior in `BaseServlet` as well. `checkInitialized` looks like this:

```
protected void checkInitialized()
    throws ServletException {
    ServletContext servletContext = getServletContext();
    String rulesFile =
      servletContext.getInitParameter("rulesfile");
```

```
      String factsFile =
       servletContext.getInitParameter("factsfile");
      if (servletContext.getAttribute("engine") == null) {
          try {
              Rete engine = new Rete(this);
              new Batch().batch(rulesFile, engine);
              engine.reset();
              if (new File(factsFile).exists())
                  engine.executeCommand("(load-facts " +
                      factsFile + ")");
              servletContext.setAttribute("engine", engine);
          } catch (Exception je) {
              throw new ServletException(je);
          }
      }
  }
```

This listing introduces the `ServletContext` class. Every web application has a single `ServletContext`, shared by all the servlets in the application. `getInitParameter` returns named configuration values from the `web.xml` file; here they're used to provide filenames for the rules and the catalog data. The methods `getAttribute` and `setAttribute` let servlets store arbitrary Java objects in the `ServletContext`; these objects last as long as the web server is running. The `checkInitialized` method creates a `Rete` object, loads it with the necessary rules and facts, and then stores it in the `ServletContext`.

The `BaseServlet` class has a few other methods, as you'll see. One simple method I should mention right now is its implementation of `doPost`:

```
  public void doPost(HttpServletRequest request,
                     HttpServletResponse response)
  throws IOException, ServletException {
      doGet(request, response);
  }
```

The `doGet` method handles HTTP GET requests, and `doPost` handles POST requests. This base class method lets you implement one of these and get the other for free.

19.8.2 *Getting the login name*

Now you'll continue with the implementation of the `Catalog` servlet's `doGet` method. The name the customer provides on the login screen will be available as a named parameter in the `HttpServletRequest` argument to the servlet's `doGet` method; in general, this is how HTML form data is received by a servlet:

```
      String customerId =
              (String) request.getParameter("customerId");
      if (customerId == null || customerId.length() == 0) {
```

```
                dispatch(request, response, "/index.html");
                return;
          }
```

If there's no login name (because the customer didn't enter one, or because the customer came directly to the `Catalog` servlet by typing its URL without logging in), the servlet invokes the login screen using the utility routine `dispatch` that you wrote in section 19.5.2. `dispatch` belongs in `BaseServlet`, because all of your servlets will use it.

19.8.3 *Starting a user session*

The set of browser requests generated by a single customer visiting TekMart.com is called a *session*. A session lasts longer than a single browser request, but not as long as the whole lifetime of the web application. The requests in a session are usually identified using *session cookies*: small bits of data that are transmitted along with the HTTP header data and stored in the browser. If a server sends a session cookie to a browser, the browser is supposed to send it back with each request it makes in the same session. The server can then use the cookies to provide some kind of context for the collection of requests in a session. A servlet container should manage all of this transparently: All a servlet needs to do is to request a `Session` object. The servlet can then store information in the `Session`, and the servlet can then use the `Session` information to identify the individual user.

The next two lines of `Catalog.doGet()` erase any previous session data and create a new `HttpSession`. Then the login name and a new order number are installed in the session, so the other servlets will be able to find them:

```
          request.getSession().invalidate();
          HttpSession session = request.getSession();

          session.setAttribute("customerId", customerId);
          session.setAttribute("orderNumber",
                          String.valueOf(getNewOrderNumber()));
```

The `getNewOrderNumber` method invokes a `defquery` on the shared `Rete` object:

```
     private int getNewOrderNumber() throws JessException {
          ServletContext servletContext = getServletContext();
          Rete engine = (Rete) servletContext.getAttribute("engine");
          String command = "(get-new-order-number)";
          int nextOrderNumber =
              engine.executeCommand(command).intValue(null);
          return nextOrderNumber;
     }
```

You wrote the `deffunction` named `get-new-order-number` in section 17.7.1.

19.8.4 *Querying the product list*

After the customer logs in, you want her to see a catalog of all the available products (this is obviously oversimplified; a real site would have a search capability, because there would be more products than could be listed easily on one page). The name of each product should be listed along with its catalog number, price, and a checkbox for ordering. The Catalog servlet prepares the list of products, and a JSP renders them as HTML. Because you're using Jess as your product database, the code to prepare the list of products should simply run the all-products query; it looks like this:

```
ServletContext servletContext = getServletContext();
Rete engine = (Rete) servletContext.getAttribute("engine");
Iterator result =
    engine.runQuery("all-products", new ValueVector());
request.setAttribute("queryResult", result);
```

All this code does is to invoke the `defquery` and then store the `java.util.Iterator` that comes back as an attribute `queryResult` in the request object, where the JSP can find it.

Note that there are three different ways to share information between the pieces of a web application, and you're using them all:

- The `Rete` object is stored in the `ServletContext`; it is shared among all invocations of all servlets and JSPs for the whole lifetime of the web application.
- You put the login name and order number in the `HttpSession` object, so these are available only within a single browser session.
- You use the `HttpServletRequest` to pass data from a servlet to a JSP; this data exists only during the chain of servlets and JSPs fired off in response to a single browser request.

Each way of communicating between servlets and JSPs has its purpose, and by using them properly, you can make your application easier to understand.

19.8.5 *Invoking the JSP*

All that's left for `Catalog.doGet()` to do is catch any thrown exceptions and then, if all is well, forward the query results on to the JSP for rendering:

```
    } catch (JessException je) {
        throw new ServletException(je);
    }

    dispatch(request, response, "/catalog.jsp");
}
```

The `ServletException` class has a constructor that accepts another exception object as an argument, which makes it easy to report errors from Jess. If a servlet throws a `ServletException`, Tomcat returns an error page that shows the stack trace and error message from both the `ServletException` and any nested exception object. You can then see all this information in your browser. In a real application, you'd want to replace the server's default error pages with custom ones that hide the true nature of the error, but the defaults are handy during debugging.

19.8.6 *The catalog JSP*

The `Catalog` servlet packages a product list and forwards it to the `catalog` JSP for display. (I'm following the convention that Java class names start with an uppercase letter, whereas JSP filenames start with a lowercase letter; hence `Catalog.java` and `catalog.jsp`.) Because we're not web designers, the JSPs are simple and to the point.

This `jsp:useBean` tag fetches the `Iterator` that the servlet put into the `HttpServletRequest`:

```
<HTML>
    <%@ page import="jess.*" %>
    <jsp:useBean id="queryResult"
                class="java.util.Iterator" scope="request"/>
```

The next part is pure HTML. You have a page title, a headline, a little text, and the header row for the table:

```
<HEAD>
    <TITLE>Ordering from Tekmart.com</TITLE>
</HEAD>

<BODY>
    <H1>Tekmart.com Catalog</H1>
    Select the items you wish to purchase and press
"Check Order" to continue.
    <FORM action="/Order/recommend" method="POST">
        <TABLE border="1">
            <TR>
                <TH>Name</TH>
                <TH>Catalog #</TH>
                <TH>Price</TH>
                <TH>Purchase?</TH>
            </TR>
```

Nothing fancy, but it still would be a pain to modify if it were embedded in `println` statements in a servlet!

Now comes the real meat of this JSP. It uses a Java `while` loop to render the rows of the table. Each row contains some text cells plus an HTML `INPUT` widget of type `checkbox`. Each checkbox is labeled with the part number of the corresponding product:

```
<% while (queryResult.hasNext()) {
    Token token = (Token) queryResult.next();
    Fact fact = token.fact(1);
    String partNum =
        fact.getSlotValue("part-number")
        .stringValue(null); %>
<TR>
    <TD><%= fact.getSlotValue("name")
            .stringValue(null) %></TD>
    <TD><%= partNum %></TD>
    <TD><%= fact.getSlotValue("price")
            .floatValue(null) %></TD>
    <TD><INPUT type="checkbox" name="items"
            value=<%= '"' + partNum + '"'%>></TD>
</TR>
<% } %>
```

All that is left is to provide a button to submit the form, and a bunch of closing tags. This part is, again, plain HTML:

```
    </TABLE>
    <INPUT type="submit" value="Check Order">
</FORM>
</BODY>
</HTML>
```

Figure 19.3 shows what the rendered page looks like in a browser.

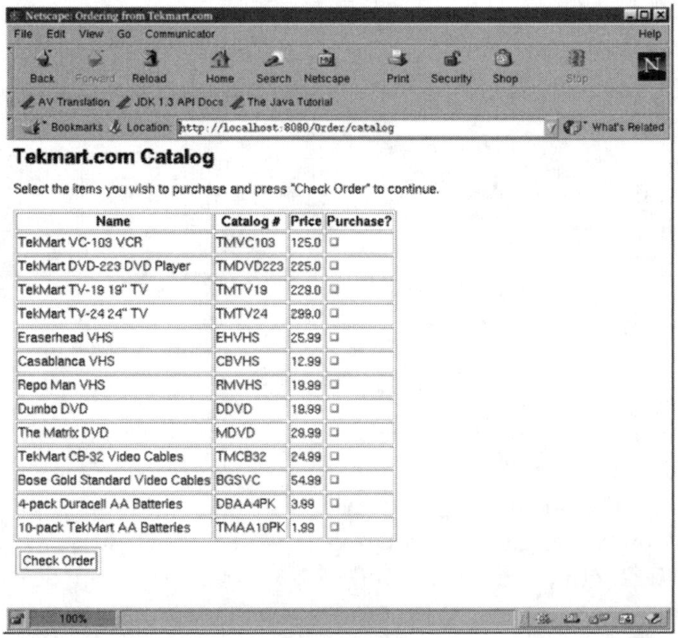

Figure 19.3
The output of the
`catalog` **JSP**

19.9 *Testing*

You can of course test a web application using a web browser, but doing so can be both tedious and error-prone. Thankfully, many automated testing tools are available for web sites. These come in two (often overlapping) categories:

- *Load-testing tools*—Simulate large numbers of simultaneous users visiting your site
- *Page-testing tools*—Invoke specific URLs and check that the resulting pages are correct

The latter kind of testing is more interesting to developers, at least in the early stages. I like to use the open-source HttpUnit/ServletUnit framework for testing web applications (http://httpunit.sourceforge.net/). The HttpUnit part of the framework lets you easily impersonate a browser and make requests to your web application, and then test the generated pages for correctness. The ServletUnit part is a simple servlet container; it lets you put a servlet through its paces directly, and then test things like the values of the servlet's member variables afterward. Both can be valuable, although I personally find that I use the HttpUnit approach more often.

TIP   One word of advice: before you begin writing and testing a large application like this, you'll want to first carefully test and debug your rules as much as possible using Jess's command-line interface!

19.10 *The Recommend servlet*

Recall that when the login form is submitted, the `Catalog` servlet gets a single request parameter named `customerId`. When the `catalog` form is submitted, there is an `items` request parameter for each product the customer purchases, and that will serve as the input to the `Recommend` servlet. The `customerId` and `orderNumber` will still be in the `HttpSession`, and the `Rete` object will be already initialized and stored in the `ServletContext`.

The `Recommend` servlet has several tasks to do:

1   Gather the `items`, `customerId`, and `orderNumber`
2   Make sure the customer is logged in and is ordering something
3   Reset the order, in case the form is resubmitted
4   Create an `order` fact

5   Create a series of `line-item` facts

6   Get recommendations from Jess

7   Pass the recommendations on to a JSP for display

This servlet has to use more of Jess's Java APIs than the `Catalog` servlet does. Let's go through these steps in order as we walk though the `Recommend` source.

19.10.1   *Getting started*

The `Recommend` servlet extends the `BaseServlet` class. It calls `checkInitialized` to make sure the `Rete` object is ready, and then launches into its own initialization:

```
public class Recommend extends BaseServlet {

    public void doGet(HttpServletRequest request,
                      HttpServletResponse response)
    throws IOException, ServletException {
        checkInitialized();

        ServletContext servletContext = getServletContext();
        String[] items = (String[])
            request.getParameterValues("items");
        String orderNumberString = (String)
            request.getSession().getAttribute("orderNumber");
        String customerIdString = (String)
            request.getSession().getAttribute("customerId");
        if (items == null ||
            orderNumberString == null || customerIdString == null) {
            dispatch(request, response, "/index.html");
            return;
        }
```

The call to `getParameterValues` returns the list of purchased items. If the shopping cart is empty, the customer hasn't logged in, or there's no order number, then `Recommend` plays it safe and sends the customer to the login screen to start over. Note that you always have to use `return` after you call `dispatch`—otherwise this servlet will try to append its output to the login screen!

19.10.2   *Creating the order*

Next you need to set up the order in Jess's working memory:

```
try {
    Rete engine = (Rete) servletContext.getAttribute("engine");
    engine.executeCommand("(assert (clean-up-order " +
                              orderNumberString + "))");
    engine.run();
```

By asserting the fact (clean-up-order NNNN), where *NNNN* is the order number, you trigger the CLEANUP module to delete any previous partial order with this number. Calling run lets the engine fire the CLEANUP rules.

Next, the Recommend servlet needs to compose the order fact. Several jess.Value objects are needed for slot values, so they're constructed first. Next a Fact object is created, and its slots are filled with setSlotValue. Finally, the completed fact is asserted with assertFact:

```
int orderNumber = Integer.parseInt(orderNumberString);
Value orderNumberValue =
    new Value(orderNumber, RU.INTEGER);
Value customerIdValue =
    new Value(customerIdString, RU.ATOM);
Fact order = new Fact("order", engine);
order.setSlotValue("order-number", orderNumberValue);
order.setSlotValue("customer-id", customerIdValue);
engine.assertFact(order);
```

Now that the order is in place, the Recommend servlet builds the individual line-item facts to represent the products being purchased:

```
for (int i=0; i<items.length; ++i) {
    Fact item = new Fact("line-item", engine);
    item.setSlotValue("order-number", orderNumberValue);
    item.setSlotValue("part-number",
                    new Value(items[i], RU.ATOM));
    item.setSlotValue("customer-id", customerIdValue);
    engine.assertFact(item);

}
```

Note that it's OK to use the Value objects you created earlier, because Value objects are *immutable*—the data in a Value object can't be changed.

19.10.3 *Getting the recommendations*

Once all the line items are asserted, the Recommendations Agent can be invoked. Calling run is enough to do it. Behind that call to run, all the rules you developed in chapter 17 get a chance to fire. When they do, they create recommend facts, and the query recommendations-for-order retrieves them:

```
engine.run();
Iterator result =
    engine.runQuery("recommendations-for-order",
            new ValueVector().add(orderNumberValue));
```

> **NOTE** A note about calling run here. Your web application might have multiple users at the same time, each running doGet in a separate thread. However, each user has a unique customer ID/order number pair, so the Recommendations Agent can keep track of them separately. Sometimes, one thread might call run, resulting in rules being fired in response to facts asserted from another thread, but this is OK. Other times, one thread might call run right after another thread already has done so, and this second call to run will have no effect; this is also OK. As long as the rules aren't specifically written to expect run to be called only from certain states, everything will work fine. Jess is meant to be used in multithreaded environments, and it uses synchronization to protect potentially fragile code from being corrupted by concurrent access.

19.10.4 Forwarding to JSPs

If there are recommendations, you want to give the customer the chance to purchase the recommended products. If not, you can go straight to the purchase page to get shipping information. In this last bit of code from the Recommend servlet, the choice is between rendering the recommendations in the recommend JSP or checking out via the Purchase servlet, based on whether the recommendations-for-order query returned results. In either case, you dispatch to the new URL. If there were recommendations, you store them in the HttpServletRequest first:

```
        if (result.hasNext()) {
            request.setAttribute("queryResult", result);
            dispatch(request, response, "/recommend.jsp");
        } else
            dispatch(request, response, "/purchase");

    } catch (JessException je) {
        throw new ServletException(je);
    }

    }
}
```

19.11 The recommend JSP

The JSP you need to render the recommendations looks a lot like the catalog JSP. The only substantial difference in the output is the presence of a "Because you bought…" column that links each recommendation back to some other product. The code to produce the display is marginally different because each individual query result contains two facts instead of one (a recommendation fact and a product fact), but the technique for accessing their slots is identical. When the customer submits the form generated by the recommend JSP, the list of selected items is sent to the Purchase servlet. The text of recommend.jsp is shown in listing 19.1.

Listing 19.1   recommend.jsp renders the output of the Recommendations Agent

```
<HTML>
    <%@ page import="jess.*" %>
    <jsp:useBean id="queryResult" class="java.util.Iterator"
            scope="request"/>
<HEAD>
    <TITLE>Some recommendations for you from Tekmart.com</TITLE>
</HEAD>

<BODY>
    <H1>Your Recommendations</H1>
    You may also wish to purchase the following items:
    <FORM action="/Order/purchase" method="POST">
        <TABLE border="1">
            <TR>
                <TH>Name</TH>
                <TH>Catalog #</TH>
                <TH>Because you bought...</TH>
                <TH>Price</TH>
                <TH>Purchase?</TH>
            </TR>
        <% while (queryResult.hasNext()) {
                Token token = (Token) queryResult.next();
                Fact fact1 = token.fact(1);
                Fact fact2 = token.fact(2);
                String partNum =
                    fact2.getSlotValue("part-number")
                    .stringValue(null); %>
            <TR>
                <TD><%= fact2.getSlotValue("name")
                        .stringValue(null) %></TD>
                <TD><%= partNum %>
                <TD><% ValueVector vv =
                        fact1.getSlotValue("because")
                        .listValue(null);
                for (int i=0; i<vv.size(); ++i) { %>
                    <%= vv.get(i).stringValue(null) %>
                    <% if (i != vv.size()-1) %>,
                    <% } %>
                </TD>
                <TD><%=
                        fact2.getSlotValue("price")
                        .floatValue(null) %></TD>
                <TD><INPUT type="checkbox" name="items"
                        value=<%= '"' + partNum + '"'%>></TD>
            </TR>
```

```
          <% } %>
          </TABLE>
          <INPUT type="submit" value="Purchase">
       </FORM>

     </BODY>
   </HTML>
```

19.12 *The Purchase servlet*

The Purchase servlet is a combination of the other two servlets; it makes sure the customer is logged in, asserts any items request parameters as line-item facts, runs the items-for-order query, and then passes the Iterator along to the purchase JSP. In a full-fledged e-commerce system, the purchase JSP would collect shipping and credit-card information; here it just displays the items and sums their prices. The Purchase servlet is shown in listing 19.2, and the JSP is in listing 19.3.

Listing 19.2 Purchase servlet

```java
public class Purchase extends BaseServlet {

    public void doGet(HttpServletRequest request,
                      HttpServletResponse response)
    throws IOException, ServletException {
        checkInitialized();

        ServletContext servletContext = getServletContext();

        String orderNumberString = (String)
            request.getSession().getAttribute("orderNumber");
        String customerIdString = (String)
            request.getSession().getAttribute("customerId");
        if (orderNumberString == null || customerIdString == null) {
            dispatch(request, response, "/index.html");
            return;
        }

        try {
            Rete engine =
                (Rete) servletContext.getAttribute("engine");

            int orderNumber = Integer.parseInt(orderNumberString);
            Value orderNumberValue =
                new Value(orderNumber, RU.INTEGER);
            Value customerIdValue =
                new Value(customerIdString, RU.ATOM);

            String[] items = (String[])
                request.getParameterValues("items");
            if (items != null) {
```

```
            for (int i=0; i<items.length; ++i) {
                Fact item = new Fact("line-item", engine);
                item.setSlotValue("order-number",
                                    orderNumberValue);
                item.setSlotValue("customer-id",
                                    customerIdValue);
                item.setSlotValue("part-number",
                    new Value(items[i], RU.ATOM));
                engine.assertFact(item);
            }
        }

        Iterator result =
            engine.runQuery("items-for-order",
                    new ValueVector().add(orderNumberValue));
        request.setAttribute("queryResult", result);

    } catch (JessException je) {
        throw new ServletException(je);
    }

    dispatch(request, response, "/purchase.jsp");
    }
}
```

Listing 19.3 purchase JSP

```
<HTML>
    <%@ page import="jess.*" %>
    <jsp:useBean id="queryResult" class="java.util.Iterator"
                                scope="request"/>

    <HEAD>
        <TITLE>Thank you for your order</TITLE>
    </HEAD>

    <BODY>
        <H1>Thanks for shopping at TekMart.com!</H1>
        These are the items you are purchasing. If this
        were a real web site, I'd be asking for your credit
        card number now!
        <P>
        <TABLE border="1">
            <TR>
                <TH>Name</TH>
                <TH>Catalog #</TH>
                <TH>Price</TH>
            </TR>
            <% double total = 0;
            while (queryResult.hasNext()) {
                Token token = (Token) queryResult.next();
                Fact fact = token.fact(2);
                double price =
```

```
                    fact.getSlotValue("price").floatValue(null);
                total += price; %>
        <TR>
            <TD><%= fact.getSlotValue("name").
                    stringValue(null) %></TD>
            <TD><%= fact.getSlotValue("part-number").
                    stringValue(null) %></TD>
            <TD><%= price %></TD>
        </TR>
        <% } %>
        <TR><TD></TD><TD>
            <B>Total:</B></TD><TD><%= total %>
        </TD></TR>
    </TABLE>
  </BODY>
</HTML>
```

19.13 *Persistence*

One detail that may have occurred to you is that the web application won't run
forever. Sometimes, it will be taken offline. When it is, the Rete object containing
all the past purchases and recommendations will be lost. This is bad, because this
kind of customer information is valuable. How can you preserve it?

The Servlet class has a destroy method. The servlet container calls destroy
when it's being shut down or the web application is being taken offline. You can
implement destroy to save all this data so it can be restored later. In this implementation the catalog is being read from a flat file (it's actually stored in the same
file as the rules, as a deffacts), so you'll save the order information in a flat file,
too. If you look back at the definition of checkInitialized in section 19.8.1,
you'll see that that method attempts to load facts from the file named in the initialization parameter factsfile. Here's an implementation of destroy that
writes the facts out to that same file:

```
public void destroy() {
    try {
        ServletContext servletContext = getServletContext();
        Rete engine = (Rete)
            servletContext.getAttribute("engine");
        String factsFileName =
            servletContext.getInitParameter("factsfile");
        File factsFile = new File(factsFileName);
        File tmpFile =
            File.createTempFile("facts",
                                "tmp",
                                factsFile.getParentFile());
```

```
            engine.executeCommand("(save-facts " +
                tmpFile.getAbsolutePath() +
                " order recommend line-item next-order-number)");
            factsFile.delete();
            tmpFile.renameTo(factsFile);

        } catch (Exception je) {
            // Log error
        }
    }
```

This implementation tries to be careful about losing data; it writes the facts to a temporary file and then renames the temporary file to `factsfile` only if it succeeds.

The method `checkInitialized` is called by all the servlets, but you want this version of `destroy` to be called only once. I put it into the `Catalog` servlet, although it could go into any of them.

After extensive use, writing and reading the accumulated facts from flat files could become prohibitively slow. Also, loading all the data at startup and saving it all at shutdown may incur too great a risk of data loss in the event of a crash. Instead of using a flat file, the application could be changed to use a relational database. Orders relevant to a particular user could be loaded from a database on demand by the `Recommend` servlet. The `Purchase` servlet could save those facts relevant to a particular order just as the order was being placed, and then remove all the user's facts from the `Rete` object.

19.14 *Deploying the application*

Deploying this web application is no more complex than deploying the single servlets you worked with before. The files need to be installed like this:

```
$(TOMCAT)/
    lib/
        jess.jar
    webapps/
        Order/
            catalog.jsp
            index.html
            purchase.jsp
            recommend.jsp
            WEB-INF/
                web.xml
                classes/
                    tekmart.clp
                    Catalog.class
                    Purchase.class
                    Recommend.class
```

> **NOTE**   The JSPs are all at the top level of the application. The rule file `tek-mart.clp` is in the `WEB-INF/classes` directory so the class loader can find it. One of the most confusing things about beginning servlet development is remembering that the current directory of the servlet is likely to be the directory from which the servlet container was launched; the servlet may not have read or write access to that directory. As a result, you can't expect to use the current directory to find files via relative paths.

The `web.xml` file for the application is no more complex than the one for the first `Hello` servlet. There is one `servlet` element and one `servlet-mapping` tag for each servlet; the servlet `Catalog` is mapped to the URL `/catalog`, and the mappings for the other two are similar. The only new element is the `context-param` element, which is used to pass initialization parameters to the application:

```
<context-param>
    <param-name>rulesfile</param-name>
    <param-value>tekmart.clp</param-value>
</context-param>

<context-param>
    <param-name>factsfile</param-name>
    <param-value>/var/tekmart/data</param-value>
</context-param>
```

These are the two parameters read by the `checkInitialized` method. `/var/tek-mart/data` is the absolute path to a file `data` where the order information should be persisted.

19.15 *What's next?*

This is a book about rule-based application development, not a book about building e-commerce systems, so the web application you've developed here is lacking in many important respects. Security, for example, is nonexistent; and, of course, the system doesn't *do* anything with the order the customer eventually places. These kinds of enhancements are straightforward, though, and many other books discuss them. There's no point in going into them here.

On the other hand, there *are* some ways in which the use of Jess in this application could be improved. You could encapsulate all the knowledge about Jess in the servlets themselves, so the JSPs don't depend on the specific rule engine being used. The JSPs work with `Iterator` objects passed in as `HttpServletRequest` attributes. Instead of passing the iterators returned from Jess, the servlets could construct neutral data structures, using only generic containers of strings and numbers, and pass iterators over these neutral structures instead. This would make it possible to radically modify the templates and rules, or even to use a different rule engine, without touching the JSPs. This encapsulation would have made the sample implementation longer, so I didn't use this technique here; but it's a good idea from a software-engineering standpoint.

Another related possibility would be to use the `javax.rules` API first mentioned in section 2.5. The `javax.rules` API doesn't offer access to many of the features you used in this application, however (notably, queries are not supported). We'll look at using `javax.rules` in the last part of this book.

Finally, I have already mentioned the possibility of using a relational database together with Jess to provide long-term persistence. A database would provide faster, more robust access to historical data than the flat file used here.

19.16 *Summary*

In chapter 17, you developed a rule-based Recommendations Agent for e-commerce. The Recommendations Agent rules are the most complex individual rules presented in this book. You wrote the rules along with a number of queries that the web application needs to probe Jess's working memory.

Many of Jess's Java APIs were presented in chapter 18. You saw how Jess is really a programmer's library rather than an application, and you learned how to embed Jess in other software.

In this chapter, you embedded the Recommendations Agent in a web application built from three servlets, three JavaServer Pages, and one HTML file. The resulting application is the largest one you've developed so far, and the first one you've written that doesn't use `jess.Main`. Many details of a proper e-commerce application are omitted, but the embedded Recommendations Agent could form the core of an industrial-strength online ordering web site.

In the next (and final) part of this book, you'll see how rule engines in general, and Jess in particular, can be used in enterprise applications.

Part 7

Enterprise systems

Business rules are policies and procedures by which corporations conduct their affairs. Capturing business rules in a rule engine makes great sense. This is but one of the many applications for rule engines in *enterprise systems*—large-scale, mission-critical software that supports business operations. At the heart of many enterprise applications these days is the *Java 2 Enterprise Edition* (J2EE) environment. J2EE is an enabling technology that combines access to data and computing resources into a standard service called an *application server*. Part 7 of this book concerns the interaction between rule engines and application servers. We'll touch on a wide range of relevant topics, including using Jess with Enterprise Java-Beans and with XML.

20

Jess, XML, and the enterprise

In this chapter you'll...

- Learn about rule engines in enterprise applications
- Look at XML representations for rules
- Transform Jess rules into XML and back

With this chapter, we begin part 7 of this book. This last part is different from the others in that it's not structured around the development of a single application. Instead, we'll look at many of the pieces that might be used to build applications based on the Java 2 Enterprise Edition (J2EE) platform. The J2EE is simply too big and too complex, and offers too many possibilities, to be covered by one big example.

Therefore, this part will be a kind of grab-bag of individual topics. It includes small programs and program fragments you can use to develop your own applications. In this chapter, we'll look at an overview of enterprise applications and cover representing rules in XML and software for editing rules. In the next chapter, we'll look at using rules in Enterprise JavaBeans applications, the `javax.rules` rule engine API, and more.

You can use the techniques we'll discuss to create new kinds of applications or develop enterprise-ready versions of the applications we've looked at so far. These techniques are all aimed at providing practical solutions for the problem of deploying a rule-based application in a business environment.

20.1 *Enterprise applications*

The word *enterprise* has been the most durable information technology buzzword of the last decade. Simply put, an enterprise application is any large software application that your business depends on. Enterprise applications aren't applications that individual employees use, like Microsoft Word or Adobe Photoshop. An enterprise application is run on behalf of the business itself. Payroll applications, customer databases, resource-planning applications, inventory applications, and online-ordering applications all fit this definition.

Enterprise applications have to perform well and be reliable. This is traditionally described in terms of a long list of additional buzzwords. Generally, enterprise applications are expected to be

- *Scalable*—As the business grows, the application should grow with it. You'll typically add more computers for it to run on, or upgrade the software infrastructure around it.

- *Available*—Users should be able to get at the application 24 hours a day, 7 days a week. Downtime should be minimal or nonexistent.

- *Transactional*—It should be possible to undo complete user interactions up until the last moment. For example, if an ATM machine goes offline while a customer is using it, any incomplete transactions should be cancelled cleanly.

Furthermore, many enterprise applications are

- *Distributed*—An enterprise application may consist of individual components running on many different computers, sometimes physically separated by great distances.
- *Seamless*—This buzzword usually means that many unrelated components work well together to create one application.

20.1.1 *What is the J2EE?*

The *Java 2 Enterprise Edition* (J2EE; http://java.sun.com/j2ee/index.html) is a specification for a software infrastructure for enterprise applications written in Java. It includes more than a dozen APIs, each of which has its own acronym and its own detailed specification. An implementation of the J2EE specification is called an *application server*, and many commercial J2EE application servers are available. JBoss (http://www.jboss.org/) is a very popular open-source implementation. An application server provides services and infrastructure common to many enterprise applications. The J2EE provides a standard, vendor-neutral mechanism for deploying enterprise applications on an application server, making it easy (at least in theory!) to migrate an application to a new application server.

The term *J2EE* is also sometimes used to refer to Sun's own reference implementation of the J2EE specification. This freely available reference implementation makes an excellent standards-compliant, vendor-neutral development platform, but it is not intended to be suitable for deploying enterprise applications (Sun doesn't support it as a deployment platform, and it doesn't have important features like the ability to distribute an application over multiple processors). Much of the J2EE reference implementation is based on components from the Apache Jakarta project, an exemplary open-source project that develops high-quality server-side solutions for the Java platform. In this book, we'll always refer to this software as the *J2EE reference implementation*. Note that the J2EE is the subject of many books. I don't have room here to teach much about J2EE—we're only interested in how rule engines fit into the J2EE environment. I will not provide listings of the classes or methods in any of the J2EE APIs, although here and there I'll discuss a small part of one of these APIs to provide context for the discussion. I assume that you have some experience with the J2EE, but I'll refresh your memory as appropriate.

20.1.2 *What does that stand for?*

You're going to meet a bewildering collection of acronyms in this chapter and the next. I've collected them into table 20.1 for easy reference. Note that this table doesn't include *all* the acronyms related to J2EE development—only the ones I've used in this book!

Table 20.1   Acronyms used in our discussions of J2EE

Acronym	Definition	Meaning
DAML	DARPA Agent Markup Language	An XML-based language for representing general knowledge
DOM	Document Object Model	A standard representation of an XML document as a tree of objects
DTD	Document Type Definition	A way of specifying the allowed contents of an XML document
EJB	Enterprise JavaBeans	A component model for server-side Java programming
J2EE	Java 2 Enterprise Edition	A specification for a Java enterprise application architecture
J2SE	Java 2 Standard Edition	The main Java software developer's kit
JCA	J2EE Connector Architecture	A generic API for accessing resources from EJBs
JDBC	Java Database Connectivity	The standard Java API for working with relational databases
JNDI	Java Naming and Directory Interface	The standard Java naming service in the J2EE environment
JSR 94	The `javax.rules` API	A developing standard API for rule engines
LDAP	Lightweight Directory Access Protocol	A standard enterprise naming service
RMI	Remote Method Invocation	A Java API for connecting Java applications over a network
XML	Extensible Markup Language	A self-describing, structured text document format
XSLT	Extensible Style Language Transformations	A declarative pattern language for transforming XML documents

Just as J2EE is a universal software architecture for building enterprise applications, XML can be seen as a universal data-structuring architecture for the enterprise. To use Jess in the enterprise, you'll want to embed it in a J2EE application; likewise, you'll want to represent the rules themselves in XML.

20.2   *Rules and XML*

A number of projects exist with the aim of defining a standard rule language based on XML, the Extensible Markup Language. XML is a self-describing, text-based structured data file format. The power of XML lies not so much with XML itself, but with the wealth of available tools for working with it. Web browsers can visualize it. Commercial XML editors are available. The XSLT pattern language can be used to write simple scripts that transform an XML document into a new XML document in a different format, or into a non-XML document. And, many high-quality parsers and APIs are available for working with XML from your Java programs.

Representing rules as XML makes sense for several reasons, among them *interoperability*, *editability*, and *searchability*. We'll visit these ideas in the following sections. The availability of XML parsers and of the XSLT scripting language means that transforming rules from XML into the language used by any given rule engine is straightforward. Transforming in the other direction, however, requires you to have a parser for the rule language, and sometimes this is not a trivial thing to write or to obtain. Therefore, it makes the most sense to create and store rules as XML, transforming them into the native format of a rule engine for execution.

Note that although XML has its advantages, it's not very readable. Complex logic represented in XML will always be harder to read than the same logic expressed in a dedicated rule language like the Jess language.

20.2.1 *Interoperability*

Quite a few rule engines are available that are suitable for use in enterprise applications; Jess is only one of them (it's difficult for me not to inject my opinion that Jess is the *best* one, but I hope you'll agree). Each rule engine has its own strengths and weaknesses, of course. In general, especially in the early stages of a large project, it's good to avoid being locked into using one vendor's product. If possible, it makes sense to develop your rules in a vendor-neutral language. Unfortunately, no standard rule language is supported by all (or even some) of the major rule-engine vendors.

In the Jess language, rules are represented as `defrule` constructs. Other rule engines have their own ways of representing rules, including constructs in other programming languages, text that's like natural language, or graphical diagrams and flowcharts. Each of these representations has advantages and disadvantages, but it's important to remember that they're just that: *representations*. In general, a core of common concepts can be expressed in all rule languages. Although each language represents these concepts differently, they all represent the same underlying information.

If rules that only use this common core of concepts are developed in a neutral, flexible representation like XML, then they can easily be translated into the native format supported by a specific rule engine as needed. (Of course, this works only if the rule engine supports a textual representation for their rules. If the only way to enter rules is through a GUI, then the rule engine can't be used this way.)

Unfortunately, restricting your development to that common core can be frustrating, because rule engines vary quite a bit in their capabilities. Furthermore, standard rule representations may not be capable of expressing everything that any one specific engine can. Still, the benefits of interoperability often outweigh these disadvantages.

20.2.2 *Editing and other processing*

In each of the applications you've developed in this book, the programmer has written all the rules after consultation with experts. Some applications, though, are simple enough that nontechnical people can add rules—at least, they could if they understood how to program in a rule language.

In general, you won't be able to teach programming to the folks in marketing, and you shouldn't have to. As a programmer, there's no reason why you can't put together a *rule editor*—a graphical interface that allows nontechnical people to add and modify the rules by pointing and clicking instead of programming.

Some rule engines come with an integrated rule editor or a toolkit for developing rule editors. Sometimes these editors only let you create rules in the native language of the rule engine, not in vendor-independent XML. If you want to keep interoperability, you may need to develop an editor yourself.

The good news is that XML makes this development fairly painless. An editor that works with XML doesn't need to worry about parsing existing rules or writing out completed rules, because it can use existing XML-parsing and -writing libraries to do the hard work. We'll discuss XML-based rule editors in section 20.5.

20.2.3 *Storage and retrieval*

One important use for rule engines in an enterprise environment is to implement *business rules.* Business rules are stated procedures that a business follows to accomplish its work. A business rule is like a policy, but more concrete: It specifies a situation and the action that must be taken in that situation—obviously a great match for the capabilities of a forward-chaining rule engine. Many businesses have a collection of numbered or otherwise indexed business rules. The collection is constantly modified as rules are added, removed, or changed. If a rule engine is being used to carry out business rules, then there must be some way to identify the rule or rules that implement a given business rule. If a whole category of rules is to be removed or temporarily suspended, then the ability to search rules in a flexible way becomes important.

Rules represented as XML are ideal for this kind of environment. If the rules are stored as one large XML document, then XML-based tools can be used to search for specific rules. If individual rules are stored in their own XML files, then these textual snippets can be stored in a relational database and searched using the database's own mechanisms. In either case, XML reporting tools can be used to display the rules found by a query.

Obviously, the whole package we've just described is greater than the sum of the parts. If rules are developed in XML and stored in a searchable fashion, then they can be edited, transformed into executable form, and deployed on demand. In the rest of this chapter, we'll flesh out these ideas by looking at XML-based rule formats and developing an XML-based rule editor.

20.3 XML-based rule representations

In the previous section, we looked at reasons for wanting to store rules in an XML format. In this section, we'll address the question of exactly what format to use. You have several emerging standards to choose from, or you may define your own format. Let's look at each of the alternatives in turn.

20.3.1 RuleML

The RuleML project (http://www.dfki.uni-kl.de/ruleml/) is defining a standard representation for rules of all kinds. The proposed RuleML standard is very broad in its reach: It not only covers forward- and backward-chaining rules of the sort appropriate for rule engines like Jess, but also transformation and mapping rules and rules that define web services.

The following example is by Said Tabet, who has written an XSLT stylesheet that converts a subset of RuleML into Jess rules (http://www.dfki.uni-kl.de/ruleml/jess). Here's a simple Jess rule that says, "If an animal has hair, then it is a mammal":

```
(defrule AnimalsRule1
    (declare (salience 10))
    (has ?x hair)
    =>
    (assert (isa ?x mammal)))
```

Here's the same rule in RuleML:

```
<imp label="AnimalsRule1" priority="10">
    <_head>
        <conclusions>
                <assert>
                <fact>
                    <atom>
                        <_opr>
                            <rel>isa</rel>
```

```
                            </_opr>
                            <var>x</var>
                            <ind>mammal</ind>
                        </atom>
                    </fact>
                    </assert>
                </conclusions>
            </_head>
            <_body>
                <and>
                    <fact>
                        <atom>
                            <_opr>
                                <rel>has</rel>
                            </_opr>
                            <var>x</var>
                            <ind>hair</ind>
                        </atom>
                    </fact>
                </and>
            </_body>
        </imp>
```

You'll notice right away that the RuleML version is much longer. This is typical of most uses of XML; the reason is simply that the XML contains more information. The individual tags explicitly state the purpose of each component of the rule, whereas in the Jess format, that purpose is implicit in the syntax. The explicit tags make translating the XML representation into other rule languages much easier; the verbosity is just the price you have to pay.

20.3.2 *DAML*

DAML (http://www.daml.org/) is the DARPA Agent Markup Language. DAML is an ambitious project to create a language for describing general knowledge on the World Wide Web. DAML contains specific primitives for expressing relationships like *implies* and *is a kind of.* The most important aspect of DAML is that it is a self-contained logical system: Because the relationships are built into the language, any software that understands DAML can make inferences based on the data, without any additional information. Although DAML currently doesn't include a specification for representing rules, one is in the works.

As with RuleML, people have written tools that translate between DAML and Jess. In particular, Mike Dean has several examples on the DAML web site that demonstrate conversion of DAML into Jess facts.

20.3.3 *Homegrown representations*

The RuleML and DAML projects are promising, but they're also still being actively developed. Tools for working with either of these complex standards are still evolving, and it will probably be some time before they come into widespread use.

One of the more serious limitations of existing standard rule languages is their minimal support for describing actions on the right-hand side (RHS) of a rule. As you've seen, in many practical Jess applications, the RHSs of rules can be complex, and working within the confines of a standard representation can be limiting. The situation will doubtless improve in the future, but for now this is a significant problem.

Currently, most people using XML and rules together use a homegrown representation of their own devising. If you come up with your own way of describing rules in XML, it's likely to be simpler than either of the standards we've just described, because it will be tailored for your specific application. With a bit of care, it will be expandable to handle new requirements as your application evolves.

The best part about using a custom representation is that transforming XML from one representation to another can be easily accomplished using an XSLT script. You can rest assured that it will be straightforward to translate your format into a future standard format—or even into an improved version of your own format—when the time comes.

Several of the commercial rule engines have their own XML-based rule format, but Jess does not. You'll remedy this situation by developing one in the next section.

20.3.4 *Strategies for representing rules in XML*

There are two broadly different strategies for representing rules in XML. The most general strategy is the one taken by the DAML and RuleML projects. In this strategy, an XML element represents the concept of a pattern, and the contents of the pattern are data inside the element. As you've seen, the Jess pattern

```
(isa ?x mammal)
```

is represented in RuleML as

```
<fact>
    <atom>
        <_opr>
            <rel>isa</rel>
        </_opr>
        <var>x</var>
        <ind>mammal</ind>
    </atom>
</fact>
```

The interesting thing about this representation is that the data could change, and the elements themselves could stay the same. For example, the pattern

```
(hasa ?x snout)
```

would look like this in RuleML:

```
<fact>
    <atom>
        <_opr>
            <rel>hasa</rel>
        </_opr>
        <var>x</var>
        <ind>snout</ind>
    </atom>
</fact>
```

This means that rule editors and, in general, all rule-processing software can work with this kind of pattern without knowing anything about the meaning of the data. The *metadata* about the pattern (the pattern names, slot names, and so on) is explicit; indeed, it's the important part. This approach is powerful in its generality. The downside to this kind of rule language, however, is that it is verbose, and that some of the software needed to work with it is fairly complex.

An alternate approach is to represent the specifics of the pattern not as data but in the elements. Many people use this approach in specialized domains to good effect; for example, Laurence Leff of Western Illinois University has published extensively on using such an approach with XML representations of legal documents (and he uses Jess in his work).[1]

Using this approach, the original pattern might look like this:

```
<isa>
    <variable>x</variable>
    <symbol>mammal</symbol>
</isa>
```

This XML is much simpler, but less general. Each new `deftemplate` implies a new XML tag, and in the case of an unordered `deftemplate`, new tags for the slots, too, like this:

```
<animal>
    <number-of-feet>4</number-of-feet>
```

---

[1] See Go Eguchi and Laurence Leff, "XML Rule Editor for Java Expert Systems" (Proceedings of the International Conference on Artificial Intelligence and Law (ICAIL) 2002, 66–71; Laurence Leff, "Automated Reasoning with Legal XML Documents," in ICAIL 2001, 215–216; and Laurence Leff, "Rule-Processing in the Legal XML Context", in ICAIL 2001, 27–30.

```
    <hair>yes</hair>
    <color>black and white</color>
</animal>
```

Code to work with this kind of XML is shorter and more efficient than code to work with the more general representation we looked at earlier. In a specialized domain, this kind of representation allows you to develop dedicated tools more quickly and easily. The downside, of course, is the loss of generality.

In the next section, you'll develop an XML format for Jess rules that uses the first of these two approaches. You shouldn't interpret this to mean that I think the first approach is superior. Each approach has advantages and disadvantages, and you should select an approach after considering the alternatives carefully.

20.4 *Representing Jess rules in XML*

In this section, you're going to develop an XML representation for rules. Rather than being motivated by theoretical goals, this representation has the modest goal of being useful as a file format for editing and storing Jess rules. You'll develop an XML DTD (Data Type Definition) to describe this new XML type, and we'll look at some examples. I'll also show you an XSLT script that turns the XML version into Jess rules.

If you haven't seen DTDs before, they are a way to indicate the allowed structure for a specific kind of XML document. DTDs are defined in a kind of pidgin XML—a language that is similar to, but isn't quite, proper XML. ELEMENT lines describe individual XML elements and their contents. ATTLIST lines list the XML attributes an element is allowed to have.

A list of rule elements is called a rulebase; a rule element has a name attribute and optionally a priority (salience) attribute. A rule's content consists of an lhs element and an rhs element:

```
<!ELEMENT rulebase (rule)*>
<!ELEMENT rule (lhs,rhs)>
<!ATTLIST rule name CDATA #REQUIRED priority CDATA "">
```

The * means "zero or more."

An lhs element is a list of zero or more pattern and group elements. A group is a list of one or more other groups or patterns (the + means "one or more"). A pattern element is a list of zero or more slot elements; patterns, and groups have name attributes. A pattern can have a binding. An rhs is a list of zero or more function-call elements:

```
<!ELEMENT rhs (function-call)*>
<!ELEMENT lhs (group | pattern)*>
```

```
<!ELEMENT group (group | pattern)+>
<!ATTLIST group name CDATA #REQUIRED>

<!ELEMENT pattern (slot*)>
<!ATTLIST pattern name CDATA #REQUIRED binding CDATA "">
```

Next, `slot` elements have `name` attributes and contain zero or more `variable`, `constant`, and `function-call` elements:

```
<!ELEMENT slot (variable | constant | function-call)*>
<!ATTLIST slot name CDATA #REQUIRED>
```

Note that this restricts the kind of Jess constructs you can use. You have to use named slots, so you can only use unordered facts. Furthermore, you can't use the | (or) connective. Although this restricts the syntax you can use, it doesn't restrict the patterns that can be expressed. For instance, instead of writing a pattern like

```
(ball (color red | blue))
```

you can write instead the following equivalent:

```
(ball (color ?color&:(or (eq ?color red) (eq ?color blue))))
```

Remember that the Jess code is generated automatically from the XML, so this restriction really doesn't matter.

Finally, a `variable` only has a name, whereas a `function-call` contains a `head` followed by zero or more `constants`, `variables`, or other `function-calls`. The `head` and `constant` elements both contain plain text:

```
<!ELEMENT variable EMPTY>
<!ATTLIST variable name CDATA #REQUIRED>

<!ELEMENT function-call (head,(constant|variable|function-call)*)>
<!ELEMENT head (#PCDATA)>
<!ELEMENT constant (#PCDATA)>
```

20.4.1 *An example rule*

Using this DTD, you can easily write many Jess rules in XML. A rule like this:

```
(defrule AnimalRule2
    (declare (salience 10))
    ?animal <- (animal (has-hair TRUE))
    =>
    (modify ?animal (type mammal)))
```

can be represented as shown by the XML document in listing 20.1.

Listing 20.1   The rule `AnimalRule2` represented as XML

```xml
<?xml version="1.0"?>
<!DOCTYPE rulebase SYSTEM "jess.dtd">
<rulebase>
    <rule name="AnimalRule2" priority="10">
        <lhs>
            <pattern name="animal" binding="animal">
                <slot name="has-hair">
                    <constant>TRUE</constant>
                </slot>
            </pattern>
        </lhs>
        <rhs>
            <function-call>
                <head>modify</head>
                <variable>animal</variable>
                <constant>(type mammal)</constant>
            </function-call>
        </rhs>
    </rule>
</rulebase>
```

20.4.2 *Transforming the XML rules into Jess rules*

The XML rule format can be transformed into Jess rules using an XSLT script of about 100 lines. XSLT programs are declarative rather than procedural—just like rules in Jess. In fact, an XSLT program is precisely a list of rules for transforming specific parts of an XML document into some desired result format. This isn't a book about XSLT programming, so I won't go over the code and try to explain it; but because XSLT is rule-based, it seems appropriate to include this script here (see listing 20.2) along with a brief explanation of a single rule.

NOTE   If you're interested in learning more about XSLT, there are many excellent books on the topic; my favorite is by Michael Kay: *XSLT Programmer's Reference*, 2d ed. (Birmingham, UK: Wrox, 2001). XSLT is a powerful technology, and learning to use it helps you think declaratively, a useful skill relevant to all rule-based programming.

Here is an XSLT transformation rule from the script; it's responsible for processing `variable` nodes:

```xml
<xsl:template match="variable">
    <xsl:text> ?</xsl:text>
```

```
        <xsl:value-of select="@name"/>
    </xsl:template>
```

An `xsl:template` element specifies a rule. The `match` attribute is a pattern that specifies where this rule applies; this one applies to all `variable` elements in the XML. `xsl:text` is an XSLT command that emits its contents verbatim. When this script sees a `variable` element in the XML, it prints a space and then a question mark, which is how variable names in Jess begin. By not including the question mark in the XML, you make it easier to generate rules in other rule languages that don't use the question-mark convention.

The `xsl:value-of` element emits a value derived from an element in the XML. The `select` attribute dictates what the `xsl:value-of` will do; here it says to use the value of the `name` attribute of the current node (the @ character indicates that the following string is an attribute name).

Taken together, this rule transforms the XML fragment

```
<variable name="color"/>
```

into the Jess snippet

```
" ?color"
```

(including that leading space).

Listing 20.2   XSLT script to transform the XML rule format into Jess rules

```
<xsl:stylesheet xmlns:xsl="http://www.w3.org/1999/XSL/Transform"
    version="1.0">
    <xsl:output method="text" indent="no"/>
    <xsl:strip-space elements="*"/>

    <!- Top-level rule template ->
    <xsl:template match="rule">
        <xsl:text>(defrule </xsl:text>
        <xsl:value-of select="@name"/>
        <xsl:text>&#xA;</xsl:text>
        <xsl:if test="@priority != ''">
            <xsl:text> (declare (salience </xsl:text>
            <xsl:value-of select="./@priority"/>
            <xsl:text>))&#xA;</xsl:text>
        </xsl:if>
        <xsl:apply-templates select="./lhs"/>
        <xsl:text> =&gt;</xsl:text>
        <xsl:apply-templates select="./rhs"/>
        <xsl:text>)&#xA;</xsl:text>
    </xsl:template>
```

```
<!- Rule left hand sides ->
<xsl:template match="lhs">
    <xsl:for-each select="./group | ./pattern">
        <xsl:text> </xsl:text>
        <xsl:apply-templates select="."/>
        <xsl:text>&#xA;</xsl:text>
    </xsl:for-each>
</xsl:template>

<xsl:template match="group">
    <xsl:text>(</xsl:text>
    <xsl:value-of select="./@name"/>
    <xsl:text> </xsl:text>
    <xsl:apply-templates/>
    <xsl:text>)</xsl:text>
</xsl:template>

<xsl:template match="pattern">
    <xsl:if test="@binding != ''">
        <xsl:text>?</xsl:text>
        <xsl:value-of select="@binding"/>
        <xsl:text> &lt;- </xsl:text>
    </xsl:if>
    <xsl:text>(</xsl:text>
    <xsl:value-of select="./@name"/>
    <xsl:apply-templates select="./slot"/>
    <xsl:text>)</xsl:text>
</xsl:template>

<xsl:template match="slot">
    <xsl:text> (</xsl:text>
    <xsl:value-of select="./@name"/>
    <xsl:for-each select="./*">
        <xsl:if test="position() != 1">
            <xsl:text>&amp;</xsl:text>
        </xsl:if>
        <xsl:apply-templates select="."/>
    </xsl:for-each>
    <xsl:text>)</xsl:text>
</xsl:template>

<xsl:template match="slot/function-call">
    <xsl:text>:</xsl:text>
    <xsl:call-template name="funcall"/>
</xsl:template>

<!- Rule right hand sides ->
<xsl:template match="rhs/function-call">
    <xsl:text>&#xA; </xsl:text>
    <xsl:call-template name="funcall"/>
    <xsl:text></xsl:text>
</xsl:template>
```

```
<!- Function calls ->
<xsl:template match="function-call">
    <xsl:call-template name="funcall"/>
</xsl:template>

<xsl:template name="funcall">
    <xsl:text>(</xsl:text>
    <xsl:apply-templates select="./*"/>
    <xsl:text>)</xsl:text>
</xsl:template>

<xsl:template match="function-call/function-call">
    <xsl:text> </xsl:text>
    <xsl:call-template name="funcall"/>
</xsl:template>

<!- Miscellaneous ->
<xsl:template match="variable">
    <xsl:text> ?</xsl:text>
    <xsl:value-of select="@name"/>
</xsl:template>

<xsl:template match="constant">
    <xsl:text> </xsl:text>
    <xsl:value-of select="."/>
</xsl:template>
</xsl:stylesheet>
```

Now that you've decided on an XML representation and come up with a way to translate XML rules into Jess rules, you need a way to create and modify rules in the XML format. XML is a text-based format, so you could simply fire up your favorite text editor—but there are definitely better alternatives.

20.5 *Rule editors*

If rules are represented in XML documents, then it follows that you can use XML editors to create rules. Some XML editors are graphical in nature, and you can edit a document by dragging appropriate elements into a tree. If your XML format is described rigorously by a DTD, then many editors can use it to restrict the documents you create to only well-formed rule documents. Although using an XML editor is certainly a possibility, in general doing so is too complicated for nontechnical users. An editor that allows you to customize the display for rule editing would be easier to use.

Some rule engines come with rule editors, and others come with toolkits that let you create your own custom rule editor. Current versions of Jess don't come with a rule editor, but you can write your own custom editor in Java. Using an

XML rule format simplifies this approach quite a bit, because you don't need to worry about parsing input files or writing output files; standard XML libraries handle this for you easily. For example, to load an XML file as a tree of Java objects (a DOM tree), you can use the following:

```
import java.io.*;
import org.w3c.dom.*;
import org.xml.sax.InputSource;
import javax.xml.parsers.*;
//...
    public Document readInRules(String filename)
        throws Exception {
        DocumentBuilderFactory dfactory =
            DocumentBuilderFactory.newInstance();

        DocumentBuilder docBuilder =
            dfactory.newDocumentBuilder();

        FileReader reader = new FileReader(filename);
        try {
            return docBuilder.parse(new InputSource(reader));
        } finally {
            reader.close();
        }
    }
```

You can then use the interfaces in the `org.w3c.dom` package to examine and modify the DOM tree. To write the modified DOM tree back out to disk, you can use the following:

```
import javax.xml.transform.*;
import javax.xml.transform.dom.DOMSource;
import javax.xml.transform.stream.StreamResult;
//...
    public void writeOutRules(Document rules, String filename)
        throws Exception {
        TransformerFactory tFactory =
            TransformerFactory.newInstance();
        Transformer transformer = tFactory.newTransformer();

        DOMSource source = new DOMSource(rules);

        FileWriter writer = new FileWriter(filename);
        StreamResult result = new StreamResult(writer);
        try {
            transformer.transform(source, result);
        } finally {
            writer.close();
        }
    }
```

In between reading and writing, of course, would be code to allow editing of the rules. This could be a Swing GUI, or it could be a web interface using servlets and JSPs. The important thing to remember is that although creating a fully general rule editor might be a difficult undertaking, it's much simpler to create a limited editor that allows your users to add rules within a set of constraints appropriate to your application.

20.6 *Summary*

XML is an excellent way to store rules. It can easily be translated into the native rule language of almost any rule engine. It is easy to parse using one of the many available high-quality XML parsers, and you can write XML documents easily using the `javax.xml.transform` APIs. XML can easily be searched using XSLT scripts or from Java code. Together, these qualities make XML an excellent native format for a rule editor. A rule editor that can be used by nonprogrammers is sometimes an important component of an enterprise system.

In the next chapter, we'll examine ways in which rule engines in general, and Jess in particular, can be used with applications based on Enterprise JavaBeans.

Jess in the J2EE environment

375

Most of the time, when people talk about working in the J2EE environment, they actually mean they are working with Enterprise JavaBeans (EJBs). Programming EJBs can be a real challenge, but they offer powerful capabilities. In this chapter, we'll briefly review what EJBs are and how they are programmed, and then we'll look at several strategies for incorporating rule engines in general, and Jess in particular, into EJB applications.

21.1 A quick tour of EJB concepts

Enterprise JavaBeans is a component architecture for server-side Java programming. The *Beans* referred to are the individual components. They are the relatively small, relatively self-contained pieces of code that implement your application. EJBs are embedded in a *container*—an application that provides essential services to the Beans. These services include things like lifecycle management (creating and deleting beans), network connectivity (so client software can make requests on the beans), database access, persistence, replication, transactions, and more.

21.1.1 Kinds of EJBs

There are three different kinds of EJBs: *entity beans*, *session beans*, and *message-driven beans*. Entity beans represent concrete objects or concepts like people or products. Generally, each entity bean corresponds to a single row in an underlying database, so that changes to the bean are reflected automatically in persistent storage. The EJB container can take care of this persistence automatically, without your writing any database code.

If entity beans represent *things*, session beans represent *actions*. They contain business logic that coordinates the components of an application. *Stateful* session beans have short-term persistence; they are used for things like shopping carts. If you restart the application server, stateful session beans disappear, whereas entity beans survive. *Stateless* session beans merely encapsulate code, and contain no client-specific data.

Message-driven beans are new with the EJB 2.0 specification. They are stateless components that help integrate Java Message Service (JMS) services into the EJB container. JMS is an asynchronous, event-based communication mechanism.

21.1.2 EJB restrictions

To provide the services that it does, an EJB container needs to maintain strict control over its internal state. As a result, there are certain prohibitions on what EJBs are allowed to do. In general, EJBs aren't supposed to do the following:

- Use threads or synchronization
- Use the `java.io` package to access files
- Display a GUI
- Receive incoming socket connections
- Set global objects like socket factories and `System.out`
- Load native libraries
- Use static variables

Some of these limitations are trivial (who would expect to be able to display a GUI from a server-side component?), but others can cause headaches. Not being able to use synchronized methods is one of these; most nontrivial code uses at least some synchronization, Jess included. The restrictions on accessing files, loading native libraries, and especially using static data can severely complicate many applications.

To be fair, *some* of the restrictions can be safely ignored, *if* you understand them. For example, if you know that an application won't use replication services—that is, the J2EE container will always consist of just one process—then you can ignore the admonition about static data.

21.1.3 Do you need to use EJBs?

If servlets and JSPs are the bread and butter of Java programming on the server, EJBs must be the caviar. By writing your program to the EJB specification, you get a wealth of industrial-strength qualities and services for free: scalability, availability, object persistence, transaction management, and more.

But there's no such thing as a free lunch, and with EJBs, as in life, you have to pay for what you get. First, there are those restrictions. If your application meets the definition of a traditional EJB application (a database-driven application that doesn't need to do any substantial computation), then the restrictions aren't bad. But if you need to work with code in a native library, or interface to a legacy system without an EJB interface, or link in substantial amounts of existing Java code, you may have a hard row to hoe to work around them.

Second, programming with EJBs is complex. The J2EE reference implementation comes with almost a dozen command-line tools for managing parts of EJB development (commercial J2EE environments often provide the same functionality via graphical interfaces). There is a substantial market for expensive Enterprise Editions of Java development environments that include graphical tools for automating the EJB development process.

All the infrastructure costs something in performance, as well. Scalability—the ability to perform as well for 1,000 clients as for a single one—doesn't imply high performance.

Given all this, a question suggests itself: "Should I be using EJBs?" That can be a hard question to answer, but it boils down to this: If you need many of the advanced services EJBs make available, then yes, you should use them. If you're only considering EJBs because "it's the thing to do," then you're asking for trouble.

21.1.4 *Accessing external resources from EJBs*

If you decide to use EJBs, you'll almost certainly find that you need to connect them to some external resources—software that can't be directly integrated into the EJB environment. Often, doing so is necessary because of the EJB programming restrictions. Jess uses multiple threads and synchronized methods, and therefore technically can't be used inside an EJB container.

There are a number of possibilities for integrating external resources into EJB applications. One is to ignore the restrictions and directly use the resource from your EJBs; this approach, while not recommended, is widely used, apparently with great success. Although it might work when the application is run on the reference implementation or on a single processor using another application server, it is likely to fail spectacularly if the application is later deployed on a server farm. The application server's persistence and replication services almost certainly won't work if you break these rules.

A more robust way is to run the resource in a separate application, and let the EJB communicate with it through some form of interprocess communication. In the rest of this chapter, we'll look at several approaches to doing this with Jess.

Finally, there's the J2EE Connector Architecture (JCA), a standard Java API for connecting external resources to J2EE servers. The JCA is rather complex, and implementing a JCA connector is far beyond the scope of this book. However, using a connected resource can be simple: Often, it's just a matter of obtaining a reference to the resource from the Java Naming and Directory Interface (JNDI). Commercial application servers that include an integrated rule engine generally make it available in the same way: as an object you can retrieve from JNDI.

21.2 *An RMI-based rule server*

One way to use an external resource (like a rule engine) from an EJB environment is to wrap that resource in a Remote Method Invocation (RMI) server. RMI is a J2EE API for communicating between separate Java applications, either on one machine or over a network.[1] Most EJB environments use RMI for client/server communications. By letting the external resource run in its own separate process, you can avoid problems due to EJB programming restrictions that the resource might violate.

RMI creates the illusion that an object in one Java application exists inside a second application, so that that second application can call the methods of the remote object in the normal fashion. The magic is accomplished by special classes called *stubs* and *skeletons*. An instance of a stub class masquerades as a local object, but its methods package up their arguments in a network request and forward the request to a remote object. A skeleton class receives such a request, unpacks the arguments, and calls the method on the real object. The return value, if any, is then packaged and returned to the stub's method, which returns it as its own return value. The end result is that, for example, an EJB could invoke methods on a rule engine as if it were running inside the J2EE server, when in fact the rule engine was in a separate process—maybe even on a dedicated machine.

The good news is that, unlike writing EJBs, writing RMI servers is simple. In this section you'll develop a flexible and powerful RMI-based rule server in less than 100 lines of code. There are basically four steps to writing an RMI server:

1 Define a remote interface.

2 Implement the remote interface.

3 Write a server mainline.

4 Run the `rmic` tool to create the stub and skeleton classes.

In the remainder of this section, you'll develop an RMI-based rule server that can be used with EJBs or in other situations.

21.2.1 *The remote interfaces*

A remote interface, not surprisingly, defines the methods of an object that are available remotely. For your Jess server, you need two kinds of remote objects: a

---

[1] A good place to learn about RMI is from the RMI chapter of Sun's Java Tutorial; see http://java.sun.com/docs/books/tutorial/rmi/index.html.

remote version of `jess.Rete`, the main class you want to interact with; and a *factory class* that can create instances of your remote `Rete`. A typical client contacts the factory to get a single instance of the rule engine for its own private use, loads it with rules, and then makes repeated method calls to it.

A remote interface has to extend `java.rmi.Remote`, and all of its methods must be declared as throwing `java.rmi.RemoteException`. In addition, any argument or return value types must either be serializable or be themselves remote interfaces.

The remote interface for the factory therefore looks like this:

```
import java.rmi.*;

interface JessFactory extends Remote {
    Jess create() throws RemoteException;
}
```

`Jess` is the name you'll give the remote `Rete` interface. You can make this interface as simple or complex as desired. A version that had only a single `executeCommand` method would be quite useful. To make it more general, however, it at least needs a way to transfer Java objects back and forth, because `executeCommand` only accepts strings as an argument. To do this, you can add support for calling `store` and `fetch`. Here's the resulting interface:

```
import java.rmi.*;
import jess.*;

interface Jess extends Remote {
    Value executeCommand(String command)
        throws RemoteException, JessException;

    void store(String name, Object object) throws RemoteException;

    Value fetch(String name) throws RemoteException;
}
```

You might want to add more methods, but this simple interface gives you access to almost all of Jess's capabilities.

21.2.2 *Implementing the interfaces*

Implementing these two interfaces is easy, because all they do is call a constructor (`JessFactory`) or forward methods to a `Rete` object (`Jess`). Here's an implementation of the `JessFactory` interface:

```
import jess.*;
import java.rmi.*;
import java.rmi.server.*;
```

```
public class JessFactoryImpl extends UnicastRemoteObject
    implements JessFactory {

    private JessFactoryImpl() throws RemoteException {
    }

    public Jess create() throws RemoteException {
        return new JessImpl();
    }
}
```

Remote object implementations often extend the `UnicastRemoteObject` class, but this is not required. By extending UnicastRemoteObject, a remote object implementation class gains the ability to automatically *export* itself, or connect to a network. Because `UnicastRemoteObject`'s constructor throws `RemoteException`, `JessFactoryImpl`'s constructor must throw it as well. The implementation of the single remote method is about as simple as you can get. Improvements might include a pooling mechanism—`create` could check a collection of previously created `Rete` objects before making a new one.

Here's an implementation of the `Jess` remote interface; it's only slightly more complex than `JessFactory`:

```
import java.rmi.*;
import java.rmi.server.*;
import jess.*;

public class JessImpl extends UnicastRemoteObject
    implements Jess {
    private Rete m_rete = new Rete();

    JessImpl() throws RemoteException {}

    public Value executeCommand(String command)
        throws JessException {
        return m_rete.executeCommand(command);
    }

    public void store(String name, Object object) {
        m_rete.store(name, object);
    }

public Value fetch(String name) {
        return m_rete.fetch(name);
    }
}
```

Each instance of `JessImpl` contains a single instance of `jess.Rete`, so `JessImpl` objects are independent.

21.2.3 *Implementing a main method*

When you write an RMI server, you need to supply a main method that creates any objects that should exist when the server starts up. The main method then registers those objects with a naming service so clients can find them. The naming service can either be the standalone program rmiregistry that comes with the J2SE, or an enterprise directory service like LDAP. Here you'll use rmiregistry, accessed via the java.rmi.Naming class. Your main will create a single JessFactoryImpl object and register it under the name Jess. You can put this method in the JessFactoryImpl class:

```
public static void main(String[] argv) throws Exception {
    JessFactoryImpl impl = new JessFactoryImpl();
    Naming.rebind("Jess", impl);
    System.out.println("Jess server running");
}
```

Here you ignored the fact that most RMI servers install a special RMI security manager; a full implementation would certainly do so. You won't use one here because doing so would complicate the deployment step by requiring you to write a security policy file.

21.2.4 *Generating the stubs*

The rmic stub compiler operates on the compiled implementation classes—not, as you might expect, on the remote interfaces. Once you have compiled JessImpl and JessFactoryImpl, you can run rmic like this:

```
rmic JessImpl JessFactoryImpl
```

This command creates JessImpl_Stub.class, JessImpl_Skel.class, and the stub and skeleton classes for JessFactoryImpl.

The RMI rule server is now ready to launch. First, run the rmiregistry program, and then execute the JessFactoryImpl class with your JVM. You should see the *Jess server running* message if everything worked OK.

21.2.5 *A sample client*

You're done writing the rules server, and it's ready to be used from an EJB acting as a client. Although you won't be writing any EJBs here, of course you want to see what the client code would look like. Here's a simple client application that builds a Jess command from its arguments and executes the result in a remote Jess object:

```
import java.rmi.*;

public class JessClient {
```

```
    public static void main(String[] argv)
        throws Exception {
        JessFactory factory = (JessFactory) Naming.lookup("Jess");
        Jess jess = factory.create();
        StringBuffer sb = new StringBuffer();
        for (int i=0; i<argv.length; ++i) {
            sb.append(argv[i]);
            sb.append(" ");
        }
        System.out.println(jess.executeCommand(sb.toString()));
    }
}
```

You need the two remote interface classes to compile this client, and to run it you need the two stub class files as well. Here's a sample run:

```
% java JessClient "(+ 2 3)"
5
```

21.2.6 *Final polishing*

We've ignored many of RMI's subtle points in this section. For example, RMI includes a mechanism for loading stub class files (and other classes) remotely using a web server as a *class server*. This makes it easier to modify the server over time, because otherwise every client installation would need to be updated with a new set of stub files every time the server changed. To enable this mechanism, you need to install a special RMI security manager, define a security policy, and set several system properties defining the location of the class server. You can read all about this and other details in Sun's RMI tutorial (http://java.sun.com/docs/books/tutorial/rmi/index.html).

21.3 *JSR 94: the* **javax.rules** *API*

The `javax.rules` package is a standard, lightweight API for attaching to and using a rule engine. It can be used in both J2SE and J2EE applications. It includes mechanisms for storing and managing rule bases as well as classes that represent individual sessions with a rule engine. Using the `javax.rules` package, you can write Java code to work with rule engines in a generic manner, so that changing from one rule engine to another won't necessitate changes to the code. The name *JSR 94* refers to the standards committee that developed this new API; its members represent many of the major rule engine vendors. I was a member of the committee.

  `javax.rules` is *not* a standard rule language; it says nothing about rule languages. Therefore, if you change rule engine vendors, you will probably have to rewrite your rules, even if you don't need to change your Java code. The `javax.rules` API also doesn't provide an escape mechanism by which vendors can expose nonstandard interfaces, although many of its methods accept property lists as a customization mechanism. Jess is more than just a rule engine, so the `javax.rules` interface limits what you can do with Jess.

Implementations of JSR 94 intended for use with J2EE containers deal with the programming restrictions imposed by that environment. For example, some JSR 94 implementations are built on top of an RMI service like the one you built in the last section. Other JSR 94 implementations are targeted toward high performance in J2SE applications, and some can switch between the two.

At the time of this writing, the JSR 94 specification is being readied for public release, and the only implementation is the reference implementation—which, incidentally, is a driver for Jess! Some of what I'll present here will probably change, but much of this material will still be valid when the `javax.rules` API becomes official.

21.3.1 *Working with javax.rules*

The `javax.rules` API divides interaction with rule engines into *administrative* and *runtime* interactions. Administrative tasks include instantiating the rule engine and loading rules, and runtime tasks include manipulating working memory and executing rules. If you use `javax.rules` from a J2SE program, you'll probably need to perform all of these tasks from your code. On the other hand, in the J2EE environment, the administrative tasks are part of application deployment. Eventually, `javax.rules`-compliant application servers should offer dedicated mechanisms—GUIs—for installing a rule engine and preparing rule sessions, just as they currently include tools for plugging in databases and other resources. The JSR 94 reference implementation includes a JCA connector that makes a `RuleService-Provider` accessible through JNDI.

Setting things up

The administrative phase begins with finding an appropriate `javax.rules.Rule-ServiceProvider` object, which gives the programmer access to the rest of the `javax.rules` implementation. In a J2EE environment, you may be able to retrieve the `RuleServiceProvider` using JNDI. Otherwise, you can get one from the `javax.rules.RuleServiceProviderManager` class:

```
String implName = "org.jcp.jsr94.ri.RuleServiceProvider";
  Class.forName(implName);
RuleServiceProvider serviceProvider =
   RuleServiceProviderManager.getRuleServiceProvider(implName);
```

This is a little like loading a JDBC driver—it's a similar concept, in that both provide access to an external resource, and you need to do some general initialization before you instantiate any of the classes.

Once you have the `RuleServiceProvider`, you can retrieve a `javax.rules.admin.RuleAdministrator`. From the `RuleAdministrator`, you can get a `RuleExecutionSetProvider`, which, as the name suggests, creates `javax.rules.RuleExecutionSets`. A `RuleExecutionSet` is basically a loaded set of rules, ready to be executed.

The `javax.rules.admin` package includes two different `RuleExecutionSetProvider` classes. `RuleExecutionSetProvider` itself includes methods for creating `RuleExecutionSets` from serializable objects, and therefore can be used when the rule engine is located in a remote server; the constructor arguments can be sent via RMI. Another class called `LocalRuleExecutionSetProvider` includes additional methods to create `RuleExecutionSets` from nonserializable resources like `java.io.Reader` objects (local files). Given a `RuleServiceProvider`, you can create a `RuleExecutionSet` from a local file `rules.xml` like this:

```
RuleAdministrator admin = serviceProvider.getRuleAdministrator();
HashMap properties = new HashMap();
properties.put("name", "My Rules");
properties.put("description", "A trivial rulebase");

FileReader reader = new FileReader("rules.xml");
RuleExecutionSet ruleSet = null;
try {
    LocalRuleExecutionSetProvider lresp =
        admin.getLocalRuleExecutionSetProvider(properties);

    ruleSet = lresp.createRuleExecutionSet(reader, properties);
} finally {
    reader.close();
}
```

You then register the `RuleExecutionSet` with the `RuleAdministrator` under a well-known name. At runtime, you use the same name to create a `RuleSession`; the `RuleSession` uses the named `RuleExecutionSet`. This example uses the well-known name `rules`:

```
admin.registerRuleExecutionSet("rules", ruleSet, properties);
```

Executing the rule engine

In the runtime phase, you create a `RuleSession`. A `RuleSession` is basically an instance of a rule engine with a specific set of rules loaded into it. You get `RuleSessions` from the `javax.rules.RuleRuntime` object, and you get the `RuleRuntime`, in turn, from the `RuleServiceProvider`.

There are two kinds of `RuleSessions`: *stateful* and `stateless`. They differ in the capabilities they offer. The working memory of a `StatefulRuleSession` persists between method calls. You can add objects to working memory in a series of invocations, then run the engine, and then add more objects and run again. In contrast, a `StatelessRuleSession` is a one-shot affair: To call its `executeRules` methods, you must supply the entire initial contents of working memory, and you will receive a list of the final contents as a return value.

Here you create a `StatefulRuleSession`, add two objects (an `Integer` and a `String`) to working memory, execute the rules, and then retrieve the entire contents of working memory as a `java.util.List`. Finally, you dispose of the `RuleSession` by calling `release`:

```
RuleRuntime runtime = rsp.getRuleRuntime();
StatefulRuleSession session = (StatefulRuleSession)
    runtime.createRuleSession("rules", properties,
    RuleRuntime.STATEFUL_SESSION_TYPE);
session.addObject(new Integer(1));
session.addObject("A string");
session.executeRules();
List results = session.getObjects();
session.release();
```

The `javax.rules` API is clearly designed to be used in a managed environment like the J2EE. For a simple application like the one we're imagining here, it could be overkill. Consider that by using Jess's native API, all the code in this section and the preceding one can be expressed as follows (assuming the appropriate `defclasses` are defined in `rules.clp`):

```
Rete session = new Rete();
session.executeCommand("(batch rules.clp)");
session.definstance("java.lang.Integer", new Integer(1), false);
session.definstance("java.lang.String", "A string", false);
session.run();
Iterator results = engine.listDefinstances();
```

On the other hand, both in the J2EE environment and in standalone applications, `javax.rules` gives you some measure of vendor independence.

21.3.2 *The reference implementation*

The first implementation of `javax.rules` is the reference implementation (RI) included as part of the specification. This RI is, as I mentioned earlier, a wrapper for Jess. It's an interesting case study, because the mapping of the `javax.rules` API forces a specific interpretation onto Jess's more general facilities. Here I'm not concerned with describing how it is implemented, but simply with filling in the missing information that allows you to use it.

Working memory elements in a `RuleSession` are arbitrary Java objects. Because Jess doesn't let you add arbitrary objects to working memory without providing extra information in the form of a `definstance` call, the RI has to make some assumptions and provide the extra information. Every time an object is added to working memory, Jess automatically defines a `defclass` for it; the `defclass` name is the full class name of the object: `java.lang.Integer`, for example. Therefore, a program to add two `Integers` would look like this:

```
(defclass java.lang.Integer java.lang.Integer nil)
(defrule add-two-integers
    (java.lang.Integer (OBJECT ?i1))
    (java.lang.Integer (OBJECT ?i2&~?i1))
    =>
    (undefinstance ?i1)
    (undefinstance ?i2)
    (bind ?i3 (new Integer (+ (?i1 intValue) (?i2 intValue))))
    (definstance java.lang.Integer ?i3 static))
```

Working memory elements that are not JavaBeans call for a different programming style, compared to normal Jess. You can use individual patterns to bind objects, as is the case here, but most tests will be fairly verbose and so should be expressed as `test` conditional elements, as in the following example:

```
(defrule find-number-3
    (java.lang.Integer (OBJECT ?i1))
    (test (eq 3 (?i1 intValue)))
    =>
    ;; Found 3, do something...
```

One other thing about the RI is special: The input files must be XML, rather than normal Jess input files. The format is exceedingly simple. Each XML file must contain a `rule-execution-set` element, which contains three children: a `name` (the name of the set of rules); a `description` (a brief summary of the rule's purpose); and a `code` element, which contains Jess code. Note that the Jess code has to use normal XML encoding, so that special characters like & and > must be represented as `&amp;` and `&lt;`, respectively. Here's a rule base containing the single add-two-integers rule:

```
<?xml version="1.0" encoding="UTF-8"?>

<rule-execution-set>
    <name>Mathemetical rules</name>
    <description>One rule that adds two Integers/description>
    <code>
        (defclass java.lang.Integer java.lang.Integer nil)
        (defrule add-two-integers
```

```
            (java.lang.Integer (OBJECT ?i1))
            (java.lang.Integer (OBJECT ?i2&amp;~?i1))
            =&gt;
            (undefinstance ?i1)
            (undefinstance ?i2)
            (bind ?i3 (new Integer (+ (?i1 intValue) (?i2 intValue))))
            (definstance java.lang.Integer ?i3 static))
        </code>
    </rule-execution-set>
```

The RI is bound by the limitations of the `javax.rules` API. As such, there are no hooks to give you access to queries, `store/fetch`, or other Jess features. When the `javax.rules` API is finalized, Jess will offer native support for it, including extensions to allow access to these features and more.

21.4 *Summary*

This chapter has had a bit of a shotgun quality to it—it hits a bit here and a bit there, and misses little bits in between—and there was no way to avoid writing it this way. The J2EE specification is vast, and there are many different ways you can build applications with it. I hope that what I've described in this chapter can serve as a sourcebook when you design your own rule-based J2EE applications, and that I've brought out some of the important issues.

After an overview of Enterprise JavaBeans, we looked at building a custom rule server using Jess and Java RMI. Servers like this one are in widespread use. You can customize this simple rule server for your own needs by adding more methods or by adding an object pool or other lifecycle services.

The `javax.rules` API, which as of this writing is still being developed, promises to provide portable, generic access to rule engines from multiple vendors. The API includes sophisticated features for managing rule bases in the J2EE environment but is still fairly simple to use in runtime components.

Jess in Action has taught you to program in the Jess language and build a wide variety of rule-based software. From the simple command-line Tax Forms Advisor to the sophisticated web-based Recommendations Agent, from the interactive PC Repair Assistant to the autonomous HVAC Controller, you've seen how rule technology can be applied to many different kinds of applications. Each of the systems you've developed in this book can serve as a launching point for a whole family of software, and still you've barely scratched the surface of the practically unlimited potential of Jess.

Jess functions

This appendix lists every function included with Jess 6.1. In the argument lists, *number* means any number, and *lexeme* means any symbol or string. *boolean* arguments can be anything; all values but the symbol FALSE are interpreted as "true." An argument type of *expression* means that anything is acceptable. A *fact* argument means the actual text of a fact, whereas a *fact-id* is either a reference to a jess.Fact object or the integer ID of a fact. Square brackets denote optional arguments. + means one or more of the preceding argument, * means zero or more, and | means "or." Most of these functions are very flexible about the arguments they'll accept. Extra arguments are generally ignored, and missing arguments are defaulted in some cases.

Arguments that are filenames deserve special care. A filename argument must follow Jess's rules for a valid symbol or string. On UNIX systems, this presents no particular problems, but Win32 filenames may need special treatment. In particular: Pathnames should use either \\ (double backslash) or / (forward slash) instead of \ (single backslash) as directory separators; and pathnames that include a colon (:) or a space character ( ) *must* be enclosed in double quotes.

Some "functions" are actually *constructs*—special forms built into the Jess language—and so don't appear in this list. Constructs can't be called like regular functions; for example, they can't appear on the right-hand side (RHS) of a rule. The complete list of constructs includes defrule, deftemplate, defglobal, deffacts, deffunction, and defquery; they are all discussed in part 2 of this book.

Jess functions throw an exception of type jess.JessException if the arguments are of the wrong type.

(- *<number>* *<number>*+)

Returns the first argument minus all subsequent arguments. The return value is an INTEGER unless any of the arguments are FLOAT, in which case it is a FLOAT.

(/ *<number>* *<number>*+)

Returns the first argument divided by all subsequent arguments. The return value is a FLOAT.

(* *<number>* *<number>*+)

Returns the products of its arguments. The return value is an INTEGER unless any of the arguments are FLOAT, in which case it is a FLOAT.

(** <number> <number>)

Raises its first argument to the power of its second argument (using Java's `Math.pow()` function). The return value is `NaN` (not a number) if both arguments are negative.

(+ <number> <number>+)

Returns the sum of its arguments. The return value is an `INTEGER` unless any of the arguments are `FLOAT`, in which case it is a `FLOAT`.

(< <number> <number>+)

Returns `TRUE` if each argument is less than the argument following it; otherwise, returns `FALSE`.

(<= <number> <number>+)

Returns `TRUE` if the value of each argument is less than or equal to the value of the argument following it; otherwise, returns `FALSE`.

(<> <number> <number>+)

Returns `TRUE` if the value of the first argument is not equal in value to all subsequent arguments; otherwise, returns `FALSE`.

(= <number> <number>+)

Returns `TRUE` if the value of the first argument is equal in value to all subsequent arguments; otherwise, returns `FALSE`. The integer 2 and the float 2.0 are =, but not `eq`.

(> <number> <number>+)

Returns `TRUE` if the value of each argument is greater than that of the argument following it; otherwise, returns `FALSE`.

(>= <number> <number>+)

Returns `TRUE` if the value of each argument is greater than or equal to that of the argument following it; otherwise, returns `FALSE`.

(abs <number>)

Returns the absolute value of its only argument.

(agenda [<module name>])

Displays a list of rule activations to the WSTDOUT router. If no argument is specified, the activations in the current module (not the focus module) are displayed. If a module name is specified, only the activations in that module are displayed. If * is specified, then all activations are displayed.

(and <expression>+)

Returns TRUE if none of the arguments evaluate to FALSE; otherwise, returns FALSE.

(apply <expression>+)

Returns the result of calling the first argument, as a Jess function, on all the remaining arguments. The strength of this function lies in the fact that you can call a function whose name, for instance, is in a Jess variable. In this example, a mathematical function is applied to a list of numbers; Jess gets the name of the function from the console by calling read:

```
Jess> (bind ?function (read))
+ ;; You enter "+"
"+"
Jess (apply ?function 1 2 3 4 5)
15
```

(asc <lexeme>)

Returns the Unicode value of the first character of the argument, as an RU.INTEGER.

(assert <fact>+)

Asserts all facts into working memory; returns the fact-ID of the last fact asserted or FALSE if no facts were successfully asserted (for example, if all facts given are duplicates of existing facts).

(assert-string <string>)

Converts a string into a fact and asserts it. Attempts to parse the string as a fact and, if successful, returns the value returned by assert with the same fact. Note that the string must contain the fact's enclosing parentheses:

```
Jess> (assert-string "(grocery-list milk bread soup)")
<Fact-0>
```

(bag <command> <expression>+)

Lets you manipulate Java hash tables from Jess. The net result is that you can create any number of associative arrays or property lists. Each such array or list has a name by which it can be looked up. The lists can contain other lists as properties, or any other Jess data type.

The bag command does different things based on its first argument. It's really seven commands in one:

- create accepts a string, the name of a new bag to be created. The bag object itself is returned. For example:

```
Jess> (bag create my-bag)
<External-Address:java.util.Hashtable>
```

- delete accepts the name of an existing bag and deletes it from the list of bags.

- find accepts the name of a bag and returns the corresponding bag object, if one exists, or nil.

- list returns a list of the names of all the existing bags.

- set accepts as arguments a bag, a String property name, and any Jess value. The named property of the given bag is set to the value, and the value is returned.

- get accepts as arguments a bag and a String property name. The named property is retrieved and returned, or nil if there is no such property. For example:

```
Jess> (defglobal ?*bag* = 0)
TRUE
Jess> (bind ?*bag* (bag create my-bag))
<External-Address:java.util.Hashtable>
Jess> (bag set ?*bag* my-prop 3.0)
3.0
Jess> (bag get ?*bag* my-prop)
3.0
```

- props accepts a bag as the single argument and returns a list of the names of all the properties of that bag.

Bag objects are local to each Rete object.

(batch <filename>)

Attempts to parse and evaluate the given file as Jess code. If successful, returns the return value of the last expression in the file. In an applet, batch will try to find the file relative to the applet's document base. In any program, if the file is not found, the name is then passed to ClassLoader.getSystemResourceAsStream(). This allows files along the class path, including files in JARs, to be batched. Jess uses the class loader that loaded the *application object*. You can supply this special object as a constructor argument when you create a jess.Rete object.

(bind <variable> <expression>)

Assigns the given value to the given variable, creating the variable if necessary. Returns the given value.

(bit-and <integer>+)

Performs the bitwise AND of the arguments. `(bit-and 7 4)` is 4, and is equivalent to the Java `7 & 4`.

(bit-not <integer>)

Performs the bitwise NOT of the argument. `(bit-not 0)` is –1, and is equivalent to the Java `~0`.

(bit-or <integer>+)

Performs the bitwise OR of the arguments. `(bit-or 2 4)` is 6, and is equivalent to the Java `2 | 4`.

(bload <filename>)

Decompresses and deserializes a file to restore the state of the current `Rete` object. The argument is the name of a file previously produced by the `bsave` command. I/O routers are not restored from the file; they retain their previous state. Furthermore, `JessListener` objects are not restored from the file; again, they are retained from their state prior to the `bload`. If the filename contains special characters, it must be passed as a double-quoted string.

(bsave <filename>)

Dumps the engine in which it is called to the given filename argument in a format that can be read using `bload`. Any input/output streams and event listeners are not saved during the serialization process. If the filename contains special characters, it must be passed as a double-quoted string.

(build <string>)

Evaluates a string as though it were entered at the command prompt. Attempts to parse and evaluate a single expression from the given string as Jess code. If successful, returns the return value of the expression. This function is typically used to define rules or other constructs from Jess code at runtime. For instance:

```
(build "(defrule my-rule (foo) => (bar))")
```

Note that the string must consist of a single expression.

(call (<external-address> | <lexeme>) <lexeme> <expression>+)

Calls a Java method on the given object, or a static method of the class named by the first argument. The second argument is the name of the method, and subsequent arguments are passed to the method. Arguments are promoted, and overloaded methods are selected precisely as for new. The return value is converted to a suitable Jess value before being returned. Array return values are converted to Jess lists.

The functor call may be omitted if the method being called is nonstatic. The following two method calls are equivalent:

```
;; These are both legal and equivalent
(call ?vector addElement (new java.lang.String "Foo"))
(?vector addElement (new java.lang.String "Foo"))
```

(call-on-engine <external-address> <jess-code>)

Executes some Jess code in the context of the given Rete object (the *external-address*). This is a nice way to send messages between multiple Rete engines in one process. Note that the current variable context is used to evaluate the code, so (for instance) all defglobal values will be from the calling engine, not the target:

```
Jess> (bind ?engine (new jess.Rete))
<External-Address:jess.Rete>
Jess> (call-on-engine ?engine (+ 2 2))
4
```

(clear)

Clears the rule engine. Deletes all rules, deffacts, defglobals, templates, facts, activations, and so forth. User functions written in Java are *not* deleted.

(clear-focus-stack)

Removes all modules from the focus stack.

(clear-storage)

Clears the hash table used by store and fetch.

(close [<lexeme>+])

Interprets each argument as an I/O router name. Closes any I/O routers associated with the given names by calling close() on the underlying stream, and then removes the routers. Any subsequent attempt to use a closed router will report bad router. See open.

(complement$ <list> <list>)

Returns a new list consisting of all elements of the second list not appearing in the first list.

(context)

Returns the execution context (a jess.Context object) in which it is called. This provides a way for deffunctions to get a handle to this useful class.

(count-query-results <lexeme> <expression>+)

Runs the query whose name is given by the first argument and returns a count of the matches. See the documentation for defquery for more details. Also see run-query for caveats concerning calling count-query-results from a rule.

(create$ <expression>*)

Returns a new list containing all the given arguments, in order. For each argument that itself is a list, the individual elements of the list are added to the new list; this function will not create nested lists (which are not meaningful in the Jess language). Note that lists must be created explicitly using this function or others that return them; ordinary lists cannot be directly parsed from Jess input.

(defadvice (before | after) (<lexeme> | <list>) <expression>+)

Lets you supply extra code to run before or after the function(s) named by the second argument. The list of expressions is taken as a block of code to execute. If *before* is specified, the code executes before the named function(s); the variable ?argv holds the entire function call vector (function name and parameters) on entry to and exit from the code block. If *after* is specified, the function is called before the code block is entered. When the block is entered, the variable ?retval refers to the original function's return value.

Whether before or after is specified, if the code block explicitly calls return with a value, the returned value appears to the caller to be the return value of the original function. For before advice, this means the original function is not called.

(defclass <lexeme> <lexeme> [extends <lexeme>])

Defines a template based on a Java class. The first argument is the template tag, and the second argument is the name of a Java class. The names of the template's slots are based on the JavaBeans properties found in the named class. If the optional *extends* clause is included, the last argument is the name of another template; it becomes the parent template of the new template. The common slots in the two templates are in the same order, at the beginning of the new template.

Rules defined to match instances of the parent template also match instances of the new child template.

(definstance <lexeme> <object> [static | dynamic])

Creates a shadow fact representing the given Java object, according to the template named by the first argument (which should have come from defclass). If the symbol static is *not* supplied as the optional third argument, a PropertyChangeListener is installed in the given object, so that Jess can keep the shadow fact updated if the object's properties change (dynamic is the default). The shadow fact is returned.

Note that it is an error for a given Java object to be installed in more than one definstance at a time. The second and subsequent definstance calls for a given object will return a fact with an ID of –1.

(delete$ <list> <integer> <integer>)

Deletes the specified range from a list. The first integer expression is the one-based index of the first element to remove; the second is the one-based index of the last element to remove.

(div <number> <number>+)

Returns the first argument divided by all subsequent arguments using integer division.

(do-backward-chaining <lexeme>)

Marks a template as being eligible for backward chaining. If the template is unordered—that is, if it is explicitly defined with deftemplate or defclass—then it must be defined *before* calling do-backward-chaining. In addition, this function must be called *before* defining any rules that use the template.

(duplicate <fact-id> (<symbol> <expression>)+)

Makes a copy of the given fact, with the values of slots modified as indicated by the (symbol, expression) pairs. The fact-id must refer to an unordered fact. Each list is taken as the name of a slot in this fact and a new value to assign to the slot. A new fact is asserted, which is similar to the given fact but which has the specified slots replaced with new values. The fact-id of the new fact is returned. It is an error to call duplicate on a shadow fact.

(e)

Returns the transcendental number *e*.

(engine)

Returns the `jess.Rete` object in which the function is called.

(eq <expression> <expression>+)

Returns TRUE if the first argument is equal in type and value to all subsequent arguments. For strings, this means identical contents. Uses the Java `Object.equals()` function, so it can be redefined for external types. Note that the integer 2 and the floating-point number 2.0 are *not* eq, but they are eq* and =.

(eq <expression> <expression>+)*

Returns TRUE if the first argument is equivalent to all the others. Uses numeric equality for numeric types, unlike eq. Note that the integer 2 and the floating-point number 2.0 are *not* eq, but they are eq* and =.

(eval <string>)

Synonym for `build`.

(evenp <number>)

Returns TRUE for even numbers; otherwise, returns FALSE. Results with nonintegers are unpredictable.

(exit)

Exits Jess and halts Java by calling `System.exit(0)`.

(exp <number>)

Raises the value *e* to the power of the argument.

(explode$ <string>)

Creates a list value from a string. Parses the string as if by a succession of read calls, and then returns these individual values as the elements of a list.

(external-addressp <expression>)

Returns TRUE or FALSE depending on whether the given expression is an external address.

(fact-id <integer>)

If the argument is the fact-id of an existing fact, returns the actual `jess.Fact` object; otherwise, throws an exception.

(facts [symbol | *])

Prints a list of all facts in working memory. If an argument is given, it should be the name of a module; only the facts from that module are printed. The symbol * indicates all modules. With no argument, only the facts from the current module are listed.

(fact-slot-value <fact-id> <symbol>)

Returns the value in the named slot of the fact with the given fact-id.

(fetch <lexeme>)

Retrieves and returns any value previously stored by the store function under the given name, or nil if there is none. Analogous to the fetch() member function of the Rete class. Note that the storage used by store and fetch is local to each individual Rete object.

(first$ <list>)

Returns the first field of a list as a new single-element list; like car in traditional LISP.

(float <number>)

Converts its only argument to a Jess floating-point number.

(floatp <expression>)

Returns TRUE for arguments of type RU.FLOAT; otherwise, returns FALSE.

(focus <symbol>+)

Changes the focus module. The next time the engine runs, the first rule to fire will be from the first module named as an argument (if any rules are activated in this module). The previously active module is pushed down on the focus stack. If more than one module is listed, they are pushed onto the focus stack in order from right to left. If the engine is running at the time of the call, the focus changes immediately and the next rule to fire will be from the first named module.

(foreach <variable> <list> <expression>*)

Sets the named variable to each of the values in the list in turn; for each value, all the other expressions are evaluated in order. The return function can be used to break the iteration. This example uses foreach to print each item in the list:

```
(foreach ?x (create$ a b c d) (printout t ?x crlf))
```

(format <symbol> <string> <expression>*)

Creates a formatted string. Formats the third and subsequent arguments according to the format string (the second argument), which is identical to that used by `printf` in the C language (refer to a C book for more information). Returns the string, and optionally prints the string to the I/O router named by the first argument. If you pass `nil` for the router name, no printing is done.

(gensym*)

Returns a special unique sequenced value consisting of the letters *gen* plus an integer. Use `setgen` to set the value of the integer to be used by the next `gensym` call.

(get <object> <symbol>)

Retrieves the value of a JavaBean's property. The first argument is the object, and the second argument is the name of the property. The return value is converted to a suitable Jess value exactly as for `call`. You can refer to the JavaBeans specification for the complete definition of a *property*, but often a property *X* implies a method `getX()`.

(get-current-module)

Gets the current module (see `set-current-module`).

(get-focus)

Returns the name of the current focus module (see `focus`).

(get-focus-stack)

Returns the module names on the focus stack as a list. The top module on the stack is the first entry in the list.

(get-member (<object> | <lexeme>) <symbol>)

Retrieves the value of a Java member variable. The first argument is a Java object (or the name of a class, for a static member), and the second argument is the name of the variable. The return value is converted to a suitable Jess value exactly as for `call`.

(get-multithreaded-io)

Returns TRUE if Jess is currently using a separate thread to flush I/O streams. Turning this on can lead to a modest performance enhancement, but may result in loss of output on program termination.

(get-reset-globals)

Indicates the current setting of global variable reset behavior. See `set-reset-globals` for an explanation of this property.

(get-salience-evaluation)

Indicates the current setting of salience evaluation behavior. See `set-salience-evaluation` for an explanation of this property.

(halt)

Halts the rule execution cycle. Has no effect unless the rule engine is running.

(if <boolean> then <expression>+ [else <expression>+])

Allows conditional execution of a group of actions. The Boolean expression is evaluated. If it does not evaluate to FALSE, the first list of expressions is evaluated, and the return value is whatever is returned by the last expression of that list. If the Boolean expression evaluates to FALSE and the optional second list of expressions is supplied, then those expressions are evaluated, and the value of the last is returned.

(implode$ <list>)

Creates a string from a list. Converts each element of the list to a string and returns these strings concatenated with single intervening spaces.

(import <lexeme>)

Works like the Java `import` statement. You can import either a whole package using (`import java.io.*`) or a single class using (`import java.awt.Button`). After a call to `import`, all functions that can accept a Java class name (`new`, `defclass`, `call`, and so on) refer to the import list to try to find the class that goes with a specific name. Note that as in Java, `java.lang.*` is implicitly imported.

(insert$ <list> <integer> <expression>+)

Inserts one or more values in a list. Inserts the elements of the second and later arguments so that they appear starting at the given one-based index of the first list. If any of the expressions are themselves lists, the individual elements of these lists are inserted, not the lists themselves.

(instanceof <object> <lexeme>)

Returns TRUE if the object could legally be assigned to a Java variable whose class type is given by the second argument, a Java class name. Implemented using `java.lang.Class.isInstance()`. The class name can be fully qualified or it can be an imported name; see `import`.

(integer <number>)

Converts its only argument to an integer. Truncates any fractional component of the value of the given numeric expression and returns the integral part.

(integerp <expression>)

Returns TRUE for INTEGER values; otherwise, returns FALSE.

(intersection$ <list> <list>)

Returns the intersection of two lists: a list consisting of the elements the two argument lists have in common.

(jess-version-number)

Returns a version number for Jess; currently 6.1.

(jess-version-string)

Returns a human-readable string descriptive of this version of Jess.

(length$ <list>)

Returns the number of fields in a list value.

(lexemep <expression>)

Returns TRUE for symbols and strings; otherwise, returns FALSE.

(list-deftemplates [* | module-name])

With no arguments, prints a list of all deftemplates in the current module (not the focus module) to the t router. With a module name for an argument, prints the names of the templates in that module. With * as an argument, prints the names of all templates.

(list-focus-stack)

Displays the module focus stack, one module per line; the top of the stack (the focus module) is displayed first.

(list-function$)

Returns a list of all the functions currently callable, including intrinsics, deffunctions, and Java user functions. Each function name is a symbol. The list is sorted in alphabetical order.

(load-facts <lexeme>)

Asserts facts loaded from a file. The argument should name a file containing a list of facts (not deffacts constructs, and no other commands or constructs). Jess parses the file and asserts each fact. The return value is the return value of `assert` when asserting the last fact. `load-facts` looks for the named file the same way the `batch` command looks for scripts. If the filename contains special characters, it must be passed as a double-quoted string.

(load-function <lexeme>)

Loads a class into Jess and adds it to the engine, thus making the corresponding command available. The argument must be the fully qualified name of a Java class that implements the `jess.Userfunction` interface.

(load-package <lexeme>)

Loads a class into Jess and adds it to the engine, thus making the corresponding package of commands available. The argument must be the fully qualified name of a Java class that implements the `jess.Userpackage` interface.

(log <number>)

Returns the logarithm base *e* of its only argument.

(log10 <number>)

Returns the logarithm base 10 of its only argument.

(long <expression>)

Interprets the expression as a Java `long` (if possible) and returns a LONG value. Use strings or symbols for precise values that can't be expressed as an integer. Longs in Jess are second-class citizens in the sense that you can't directly do math on them. You can assign them to variables, pass them to function calls, and convert them to strings or floating-point numbers.

(longp <expression>)

Returns TRUE if the expression is of type RU.LONG; otherwise, returns FALSE.

(lowcase <lexeme>)

Converts uppercase characters in a string or symbol to lowercase. Returns the argument as an all-lowercase string.

(matches <lexeme>)

Produces an ugly printout, useful for debugging, of the contents of the left and right memories of each two-input node on the named rule or query's left-hand side.

(max <number>+)

Returns the value of its largest numeric argument.

(member$ <expression> <list>)

Returns the position (one-based index) of a value within a list; otherwise, returns FALSE.

(min <number>+)

Returns the value of its smallest numeric argument.

(mod <number> <number>)

Returns the remainder of the result of dividing the first argument by the second.

(modify <fact-id> (<lexeme> <expression>)+)

Modifies the given unordered fact in working memory. Each of the *(lexeme, expression)* lists is taken as the name of a slot in this fact and a new value to assign to the slot. The numeric ID of the fact is preserved. The jess.Fact object is returned. Modifying a shadow fact causes the appropriate object properties to be set as well. (See duplicate.)

(listp <expression>)

Returns TRUE for list values; otherwise, returns FALSE.

(neq <expression> <expression>+)

Returns TRUE if the first argument is not equal in type and value to any of the subsequent arguments (see eq); otherwise, returns FALSE.

(new <lexeme> <expression>*)

Creates a new Java object and returns an EXTERNAL_ADDRESS value containing it. The first argument is the class name: java.util.Vector, for example. The new function looks in the table maintained by the import function to resolve class names that don't include a package name. Any additional arguments are taken to be constructor arguments. The constructor is chosen from among all constructors for the named class based on a *first-best fit* algorithm, as discussed in section 5.1 of the text. Built-in Jess types are converted as necessary to match available constructors.

(not <expression>)

Returns TRUE if its only argument evaluates to FALSE; otherwise, returns FALSE.

(nth$ <integer> <list>)

Returns the value of the specified field of a list value. The first argument is the one-based index of the field to return.

(numberp <expression>)

Returns TRUE for numbers; otherwise, returns FALSE.

(oddp <integer>)

Returns TRUE for odd numbers; otherwise, returns FALSE. (See evenp.)

(open <lexeme> <lexeme> [r | w | a])

Opens a file; the first argument names the file. Subsequently, the router identifier (the second argument) can be passed to printout, read, readline, or any other functions that accept I/O routers as arguments. By default, the file is opened for reading; if a mode string is given, it may be opened for reading only (r), writing only (w), or appending (a). If the filename contains special characters, it must be passed as a double-quoted string.

(or <expression>+)

Returns TRUE if any of the arguments evaluate to a non-FALSE value; otherwise, returns FALSE.

(pi)

Returns the irrational number pi.

(pop-focus)

Removes the top module from the focus stack and returns its name.

(ppdeffacts <lexeme>)

Returns a pretty-print rendering of a deffacts, as a string.

(ppdeffunction <lexeme>)

Returns a pretty-print representation of a deffunction, as a string.

(ppdefglobal <symbol>)

Returns a pretty-print representation of a defglobal, as a string.

(ppdefquery <symbol>)

Returns a pretty-print rendering of a defquery, as a string.

(ppdefrule <symbol>)

Returns a pretty-print rendering of a defrule, as a string.

(ppdeftemplate <symbol>)

Returns a pretty-print representation of a deftemplate, as a string.

(printout <lexeme> <expression>+)

Prints its second and subsequent arguments to the router named by the first argument, which must be open for output. No spaces are added between arguments. The special symbol crlf prints as a newline. The special router name t can be used to signify standard output.

(progn <expression>+)

Evaluates each of its arguments in turn, and returns the value of the last expression.

(random)

Returns a pseudo-random integer between 0 and 65536.

(read [<lemexe>])

Reads a single symbol, string, or number from the named router and returns this value. The router t is the default if no argument is given. By default, newlines are treated as ordinary whitespace. If you need to parse text line by line, use readline and explode$.

(readline [<lexeme>])

Reads an entire line as a string from the specified I/O router. If no argument is given, the default is t.

(replace$ <list> <integer> <integer> <list>+)

Replaces the specified range of a list value with a set of values. The variable number of final arguments is inserted into the first list, replacing elements between the one-based indices given by the two numeric arguments, inclusive. Here's an example:

```
Jess> (replace$ (create$ a b c) 2 2 (create$ x y z))
(a x y z c)
```

(reset)

Removes all facts from working memory and all activations from the agenda, asserts the fact (initial-fact), asserts all facts found in deffacts constructs, asserts a fact representing each registered definstance, and (if the set-reset-globals property is TRUE) initializes all defglobals.

(rest$ <list>)

Returns all but the first field of a list as a new list; like cdr in traditional LISP.

(retract <fact-id>+)

Removes the given facts from working memory. Retracting a shadow fact results in an implicit call to undefinstance for the corresponding object.

(retract-string <string>)

Parses the string as a fact; if such a fact exists in working memory, calls `retract` on it.

(return [<expression>])

From a `deffunction`, returns the given value and exits the `deffunction` immediately. From the right-hand side of a rule, terminates the rule's execution immediately and pops the current focus module from the focus stack. The argument is meaningless when `return` is called from a rule.

(round <number>)

Rounds its argument toward the closest integer, or toward negative infinity if exactly between two integers.

(rules [<lexeme> | *])

With no arguments, prints a list of all rules and queries in the current module (not the focus module) to the `t` router. With a module name for an argument, prints the names of the rules and queries in that module. With * as an argument, prints the names of all rules and queries.

(run [<integer>])

Starts the inference engine. If no argument is supplied, Jess keeps running until no more activations remain or `halt` is called. If an argument is supplied, it gives the maximum number of rules to fire before stopping.

(run-query <lexeme> <expression>+)

Runs a `defquery` and returns a `java.util.Iterator` of the matches. The first argument is the name of the query, and the later ones are the arguments to the query. Note that `run-query` can lead to backward chaining, which can cause rules to fire; thus if `run-query` is called on a rule's right-hand side, other rules' right-hand sides may run to completion before the instigating rule completes. Putting `run-query` on a rule's right-hand side can also cause the count of executed rules returned by `run` to be low. Calling `run-query` on the left-hand side of a rule can cause strange effects; be sure you know what you're doing.

Note that the `Iterator` returned by this function should be used immediately. It will become invalid if any of the following functions are called before you've used it: `reset`, `count-query-results`, or `run-query`. It *may* become invalid if any of the following are called: `assert`, `retract`, `modify`, or `duplicate`; and any of the affected facts are involved in the active query's result.

Each match is a `jess.Token` object, as described in section 7.7 of the text.

(run-until-halt)

Runs the engine until `halt` is called. Returns the number of rules fired. When there are no active rules, the calling thread is blocked, waiting on the engine's activation semaphore until new activations become available. This function is typically called either as the last expression in a script or from its own thread.

(save-facts <filename> [<lexeme>])

Saves facts to a file. Attempts to open the named file for writing, and then writes a list of all facts in working memory to the file. This file is suitable for reading with `load-facts`. If the optional second argument is given, only facts whose head matches this symbol will be saved. `save-facts` does not work in applets; the argument must be a valid path to a writeable, local file. If the filename contains special characters, it must be passed as a double-quoted string.

(set <object> <lexeme> <expression>)

Sets a JavaBean's property to the given value. The first argument is the Bean object; the second argument is the name of the property. The third value is the new value for the property; the same conversions are applied as for `new` and `call`. See `get`.

(set-current-module <lexeme>)

Sets the current module. Any constructs defined without explicitly naming a module are defined in the current module. Note that defining a `defmodule` also sets the current module.

(set-factory <object>)

Sets the *thing factory* for the active Rete object, an instance of `jess.factory.Factory`. Providing an alternate thing factory is a very advanced, and currently undocumented, way to extend Jess's functionality.

(setgen <number>)

Sets the starting number used by `gensym*`. Note that if this number has already been used, `gensym*` uses the next larger number that has not been used.

(set-member (<object> | <lexeme>) <lexeme> <expression>)

Sets a Java member variable to the given value. The first argument is the object (or the name of the class, in the case of a static member variable). The second argument is the name of the variable. The third value is the new value for the variable; the same conversions are applied as for `new` and `call`. See `get-member`.

(set-multithreaded-io (TRUE | FALSE))

Specifies whether Jess should use a separate thread to flush I/O streams. Turning this on can lead to a modest performance enhancement, but may result in loss of output on program termination. Returns the previous value of this property.

(set-node-index-hash <integer>)

Sets the default hashing key used in all Rete network join node memories defined after the function is called; this function will not affect parts of the network already in existence at the time of the call. A small value gives rise to memory-efficient nodes; a larger value uses more memory and increases performance (up to a point). If the created nodes will generally have to remember many partial matches, large numbers will lead to faster performance; the opposite may be true for nodes that will rarely hold more than one or two partial matches. This function sets the default; explicit `declare` statements can override this for individual rules. The default value is 101.

(set-reset-globals (TRUE | FALSE | nil))

Changes the current setting of the global variable reset behavior. If this property is set to TRUE (the default), then the `reset` command reinitializes the values of global variables to their initial values (if the initial value was a function call, the function call is reexecuted). If the property is set to FALSE or nil, then `reset` does not affect global variables.

(set-salience-evaluation (when-defined | when-activated | every-cycle))

Changes the current setting of the salience evaluation behavior. By default, a rule's salience is determined once, when the rule is defined (`when-defined`). If this property is set to `when-activated`, then the salience of each rule is redetermined immediately before each time it is placed on the agenda. If the property is set to `every-cycle`, then the salience of every rule is redetermined immediately after any rule fires; this can be very computationally expensive.

(set-strategy (depth | breadth | <lexeme>))

Lets you specify the *conflict-resolution strategy* Jess uses to order the firing of rules of equal salience. Two strategies are built into Jess: *depth (LIFO)* and *breadth (FIFO)*. When the `depth` strategy is in effect (the default), more recently activated rules are fired before less recently activated rules of the same salience. When the `breadth` strategy is active, rules of the same salience fire in the order in which they are activated. Note that in either case, if several rules are activated simultaneously (by the same fact-assertion event), the order in which they fire is unspecified, implementation-dependent, and subject to change.

You can implement your own strategies in Java by creating a class that implements the jess.Strategy interface and then specifying its fully-qualified class name as the argument to set-strategy.

(show-deffacts)

Displays all defined deffacts to the t router.

(show-deftemplates)

Displays all defined deftemplates to the t router.

(show-jess-listeners)

Displays all JessListeners registered with the engine to the t router.

(socket <lexeme> <integer> <lexeme>)

Somewhat equivalent to open, except that instead of opening a file, opens an unbuffered TCP network connection to the host named by the first argument at the numbered port given by the second argument, and installs it as a pair of read and write routers under the name given by the last argument. Because Jess routers can't work with binary data, this method is mostly useful to let instances of Jess communicate over a network. For general networking, it would make sense to use the java.net package directly.

(sqrt <number>)

Returns the square root of its argument.

(store <lexeme> <expression>)

Associates the expression with the name given by the first argument, such that later calls to fetch using that same name will retrieve it. Storing the symbol nil clears any value associated with the name. Analogous to the store() member function of the jess.Rete class. The storage area is local to the Rete engine where store is called.

(str-cat <expression>*)

Concatenates its arguments as strings to form a single string, without intervening spaces. For Java objects, the toString method is called.

(str-compare <lexeme> <lexeme>)

Lexicographically compares two strings. Returns 0 if the strings are identical, a negative integer if the first is lexicographically less than the second, or a positive integer if the first is lexicographically greater.

(str-index <lexeme> <lexeme>)

Returns the position of the first argument within the second argument. This is the one-based index at which the first string first appears in the second; otherwise, returns FALSE.

(stringp <expression>)

Returns TRUE for strings; otherwise, returns FALSE.

(str-length <lexeme>)

Returns the length of the argument in characters.

(subseq$ <list> <integer> <integer>)

Extracts the specified range from a list consisting of the elements between the two one-based indices of the given list, inclusive, and returns this range as a new list.

(subsetp <list> <list>)

Returns TRUE if the first argument is a subset of the second (that is, all the elements of the first list appear in the second list); otherwise, returns FALSE.

(sub-string <integer> <integer> <string>)

Retrieves a subportion from a string. Returns the string consisting of the characters between the two one-based indices of the given string, inclusive.

(symbolp <expression>)

Returns TRUE for symbols; otherwise, returns FALSE.

(sym-cat <expression>+)

Concatenates its arguments as strings to form a single symbol. For Java objects, the toString method is called.

It's easy to create unparseable symbols using this function. For example, although a Jess symbol normally can't contain a space, the symbol returned by (sym-cat "a space") does contain a space. If you use this symbol as the name of a rule (for example) and then save the rule's text into a file, Jess will report a syntax error if you later try to read that file back in. Therefore, you should use sym-cat carefully. This advice also applies to the jess.Value constructor that takes a string as an argument; it can also be used to create invalid symbols.

(system <lexeme>+ [&])

Sends a command to the operating system. Each argument becomes one element of the argument array in a call to the Java java.lang.Runtime.exec(String[])

method; therefore, to execute the command edit myfile.txt, you should call (system edit myfile.txt), not (system "edit myfile.txt"). Normally blocks (Jess stops until the launched application returns), but if the last argument is an ampersand (&), the program runs in the background. The standard output and standard error streams of the process are connected to the t router, but the input of the process is not connected to the terminal. Returns the Java Process object. You can call waitFor and then exitValue to get the exit status of the process.

(throw <object>)

Throws the given object, which must be an instance of java.lang.Throwable or one of its subclasses. If the object is a JessException, throws it directly. If the object is some other type of exception, it is wrapped in a JessException before throwing. The object's stack trace is filled in such that the exception appears to have been created by the throw function.

(time)

Returns the number of seconds (*not* milliseconds) since 12:00 A.M., January 1, 1970.

(try <expression>* [catch <expression>*] [finally <expression>*])

Works something like Java try, with a few simplifications. The biggest difference is that the catch clause can specify neither a type of exception nor a variable to receive the exception object. All exceptions occurring in a try block are routed to the single catch block. The variable ?ERROR is made to point to the exception object as an EXTERNAL_ADDRESS. For example:

```
(try
    (open NoSuchFile.txt r)
catch
    (printout t (call ?ERROR toString) crlf))
Jess reported an error in routine open
    while executing (open NoSuchFile.txt r).
    Message: I/O Exception.
```

An empty catch block is fine; it signifies ignoring possible errors. The expressions in the finally block, if present, are executed after all try and/or catch code has executed, immediately before the try function returns.

(undefadvice (<lexeme> | ALL | <list>))

Removes advice from the named function(s); see defadvice. ALL indicates that advice should be removed from all functions.

*(undefinstance (<object> | *))*

If the object currently has a shadow fact, removes the shadow fact from working memory. Furthermore, if the object has a `PropertyChangeListener` installed, this is removed as well. If the argument is `*`, this is done for all `definstances`.

(undefrule <lexeme>)

Deletes a rule. Removes the named rule from the Rete network and returns TRUE if the rule existed. This rule will never fire again. If the rule has subrules generated by compiling the `or` conditional element, they are removed as well.

(union$ [<list>]+)

Returns a new list consisting of the union of all its list arguments (that is, of all the elements that appear in any of the arguments, with duplicates removed).

(unwatch [all | rules | compilations | activations | facts | focus])

Causes trace output to not be printed for the given indicator. See `watch`.

(upcase <lexeme>)

Converts lowercase characters in a string or symbol to uppercase. Returns the argument as an all-uppercase string.

(view)

Displays a live snapshot of the `Rete` network in a graphical window. You can double-click on individual nodes in the network to get information about them.

(watch [all | rules | compilations | activations | facts | focus])

Produces debug output when specific events happen in Jess, depending on the argument. Any number of different watches can be active simultaneously:

- `rules`—Prints a message when any rule fires
- `compilations`—Prints a message when any rule is compiled
- `activations`—Prints a message when any rule is activated or deactivated, showing which facts have caused the event
- `facts`—Prints a message whenever a fact is asserted or retracted
- `focus`—Prints a message for each change to the module focus stack
- `all`—All of the above

(while <boolean> [do] <expression>)*

Allows conditional looping. Evaluates the Boolean expression repeatedly. As long as it does not equal FALSE, the list of other expressions is evaluated. The value of the last expression evaluated is the return value. The symbol do after the Boolean expression is optional. If present, it is ignored.

Abridged Java API for Jess

The Jess library contains about 75 public classes. Many of them are used only rarely by Jess programmers. Even among the most-used classes, plenty of methods are used very infrequently. This appendix lists only the most important methods of the most important classes—a 20,000-foot view that should be a big help to anyone just getting started with the Jess library.

B.1 *jess.Context*

This class represents the execution context of a function. If you write your own Jess functions in Java, you get a `Context` object as an argument to the `call` method. The `Context` gives you access to the `Rete` object the function is executing in, as well as the values of relevant variables.

public Rete getEngine()

Returns the `Rete` object relevant to the calling code.

public Value getVariable(String name)

Returns the value of a variable. The parameter is the name of the variable with no leading ? or $ characters. You can use this method to get the current value of a `defglobal`.

public void setVariable(String name, Value value)

Sets the value of a variable. The first parameter is the name of the variable with no leading ? or $ characters.

B.2 *jess.Fact*

The `Fact` class represents one entry in Jess's working memory. Fact is a subclass of `ValueVector`.

public Fact(String name, Rete engine)

Asks the `Rete` object for a template by the given name; if one doesn't exist, an ordered one is created. This is the most commonly used constructor.

public Deftemplate getDeftemplate()

Returns the `Deftemplate` for a `Fact,` which can tell you the name of the `Fact`, the number of slots, and the names of its slots.

public int getFactId()

Returns a `Fact`'s numeric identifier; every `Fact` has one.

public int getShadowMode()

If this `Fact` is not a shadow fact, returns the constant `Fact.NO`. Otherwise, returns `Fact.DYNAMIC` or `Fact.STATIC`, depending on the type of shadow fact it is.

public Value getSlotValue(String name)

Returns the value held by the named slot. Ordered facts have a single slot named __data containing a list of items.

public void setSlotValue(String name, Value value)

Sets the value in a slot by name. Don't call this method on a `Fact` that is currently in Jess's working memory!

B.3   jess.Funcall

A `Funcall` is a specialized list representing a function call. If you need to call a Jess function from Java repeatedly with no or only minor changes, it's generally more efficient to build a `Funcall` object yourself and call `execute` on it.

Funcall also includes a number of useful constants as static `Value` objects: `Funcall.TRUE`, `Funcall.FALSE`, and `Funcall.NIL` are all symbols, and `Funcall.NILLIST` is an empty list.

public Funcall(String name, Rete engine)

Accepts the name of the function to call. Note that the function doesn't have to be defined at the time; as long as it is defined when `execute` is called, everything will work.

public Funcall arg(Value v)

Appends an argument to the `Funcall`. Note that because this method returns the modified `Funcall` object, you can chain calls to `arg` together.

public Value execute(Context context)

Executes the `Funcall` using the given `Context`. If you don't have a `Context` handy, you can get one by calling `Rete.getGlobalContext()`.

B.4   jess.Jesp

`Jesp` is the Jess parser. You might use this class if you wanted Jess to read input from a network stream or some other unusual source.

public Jesp(java.io.Reader reader, Rete engine)

Takes a `Reader` object, the source for all the input this object will parse. The stream of Jess code is executed and applied to the given `Rete` object.

public Value parse(boolean prompt)

Does the parsing. Returns the value of the last expression evaluated. If prompt is true, the Jess> prompt is printed to the WSTDOUT router before each expression is read.

B.5 jess.JessEvent

If you request it using the setEventMask method in the Rete class, Jess sends JessEvent objects as notifications when certain things happen. Every JessEvent has a *type* that indicates what happened, and an *object* that provides more information (usually, it's the object most affected by the event). The possible types, their meanings, and their associated objects are given in table B.1.

Table B.1   Types of JessEvent. Each type is a public, static, int variable in the JessEvent class.

Type	Object type	Description
ACTIVATION	jess.Activation	A defrule has been activated or deactivated.
CLEAR	jess.Rete	A (clear) has been executed.
DEFCLASS	The name of the defclass	A defclass has been added or removed.
DEFFACT	jess.Deffacts	A deffacts has been added or removed.
DEFGLOBAL	jess.Defglobal	A defglobal has been added or removed.
DEFINSTANCE	The JavaBean	A definstance has been added or removed.
DEFRULE	jess.Defrule	A defrule has been added or removed.
DEFRULE_FIRED	jess.Activation	A defrule has been fired.
DEFTEMPLATE	jess.Deftemplate	A deftemplate has been added or removed.
FACT	jess.Fact	A fact has been asserted or retracted.
FOCUS	The name of the module	The module focus has changed.
HALT	jess.Rete	A (run) has been executed.
RESET	jess.Rete	A (reset) has been executed.
RUN	jess.Rete	A (run) has been executed.
USERFUNCTION	jess.Userfunction	A Userfunction has been added or removed.
USERFUNCTION_CALLED	jess.Userfunction	A Userfunction has been called.
USERPACKAGE	jess.Userpackage	A Userpackage has been added or removed.

These flags are all powers of two, so you can combine them with the Java | operator and test for individual types within a combined type with the & operator. Jess combines two more constants—MODIFIED and REMOVED—with the others to mean, for instance, that a fact was retracted (FACT | REMOVED).

public int getType()

Returns the type of event, one of the constants in table B.1.

public Object getObject()

Returns data associated with the event.

public Object getSource()

Returns the source of the event—the Rete object that generated it.

B.6 jess.JessListener

This is the interface you implement if you want to receive JessEvents. It works just like the event listeners in the java.awt.event package.

public void eventHappened(JessEvent je) throws JessException

Handles events of event type. This is the only handler method in this interface. Your handler should test the getType() method in the JessEvent to decide what action to take.

B.7 jess.PrettyPrinter

This class knows how to format many Jess constructs so that they look nice to a human reader. It uses the Visitor pattern,[1] so it includes many methods named visit*XXX*, but you won't need to use them. To use PrettyPrinter, you just need to pass the construct to print as the constructor argument and then call toString() to get the formatted version. You have to construct a new PrettyPrinter for each construct you need to format.

public PrettyPrinter(Visitable v)

Argument can be an instance of any of the Jess classes that implement the Visitable interface, which include Deffacts, Deffunction, Defglobal, Defquery, Defrule, and Deftemplate.

---

[1] E. Gamma, R. Helm, R. Johnson, and J. Vlissides, *Design Patterns: Elements of Reusable Object-Oriented Software* (Reading, MA: Addison-Wesley, 1995).

public String toString()

Returns a nicely formatted rendition of the construct that was passed in as a constructor argument.

B.8 jess.Rete

This class acts as a facade for all the most important parts of Jess. There are methods in `Rete` for managing working memory, the agenda, the rule base, and more. In this appendix, I'll only mention the most important methods that have no direct equivalent in the Jess language. More methods are covered in chapter 18.

public Rete(Object appObject)

Constructs a new `Rete` object. The argument's `ClassLoader` is used to load any classes used by commands like `new`, `call`, and `defclass`.

public Rete()

Uses `this` as the application object.

B.8.1 Working with events

These methods let you work with the Jess event system. You can set the event mask to some combination of the constants in the `JessEvent` class, and then register an instance of the `JessListener` class. That instance will then receive all events that are generated.

public void addJessListener(JessListener jel)

Registers a `JessListener` to receive events.

public void removeJessListener(JessListener jel)

Unregisters a `JessListener`, so it receives no more events.

public int getEventMask()

Gets the current value of the event mask.

public void setEventMask(int mask)

Sets the event mask. In general, you should compose this value with the value returned by `getEventMask` using the | operator.

B.8.2 Exchanging Java values with Jess language code

These methods work with the same storage area accessed by the `store` and `fetch` commands in Jess. By calling `store` in one language and `fetch` in the other, you can easily move data back and forth between the two.

public void clearStorage()

Clears the storage area, so that `store` returns `null` for any name.

public Value fetch(java.lang.String name)

Retrieves an object previously stored with `store`.

public Value store(java.lang.String name, java.lang.Object val)

Stores an object under the given name. The object is wrapped in a `Value` object before being stored.

public Value store(java.lang.String name, Value val)

Stores a `Value` under the given name.

B.8.3 The import table

When you name a Java class in Jess, the *import table* is consulted, as necessary, to figure out the fully qualified name. These methods add to the import table and use it to resolve classes.

public java.lang.Class findClass(String clazz)

Given the name of a class, uses the import table to come up with the fully qualified name. If you pass `"String"` as the argument, the `Class` for `java.lang.String` is returned.

public void importClass(String clazz)

Adds a fully qualified class name to the import table.

public void importPackage(String pack)

Imports every class in a package by adding the package name to the import table.

B.8.4 Finding things

A whole set of methods is available for retrieving constructs like instances of `Defrule` and `Deffacts` from the engine. They all accept the name of the construct as an argument. If the name doesn't include a module name, the name of the current module is used. This set of methods includes `findDeffacts`, findDefrule, findDeftemplate, and findUserfunction. findDefrule can find Defquery objects as well as Defrules.

There are several methods for finding specific facts in the working memory.

public Fact findFactByFact(Fact f)

Finds fast. Can be used to find out quickly if a given fact is on the fact-list and, if so, to obtain a reference to it. The argument is a Fact that is identical to the one you're looking for.

public Fact findFactByID(int id)

Finds a fact given its numeric identifier. This method is very slow; don't use it unless you have to.

public Iterator listXXX()

Many methods return java.util.Iterators over collections of Jess constructs. These include listActivations, listDeffacts, listDefglobals, listDefinstances, listDefrules, listDeftemplates, listFacts, listFocusStack, listFunctions, listJessListeners, and listModules.

B.8.5 Waiting for rules to fire

Many multithreaded programs need to be able to pause indefinitely until Jess is ready to fire some rules. These methods let you do that.

public Object getActivationSemaphore()

Returns the *activation semaphore* for this engine. The monitor of the activation semaphore is signaled whenever an activation appears. You can therefore call wait() on this object, and the wait() call will return only when Jess is ready to fire a rule.

public void waitForActivations()

Doesn't return until there are rules on the agenda ready to fire.

B.9 jess.RU

RU stands for Rete Utilities. This is a catch-all class that contains some useful constants. Most of these constants enumerate the allowed return values for Value.getType—the different kinds of Value objects. The most important ones are (all static, final, int variables) ATOM (a symbol), EXTERNAL_ADDRESS, FACT, FLOAT, FUNCALL, INTEGER, LIST, LONG, MULTIVARIABLE, STRING, and VARIABLE.

B.9.1 *public static String gensym(String prefix)*

Returns a unique symbol starting with the given prefix. This method is useful if your Java code is automatically generating Jess rules, variables, or other entities, and needs to come up with a unique name.

B.10 jess.Token

The `Token` class represents a group of facts as they travel together through Jess's Rete network. The iterator returned by `Rete.runQuery()`, or the `run-query` function in Jess, returns a series of `Token` objects; otherwise, you shouldn't need to deal with this class.

public Fact getFact(int index)

Returns a single `Fact` from the token. The fact that matches the first pattern in a rule has index 0.

public int size()

Returns the number of facts in a `Token`.

public Fact topFact()

Equivalent to `token.getFact(token.size() - 1)`.

B.11 jess.Value

This is an important class, because every piece of information that travels through Jess (a number, a string, a Java object) does so wrapped in an instance of `jess.Value` or one of its subclasses. Nevertheless, I won't say much about it here, because it is covered well in chapter 15. Note that the type constants are defined in the class `RU`.

public Value(boolean b)

Constructs a Boolean value object (one of the symbols `TRUE` or `FALSE`).

public Value(double d, int type)

Constructs a numeric value. The type can be any `INTEGER` or `FLOAT`.

public Value(int value, int type)

Constructs a numeric value. The type can be `INTEGER` or `FLOAT`. Uses the class `LongValue` to construct a `Value` of type `LONG`.

public Value(java.lang.Object o)

Constructs a value containing a Java object (type EXTERNAL_ADDRESS).

public Value(java.lang.String s, int type)

Constructs a lexeme value—either STRING or ATOM.

public Value(Value v)

Copies a value.

public Value(ValueVector f, int type)

Constructs a value of type LIST.

public int type()

Returns the type of this variable—one of the constants in RU.

public Value resolveValue(Context c)

Given an evaluation context, returns the true value of this Value. For variables, this means the value of the variable. For Value objects containing function call objects, the function is called and the return value provided.

public String atomValue(Context c)

Returns the contents of this value, as a symbol.

public Object externalAddressValue(Context c)

Returns the contents of this value, as a Java object.

public Fact factValue(Context c)

Returns the contents of this value, as a fact.

public double floatValue(Context c)

Returns the contents of this value, as a number.

public Funcall funcallValue(Context c)

Returns the contents of this value, as a function call.

public int intValue(Context c)

Returns the contents of this value, as an int.

public ValueVector listValue(Context c)

Returns the contents of this value, as a list.

public long longValue(Context c)
Returns the contents of this value, as a `long`.

public double numericValue(Context c)
Returns the contents of this value, as a number.

public String stringValue(Context c)
Returns the contents of this value, as a `string`.

public String variableValue(Context c)
Returns the contents of this value, as a string (a variable name).

B.12 jess.ValueVector

A `ValueVector` is a list of `Value` objects. This class is used both as is and also as base class for `Fact` and other important Jess classes. `ValueVector` is very similar to the `java.util.Vector` and `java.util.ArrayList` classes. It has separate notions of a *capacity* and a *size*. A `ValueVector` contains an array of `Value` objects. The capacity is the length of the array; the size is the number of `Value` objects actually in the array. The capacity is automatically expanded if you use `add` to add `Value` objects.

public ValueVector()
Constructs a `ValueVector` with the default capacity (10).

public ValueVector(int size)
Constructs a `ValueVector` with the given capacity.

public ValueVector add(Value val)
Adds a new element to the end of this `ValueVector`.

public Value get(int i)
Fetches the entry at position `i` in the list.

public ValueVector remove(int i)
Removes the item at the given index from the list; moves all the higher-numbered elements down.

public ValueVector set(Value val, int i)
Sets the entry at position `i` to `val`.

public ValueVector setLength(int i)

Sets the size of the list. `Value` objects at this index and above are no longer part of the list.

public int size()

Returns the number of `Value` objects in this `ValueVector`.

C

An automated testing framework

When you're doing iterative development, automated testing gives you confidence that each addition or modification does not introduce errors into a previously working program. You make a change, you run your tests, and you find out immediately whether your changes broke the existing code. Having a good suite of automated tests that you can run quickly and easily helps you write better code more quickly.

This is as true for rule-based programming as it is for any other kind. Whether I'm working on extensions to Jess or writing rule-based programs, I find that automated testing helps keep the quality of the software I write as high as it can be. In this appendix, I'll describe a framework I use to write tests for Jess language code. The actual code for the framework is included with the sample code for this book.

Note that for Java application programming, server-side Java programming, and programming in many other languages, a number of excellent free testing frameworks are available.[1] JUnit (http://www.junit.org/index.htm) was the first of a large family of these frameworks; it helps you automate unit tests for Java software. There is no "JessUnit," per se, as of this writing. The framework I'll present here is the closest thing there is for now.

C.1 *Architecture*

My Jess testing framework is based on Bourne shell scripts. Therefore, it's easy to use on UNIX-like systems. It can also be used on Windows systems by installing a UNIX emulation toolkit like the excellent, free Cygwin environment.[2] Given the simplicity of the framework, however, you also could simply write your own using batch files.

The overall architecture of the test harness uses a top-level tests directory containing several template subdirectories and one additional subdirectory for each test. To add a test, you copy one of the template directories and edit the files in the copy. Each directory (including the top-level directory) contains a Makefile and a shell script named runtest.sh. The test directories contain additional files; I'll describe these later. Here's the directory structure for the framework before any tests have been added:

---

[1] A listing of some of these frameworks, with links to more information, is located at http://xprogramming.com/software.htm.

[2] Cygwin is a porting layer that lets UNIX tools run on Windows. The Cygwin home page is at http://www.cygwin.com.

```
tests/
    runtest.sh
    run1test.sh
    clean.sh
    shelldefs.mk
    JessTemplate/
        Makefile
        README
        runtest.sh
        runtest.ref
        test.clp
        test.ref
    JavaTemplate/
        Makefile
        README
        runtest.sh
        runtest.ref
        test.java
        test.ref
```

The framework works as follows. The top-level runtest.sh finds all the runtest.sh files in subdirectories and executes them, one at a time. Each runtest.sh in a subdirectory runs its own test. You can edit the script in a particular subdirectory to do whatever you want, but the default scripts run a program, capture the output in a file, and compare that to a reference file. If the files match, *Test succeeded* is displayed; if they don't, a failure message shows up instead.

The top-level runtest.sh skips any subdirectory in which it finds a file named runtest.sh.disable; this lets you turn off tests if necessary.

There is a README file in each template directory. It's a good idea to use it to write down a short description of what's being tested whenever you create a new test.

In the text, as we developed the tutorial applications throughout this book, I described various tests you could do and showed example dialogs confirming that functions or rules behaved as expected. If I were developing these systems by myself, I'd make each of those examples into an individual test. Then, each time I added a new test, I'd run all the existing tests to be sure everything still worked. You can never have too many tests. Now, let's look at the two test templates.

C.2 *The Jess template*

The two test templates are similar. The Jess template's runtest.sh script runs Jess using test.clp as the input and captures the output in a file, and then compares the result against test.ref. The file runtest.ref contains the output of a successful run of runtest.sh; it's used by the top-level scripts to determine whether the test passed. The runtest.sh script looks like this:

```
. ../shelldefs.mk

echo "Running the test program..."
${JAVA} jess.Main -nologo test.clp > test.out 2>&1

if diff -ignore-space-change test.out test.ref > /dev/null ; then
    # files are the same
    echo "Test succeeded"
else
    # files are different
    echo "Test failed. Try:"
    echo " diff -ignore-space-change test.out test.ref"
fi
```

The variable JAVA is defined in the top-level file shelldefs.mk, which is read in at the beginning of this script. All sorts of variable definitions can be collected in this file, which helps you to write portable tests.

One important point about this script is that it uses the -ignore-space-change option of GNU diff. The diff program compares files, and this option tells it to be lenient if the only changes involve extra spaces or blank lines. This option makes it easier to write reference files—you don't have to worry about getting the spacing precisely right.

The file test.clp looks like this:

```
(deffunction test-something ()
)

(printout t "Testing *** :" crlf)
(test-something)
(printout t "Test done." crlf)
(exit)
```

When you make a copy of the template, you should replace *** with a description of your test, and put the test code into test-something. The test code should display relevant results using printout, so they can be compared to the reference file. You need to create test.ref as well. One way to do this is to run the test without it; of course, the test will fail. Carefully check over the test.out file to make sure the output is correct. If it is, simply copy it to test.ref. If it is not, but you understand what the correct output should be, you might want to make a copy anyway and edit it to create a correct version in test.ref.

C.3 *The Java template*

The Jess template is for tests that consist entirely of scripts, and the Java template is for tests written as Java code. Otherwise, the functionality is very similar. The runtest.sh for JavaTemplate looks like this:

```
. ../shelldefs.mk
echo "Building..."
make clean > /dev/null 2>&1
make > test.errs 2>&1
echo "Build done"

if test ! -f test.class ; then
    echo "Build failed:"
    cat test.errs
    exit
else
    echo "Build Succeeded."
    rm test.errs
fi
echo "Running the test program..."
${JAVA} test >test.out 2>&1

if diff -ignore-space-change test.out test.ref > /dev/null ; then
    # files are the same
    echo "Test succeeded"
else
    # files are different
    echo "Test failed. Try:"
    echo " diff -ignore-space-change test.out test.ref"
fi
```

The only substantial difference is that before running the test, this script builds the Java class test. If the build fails, the test fails too.

The file test.java looks like this:

```
public class test {
    public static void main(String[] argv) {
        System.out.println("Testing XXXXX:");
        TestMyFeature();
        System.out.println("Test done.");
    }

    static void TestMyFeature() {
        System.out.println("This is the test!!");
    }
}
```

When you create a new Java-based test from this template, you need to replace XXXXX with a description of your test and implement the method TestMyFeature so that the output it prints demonstrates whether some feature of your code works correctly. See the earlier discussion of the Jess template for ideas about creating the test.ref file.

index

More Java Titles from Manning!

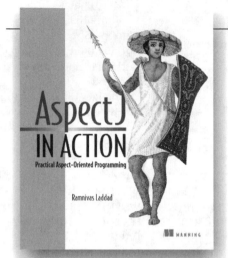

AspectJ in Action

Ramnivas Laddad
1-930110-93-6
Softbound, 512 pages, $44.95
July 2003

A practical guide to Aspect Oriented Programming (AOP) and AspectJ. The reusable code examples that are provided will enable quick implementation of functionality in your system.

More Java Titles from Manning!

Eclipse in Action

David Gallardo, Ed Burnette,
and Robert McGovern
ISBN 1-930110-96-0
Softbound, 416 pages, $44.95
May 2003

This book provides a thorough guide to using Eclipse features and plugins effectively in the context of real-world Java development. Inside, you'll learn how to use plugin tools for using Eclipse in a team environment, including using Ant and CVS for source control.

More Java Titles from Manning!

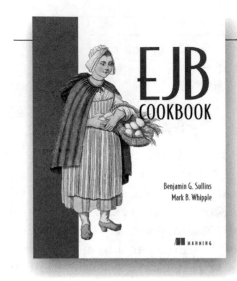